TRANSIT COOPERATIVE RESEARCH PROGRAM

Report 24

Guidebook for Attracting Paratransit Patrons to Fixed-Route Services

JOHN N. BALOG
KETRON, Division of the Bionetics Corporation
Exton, PA

Subject Area

Public Transit

Research Sponsored by the Federal Transit Administration in Cooperation with the Transit Development Corporation

TRANSPORTATION RESEARCH BOARD
NATIONAL RESEARCH COUNCIL

NATIONAL ACADEMY PRESS
Washington, D.C.   1997

TRANSIT COOPERATIVE RESEARCH PROGRAM

The nation's growth and the need to meet mobility, environmental, and energy objectives place demands on public transit systems. Current systems, some of which are old and in need of upgrading, must expand service area, increase service frequency, and improve efficiency to serve these demands. Research is necessary to solve operating problems, to adapt appropriate new technologies from other industries, and to introduce innovations into the transit industry. The Transit Cooperative Research Program (TCRP) serves as one of the principal means by which the transit industry can develop innovative near-term solutions to meet demands placed on it.

The need for TCRP was originally identified in *TRB Special Report 213—Research for Public Transit: New Directions,* published in 1987 and based on a study sponsored by the Urban Mass Transportation Administration—now the Federal Transit Administration (FTA). A report by the American Public Transit Association (APTA), *Transportation 2000,* also recognized the need for local, problem-solving research. TCRP, modeled after the longstanding and successful National Cooperative Highway Research Program, undertakes research and other technical activities in response to the needs of transit service providers. The scope of TCRP includes a variety of transit research fields including planning, service configuration, equipment, facilities, operations, human resources, maintenance, policy, and administrative practices.

TCRP was established under FTA sponsorship in July 1992. Proposed by the U.S. Department of Transportation, TCRP was authorized as part of the Intermodal Surface Transportation Efficiency Act of 1991 (ISTEA). On May 13, 1992, a memorandum agreement outlining TCRP operating procedures was executed by the three cooperating organizations: FTA; the National Academy of Sciences, acting through the **Transportation Research Board (TRB)**; and the Transit Development Corporation, Inc. (TDC), a nonprofit educational and research organization established by APTA. TDC is responsible for forming the independent governing board, designated as the TCRP Oversight and Project Selection (TOPS) Committee.

Research problem statements for TCRP are solicited periodically but may be submitted to TRB by anyone at any time It is the responsibility of the TOPS Committee to formulate the research program by identifying the highest priority projects. As part of the evaluation, the TOPS Committee defines funding levels and expected products.

Once selected, each project is assigned to an expert panel, appointed by the Transportation Research Board. The panels prepare project statements (requests for proposals), select contractors, and provide technical guidance and counsel throughout the life of the project. The process for developing research problem statements and selecting research agencies has been used by TRB in managing cooperative research programs since 1962. As in other TRB activities, TCRP project panels serve voluntarily without compensation.

Because research cannot have the desired impact if products fail to reach the intended audience, special emphasis is placed on disseminating TCRP results to the intended end users of the research: transit agencies, service providers, and suppliers. TRB provides a series of research reports, syntheses of transit practice, and other supporting material developed by TCRP research. APTA will arrange for workshops, training aids, field visits, and other activities to ensure that results are implemented by urban and rural transit industry practitioners.

The TCRP provides a forum where transit agencies can cooperatively address common operational problems. The TCRP results support and complement other ongoing transit research and training programs.

TCRP REPORT 24

Project B-5 FY'93
ISSN 1073-4872
ISBN 0-309-06068-0
Library of Congress Catalog Card No. 97-61131

©1997 Transportation Research Board

Price $65.00

NOTICE

The project that is the subject of this report was a part of the Transit Cooperative Research Program conducted by the Transportation Research Board with the approval of the Governing Board of the National Research Council. Such approval reflects the Governing Board's judgment that the project concerned is appropriate with respect to both the purposes and resources of the National Research Council.

The members of the technical advisory panel selected to monitor this project and to review this report were chosen for recognized scholarly competence and with due consideration for the balance of disciplines appropriate to the project. The opinions and conclusions expressed or implied are those of the research agency that performed the research, and while they have been accepted as appropriate by the technical panel, they are not necessarily those of the Transportation Research Board, the National Research Council, the Transit Development Corporation, or the Federal Transit Administration of the U.S. Department of Transportation.

Each report is reviewed and accepted for publication by the technical panel according to procedures established and monitored by the Transportation Research Board Executive Committee and the Governing Board of the National Research Council.

Special Notice

The Transportation Research Board, the National Research Council, the Transit Development Corporation, and the Federal Transit Administration (sponsor of the Transit Cooperative Research Program) do not endorse products or manufacturers. Trade or manufacturers' names appear herein solely because they are considered essential to the clarity and completeness of the project reporting.

Published reports of the

TRANSIT COOPERATIVE RESEARCH PROGRAM

are available from:

Transportation Research Board
National Research Council
2101 Constitution Avenue, N.W.
Washington, D.C. 20418

and can be ordered through the Internet at
http://www.nas.edu/trb/index.html

Printed in the United States of America

FOREWORD

By Staff
Transportation Research
Board

TCRP Report 24, "Guidebook for Attracting Paratransit Patrons to Fixed-Route Services," will be of interest to transit managers and planners in transit systems that provide complementary paratransit services under the Americans With Disabilities Act (ADA). Paratransit services are more expensive to provide on a per-trip basis than fixed-route transit, so operating efficiencies could be achieved by attracting some paratransit riders to fixed route. The Guidebook identifies the characteristics and preferences of four distinct market segments: people with disabilities who use fixed-route transit; people with disabilities who use paratransit; others who currently use paratransit; and people with disabilities who normally do not use transit. The Guidebook also provides step-by-step procedures for estimating demand, locating bus stops, training drivers, providing travel training for patrons, marketing services, and evaluating successes.

Under TCRP Project B-5, research was undertaken by KETRON, a Division of the Bionetics Corporation, to identify the characteristics of paratransit riders with and without disabilities who could be attracted to ride fixed-route service, the features they value in fixed-route services, and the physical and institutional barriers that hinder such efforts. The research is based on consumer surveys of people with disabilities who do not use fixed-route services as well as those who do. On-board surveys, telephone surveys, and focus groups were conduced at transit agencies around the country to obtain data on passenger preferences and abilities. Survey results indicate that the top four features that can make fixed-route transit attractive to paratransit users are (1) low fares, (2) easy access (i.e., no big roads to cross) to the bus stop, (3) drivers who announce all stops, and (4) no transfers.

A demand forecasting methodology was developed using the survey data and peer systems. Systems with transit service were grouped by geographic location, population density, climate, and topography to create peer systems. Using the peer systems tables provided, reference values for a user's system can be obtained on such items as ADA-eligible population, annual paratransit trips provided, productivity, and fixed-route vehicle information. Procedures to estimate the volume of riders who might switch from paratransit to fixed-route service are provided for the peer systems.

To aid implementation, case studies were conducted of successful projects, thereby providing information on good operational practices. Route design, bus stop location, budgeting, advertising, partnerships, public involvement, and market research are all discussed in detail.

A chapter of the Guidebook is devoted to driver training. Many transit riders—especially passengers with disabilities—rely on the driver. The third highest factor for making passengers with disabilities comfortable on fixed-route buses is announcing of stops. Another chapter is devoted to travel training for passengers. Knowledge is essential to making passengers with disabilities comfortable on fixed-route transit.

This Guidebook will help transit managers and planners design and implement fixed-route services that are attractive to passengers with disabilities. An unpublished final report on this project contains the analytical support for the findings and recommendations presented in the Guidebook. This unpublished final report is available on loan through the TCRP, 2101 Constitution Avenue, NW, Washington, DC 20418.

CONTENTS

1-1 CHAPTER 1 Introduction
Purpose of This Guidebook, 1-1
Organization of the Guidebook, 1-2
Using This Guidebook, 1-3
Example, 1-4
Conclusions, 1-4

2-1 CHAPTER 2 Estimating Travel Demand
Introduction, 2-1
Comparing a System With Its Peers, 2-1
Estimating Ridership Preferences for an Improved Fixed-Route System by Paratransit Patrons and People With Disabilities, 2-18
Estimating Ridership Preferences by Market Segment, 2-21
Probability of Purchase, 2-39

3-1 CHAPTER 3 Basic Steps
Introduction, 3-1
Step 1: Identify the Need, 3-1
Step 2: Define Funding Needs and Resources, 3-4
Step 3: Conduct Public Involvement, 3-13
Step 4: Conduct Market Research, 3-18
Conclusions, 3-28

4-1 CHAPTER 4 Locating Transit Stops Close to Passengers
Introduction, 4-1
Step 1: Identify the Need, 4-2
Step 2: Define Funding Needs and Resources, 4-3
Step 3: Conduct Public Involvement, 4-11
Step 4: Conduct Market Research, 4-12
Step 5: Identify Approach to Address Need, 4-17
Step 6: Determine Personnel and Maintenance Needs, 4-24
Step 7: Develop Implementation Plan, 4-25
Step 8: Test the Routes, 4-28
Step 9: Implement Service, 4-28
Step 10: Evaluate the Results, 4-29

5-1 CHAPTER 5 Training Drivers
Introduction, 5-1
Step 1: Identify the Need, 5-2
Step 2: Define Funding Needs and Resources, 5-3
Step 3: Conduct Public Involvement, 5-4
Step 4: Conduct Market Research, 5-5
Step 5: Determine Training Contents, 5-7
Step 6: Establish a Development Team, 5-9
Step 7: Develop and Produce Materials, 5-17
Step 8: Distribute the Video, 5-25
Step 9: Evaluate the Results, 5-27

6-1 CHAPTER 6 Programming Accessible Bus Stop Improvements
Introduction, 6-1
Step 1: Identify the Need, 6-2
Step 2: Define Funding Needs and Resources, 6-10
Step 3: Conduct a Public Involvement Program, 6-14
Step 4: Conduct Market Research, 6-21
Step 5: Select Target Stops, 6-27
Step 6: Determine Improvements, 6-29
Step 7: Evaluate Enhancements, 6-32

7-1 CHAPTER 7 Teaching Passengers to Use the Fixed-Route System—Travel Training
Introduction, 7-1
Step 1: Identify the Need, 7-2
Step 2: Define Funding Needs and Resources, 7-7
Step 3: Conduct Public Involvement, 7-11
Step 4: Conduct Market Research, 7-13

Step 5: Select a Training Model and Approach, 7-23
Step 6: Develop Travel Training Materials, 7-33
Step 7: Implement the Approach, 7-37
Step 8: Evaluate the Program, 7-46
Conclusions, 7-47

8-1 CHAPTER 8 Marketing Fixed-Route Services
Introduction, 8-1
Marketing, 8-2
The Marketing Process, 8-4
Marketing to Paratransit Riders, 8-11
What Changes to the Transit System Would Encourage You to Ride It?, 8-22
The 5 Ps and Survey Responses, 8-24
Conclusions, 8-37

9-1 CHAPTER 9 Evaluating Success
Introduction, 9-1
Basic Steps, 9-1
Counting All Passengers, 9-3
Counting Passengers With Disabilities, 9-4
Specific Steps for Each Approach, 9-22
Criteria for Success, 9-28
Conclusions, 9-31

A-1 APPENDIX A System Data Tables

B-1 APPENDIX B Bibliography

COOPERATIVE RESEARCH PROGRAMS STAFF

ROBERT J. REILLY, *Director, Cooperative Research Programs*
STEPHEN J. ANDRLE, *Manager, Transit Cooperative Research Program*
STEPHANIE NELLONS ROBINSON, *Senior Program Officer*
EILEEN P. DELANEY, *Managing Editor*
KAMI CABRAL, *Production Editor*
HILARY FREER, *Assistant Editor*

PROJECT PANEL B-5

CLEMENTINE W. MORRIS, *Transit Authority of River City, Louisville, KY* (Chair)
JANET ABELSON, *AC Transit District, El Cerrito, CA*
JOSEPH ALEXANDER, *DeLeuw Cather, Washington, DC*
LISA BLOOM-PRUITT, *Durham, NC*
KAREN J. CLAYTON, *Transportation Displays, Inc., Atlanta, GA*
SHARON DENT, *Hillsborough Area Regional Transit, Tampa, FL*
DARICE GAMBLE, *Fairburn, GA*
AVON MACKEL, *WMATA, Washington, DC*
GRAYSON W. MARSHALL, JR., *County of Placer, Auburn, CA*
MAUREEN MCCLOSKEY, *Paralyzed Veterans Association, Washington, DC*
WILLIAM C. MCCARTHY, *New Mexico State University, Las Cruces, NM*
ROGER TATE, *FTA Liaison Representative* (Deceased)
JAMES A. SCOTT, *TRB Liaison Representative*

ACKNOWLEDGMENTS

The research reported herein was performed under TCRP Project B-5 by the KETRON Division of the Bionetics Corporation as prime contractor.

John N. Balog, Vice President of Transportation Research, Planning, and Operations, was the Principal Investigator. Additional authors of this report are Anne N. Schwarz, Senior Paratransit/Transit Specialist; John B. Morrison, KETRON Senior Transportation Planner; Mark M. Hood, KETRON Paratransit/Transit Specialist; James E. Maslanka, KETRON Senior Paratransit/Transit Specialist; and Jennifer E. Rimmer, KETRON Paratransit/Transit Specialist.

Jenkins & Quinn was a subcontractor. The work undertaken by Jenkins & Quinn was performed by Michael Quinn. Acting as consultants were Betsy Buxer of The Community Forum and Julian Benjamin, Professor of Economics, North Carolina A&T State University. Peter Schauer of Peter Schauer Associates also served as a subcontractor.

KETRON would like to thank the transit managers who participated in the surveys. Ms. Kimberly Kelly-Morton of the Greater Bridgeport Transit District, Mr. Paul Larrousse and Mr. Ryan Larson of the Madison Metro Transit System, Mr. Bill Welch of the San Mateo County District, Mr. Bill Morris of the Central Florida Regional Transportation Authority, and Ms. Karen Clayton and Mr. Doug Douglas of Dallas Area Rapid Transit provided invaluable assistance to the completion of this research.

Thank you to the B-5 Panel Members for their open comments on this research and to Ms. Stephanie N. Robinson, TCRP Senior Program Officer, for her leadership throughout the project.

CHAPTER 1:

INTRODUCTION

CHAPTER 1 INTRODUCTION

PURPOSE OF THIS GUIDEBOOK

The increasingly positive attitudes of the public regarding individuals with disabilities and the requirements specified in the Americans with Disabilities Act legislation have contributed to increased availability of paratransit services at over 550 existing fixed-route systems in the United States. With the increased availability of services, more people with disabilities want paratransit to satisfy their mobility needs. Increased mobility can result in a greater sense of self-worth, a higher quality of life, and the opportunity to participate in the work force -- all desirable goals. An ancillary product of increased participation in the work force is the generation of additional revenues for state and federal governments.

Paratransit tends to be more expensive than accessible fixed-route.

The cost of curb-to-curb or door-to-door paratransit services can be and almost always is higher than the cost of accessible, fixed-route services. This cost is necessary if riders cannot use fixed-route services; however, studies and experiences around the country indicate that some individuals with disabilities can use accessible, fixed-route services effectively and at a lower cost to transit systems. A well-designed program to determine eligibility and constant evaluation of the program's performance are essential. This concept includes the effective use of trip-by-trip eligibility designations and the exclusion from the eligibility rolls of individuals with disabilities who can use traditional, accessible, fixed-route transit.

It is desirable to persuade individuals who are currently not getting around at all, are riding with friends or relatives, or are taking some other mode of transportation to use accessible, fixed-route systems. If this goal is to be achieved, certain attitudes of individuals with disabilities have to be modified, and transit systems must provide those amenities and characteristics considered important by potential riders.

Individuals with disabilities do not ride accessible, fixed-route services for a variety of reasons, including, but not necessarily limited to: (1) lack of knowledge about the availability of accessible fixed-route services; (2) the need to cross wide roads to use the service; (3) ineffective policies on the part of the transit

CHAPTER 1 INTRODUCTION

system; (4) inadequate training of drivers regarding the announcement of bus stops; (5) the need to make transfers between modes or among vehicles; (6) inadequate seating; (7) lack of large, covered shelters at bus stops; and (8) the perceived lack of security.

This Guidebook, which reflects the findings of rider and non-rider surveys, is part of the Transit Cooperative Research Program's initiative to develop methods to attract paratransit patrons and other individuals with disabilities to accessible, fixed-route services.

This Guidebook provides fixed-route transit systems with step-by-step instructions on how to attract individuals with disabilities and other potential riders to fixed-route services. The information presented reflects the results of extensive original research conducted by a team of experienced paratransit and fixed-route transit consultants.

This research addresses the following four market segments:

1. People with disabilities who currently use fixed-route transit,
2. People with disabilities who currently use paratransit,
3. Others who currently use paratransit, and
4. People with disabilities who normally do not use transit.

The fourth segment, generally the largest portion of the market, may be a significant area of growth for fixed-route transit systems. This Guidebook provides information on how to attract riders from each of the four market segments.[1]

ORGANIZATION OF THE GUIDEBOOK

The Guidebook consists of eight additional chapters as follows:

- Chapter 2, *Estimating Travel Demand*, provides step-by-step instructions for developing forecasts of how proposed

---

[1] The survey results (by municipality) and other information are provided in the Final Report for this Transit Cooperative Research Program, Project B-5, "Attracting Paratransit Patrons to Fixed-Route Services."

CHAPTER 1 INTRODUCTION

- changes to an existing local system will affect demand.
- Chapter 3, *Basic Steps*, discusses the four steps necessary to implement any approach found by the research to be positively correlated with citizen attitudes on fixed-route transit use.
- Chapter 4, *Locating Transit Stops Close to Passengers*, provides a step-by-step plan for using this technique to attract passengers.
- Chapter 5, *Training Drivers*, provides a step-by-step plan to teach drivers how to be sensitive to people with disabilities and how to assist them.
- Chapter 6, *Programming Accessible Bus Stop Improvements*, provides a step-by-step plan for improving bus stops so that individuals with disabilities find it easier to use the system.
- Chapter 7, *Teaching Passengers to Use the Fixed-Route System*, provides a step-by-step approach to providing effective travel training for individuals with disabilities.
- Chapter 8, *Marketing Fixed-Route Services*, provides a step-by-step plan for making individuals with disabilities aware of changes to the fixed-route system that will increase the available level of accessibility and increase the overall amenity level.
- Chapter 9, *Evaluating Success*, discusses how transit systems can assess whether or not the approaches they have used to attract individuals with disabilities to fixed-route services have been successful.

USING THIS GUIDEBOOK

The Guidebook is designed to minimize the amount of local data collection. Expensive, time-consuming interviews with local citizens are unnecessary because the national surveys provide information that can suggest local attitudes on the attributes of a fixed-route system.

Users should read Chapter 2, *Estimating Travel Demand*. After identifying the characteristics of the local fixed-route system and selecting the attributes of a "desired" system, users can consult the tables and other materials in order to determine the volume of

CHAPTER 1 INTRODUCTION

additional trips that could be expected to be achieved if the selected changes are made. If the resultant expected growth in trips from modal split is acceptable, Chapters 4 through 9 can be investigated to identify the actual steps necessary to implement each of the desired improvements.

Chapter 3 details the steps that users should take any time the system is modified.

It is unnecessary to read this Guidebook in its entirety at one sitting. Chapters 4 through 9 describe steps in support of the individual techniques selected for implementation by a system. To this end, the later chapters can be read as needed and in no particular order.

EXAMPLE

Example information is included throughout the document. It can be easily found by looking for the thickened vertical line to the left of the text. This location device is illustrated here.

CONCLUSIONS

This Guidebook reflects research which investigated the fixed-route service features most preferred by paratransit patrons. Each chapter includes methods to attract paratransit patrons and others to the fixed-route service. By implementing these methods, transit systems will reduce their overall cost per trip because some patrons will switch from more costly paratransit service to the fixed-route service for some or all of their trips.

CHAPTER 2: ESTIMATING TRAVEL DEMAND

CHAPTER 2   ESTIMATING TRAVEL DEMAND

INTRODUCTION

The techniques in this chapter can be used to quickly develop travel demand estimates for alternative fixed-route configurations that will attract people with disabilities to fixed-route services. Decision-making efforts can then concentrate on evaluating options from a number of perspectives, including benefit-cost ratios and economic analysis. It is always preferable to invest resources in evaluating alternatives rather than in developing data.

The demand estimation methodology can be used to accomplish two fundamental goals:

1. To compare and contrast a study system's paratransit and fixed-route ridership by people with disabilities with that of the system's peers; and
2. To establish an estimate of the number of people with disabilities in the service area of a study system who are expected to be attracted to fixed-route services if a specific set of improvements is made and to estimate the number of trips they would take on the fixed-route.

COMPARING A SYSTEM WITH ITS PEERS

Compare the local system to the system data tables based on geography, population density, topography, and climate.

Comparing a system with its peers is a quick, simple process of six steps as shown in Figure 2-1. These steps are as follows:[1]

1. Define the geographic location,
2. Define the population density,
3. Define the topography,
4. Define the climate,
5. Identify peer systems, and
6. Find peer system data.

Each step is described in detail in the following subsections.

---

[1] A full description of the statistical derivation of the peer system categories is located in the Final Report for TCRP Project B-5, "Attracting Paratransit Patrons to Fixed-Route Services."

CHAPTER 2   ESTIMATING TRAVEL DEMAND

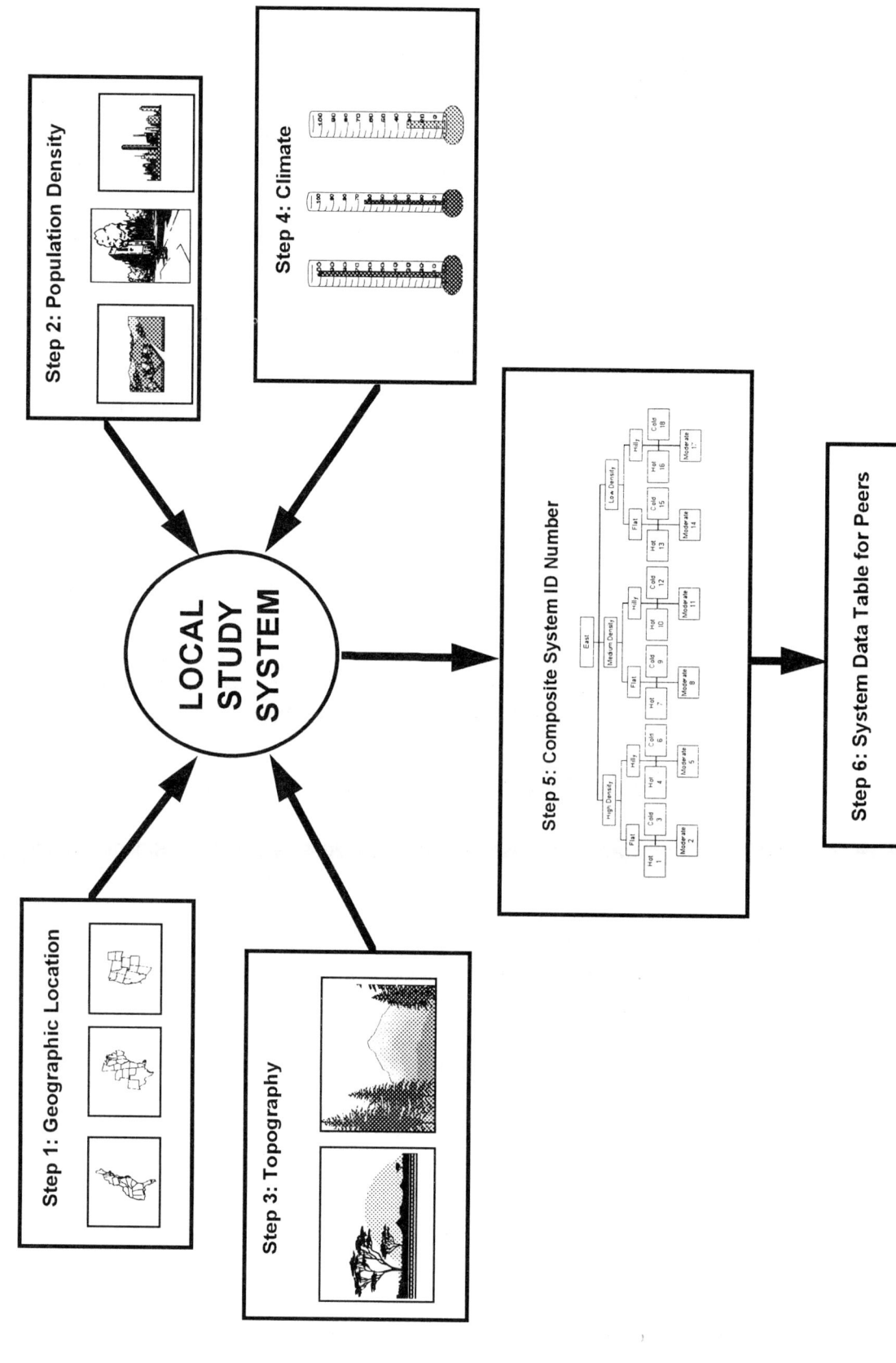

Figure 2-1. Steps to Compare a System with Its Peers

CHAPTER 2   ESTIMATING TRAVEL DEMAND

STEP 1: DEFINE GEOGRAPHIC LOCATION

Define the geographic location of the local study system. The three choices are as follows:

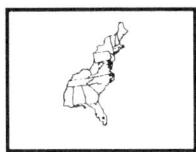

- **East** -- System is in Federal Transit Administration (FTA) Region 1, 2, 3, or 4;

- **Central** -- System is in FTA Region 5, 6, or 7; or

- **West** -- System is in FTA Region 8, 9, or 10.

The map illustrated in Figure 2-2 can be used to establish the appropriate FTA region.

Some states (such as Minnesota and Kentucky) have transit systems in two different FTA regions; this may affect which geographic location (East, Central, or West) best defines the system. In such cases, the transit system should use whichever FTA region with which it normally corresponds.

STEP 2: DEFINE POPULATION DENSITY

Define the population density of the service area of the local system. The three choices are as follows:

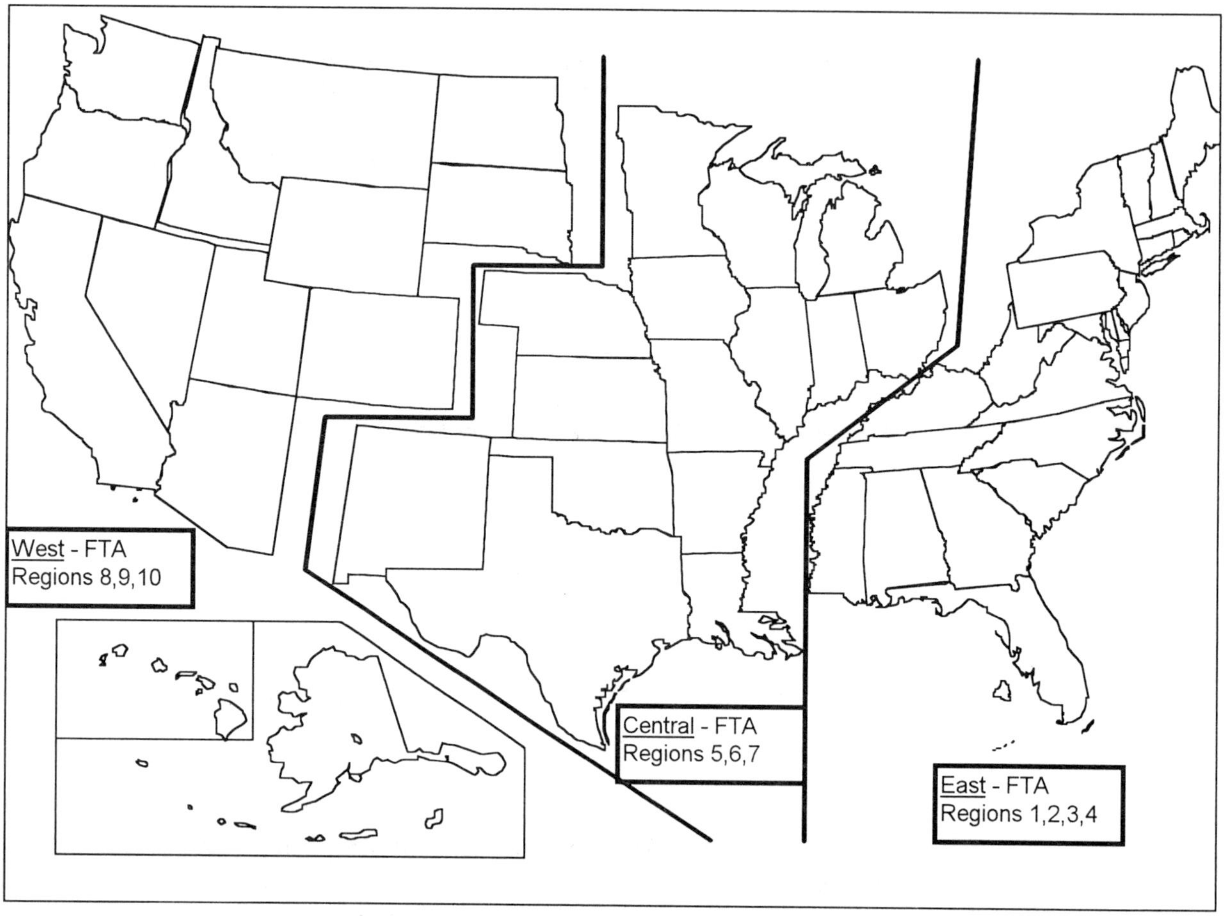

CHAPTER 2   ESTIMATING TRAVEL DEMAND

Figure 2-2. Geographic Locations of Transit Systems

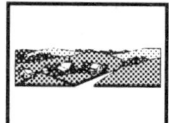

- **Low Density** -- The service area county density is less than 100 persons per square mile;

- **Medium Density** -- **(Suburban)** The service area county density is equal to or between 100 and 400 persons per square mile; or

- **High Density** -- **(Urban)** The service area county density is greater than 400 persons per square mile.

Because many transit systems operate in both urban and rural areas, such as downtown areas as well as suburban and/or rural routes, the density of the county where the transit system is

CHAPTER 2   ESTIMATING TRAVEL DEMAND

located should be used. The county population density may be obtained from the local planning commission, from any published data source (such as the current *County and City Data Book* from the U.S. Department of Commerce, Bureau of the Census, which is usually available at a local public or university library), or by dividing the total population of the county by the total land area in the county. Systems may also subjectively be categorized as rural, urban, or suburban.

STEP 3: DEFINE TOPOGRAPHY

Define the topography of the local study system. The two choices are as follows:

- **Flat** -- The topography has few hills or mountains as in some coastal areas, in plains areas, and in some desert areas; or

- **Hilly** -- The topography is characterized by large hills or mountains which can make it difficult for people with disabilities to move to and from fixed-route transit routes.

The topography of the service area is a subjective measure. Any representative from the transit system may judge whether the service area can be categorized as flat or hilly.

STEP 4: DEFINE CLIMATE

Define the climate of the local system. The three choices are as follows:

CHAPTER 2   ESTIMATING TRAVEL DEMAND

- **Hot** --   The average yearly temperature is greater than 58.7° F;

- **Moderate** -- The average yearly temperature is equal to or between 50.29° F and 58.70° F; or

- **Cold** --   The average yearly temperature is less than 50.29° F.

The data collected on average yearly temperatures from across the country exhibit a small range -- only 8.4° F separates hot from cold. If average yearly temperature data for the service area are readily available, or can easily be calculated, the transit system can categorize the climate as hot, moderate, or cold on the basis of the guidelines shown above. Sources of average annual temperature data include a local weather service at a news station or airport, a local weather almanac, an encyclopedia, or a collection of published climate data at a local or university library. Transit systems may also subjectively categorize the climate in the service area as hot, moderate, or cold.

After completing Steps 1 through 4, the local transit system should characterize itself using four descriptors: location, topography, density, and climate. This composite system description will be used to find other transit systems with similar characteristics.

CHAPTER 2   ESTIMATING TRAVEL DEMAND

STEP 5: IDENTIFY PEER SYSTEMS

From the composite system description obtained above, use the Peer Systems Chart shown in Figure 2-3 to obtain a category identification number. This identification number represents the composite transit system which most resembles the local study system. There are 54 different categories available.

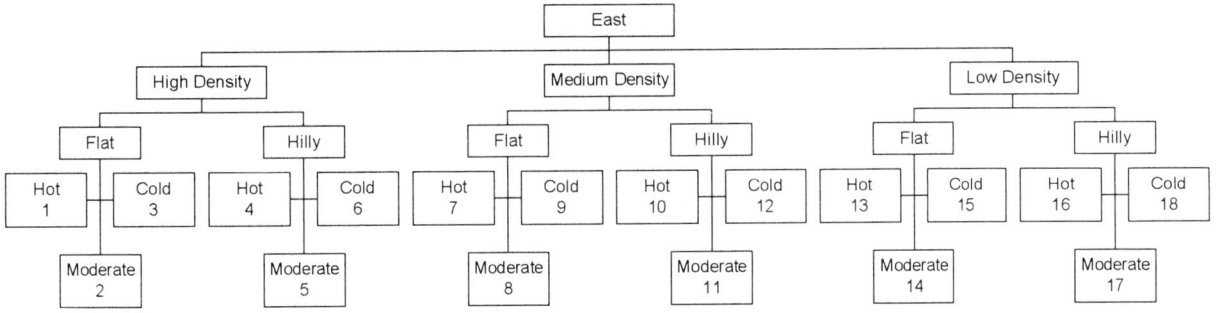

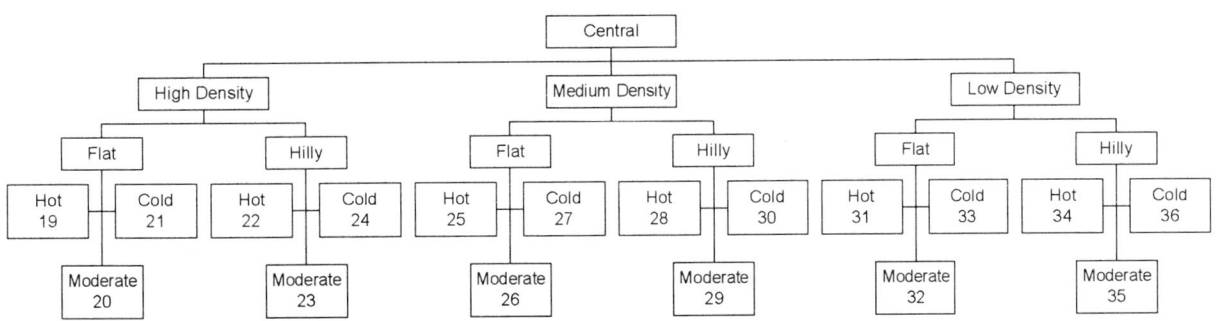

Figure 2-3. Peer Systems Chart

CHAPTER 2   ESTIMATING TRAVEL DEMAND

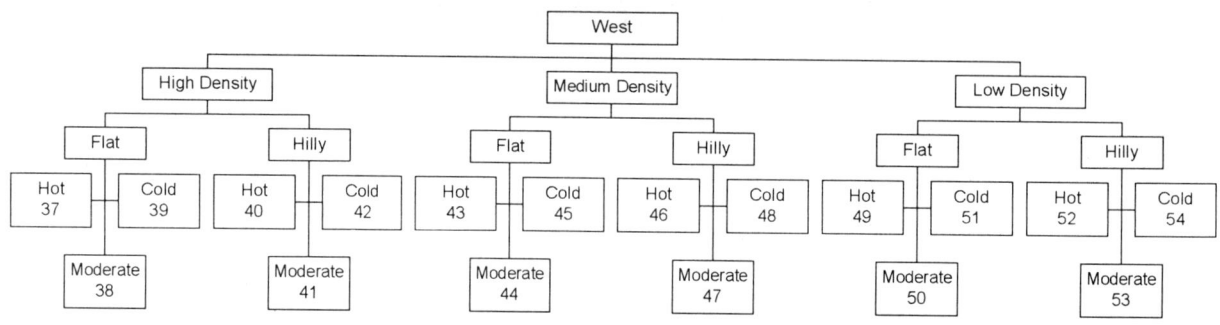

Figure 2-3. Peer Systems Chart (Concluded)

STEP 6: FIND PEER SYSTEM DATA

Once the identification number for the composite system has been determined, use the set of system data tables in Appendix A to find peer systems. Locate the system data table in Appendix A which has the corresponding identification number. This table will provide information (such as service area population, ADA-eligible population, annual paratransit trips provided, productivity, and fixed-route and paratransit vehicle fleet information) for the various transit systems from across the country that have the same composite system identification number.

COMPARISON OF A LOCAL SYSTEM WITH ITS PEERS

For an illustration of how to compare a local study system with its peers, assume that a local system has the following characteristics:

- Geographic location - Pennsylvania;
- Population density - 125 persons per square mile;
- Topography - rolling terrain; and
- Climate - average yearly temperature of 57° F.

Following Steps 1 through 4 as outlined above, the study system can be characterized by location, density, topography, and climate. Using these descriptors, the local study system is located in the **East**, with a **Medium Density (Suburban)** in the

2-8

CHAPTER 2   ESTIMATING TRAVEL DEMAND

Eastern location, medium density (suburban), hilly terrain, and moderate climate characterize System 11.

service area, a **Hilly** terrain, and a **Moderate** climate, as shown in Figure 2-4.

Figure 2-4. Composite Description of Example Study System

Following Step 5, the composite system description is compared to the Peer Systems Chart (Figure 2-3) to obtain an identification number. This identification number represents the composite transit system description which most resembles the local study system (see Figure 2-5).

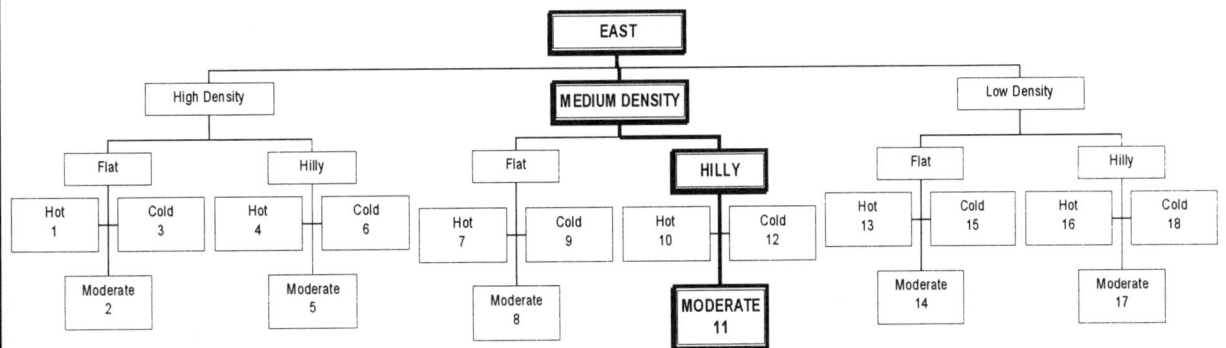

Figure 2-5. System Identification Number for the Example Study System

The Peer Systems Chart shows that the local study system has a composite system description identification number of 11. This allows the study system to compare itself with peers having the same descriptive characteristics

Following Step 6, review the system data tables in Appendix A to highlight those systems with identification number 11. The definitions for data categories (fields) used in the system data tables are included below in Tables 2-1 (population, trips, and productivity) and 2-2 (vehicle fleet) as well as in Appendix A. The system data tables for System 11 are shown in Tables 2-3 and 2-4.

CHAPTER 2   ESTIMATING TRAVEL DEMAND

Table 2-1. Population, Trips, and Productivity Definitions Used in the System Data Tables

NO. (Number): Each transit authority was assigned a number in the database. This number is only used for reference purposes.
STATE: Location state for the particular transit authority.
97 ADA ELIGIBLE: Number of individuals expected to be registered as ADA eligible in 1997 as reported by the transit authority. This number is in thousands in the tables.
SERV AREA POP: Total population of the service area as reported by the transit authority. This number is in thousands in the tables.
UZA POP: Total population of the urbanized area where the transit authority is located. This number is in thousands in the tables.
94 ADA PT TR/YR: Number of ADA paratransit trips provided in 1994 as reported by the transit authority. This number is in thousands in the tables.
97 ADA PT TR/YR: Number of ADA paratransit trips forecast to be provided in 1997 as reported by the transit authority. This number is in thousands in the tables.
97 REV HRS: Total number of paratransit (ADA and non-ADA) revenue hours forecast for 1997 as reported by the transit authority. This number is in thousands in the tables.
94 TOTAL PT TR/YR: Total number of (ADA and non-ADA) paratransit trips provided in 1994 as reported by the transit authority. This number is in thousands in the tables.
97 TOTAL PT TR/YR: Total number of (ADA and non-ADA) paratransit trips forecast to be provided in 1997 as reported by the transit authority. This number is in thousands in the tables.
97 PRODUCTIVITY: Expected paratransit productivity in trips per revenue hour for 1997. This number was calculated by dividing the total number of paratransit trips (ADA and non-ADA) forecast to be provided in 1997 by the number of total paratransit revenue hours (ADA and non-ADA) forecast for 1997.

CHAPTER 2 ESTIMATING TRAVEL DEMAND

Table 2-2. Vehicle Fleet Definitions Used in the System Data Tables

NO. (Number): Each transit authority was assigned a number in the database. This number is only used for reference purposes.
93 FR BUSES: The total number of buses in the fixed-route fleet in 1993 as reported by the transit authority.
97 FR BUSES: The total number of buses forecast to be in the fixed-route fleet in 1997 as reported by the transit authority.
93 ACC FR BUSES: The total number of accessible buses in the fixed-route fleet in 1993 as reported by the transit authority.
97 ACC FR BUSES: The total number of accessible buses forecast to be in the fixed-route fleet in 1997 as reported by the transit authority.
93 TOTAL FR BUS FLEET - PERCENT ACC: The percentage of the total fixed-route bus fleet that was accessible in 1993. This number was calculated by dividing the number of accessible fixed-route buses in 1993 by the total number of buses in the 1993 fixed-route bus fleet.
97 TOTAL FR BUS FLEET - PERCENT ACC: The percentage of the total fixed-route bus fleet forecast to be accessible in 1997. This number was calculated by dividing the number of accessible fixed-route buses forecast for 1997 by the total number of buses forecast for the 1997 fixed-route bus fleet.
BOARDINGS: This is the approximate number of boardings on the fixed-route system where lifts/ramps were deployed as reported by the transit authority. This number is in thousands in the tables.
93 ADA ACC FR BUSES: The total number of accessible buses in the fixed-route fleet in 1993 that meet ADA specifications as reported by the transit authority.
97 ADA ACC FR BUSES: The total number of accessible buses forecast to be in the fixed-route fleet that meet ADA specifications in 1997 as reported by the transit authority.
93 TOTAL PT FLEET: The total number of vehicles in the paratransit fleet in 1993 as reported by the transit authority.

CHAPTER 2   ESTIMATING TRAVEL DEMAND

Table 2-3.   System Data Tables for System 11: Data for East, Medium Density, Hilly Topography, Moderate Climate -- Population, Trips, Productivity

Note: Cells have been left blank when information has not been reported or is unavailable.

NO.	STATE	97 ADA ELIGIBLE	SERV AREA POP	UZA POP	94 ADA PT TR/YR	97 ADA PT TR/YR	97 REV HRS	94 TOTAL PT TR/YR	97 TOTAL PT TR/YR	97 PRODUC-TIVITY
57	NY	7.00	259.00	148.53	3	28	39	84	112	2.87
58	NY	0.44	29.00		0	124	27	0	124	4.57
77	MD	0.25	41.00	114.00	2	15	0	18	27	
79	MD	0.60	121.00	70.21	4	23	0.3	14	35	116.67
80	MD	1.00	75.00	54.66	8	9	0	21	22	
86	PA	0.20	80.00	19.00	5	5	32	110	135	4.22
87	PA	0.50	289.00	392.00	3	5	3.7	3	5	1.38
95	PA	5.50	25.00	186.27	21	41	49	213	247	5.04
97	PA	0.05	173.00	142.68	2	3	3.85	6	7	1.82
98	PA	0.11	43.25	77.84	0	0	11.5	39	44	3.83
100	PA	0.49	65.00	65.07	0	1	1	0	1	1.30
105	PA	0.13	106.00	0.00	1	1	46.5	124	133	2.86
106	PA	0.10		0.00	0	0	13.8	57	59	4.24
107	PA	0.15	33.00	0.00	1	1		1	1	
108	PA	0.06	38.00	0.00	0	104	3.5	0	8	2.29
109	PA	0.02	11.00	0.00	0	0	18.5	59	61	3.30
113	PA	0.30		0.00	0	1	2	0	12	5.75
118	PA	0.05		0.00	0	1		0	53	
119	PA	0.04	89.00	0.00	0	1	10.5	36	42	4.00
121	PA	0.05		0.00	0	0	0.023	0	0	6.96
132	VA	0.16	35.00	0.00	9	10	2.4	9	10	4.08
135	WV		104.00	169.59	8	9	4	8	9	2.25
136	WV	2.00	183.00	164.42	28	30	20	563	495	24.75
137	WV	0.40	70.00	84.51	10	20	13	10	20	1.54
138	WV	1.00	45.00	58.68	17	20	5	18	20	4.00
139	WV		1.00	0.00	0	4		0	4	
140	WV		4.00	0.00	0	3		0	3	
141	WV	0.30	45.00	0.00	4	6	6	4	6	1.00
142	WV		4.00	0.00	0	3		0	12	
179	KY	0.06	25.85	170.00	8	8	1.8	8	8	4.44
180	KY	0.82	53.00	60.65	16	20	11	17	20	1.82
181	KY	0.03	24.00	0.00	7	8	2.76	7	8	2.75
182	KY	0.13	36.60	0.00	1	10	3.6	7	10	2.64
198	NC	1.16	66.00	110.43	23	30	9.8	23	30	3.10
206	NC	0.01	13.00	13.00	1	1	0.4	1	1	2.50
224	TN	0.12	10.90	87.40	1	1	0.85	1	1	1.65
226	TN	0.03	23.40	52.56	0	1	7.6	21	23	2.97
228	TN	0.73	45.40	82.38	17	22	8.3	18	23	2.80

CHAPTER 2   ESTIMATING TRAVEL DEMAND

Table 2-4.   System Data Tables for System 11: Data for East, Medium Density, Hilly Topography, Moderate Climate -- Vehicle Fleet

Note: Cells have been left blank when information has not been reported or is unavailable.

NO.	93 FR BUSES	97 FR BUSES	93 ACC FR BUSES	97 ACC FR BUSES	93 TOTAL FR BUS FLEET - % ACC	97 TOTAL FR BUS FLEET - % ACC	BOARD -INGS	93 ADA ACC FR BUSES	97 ADA ACC FR BUSES	93 TOTAL PT FLEET
57	15	15	0	15	0%	100%	0	0	15	24
58	8	8	8	8	100%	100%	0.208	2	7	0
77	5	9	5	9	100%	100%	1.2	0	9	4
79	14	14	9	14	64%	100%	0.5	0	14	4
80	12	12	7	12	58%	100%	0.012	0	6	9
86	11	11	1	3	9%	27%	0.005	1	3	6
87	22	22	18	18	82%	82%	0.1	2	10	10
95	56	56	35	44	63%	79%	0.65	35	44	35
97	22	22	19	22	86%	100%	4.69	1	15	6
98	34	34	31	34	91%	100%	5.178	4	20	8
100	14	21	10	21	71%	100%	0.137	10	21	0
105	12	13	7	13	58%	100%	1.4	5	6	42
106	0	0	0	0						19
107	3	3	3	3	100%	100%	0.09	3	3	6
108	12	12	0	12	0%	100%	0	2	12	13
109	5	5	4	4	80%	80%	0	4	4	19
113	4	8	0	4	0%	50%	0	0	4	0
118	0	0	0	0						0
119	9	10	9	10	100%	100%	3	3	5	11
121	2	4	2	4	100%	100%	0.036	2	4	1
132	28	30	3	16	11%	53%	0.008	3	16	4
135	29	32	0	30	0%	94%	0	0	30	5
136	58	55	8	35	14%	64%	3	8	35	9
137	20	20	14	14	70%	70%	0.08	2	6	5
138	15	14	5	5	33%	36%	0	4	4	2
139	0	0	0	0						0
140	0	0	0	0						0
141	7	7	0	0	0%	0%	0	0	0	2
142	0	0	0	0						0
179	6	6	3	6	50%	100%	0.072	3	6	1
180	8	8	8	8	100%	100%	0.1	0	2	4
181	5	5	5	5	100%	100%	0.3	0	0	1
182	8	8	3	5	38%	63%	0.025	0	4	2
198	25	20	0	16	0%	80%	0	0	16	17
206	12	12	1	12	8%	100%	0.003	1	12	3
224	2	5	1	4	50%	80%	0	0	3	3
226	4	4	4	4	100%	100%	0	4	4	3
228	10	10	2	2	20%	20%	0	2	2	4

CHAPTER 2 ESTIMATING TRAVEL DEMAND

Transit systems should consider how a change in population density will affect them.

The system data tables for System 11 contain comparison information on 38 transit systems in New York, Maryland, Pennsylvania, West Virginia, Kentucky, North Carolina, and Tennessee. These are the transit systems (within the database of 536) that may be considered peers to the system under study.

Although geographic location, topography, and climate will not change over time for a local transit system, population density could change as a result of population growth. A transit system may want to look at a future version of the system by observing the data for systems with similar location, topography, and climate, but higher density. In the case of the study system in this example, this could be accomplished by looking at the composite system description of **East**, **High Density (Urban)**, **Hilly**, and **Moderate** climate as shown in Figure 2-6. The identification number for this system is 5 as shown in Figure 2-7.

Eastern location, high density (urban), hilly terrain, and a moderate climate characterize System 5.

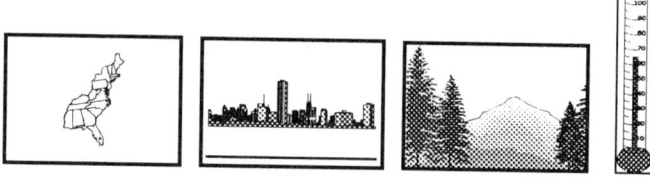

Figure 2-6. Composite Description of Example Study System with Higher Density

CHAPTER 2   ESTIMATING TRAVEL DEMAND

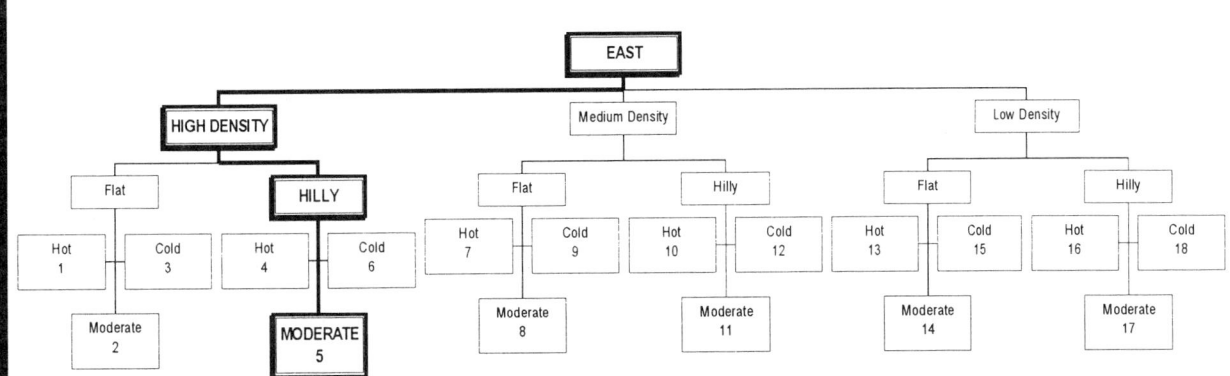

Figure 2-7. System Identification Number for the Example Study System with Higher Density

Looking at other areas of the country for comparison may be beneficial.

The system data tables for System 5 (see Tables 2-5 and 2-6) contain information on 18 transit systems from Massachusetts, Maryland, Pennsylvania, Virginia, Kentucky, North Carolina, and Tennessee. These are the transit systems (within the database of 536) that may resemble the study system if the population density increases in the future.

To compare itself with peers in other areas of the country, a system switches the location descriptor. If the example study system wanted to observe characteristics of similar systems in the west, the descriptors would become **West**, **Medium Density (Suburban)**, **Hilly**, and **Moderate**, which corresponds to identification number 47. The system data tables for System 47 are in Appendix A.

CHAPTER 2   ESTIMATING TRAVEL DEMAND

Table 2-5.   System Data Tables for System 5: Data for East, High Density, Hilly Topography, Moderate Climate -- Population, Trips, Productivity

Note: Cells have been left blank when information has not been reported or is unavailable

NO.	STATE	97 ADA ELIGIBLE	SERV AREA POP	UZA POP	94 ADA PT TR/YR	97 ADA PT TR/YR	97 REV HRS	94 TOTAL PT TR/YR	97 TOTAL PT TR/YR	97 PRODUC-TIVITY
17	MA	3.20	551.50	533.00	54	74	125	265	286	2.28
75	MD	1.74	117.00		19	19	2.4	93	93	38.75
76	MD		78.00	1889.87	168	256	0	168	256	
88	PA		99.00	204.00	22	23	16	65	66	4.13
90	PA	5.50	538.00	410.44	159	190	1100	306	360	0.33
93	PA		391.00	292.90	7	7	3	7	7	2.33
104	PA	0.09	45.00		3	7	2	3	7	3.35
125	VA	0.85	100.00	178.28	17	23	14	17	23	1.61
127	VA	0.40	78.00	98.14	15	22	4.2	15	22	5.24
129	VA	3.00	68.00	0.00	65	73	0	65	73	
131	VA	0.06	22.00	0.00	4	4	3.2	4	4	1.34
134	VA		30.00	0.00	15	19	0	15	19	
177	KY	11.00	665.00	754.96	298	335	199	322	362	1.82
178	KY	4.50	225.00	220.70	99	102	35.3	35	35	1.00
195	NC	2.70	206.00	194.51	72	83	47	92	141	3.00
221	TN	8.00	510.00	573.30	124	164	67	134	174	2.60
222	TN	1.65	208.00	304.50	41	63	29.9	41	63	2.11
231	VA	0.03	18.40		25	40	80	25	40	0.50

CHAPTER 2   ESTIMATING TRAVEL DEMAND

Table 2-6. System Data Tables for System 5: Data for East, High Density, Hilly Topography, Moderate Climate -- Vehicle Fleet

Note: Cells have been left blank when information has not been reported or is unavailable

NO.	93 FR BUSES	97 FR BUSES	93 ACC FR BUSES	97 ACC FR BUSES	93 TOTAL FR BUS FLEET - % ACC	97 TOTAL FR BUS FLEET - % ACC	BOARD INGS	93 ADA ACC FR BUSES	97 ADA ACC FR BUSES	93 TOTAL PT FLEET
17	178	178	26	93	15%	52%	0.26	11	78	47
75	8	8	8	8	100%	100%	0.208	0	0	43
76	0	0	0	0						0
88	13	15	4	5	31%	33%	0.003	4	5	22
90	70	70	3	38	4%	54%	0.012	3	38	101
93	67	65	0	24	0%	37%	0	0	24	12
104	5	10	5	10	100%	100%	0.3	5	10	2
125	38	38	10	28	26%	74%	0.431	28	28	15
127	26	26	5	20	19%	77%	0.037	5	20	3
129	16	16	3	16	19%	100%	0.26	0	13	28
131	11	10	0	7	0%	70%	0	0	7	1
134	15	16	6	13	40%	81%	0	3	10	3
177	302	302	172	260	57%	86%	1.25	0	130	65
178	40	36	7	14	18%	39%	3.12	5	14	14
195	22	27	22	27	100%	100%	1.228	22	27	12
221	132	142	29	71	22%	50%	1	29	71	35
222	58	58	8	19	14%	33%	0	7	18	7
231	5	5	2	5	40%	100%	0	0	20	4

CHAPTER 2   ESTIMATING TRAVEL DEMAND

ESTIMATING RIDERSHIP PREFERENCES FOR AN IMPROVED FIXED-ROUTE SYSTEM BY PARATRANSIT PATRONS AND PEOPLE WITH DISABILITIES

Once a system has been compared with peers, planners may want to estimate what improvements to the fixed-route system are preferred by paratransit patrons and people with disabilities. Planners can use comparisons of current systems to improved systems to estimate ridership on a fixed-route system by paratransit patrons and people with disabilities if improvements are implemented on the fixed-route service. This methodology allows decision-makers to evaluate different options using cost-benefit ratios and economic analyses. The focus is on evaluating alternative improved systems rather than collecting data.

Ridership estimates can be accomplished in the steps described below. Tables 2-7 through 2-14 are at the end of this section for the convenience of the user.

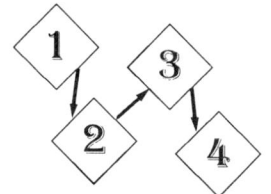

Use Tables 2-8 and 2-9 to estimate ridership preferences for a set of improvements to a fixed-route system.

STEP 1: EXAMINE CURRENT SYSTEM DESCRIPTIONS

Examine the current system descriptions in Table 2-7. These descriptions of five current fixed-route systems (Current System A through Current System E) address seven service features: transit stop distance, convenience, general atmosphere, transit stops, security, vehicle accessibility, and driver training.[2] Choosing a system which best matches the current description allows the user to develop a base line against which all other potential systems can be monitored and evaluated.

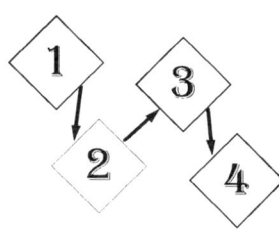

STEP 2: CHOOSE ONE CURRENT SYSTEM DESCRIPTION

Choose the system in Table 2-7 which best describes the current system. More than one of the systems in Table 2-7 may describe the current system. This is because so many variations are possible that any one current system description may not exactly match the characteristics of the study system. This may result in

---

[2] Current systems are those which include the least preferred service feature configurations, based on a conjoint analysis of the results of a survey of representative paratransit patrons.

CHAPTER 2 ESTIMATING TRAVEL DEMAND

a range of estimates being made using different systems, if appropriate.

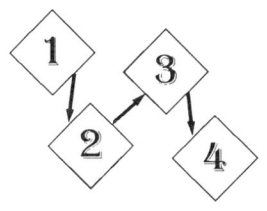

STEP 3: EXAMINE IMPROVED SYSTEM DESCRIPTION

Examine the improved system descriptions in Table 2-8. These descriptions of 20 improved fixed-route systems (Improved System A through Improved System T) illustrate what the current fixed-route system would be like if a specific set of improvements was made.[3]

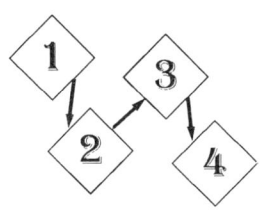

STEP 4: CHOOSE IMPROVED SYSTEM

Choose the system which best describes what the fixed-route system would look like after improvements are implemented. More than one of the systems in Table 2-8 may describe the improved system. If appropriate, the system can produce estimates for each system. This may be necessary because so many possible combinations of improved systems are possible that no one in particular will meet the exact needs of the study system.

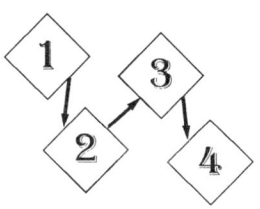

STEP 5: DETERMINE FIXED-ROUTE FARE

Determine the base fixed-route fare.

STEP 6: EXAMINE MODAL SPLIT TABLE

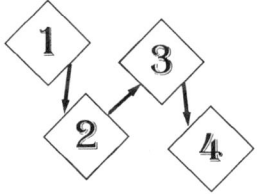

Examine Table 2-9. The current system descriptions (A-E) are listed in the left-hand column, and the Improved Systems (A-T) are in the first row. There are five fare levels associated with each current system. This table shows the percentage of all paratransit patrons and individuals with disabilities who would prefer each of the improved systems, as well as those who would prefer the current fixed-route system.

---

[3] Improved systems are those which include the preferred service configurations, based on a conjoint analysis of the results of a survey of representative paratransit patrons.

CHAPTER 2 ESTIMATING TRAVEL DEMAND

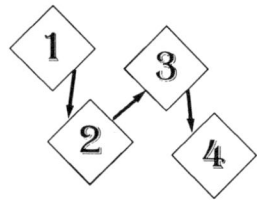

STEP 7: IDENTIFY PROPER TABLE ROW

Find the current system description and existing fixed-route fare. Applying the fixed-route fare to the current system that was chosen will identify the proper row in Table 2-9 for the system.

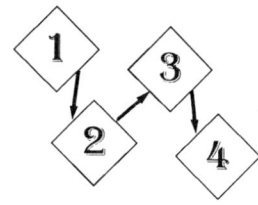

STEP 8: DETERMINE PREFERRED PERCENT

After locating the proper row describing the current system and fare, read across the row to the appropriate column with the improved fixed-route system chosen. This number indicates the percent of paratransit patrons and individuals with disabilities who would prefer the improved system over all other improved systems

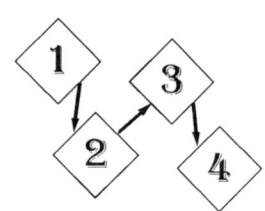

STEP 9: DETERMINE PERCENT CURRENTLY SATISFIED

Using the proper row describing the current system and fare, read across the row to the "current" column. This number indicates the percent of paratransit patrons and individuals with disabilities who would prefer the current fixed-route system (without any improvements) over all other improved systems. If individuals would prefer the current fixed-route system over the improved system as chosen by the transit system, the improvements scheduled to be made should be reevaluated, and different, more effective measures may need to be considered.

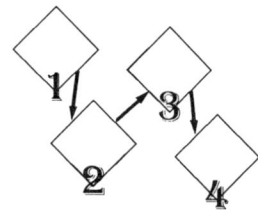

STEP 10: DETERMINE VOLUME OF RIDERS PREFERRING NEW SYSTEM

Multiply the forecast number of ADA-eligible riders in 1997 for the local study system (or from the peer systems found in the system data tables) by the appropriate percentage found from Table 2-9. This number represents the actual *total* number of ADA-eligible persons who would prefer a particular fixed-route system.

CHAPTER 2 ESTIMATING TRAVEL DEMAND

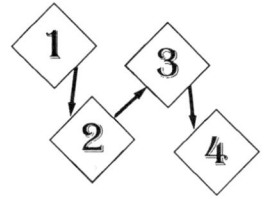

STEP 11: ESTIMATE TRIP VOLUME DIVERSIONS

The final step is to arrive at estimates for the volume of trips that may be diverted to fixed-route services. Multiply the number of persons preferring an improved fixed-route system (as determined in Step 10) by trip generation rates from local system current statistics. If the local system does not keep these statistics, data from the peer systems in the system data tables may be used.

ESTIMATING RIDERSHIP PREFERENCES BY MARKET SEGMENT

Use Tables 2-10 through 2-13 to estimate preferences by market segment.

The research for the Guidebook identified four categories of paratransit patrons. Each category or market segment had different preferences for fixed-route service. The market segments are as follows:

- Market Segment 1 consists of people with disabilities who use fixed-route.
- Market Segment 2 consists of people with disabilities who use paratransit.
- Market Segment 3 consists of others who use paratransit.
- Market Segment 4 consists of people with disabilities who do not use transit.

Transit systems may want to estimate ridership for each of the four market segments. To do so, follow the steps below.

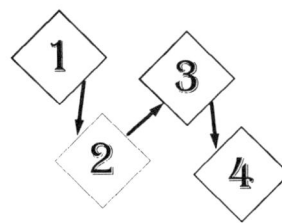

STEP 1: ESTIMATE MARKET SEGMENT SIZES

To estimate the number of paratransit-eligible individuals in each market segment who would prefer a particular fixed-route system, planners must determine the size of each market segment. This may be done by examining local system client data and trip records. Transit systems generally have disability information on clients in a database or on client lists and have a record of the trips riders have taken on paratransit. This is either on driver manifests or trip logs or in the computerized scheduling system. This information can be used to determine the sizes of some of the market segments.

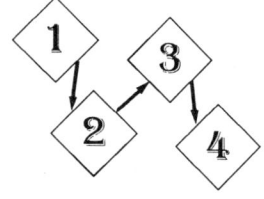

STEP 1A: ESTIMATE SIZE OF MARKET SEGMENT 1

Market Segment 1, people with disabilities who use fixed-route, is possible to determine for some systems. For those systems that use conditional or trip-by-trip eligibility, those who are conditionally eligible would be the market segment of people who use fixed-route. That segment may also include those who have been referred to the fixed-route for particular trips or those who have been referred for travel training. For those systems that do not have information on fixed-route use, a survey can be used for estimating the market segment size.

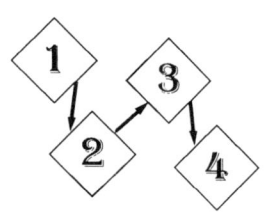

STEP 1B: ESTIMATE SIZE OF MARKET SEGMENT 2

Market Segment 2 consists of people with disabilities who use paratransit. From the client database, the transit system can list and count the clients with disabilities who have taken a paratransit trip. The transit system can determine from their experience whether they should limit that in some way, for example, to people who have taken a paratransit trip in the last year or the last 6 months.

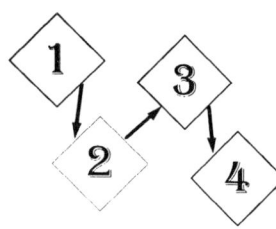

STEP 1C: ESTIMATE SIZE OF MARKET SEGMENT 3

Market Segment 3 consists of other people who use paratransit. For those systems that provide paratransit for people who are eligible on a basis other than disability, list and count the number of people without a disability who have taken a paratransit trip. This can be limited to people who have taken a paratransit trip in the last year or the last 6 months. For those systems which limit paratransit eligibility to people with disabilities, the size of Market Segment 3 is zero.

CHAPTER 2   ESTIMATING TRAVEL DEMAND

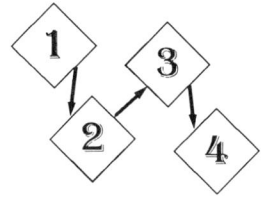

STEP 1D: ESTIMATE SIZE OF MARKET SEGMENT 4

Market Segment 4 consists of people with disabilities who do not use transit. The rider database can indicate which people with disabilities have not taken a paratransit trip in the specified period. Information on whether such people have used fixed-route can be determined through a survey.

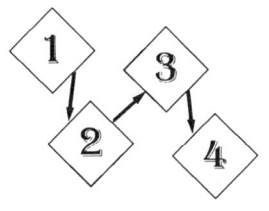

STEP 1E: USE OF DEFAULT DATA

Estimate the size of all market segments using TCRP data. If a transit system cannot estimate market segment size on the basis of its own data and survey results, the results of this research can be used as a default. Table 2-14 shows market segment sizes as reflected in surveys of five mid-sized cities. These sizes are based on the survey respondents used in this study, so more specific information can be gathered at individual transit systems.

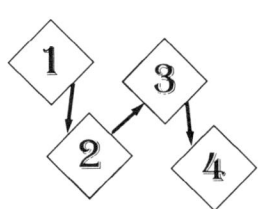

STEP 2: DETERMINE PERCENTAGE OF PEOPLE WHO PREFER FIXED-ROUTE AND CURRENT OPTIONS

Examine Tables 2-10 through 2-13. Similar to Table 2-9, Tables 2-10 through 2-13 describe percentages of people who would prefer each current or improved fixed-route system; however, Table 2-9 includes *all* paratransit patrons and people with disabilities, whereas Tables 2-10 through 2-13 group these individuals into market segments. Table 2-10 shows figures for Market Segment 1, (people with disabilities who use fixed-route services). Table 2-11 shows figures for Market Segment 2 (people with disabilities who use paratransit). Table 2-12 shows figures for Market Segment 3 (others who use paratransit). Table 2-13 shows figures for Market Segment 4 (people with disabilities who do not normally use transit).

CHAPTER 2   ESTIMATING TRAVEL DEMAND

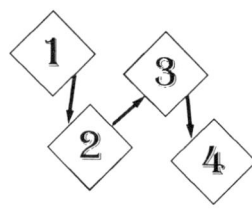

STEP 3: DETERMINE PREFERENCES BY MARKET SEGMENT

To determine preferences by market segment, follow the same procedures described to estimate preferences for all patrons with disabilities in Steps 1 through 10; however, use Tables 2-10 through 2-13 instead.

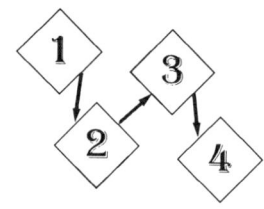

STEP 4: DETERMINE VOLUME PREFERRING FIXED-ROUTE BY MARKET SEGMENT

Multiply the calculated number of ADA-eligible riders in 1997 for each market segment as determined in Step 1 by the appropriate percentages found in Tables 2-10 through 2-13 as determined in Step 3. These numbers represent the number of ADA-eligible persons in each market segment who would prefer a particular fixed-route system.

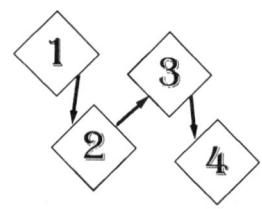

STEP 5: ESTIMATE VOLUME OF TRIPS DIVERTED

To estimate the volume of trips that may be diverted to fixed-route services, multiply the number of people in the market segment who prefer an improved fixed-route system (as determined in Step 4) by trip generation rates from local system current statistics. If the local system does not keep these statistics, data from the peer systems in the system data tables may be used.

These demand estimates give empirical, maximum numbers of diverted trips. However, the likelihood of individuals actually using the system may be somewhat different. To further refine estimates of people using improved fixed-route services, follow the directions in the next section, Probability of Purchase.

CHAPTER 2   ESTIMATING TRAVEL DEMAND

Table 2-7. Current System Descriptions

Current System A

Service Feature
A consumer has a short traveling distance to and from the vehicle
The schedules are reliable
Other passengers don't complain when a consumer needs extra time
Schedules a consumer can use are at the stops
Uniformed officers may be on the vehicles
Mobility or other equipment can be stored near the consumer
Drivers understand boarding and securing wheelchairs

Current System B

Service Feature
There are no uphill portions on the way to the vehicle
The schedules are reliable
Other passengers don't complain when a consumer needs extra time
Schedules a consumer can use are at the stops
Vehicle stops have security cameras
Mobility or other equipment can be stored near the consumer
Drivers move people out of the front seats when a consumer with a disability asks

Current System C

Service Feature
There are no uphill portions on the way to the vehicle
The schedules are reliable
Vehicle doesn't move until consumers are ready
Schedules a consumer can use are at the stops
Vehicle stops have security cameras
Mobility or other equipment can be stored near the consumer
Drivers understand boarding and securing wheelchairs

CHAPTER 2   ESTIMATING TRAVEL DEMAND

Table 2-7. Current System Descriptions (Concluded)

Current System D

Service Feature
A consumer has no big roads to cross to get to the vehicle
Vehicle stops near the consumer's home and goes where the consumer wants
Other passengers don't complain when a consumer needs extra time
Shelters are lighted
A consumer feels safe waiting for the vehicle
Vehicle is close to the ground and has no steps
Drivers move people out of the front seats when a consumer with a disability asks

Current System E

Service Feature
A consumer has a short traveling distance to and from the vehicle
Arrangements are made for consumers if the vehicle or lift breaks down
Other passengers don't complain when a consumer needs extra time
Stops have benches
Uniformed officers may be on the vehicles
Consumers can be trained on using the transit system
Drivers understand boarding and securing wheelchairs

CHAPTER 2 ESTIMATING TRAVEL DEMAND

Table 2-8. Improved System Descriptions

Improved System A

Service Feature
Trip costs up to $1.00
A consumer has no big roads to cross to get to the vehicle
Vehicle stops near the consumer's home and goes where the consumer wants
A consumer doesn't have to transfer vehicles and the trips are short
Stops have large, covered shelters
A consumer feels safe traveling to and from the vehicle
Drivers announce all stops and routes
Drivers drive safely

Improved System B

Service Feature
Trip costs up to $1.00
There are sidewalks between a consumer and the vehicle
Arrangements are made for consumers if the vehicle or lift breaks down
A consumer doesn't have to transfer vehicles and the trips are short
Shelters are lighted
A consumer feels safe traveling to and from the vehicle
Drivers announce all stops and routes
Drivers drive safely

Improved System C

Service Feature
Trip costs up to $1.00
A consumer has no big roads to cross to get to the vehicle
A consumer can always leave and arrive when he/she wants
A consumer always has a seat or a wheelchair position
Shelters are lighted
A consumer feels safe waiting for the vehicle
Drivers announce all stops and routes
Drivers don't complain when a consumer needs help

CHAPTER 2   ESTIMATING TRAVEL DEMAND

Table 2-8. Improved System Descriptions (Continued)

Improved System D

Service Feature
Trip is free
There are sidewalks between a consumer and the vehicle
The schedules are reliable
Vehicle is a comfortable temperature
Stops have large, covered shelters
Vehicle stops have security cameras
A consumer can board in his/her wheelchair and be secured in it
Driver knows how to communicate with consumers

Improved System E

Service Feature
Trips costs up to $1.00
A consumer has no big roads to cross to get to the vehicle
Vehicle stops near the consumer's home and goes where the consumer wants
The consumer doesn't have to transfer vehicles and the trips are short
Stops are clearly labeled
The consumer feels safe traveling to and from the vehicle
The consumer can board in his/her wheelchair and be secured in it
Drivers know how to communicate with consumers

Improved System F

Service Feature
Trip costs between $1.01 and $2.00
There are no curbs or steps on the way to the vehicle
A consumer can always leave and arrive when he/she wants
A consumer always has a seat or a wheelchair position
Shelters are lighted
A consumer is not exposed to crime on the vehicle
A consumer can board in his/her wheelchair and be secured in it
Drivers know how to communicate with consumers

CHAPTER 2   ESTIMATING TRAVEL DEMAND

Table 2-8. Improved System Descriptions (Continued)

Improved System G

Service Feature
Trip costs between $1.01 and $2.00
A consumer has no big roads to cross to get to the vehicle
A consumer can always leave and arrive when he/she wants
Vehicle doesn't move until consumers are ready
Stops have large, covered shelters
A consumer is not exposed to crime on the vehicle
A consumer can board in his/her wheelchair and be secured in it
Drivers don't complain when a consumer needs help

Improved System H

Service Feature
Trip costs between $1.01 and $2.00
A consumer has a short traveling distance to and from the vehicle
Vehicle stops near the consumer's home and goes where the consumer wants
A consumer doesn't have to transfer vehicles and the trips are short
Stops have benches
A consumer feels safe traveling to and from the vehicle
A consumer can board in his/her wheelchair and be secured in it
Drivers move people out of the front seats when a consumer with a disability asks

Improved System I

Service Feature
Trip costs up to $1.00
There are no curbs or steps on the way to the vehicle
Arrangements are made for consumers if the vehicle or lift breaks down
Vehicle doesn't move until consumers are ready
Stops have benches
Uniformed officers may be on the vehicles
Drivers announce all stops and routes
Drivers don't complain when a consumer needs help

CHAPTER 2   ESTIMATING TRAVEL DEMAND

Table 2-8. Improved System Descriptions (Continued)

Improved System J

Service Feature
Trip costs between $1.01 and $2.00
There are no uphill portions on the way to the vehicle
A consumer can always leave and arrive when he/she wants
A consumer always has a seat or wheelchair position
Stops have large, covered shelters
A consumer is not exposed to crime on the vehicle
Drivers announce all stops and routes
Drivers don't complain when a consumer needs help

Improved System K

Service Feature
Trip is free
There are no uphill portions on the way to the vehicle
Arrangements are made for consumers if the vehicle or lift breaks down
Vehicle is clean
Stops are clearly labeled
A consumer feels safe waiting for the vehicle
Vehicle is close to the ground and has no steps
Drivers don't complain when a consumer needs help

Improved System L

Service Feature
Trip is free
There are no curbs or steps on the way to the vehicle
Vehicle stops near the consumer's home and goes where the consumer wants
A consumer always has a seat or wheelchair position
Stops have benches
Uniformed officers may be on the vehicles
Vehicle is close to the ground and has no steps
Drivers know how to communicate with consumers

CHAPTER 2 ESTIMATING TRAVEL DEMAND

Table 2-8. Improved System Descriptions (Continued)

Improved System M

Service Feature
Trip is free
There are no curbs or steps on the way to the vehicle
Vehicle stops near the consumer's home and goes where the consumer wants
A consumer always has a seat or wheelchair position
Stops have benches
Uniformed officers may be on the vehicles
Vehicle is close to the ground and has no steps
Drivers know how to communicate with consumers

Improved System N

Service Feature
Trip costs between $2.01 and $3.00
A consumer has a short traveling distance to and from the vehicle
A consumer doesn't have to call ahead to make arrangements
A consumer always has a seat or wheelchair position
Stops are clearly labeled
A consumer feels safe traveling to and from the vehicle
Mobility or other equipment can be stored near the consumer
Drivers drive safely

Improved System O

Service Feature
Trip is free
There are no curbs or steps on the way to the vehicle
A consumer doesn't have to call ahead to make arrangements
Vehicle is clean
Schedules a consumer can use are at the stops
Vehicle stops have security cameras
Vehicle is close to the ground and has no steps
Drivers move people out of the front seats when a consumer with a disability asks

CHAPTER 2   ESTIMATING TRAVEL DEMAND

Table 2-8. Improved System Descriptions (Continued)

Improved System P

Service Feature
Trip costs over $3.00
There are sidewalks between a consumer and the vehicle
A consumer doesn't have to call ahead to make arrangements
Vehicle is a comfortable temperature
Stops have benches
Vehicle stops have security cameras
Consumers can be trained on using the transit system
Drivers move people out of the front seats when a consumer with a disability asks

Improved System Q

Service Feature
Trip costs between $2.01 and $3.00
A consumer has a short traveling distance to and from the vehicle
A consumer doesn't have to call ahead to make arrangements
Vehicle is clean
Stops are clearly labeled
A consumer feels safe waiting for the vehicle
Consumers can be trained on using the transit system
Drivers understand boarding and securing wheelchairs

Improved System R

Service Feature
Trip costs between $2.01 and $3.00
There are sidewalks between a consumer and the vehicle
A consumer doesn't have to call ahead to make arrangements
Other passengers don't complain when a consumer needs extra time
Stops are clearly labeled
Uniformed officers may be on the vehicles
Consumers can be trained on using the transit system
Drivers know how to communicate with consumers

CHAPTER 2   ESTIMATING TRAVEL DEMAND

Table 2-8. Improved System Descriptions (Concluded)

Improved System S

Service Feature
Trip costs between $1.01 and $2.00
There are no uphill portions on the way to the vehicle
A consumer can always leave and arrive when he/she wants
Vehicle is clean
Schedules a consumer can use are at the stops
A consumer is not exposed to crime on the vehicle
Consumers can be trained on using the transit system
Drivers understand boarding and securing wheelchairs

Improved System T

Service Feature
Trip costs over $3.00
There are sidewalks between a consumer and the vehicle
The schedules are reliable
Vehicle is a comfortable temperature
Shelters are lighted
A consumer feels safe waiting for the vehicle
Mobility or other equipment can be stored near the consumer
Drivers drive safely

CHAPTER 2 ESTIMATING TRAVEL DEMAND

Table 2-9. Percent of Paratransit Consumers and People With Disabilities Who Prefer Each Current or Improved System

CURRENT SYSTEMS	Current Design	IMPROVED SYSTEMS																			
		A	B	C	D	E	F	G	H	I	J	K	L	M	N	O	P	Q	R	S	T
Current A - Free	3.3	5	2.9	2.9	2	4.8	5.7	7.2	13.6	3.3	4.6	2.7	3.1	4.9	9.3	2.3	2.7	7.9	3.8	5.9	2.2
Current A - to $1.00	5.5	4.8	2.4	3	2	4.8	5.7	7.2	13.8	3.3	4.6	2.8	3.1	4.8	8.6	2.3	2.9	8	2.7	5.7	2.2
Current A - $1.00 to $2.00	4.8	5	2.8	3	1.9	4.8	5.7	7.2	13.6	3.1	4.5	2.8	3.1	4.8	8.8	2.3	2.8	7.6	3.7	5.6	2.2
Current A - $2.00 to $3.00	4	5.1	2.9	3.1	2	4.9	5.7	7.2	13.5	3.2	4.5	2.8	3.2	4.9	8.9	2.3	2.8	7.7	3.7	5.5	2.2
Current A - over $3.00	3.3	5.1	2.9	3.1	2	4.9	5.8	7.3	13.8	3.3	4.6	2.8	3.2	4.9	8.7	2.3	2.8	7.5	3.7	5.7	2.2
Current B - Free	2.8	5.1	2.9	3.1	2	4.9	5.8	7.3	13.8	3.3	4.6	2.8	3.2	4.9	9	2.3	2.8	7.7	3.8	5.7	2.2
Current B - to $1.00	5.1	4.8	2.4	3	1.9	4.8	5.8	7.2	13.8	3.3	4.5	2.8	3.2	4.8	8.8	2.1	2.8	8.3	2.8	5.7	2.2
Current B - $1.00 to $2.00	4.6	5	2.8	3	1.9	4.8	5.7	7.1	13.6	3.2	4.5	2.7	3.2	4.8	9	2.2	2.7	7.8	3.8	5.6	2.2
Current B - $2.00 to $3.00	3.7	5.1	2.9	3.1	1.9	4.9	5.7	7.2	13.5	3.3	4.5	2.8	3.2	4.9	9.1	2.2	2.7	7.9	3.8	5.5	2.2
Current B - over $3.00	3.2	5.1	2.9	3.1	1.9	4.9	5.7	7.3	13.8	3.3	4.5	2.8	3.2	4.9	8.9	2.2	2.7	7.9	3.7	5.7	2.2
Current C - Free	2.6	5.1	2.9	3.1	1.9	4.9	5.8	7.3	13.8	3.3	4.6	2.8	3.2	4.9	9.1	2.2	2.6	8	3.8	5.7	2.2
Current C - to $1.00	3.8	4.8	2.4	3	1.9	4.8	5.8	7.2	14.2	3.3	4.6	2.8	3.2	4.9	8.9	2.3	2.9	8.3	2.9	5	2.3
Current C - $1.00 to $2.00	3.4	5	2.9	3	1.9	4.9	5.7	7.2	13.9	3.2	4.5	2.8	3.2	4.9	9.1	2.3	2.7	7.8	3.9	5.5	2.2
Current C - $2.00 to $3.00	2.7	5.2	2.9	3.1	1.9	5	5.7	7.1	13.9	3.3	4.5	2.8	3.2	4.9	9.2	2.3	2.8	7.9	3.9	5.3	2.3
Current C - over $3.00	2.3	5.2	2.9	3.1	1.9	5	5.8	7.2	14.1	3.3	4.6	2.8	3.2	4.9	9	2.3	2.8	7.8	3.9	5.6	2.3
Current D - Free	1.9	5.2	2.9	3.1	2	5	5.8	7.3	14.1	3.3	4.6	2.8	3.2	5	9.2	2.3	2.7	7.9	3.9	5.6	2.2
Current D - to $1.00	6.5	4.6	2.3	2.8	2	4.6	5.6	7	13.4	3.3	4.6	2.6	3	4.7	8.9	2.2	2.9	8.2	2.8	5.9	2.2
Current D - $1.00 to $2.00	5.6	4.8	2.8	2.7	2	4.6	5.6	7	13.3	3.2	4.5	2.7	3	4.8	9.1	2.3	2.7	7.7	3.8	5.8	2.2
Current D - $2.00 to $3.00	4.8	4.9	2.9	2.9	2	4.8	5.6	7	13.1	3.3	4.5	2.7	3.1	4.8	9.2	2.3	2.7	7.8	3.8	5.7	2.2
Current D - over $3.00	4.1	5	2.9	2.9	2	4.8	5.7	7.1	13.5	3.3	4.6	2.7	3.1	4.8	9.1	2.3	2.8	7.7	3.7	5.8	2.2
Current E - Free	9.7	4.6	2.2	2.8	1.9	4.6	5.5	6.9	13	2.9	4.4	2.6	2.9	4.6	8.4	2.2	2.7	7.5	2.7	5.5	2.3
Current E - to $1.00	8	4.9	2.7	2.9	1.9	4.7	5.5	7	13	2.8	4.4	2.7	3	4.6	8.8	2.3	2.6	7.2	3.5	5.4	2.2
Current E - $1.00 to $2.00	6.7	5	2.8	3	2	4.8	5.6	7	12.8	3	4.4	2.7	3	4.7	8.9	2.3	2.6	7.3	3.6	5.4	2.3
Current E - $2.00 to $3.00	5.5	5.1	2.8	3	2	4.9	5.7	7.2	13.3	3.1	4.5	2.7	3.1	4.8	8.8	2.3	2.7	7.1	3.4	5.6	2.3
Current E - over $3.00	4.8	5.1	2.9	3	2	4.9	5.7	7.2	13.4	3.1	4.6	2.7	3.1	4.8	9	2.4	2.6	7.4	3.6	5.6	2.3

CHAPTER 2 ESTIMATING TRAVEL DEMAND

Table 2-10. Percent of People in Market Segment 1 (People With Disabilities Who Use Fixed-Route Transit) Who Prefer Each Current or Improved System

CURRENT SYSTEMS	Current Design	IMPROVED SYSTEMS																		
		A	B	C	D	E	F	G	H	I	J	K	L	M	N	O	P	Q	R	S	T
Current A - Free	6	5.2	3.1	3.5	2	4.7	5.3	7.9	12.5	3.2	4.8	3	3.1	4.8	8.1	2.3	2.5	7	3.7	5.1	2.2
Current A - to $1.00	5.2	5.2	3.1	3.4	2.1	4.7	5.4	7.9	12.6	3.1	4.9	3.1	3.2	5	8.2	2.4	2.6	7	3.8	5.2	2.2
Current A - $1.00 to $2.00	4	5.3	3.2	3.5	2.1	4.8	5.4	7.9	12.6	3.2	4.9	3.1	3.2	5	8.3	2.4	2.6	7.1	3.8	5.1	2.3
Current A - $2.00 to $3.00	3.3	5.3	3.2	3.6	2.1	4.9	5.5	8.1	12.9	3.3	5	3.1	3.2	5.1	8.1	2.4	2.6	7	3.7	5.3	2.3
Current A - over $3.00	2.9	5.3	3.2	3.6	2.1	4.9	5.5	8.1	12.9	3.3	5	3.1	3.2	5.1	8.4	2.4	2.6	7.2	3.8	5.3	2.2
Current B - Free	6	5.3	3.2	3.4	2	4.7	5.3	7.8	12.5	3.2	4.8	2.9	3.1	4.8	8.3	2.1	2.4	7.2	3.8	5.1	2.2
Current B - to $1.00	5.4	5.1	3.1	3.4	2	4.6	5.4	7.9	12.5	3.2	4.8	3	3.2	4.9	8.3	2.2	2.4	7.3	3.8	5.2	2.2
Current B - $1.00 to $2.00	4.1	5.3	3.2	3.5	2.1	4.8	5.4	7.9	12.5	3.3	4.8	3.1	3.2	5	8.5	2.3	2.5	7.4	3.9	5.1	2.2
Current B - $2.00 to $3.00	3.5	5.3	3.2	3.5	2.1	4.8	5.5	8	12.8	3.3	4.9	3.1	3.3	5	8.3	2.3	2.5	7.3	3.8	5.3	2.3
Current B - over $3.00	2.9	5.3	3.2	3.5	2.1	4.8	5.5	8.1	12.9	3.3	4.9	3.1	3.3	5.1	8.5	2.3	2.4	7.4	3.9	5.3	2.2
Current C - Free	4.1	5.3	3.2	3.5	2	4.8	5.4	7.9	12.9	3.2	4.9	3	3.2	4.9	8.4	2.3	2.5	7.2	3.9	5.1	2.2
Current C - to $1.00	3.7	5.2	3.1	3.4	2.1	4.8	5.5	7.9	13	3.2	4.9	3.1	3.3	5	8.5	2.4	2.6	7.3	4	5.1	2.2
Current C - $1.00 to $2.00	2.7	5.4	3.2	3.6	2.1	4.9	5.5	7.9	13	3.3	4.9	3.1	3.3	5.1	8.6	2.4	2.6	7.3	4	5	2.3
Current C - $2.00 to $3.00	2.3	5.4	3.2	3.6	2.1	4.9	5.5	8	13.2	3.3	4.9	3.1	3.3	5.1	8.4	2.4	2.6	7.2	4	5.2	2.3
Current C - over $3.00	1.9	5.4	3.2	3.6	2.1	4.9	5.5	8	13.2	3.3	4.9	3.1	3.3	5.1	8.6	2.4	2.5	7.4	4	5.2	2.2
Current D - Free	7.8	4.9	3	3.2	2	4.5	5.2	7.6	12.1	3.2	4.8	2.8	2.9	4.7	8.4	2.2	2.5	7.1	3.8	5.3	2.2
Current D - to $1.00	7	4.8	2.9	3	2.1	4.4	5.3	7.7	12.3	3.2	4.8	2.9	3.1	4.8	8.5	2.3	2.5	7.2	3.8	5.3	2.2
Current D - $1.00 to $2.00	5.6	5.1	3.1	3.3	2.1	4.6	5.3	7.7	12.1	3.3	4.8	3	3.1	4.9	8.6	2.3	2.5	7.2	3.9	5.3	2.2
Current D - $2.00 to $3.00	4.7	5.1	3.1	3.3	2.1	4.6	5.4	7.8	12.5	3.3	4.9	3	3.1	4.9	8.5	2.3	2.5	7.1	3.8	5.4	2.2
Current D - over $3.00	3.8	5.2	3.2	3.3	2.2	4.7	5.4	7.9	12.6	3.3	4.9	3	3.2	5	8.6	2.4	2.5	7.3	3.9	5.5	2.2
Current E - Free	9.4	5	3	3.4	2	4.6	5.2	7.6	11.9	2.9	4.7	2.8	2.9	4.6	8.1	2.3	2.4	6.6	3.5	5	2.2
Current E - to $1.00	8	5	2.9	3.3	2.1	4.6	5.3	7.7	12.1	2.8	4.8	2.9	3.1	4.8	8.2	2.3	2.4	6.7	3.6	5.1	2.2
Current E - $1.00 to $2.00	6.6	5.2	3.1	3.5	2.1	4.7	5.3	7.8	12.1	3	4.8	3	3.1	4.9	8.3	2.4	2.5	6.8	3.6	5	2.3
Current E - $2.00 to $3.00	5.4	5.3	3.1	3.5	2.1	4.8	5.4	8	12.5	3	4.9	3	3.1	4.9	8.3	2.4	2.5	6.6	3.5	5.2	2.3
Current E - over $3.00	4.6	5.3	3.2	3.5	2.1	4.8	5.4	8	12.5	3.1	4.9	3.1	3.2	4.9	8.4	2.4	2.4	6.9	3.7	5.2	2.3

CHAPTER 2   ESTIMATING TRAVEL DEMAND

Table 2-11. Percent of People in Market Segment 2 (People With Disabilities Who Use Paratransit) Who Prefer Each Current or Improved System

CURRENT SYSTEMS	Current Design	A	B	C	D	E	F	G	H	I	J	K	L	M	N	O	P	Q	R	S	T
Current A - Free	5.2	5.2	3	3.2	1.8	5	5.9	7	13.3	3.1	4.5	2.7	2.9	4.8	9	2.2	2.6	7.7	3.5	5.3	2.3
Current A - to $1.00	4.6	5.1	2.9	3.2	1.8	4.9	5.9	7	13.3	3.1	4.5	3	2.9	5	9	2.3	2.5	7.9	3.5	5.4	2.2
Current A - $1.00 to $2.00	3.8	5.3	3	3.3	1.9	5	5.9	7	13.3	3.2	4.5	2.8	3	4.9	9.2	2.3	2.6	7.8	3.6	5.2	2.3
Current A - $2.00 to $3.00	3.1	5.3	3	3.3	1.9	5.1	6	7.2	13.6	3.2	4.6	2.8	3	5	9	2.3	2.6	7.7	3.5	5.4	2.3
Current A - over $3.00	2.7	5.3	3	3.3	1.9	5.1	6	7.2	13.6	3.2	4.6	2.8	3	5	9.2	2.3	2.6	7.9	3.6	5.4	2.3
Current B - Free	4.7	5.2	3	3.2	1.8	5	5.9	7	13.3	3.2	4.5	2.7	3	4.8	9.2	2	2.5	8	3.6	5.4	2.3
Current B - to $1.00	4.4	5.1	2.9	3.2	1.8	4.9	5.9	7	13.3	3.1	4.5	3	3	5	9.2	2.2	2.4	8.2	3.6	5.4	2.2
Current B - $1.00 to $2.00	3.5	5.3	3	3.3	1.8	5	5.9	7	13.3	3.2	4.5	2.8	3	4.9	9.4	2.2	2.5	8.1	3.6	5.2	2.3
Current B - $2.00 to $3.00	3	5.3	3	3.3	1.8	5.1	6	7.1	13.6	3.2	4.6	2.8	3.1	4.9	9.2	2.2	2.5	8	3.6	5.4	2.3
Current B - over $3.00	2.5	5.3	3	3.3	1.9	5.1	6	7.2	13.6	3.2	4.6	2.8	3.1	5	9.4	2.2	2.5	8.1	3.7	5.4	2.3
Current C - Free	3.6	5.3	3	3.3	1.8	5	6	7	13.7	3.2	4.5	2.7	3	4.8	9.3	2.2	2.6	7.9	3.7	5.2	2.3
Current C - to $1.00	3.2	5.2	2.9	3.2	1.8	4.9	6	7	13.6	3.1	4.5	3	3	5.1	9.3	2.3	2.5	8.1	3.7	5.3	2.3
Current C - $1.00 to $2.00	2.6	5.3	3	3.3	1.9	5.1	6	7	13.7	3.2	4.5	2.8	3.1	5	9.4	2.3	2.6	8.1	3.7	5.1	2.3
Current C - $2.00 to $3.00	2.2	5.4	3	3.3	1.9	5.1	6.1	7.1	13.9	3.2	4.6	2.8	3.1	5	9.3	2.3	2.6	7.9	3.7	5.3	2.3
Current C - over $3.00	1.8	5.4	3	3.3	1.9	5.1	6.1	7.1	13.9	3.2	4.6	2.8	3.1	5	9.5	2.3	2.6	8.1	3.7	5.3	2.3
Current D - Free	6.4	5	2.9	3	1.8	4.8	5.8	6.9	12.9	3.1	4.5	2.6	2.8	4.6	9.3	2.1	2.5	7.8	3.5	5.4	2.3
Current D - to $1.00	5.7	4.9	2.9	2.9	1.8	4.7	5.8	6.9	13	3.1	4.5	2.9	2.9	4.9	9.3	2.2	2.5	8	3.5	5.5	2.2
Current D - $1.00 to $2.00	4.8	5.1	3	3.1	1.9	4.9	5.8	6.9	12.8	3.2	4.5	2.7	2.9	4.8	9.4	2.2	2.6	7.9	3.6	5.5	2.3
Current D - $2.00 to $3.00	4	5.1	3	3.1	1.9	4.9	5.9	7	13.3	3.2	4.6	2.7	2.9	4.9	9.3	2.2	2.6	7.8	3.6	5.6	2.3
Current D - over $3.00	3.4	5.2	3	3.1	1.9	4.9	5.9	7.1	13.3	3.2	4.6	2.7	3	4.9	9.5	2.2	2.5	8	3.6	5.6	2.2
Current E - Free	8.9	5	2.8	3.1	1.8	4.8	5.7	6.8	12.6	2.9	4.4	2.6	2.7	4.5	8.9	2.2	2.4	7.2	3.3	5.1	2.3
Current E - to $1.00	7.9	5	2.8	3.1	1.8	4.8	5.7	6.8	12.7	2.8	4.4	2.9	2.8	4.8	8.9	2.3	2.4	7.4	3.3	5.2	2.2
Current E - $1.00 to $2.00	6.6	5.2	2.9	3.2	1.9	4.9	5.8	6.9	12.6	3	4.5	2.7	2.9	4.8	9.2	2.3	2.5	7.4	3.4	5.1	2.4
Current E - $2.00 to $3.00	5.4	5.3	2.9	3.3	1.9	5	6	7.1	13.2	3	4.6	2.7	2.9	4.8	9.1	2.3	2.5	7.2	3.3	5.3	2.4
Current E - over $3.00	4.7	5.3	3	3.3	1.9	5	6	7.1	13.2	3	4.6	2.7	2.9	4.8	9.3	2.3	2.4	7.5	3.4	5.3	2.3

Header spanning: columns A–T are under **IMPROVED SYSTEMS**.

CHAPTER 2   ESTIMATING TRAVEL DEMAND

Table 2-12. Percent of People in Market Segment 3 (Others Who Use Paratransit) Who Prefer Each Current or Improved System

CURRENT SYSTEMS	Current Design	A	B	C	D	E	F	G	H	I	J	K	L	M	N	O	P	Q	R	S	T
Current A - Free	5	5.4	3.7	2.9	2	6.1	5.3	6.1	15.1	3.7	3.4	2.4	2.9	5.5	8.2	2.8	2.3	6.7	3.7	4.7	2.1
Current A - to $1.00	5	5.4	3.6	2.9	2.1	6	5.3	6.1	15.1	3.6	3.4	2.5	2.9	5.5	8.3	2.8	2.3	6.8	3.7	4.7	2.1
Current A - $1.00 to $2.00	3.5	5.6	3.7	3	2.1	6.2	5.3	6.1	15.1	3.8	3.4	2.5	3	5.6	8.4	2.9	2.4	6.9	3.8	4.6	2.1
Current A - $2.00 to $3.00	3.2	5.9	3.8	3.1	2	6.4	5.4	6.2	15.4	3.9	3.5	2.5	2.9	5.5	8.2	2.9	2.4	6.7	3.7	4.7	2.1
Current A - over $3.00	2.3	5.6	3.7	3	2.1	6.3	5.4	6.2	15.5	3.8	3.5	2.5	3	5.7	8.5	2.9	2.4	6.9	3.8	4.8	2.1
Current B - Free	4.8	5.5	3.6	2.9	2	6.1	5.3	6.1	15.1	3.7	3.4	2.4	2.9	5.5	8.4	2.6	2.2	7	3.8	4.7	2.1
Current B - to $1.00	4.9	5.4	3.6	2.9	2	6	5.3	6.1	15.1	3.7	3.4	2.4	3	5.5	8.4	2.7	2.2	7	3.8	4.7	2.1
Current B - $1.00 to $2.00	3.4	5.6	3.7	3	2	6.2	5.3	6.1	15.1	3.8	3.4	2.5	3	5.6	8.6	2.8	2.3	7.1	3.8	4.6	2.1
Current B - $2.00 to $3.00	3.3	5.8	3.7	3	2	6.4	5.3	6.2	15.3	3.9	3.4	2.4	3	5.5	8.3	2.7	2.3	6.9	3.7	4.7	2.1
Current B - over $3.00	2.3	5.6	3.7	3	2.1	6.3	5.4	6.2	15.5	3.8	3.5	2.5	3	5.7	8.6	2.8	2.2	7.1	3.9	4.8	2.1
Current C - Free	3.5	5.5	3.7	3	2	6.2	5.3	6.1	15.5	3.7	3.4	2.4	3	5.5	8.5	2.7	2.3	7	3.9	4.6	2.1
Current C - to $1.00	3.5	5.5	3.6	2.9	2	6.1	5.3	6.1	15.5	3.6	3.4	2.5	3	5.6	8.5	2.8	2.3	7	3.9	4.6	2.1
Current C - $1.00 to $2.00	2.4	5.6	3.7	3	2.1	6.3	5.3	6.1	15.5	3.8	3.4	2.5	3	5.7	8.7	2.9	2.4	7.1	3.9	4.5	2.2
Current C - $2.00 to $3.00	2.3	5.9	3.8	3.1	2	6.4	5.4	6.1	15.7	3.9	3.4	2.4	3	5.5	8.4	2.8	2.3	6.9	3.9	4.6	2.1
Current C - over $3.00	1.6	5.6	3.8	3	2.1	6.3	5.4	6.2	15.8	3.8	3.5	2.5	3	5.7	8.7	2.9	2.3	7.1	4	4.7	2.1
Current D - Free	6.3	5.3	3.6	2.7	2	5.9	5.2	6	14.7	3.7	3.4	2.3	2.8	5.4	8.5	2.7	2.3	6.8	3.7	4.8	2.1
Current D - to $1.00	6.3	5.1	3.5	2.6	2.1	5.7	5.2	6	14.7	3.6	3.4	2.4	2.8	5.5	8.5	2.8	2.3	6.8	3.8	4.8	2.1
Current D - $1.00 to $2.00	4.7	5.4	3.7	2.8	2.1	6	5.2	6	14.6	3.8	3.4	2.4	2.9	5.6	8.6	2.8	2.3	6.9	3.8	4.8	2.1
Current D - $2.00 to $3.00	4.4	5.6	3.7	2.9	2.1	6.1	5.2	6	15	3.9	3.4	2.4	2.9	5.4	8.5	2.8	2.3	6.7	3.7	4.8	2.1
Current D - over $3.00	3.2	5.4	3.7	2.8	2.1	6.1	5.3	6.1	15.2	3.8	3.5	2.4	2.9	5.6	8.7	2.9	2.3	7	3.9	4.9	2.1
Current E - Free	7.4	5.3	3.5	2.9	2	6	5.2	6	14.5	3.4	3.4	2.4	2.7	5.3	8.3	2.8	2.2	6.4	3.5	4.6	2.1
Current E - to $1.00	7.9	5.2	3.4	2.8	2	5.8	5.2	6	14.4	3.2	3.4	2.4	2.8	5.4	8.3	2.8	2.2	6.5	3.6	4.6	2.1
Current E - $1.00 to $2.00	5.1	5.5	3.6	3	2.1	6.2	5.3	6.1	14.6	3.5	3.4	2.5	2.9	5.5	8.5	2.9	2.3	6.6	3.6	4.6	2.2
Current E - $2.00 to $3.00	4.7	5.8	3.7	3	2.1	6.3	5.3	6.1	14.9	3.6	3.4	2.4	2.9	5.4	8.3	2.9	2.3	6.4	3.5	4.7	2.2
Current E - over $3.00	3.6	5.5	3.7	3	2.1	6.2	5.4	6.2	15.1	3.6	3.5	2.5	2.9	5.6	8.6	2.9	2.2	6.7	3.7	4.8	2.2

CHAPTER 2   ESTIMATING TRAVEL DEMAND

Table 2-13. Percent of People in Market Segment 4 (People With Disabilities Who Normally Do Not Use Transit) Who Prefer Each Current or Improved System

CURRENT SYSTEMS	Current Design	\multicolumn{20}{c	}{IMPROVED SYSTEMS}
		A	B	C	D	E	F	G	H	I	J	K	L	M	N	O	P	Q	R	S	T
Current A - Free	5.6	4.8	2.7	2.8	1.9	4.7	5.6	7	13.6	3.2	4.5	2.7	3.1	4.7	8.8	2.3	2.8	7.6	3.7	5.8	2.1
Current A - to $1.00	4.9	4.8	2.7	2.8	1.9	4.7	5.6	7.1	13.7	3.2	4.5	2.7	3.2	4.8	8.9	2.3	2.9	7.6	3.8	5.8	2.1
Current A - $1.00 to $2.00	4.1	4.9	2.8	2.9	2	4.8	5.6	7.1	13.6	3.3	4.5	2.8	3.2	4.8	9	2.3	2.9	7.7	3.8	5.7	2.2
Current A - $2.00 to $3.00	3.3	5	2.8	2.9	2	4.8	5.7	7.2	14	3.3	4.6	2.8	3.2	4.9	8.8	2.4	2.9	7.6	3.7	5.9	2.2
Current A - over $3.00	2.9	5	2.8	2.9	2	4.8	5.7	7.2	14	3.3	4.6	2.8	3.2	4.9	9	2.4	2.9	7.8	3.8	5.9	2.2
Current B - Free	5.1	4.9	2.7	2.8	1.8	4.7	5.6	7.1	13.7	3.3	4.4	2.6	3.1	4.7	9	2.1	2.7	7.9	3.8	5.8	2.1
Current B - to $1.00	4.6	4.8	2.7	2.8	1.9	4.7	5.6	7.1	13.7	3.3	4.4	2.7	3.2	4.8	9.1	2.2	2.8	7.9	3.8	5.8	2.1
Current B - $1.00 to $2.00	3.8	4.9	2.8	2.9	1.9	4.8	5.6	7.1	13.6	3.3	4.4	2.7	3.2	4.8	9.2	2.2	2.8	8	3.9	5.7	2.2
Current B - $2.00 to $3.00	3.2	5	2.8	2.9	1.9	4.8	5.7	7.2	13.9	3.3	4.5	2.7	3.3	4.8	9	2.2	2.8	7.9	3.8	5.9	2.2
Current B - over $3.00	2.6	5	2.8	2.9	1.9	4.8	5.7	7.2	14	3.3	4.5	2.7	3.3	4.9	9.2	2.3	2.7	8	3.9	5.9	2.1
Current C - Free	3.8	4.9	2.8	2.9	1.9	4.8	5.7	7.1	14	3.3	4.5	2.7	3.2	4.8	9.1	2.2	2.8	7.9	3.9	5.7	2.2
Current C - to $1.00	3.4	4.9	2.8	2.8	1.9	4.7	5.7	7.1	14.1	3.2	4.5	2.7	3.2	4.8	9.2	2.3	2.9	7.9	3.9	5.7	2.2
Current C - $1.00 to $2.00	2.8	5	2.8	2.9	1.9	4.9	5.7	7.1	14.1	3.3	4.5	2.8	3.3	4.9	9.3	2.3	2.9	8	3.9	5.6	2.2
Current C - $2.00 to $3.00	2	5	2.8	2.9	2	4.9	5.8	7.4	14.3	3.2	4.5	2.8	3.1	5	9	2.4	2.9	7.8	4	5.6	2.3
Current C - over $3.00	2	5	2.8	2.9	1.9	4.9	5.8	7.2	14.3	3.3	4.6	2.8	3.3	4.9	9.3	2.3	2.8	8	3.8	5.8	2.1
Current D - Free	6.3	4.7	2.7	2.7	1.9	4.5	5.5	6.9	13.3	3.3	4.4	2.5	3	4.6	9.1	2.2	2.8	7.7	4	5.9	2.1
Current D - to $1.00	5.3	4.6	2.7	2.6	2	4.5	5.6	7	13.5	3.2	4.5	2.6	3.1	4.7	9.2	2.3	2.8	7.8	3.8	6	2.2
Current D - $1.00 to $2.00	4.7	4.8	2.8	2.7	2	4.6	5.5	6.9	13.2	3.3	4.5	2.7	3.1	4.8	9.3	2.3	2.9	7.9	3.9	6	2.2
Current D - $2.00 to $3.00	3.9	4.8	2.8	2.7	2	4.7	5.6	7.1	13.7	3.3	4.6	2.7	3.1	4.8	9.2	2.3	2.9	7.8	3.8	6.1	2.2
Current D - over $3.00	3.2	4.8	2.8	2.7	2	4.7	5.7	7.1	13.7	3.4	4.6	2.7	3.2	4.8	9.4	2.3	2.8	8	3.9	6.1	2.1
Current E - Free	9.5	4.7	2.6	2.7	1.9	4.6	5.4	6.8	12.9	2.9	4.3	2.5	2.9	4.4	8.7	2.2	2.6	7.1	3.5	5.6	2.1
Current E - to $1.00	8	4.7	2.6	2.7	1.9	4.6	5.5	6.9	13.1	2.8	4.4	2.6	3	4.6	8.8	2.3	2.7	7.2	3.5	5.7	2.2
Current E - $1.00 to $2.00	6.9	4.8	2.7	2.8	1.9	4.7	5.5	6.9	13	3.1	4.4	2.7	3.1	4.7	9	2.3	2.7	7.4	3.6	5.6	2.2
Current E - $2.00 to $3.00	5.6	4.9	2.7	2.9	2	4.8	5.6	7.1	13.5	3.1	4.5	2.7	3.1	4.7	8.9	2.4	2.8	7.2	3.5	5.8	2.2
Current E - over $3.00	4.9	4.9	2.7	2.9	2	4.8	5.7	7.1	13.5	3.1	4.5	2.7	3.1	4.7	9.1	2.4	2.7	7.5	3.7	5.8	2.2

CHAPTER 2 ESTIMATING TRAVEL DEMAND

Table 2-14. Market Segment Sizes Based on Survey Results of Five Mid-Sized U.S. Cities

Market Segment	Number of Respondents	Percent of All Respondents
1	75	10
2	169	23
3	31	4
4	392	54
Total	667	92

PROBABILITY OF PURCHASE

To estimate the probability that people will actually use the system configuration they prefer, planners should follow a simple procedure using Tables 2-15 and 2-16. Table 2-15 shows the probability of purchase of the current systems for all respondents and for each of the market segments. Table 2-16 shows the probability of purchase of the improved systems for all respondents and for each of the market segments. These figures can be interpreted as percentage of likelihood of using the system. For example, a 61.6% probability of purchase can be interpreted as "a 61.6% likelihood" that the respondents who prefer the system would actually use it. This may mean that the people would choose it for 61.6% of their trips or that 61.6% of the people would use it all the time or that there is one chance in three that no one would use it at all. To estimate the probability of purchase and subsequent ridership, planners should take the number of people preferring a particular system configuration and multiply it by the appropriate factor in Tables 2-15 or 2-16.

CHAPTER 2   ESTIMATING TRAVEL DEMAND

Table 2-15. Probability of Purchase by Market Segment for Each Current System

Current Systems	Market Segments				
	All Respondents	Segment 1	Segment 2	Segment 3	Segment 4
Current A - Free	0.533	0.529	0.527	0.557	0.536
Current A - to $1.00	0.497	0.491	0.499	0.548	0.496
Current A - $1.00 to $2.00	0.452	0.439	0.45	0.46	0.456
Current A - $2.00 to $3.00	0.403	0.391	0.401	0.436	0.406
Current A - over $3.00	0.357	0.343	0.355	0.351	0.361
Current B - Free	0.523	0.527	0.518	0.563	0.526
Current B - to $1.00	0.488	0.488	0.489	0.557	0.487
Current B - $1.00 to $2.00	0.443	0.441	0.442	0.466	0.447
Current B - $2.00 to $3.00	0.395	0.395	0.392	0.441	0.398
Current B - over $3.00	0.35	0.347	0.348	0.356	0.354
Current C - Free	0.449	0.447	0.444	0.478	0.453
Current C - to $1.00	0.415	0.409	0.417	0.474	0.417
Current C - $1.00 to $2.00	0.372	0.36	0.371	0.384	0.378
Current C - $2.00 to $3.00	0.327	0.316	0.325	0.359	0.341
Current C - over $3.00	0.285	0.272	0.284	0.281	0.29
Current D - Free	0.609	0.619	0.618	0.658	0.601
Current D - to $1.00	0.574	0.58	0.591	0.646	0.563
Current D - $1.00 to $2.00	0.529	0.531	0.544	0.565	0.521
Current D $2.00 to $3.00	0.48	0.48	0.494	0.541	0.471
Current D - over $3.00	0.432	0.433	0.447	0.455	0.424
Current E - Free	0.692	0.678	0.688	0.677	0.696
Current E - to $1.00	0.66	0.643	0.663	0.66	0.661
Current E - $1.00 to $2.00	0.617	0.593	0.618	0.59	0.622
Current E - $2.00 to $3.00	0.568	0.543	0.568	0.564	0.573
Current E - over $3.00	0.52	0.493	0.521	0.481	0.526

- Market Segment 1 - People with disabilities who use fixed-route transit
- Market Segment 2 - People with disabilities who use paratransit
- Market Segment 3 - Others who use paratransit
- Market Segment 4 - People with disabilities who normally do not use transit

CHAPTER 2 ESTIMATING TRAVEL DEMAND

Table 2-16. Probability of Purchase by Market Segments for Each Improved System

Improved Systems	Market Segments				
	All	1	2	3	4
A	0.588	0.589	0.60	0.646	0.58
B	0.408	0.432	0.455	0.497	0.432
C	0.449	0.464	0.469	0.473	0.437
D	0.326	0.336	0.318	0.372	0.325
E	0.568	0.554	0.579	0.638	0.563
F	0.606	0.584	0.62	0.629	0.604
G	0.658	0.663	0.661	0.657	0.656
H	0.754	0.727	0.758	0.795	0.756
I	0.428	0.424	0.437	0.457	0.425
J	0.568	0.576	0.572	0.527	0.568
K	0.411	0.423	0.417	0.422	0.408
L	0.435	0.431	0.432	0.479	0.435
M	0.561	0.551	0.568	0.587	0.559
N	0.674	0.641	0.688	0.698	0.676
O	0.365	0.353	0.362	0.439	0.367
P	0.387	0.364	0.383	0.382	0.393
Q	0.646	0.604	0.653	0.657	0.65
R	0.393	0.463	0.462	0.474	0.472
S	0.575	0.549	0.572	0.558	0.583
T	0.334	0.326	0.342	0.346	0.33

- Market Segment 1 - People with disabilities who use fixed-route transit
- Market Segment 2 - People with disabilities who use paratransit
- Market Segment 3 - Others who use paratransit
- Market Segment 4 - People with disabilities who normally do not use transit

CHAPTER 2 ESTIMATING TRAVEL DEMAND

Eastern location, medium density (suburban), hilly terrain and a moderate climate characterize System 11.

ESTIMATION OF RIDERSHIP DEMAND AND PREFERENCES FOR A LOCAL TRANSIT SYSTEM

To illustrate how to estimate ridership and preferences for an improved fixed-route system, the local study system described previously in this chapter will be used. Remember that the example study system has the following characteristics:

- Geographic location - Pennsylvania;
- Population density - 125 people per square mile;
- Topography - rolling terrain; and
- Climate - average yearly temperature of 57° F.

The system is, therefore, in the **East**, with a **Medium Density (Suburban)** in the service area, a **Hilly** terrain, and a **Moderate** climate, as shown in Figure 2-8.

Figure 2-8. Composite Description of Example Study System

TO ESTIMATE FOR ALL PATRONS

The composite system identification number is 11 and the peer systems tables are in Appendix A. Assume that the transit system follows Steps 1 and 2 for estimating demand by examining Table 2-7 and deciding that their fixed-route system is best described by Current System A as shown in Table 2-17.

CHAPTER 2 ESTIMATING TRAVEL DEMAND

Table 2-17. Current Example Study System is Best
Described by Current System A

Current System A

Service Feature
A consumer has a short traveling distance to and from the vehicle
The schedules are reliable
Other passengers don't complain when a consumer needs extra time
Schedules a consumer can use are at the stops
Uniformed officers may be on the vehicles
Mobility or other equipment can be stored near the consumer
Drivers understand boarding and securing wheelchairs

Find appropriate "current" system and "improved" system descriptions.

Transit system personnel then examine Table 2-8 and decide that, after making improvements to the fixed-route service, the system will best be described by Improved System H (Steps 3 and 4). This system is shown in Table 2-18.

In Step 5, the transit system determines that the base fixed-route fare is $1.50. Using this information and Table 2-9, planners for the Example Study System follow Steps 6 and 7 to find the appropriate row in Table 2-9; Current System A with a $1.50 fare corresponds with the third row in Table 2-9. In Steps 8 and 9, planners locate the column for Improved H as well as the "current" column and compare these with the results of Steps 6 and 7 as shown in Figure 2-9.

Table 2-18. After Improvements are Made, Current Example Study System is Best
Described by Improved System H.

Improved System H

Service Feature
Trip costs between $1.01 and $2.00
A consumer has a short traveling distance to and from the vehicle
Vehicle stops near the consumer's home and goes where the consumer wants
The consumer doesn't have to transfer vehicles and trips are short
Stops have benches
A consumer feels safe traveling to and from the vehicle
A consumer can board in his/her wheelchair and be secured in it
Drivers move people out of the front seats when a consumer with disabilities asks

CHAPTER 2 ESTIMATING TRAVEL DEMAND

Percent of Paratransit Patrons and People With Disabilities Who Prefer Each Current or Improved System

CURRENT SYSTEMS	Current Design	A	B	C	D	E	F	G	H	I	J	K	L	M	N	O	P	Q	R	S	T
Current A - Free	3.3	5	2.9	2.9	2	4.8	5.7	7.2	13.6	3.3	4.6	2.7	3.1	4.9	9.3	2.3	2.7	7.9	3.8	5.9	2.2
Current A - to $1.00	5.5	4.8	2.4	3	2	4.8	5.7	7.2	13.8	3.3	4.6	2.8	3.1	4.8	8.6	2.3	2.9	8	2.7	5.7	2.2
Current A - $1.00 to $2.00	4.8	5	2.8	3	1.9	4.8	5.7	7.2	13.6	3.1	4.5	2.8	3.1	4.8	8.8	2.3	2.8	7.6	3.7	5.6	2.2
Current A - $2.00 to $3.00	4	5.1	2.9	3.1	2	4.9	5.7	7.2	13.5	3.2	4.5	2.8	3.2	4.9	8.9	2.3	2.8	7.7	3.7	5.5	2.2
Current A - over $3.00	3.3	5.1	2.9	3.1	2	4.9	5.8	7.3	13.8	3.3	4.6	2.8	3.2	4.9	8.7	2.3	2.8	7.5	3.7	5.7	2.2
Current B - Free	2.8	5.1	2.9	3.1	2	4.9	5.8	7.3	13.8	3.3	4.6	2.8	3.2	4.9	9	2.3	2.8	7.7	3.8	5.7	2.2
Current B - to $1.00	5.1	4.8	2.4	3	1.9	4.8	5.8	7.2	13.8	3.3	4.5	2.7	3.2	4.8	8.8	2.1	2.8	8.3	2.8	5.7	2.3
Current B - $1.00 to $2.00	4.6	5	2.8	3	1.9	4.8	5.7	7.1	13.6	3.2	4.5	2.7	3.2	4.8	9	2.2	2.7	7.8	3.8	5.6	2.2
Current B - $2.00 to $3.00	3.7	5.1	2.9	3.1	1.9	4.9	5.7	7.2	13.5	3.3	4.5	2.8	3.2	4.9	9.1	2.2	2.7	7.9	3.8	5.5	2.2
Current B - over $3.00	3.2	5.1	2.9	3.1	1.9	4.9	5.7	7.3	13.8	3.3	4.5	2.8	3.2	4.9	8.9	2.2	2.7	7.9	3.7	5.7	2.2
Current C - Free	2.6	5.1	2.9	3.1	1.9	4.9	5.8	7.3	13.8	3.3	4.6	2.8	3.2	4.9	9.1	2.2	2.6	7.9	3.8	5.7	2.2
Current C - to $1.00	3.8	4.8	2.4	3	1.9	4.8	5.8	7.2	14.2	3.3	4.6	2.8	3.2	4.9	8.9	2.3	2.9	8.3	2.9	5.7	2.3
Current C - $1.00 to $2.00	3.4	5	2.9	3	1.9	4.9	5.7	7.2	13.9	3.2	4.5	2.8	3.2	4.9	9.1	2.3	2.7	7.8	3.9	5.5	2.2
Current C - $2.00 to $3.00	2.7	5.2	2.9	3.1	1.9	5	5.7	7.1	13.9	3.3	4.5	2.8	3.2	4.9	9.1	2.3	2.8	7.9	3.9	5.3	2.3
Current C - over $3.00	2.3	5.2	2.9	3.1	1.9	5	5.8	7.2	14.1	3.3	4.6	2.8	3.2	4.9	9.2	2.3	2.8	7.9	3.9	5.6	2.3
Current D - Free	1.9	5.2	2.9	3.1	2	5	5.8	7.3	14.1	3.3	4.6	2.8	3.2	4.9	9	2.3	2.8	7.8	3.9	5.6	2.2
Current D - to $1.00	6.5	4.6	2.3	2.8	2	4.6	5.6	7	13.4	3.3	4.6	2.6	3	5	9.2	2.3	2.7	7.9	3.9	5.6	2.2
Current D - $1.00 to $2.00	5.6	4.8	2.8	2.7	2	4.6	5.6	7	13.3	3.2	4.5	2.7	3	4.7	8.9	2.2	2.9	8.2	2.8	5.9	2.2
Current D - $2.00 to $3.00	4.8	4.9	2.9	2.9	2	4.8	5.6	7	13.1	3.3	4.5	2.7	3	4.8	9.1	2.3	2.7	7.7	3.8	5.8	2.2
Current D - over $3.00	4.1	5	2.9	2.9	2	4.8	5.7	7.1	13.5	3.3	4.5	2.7	3.1	4.8	9.2	2.3	2.7	7.8	3.8	5.7	2.2
Current E - Free	9.7	4.6	2.2	2.8	2	4.8	5.7	7.1	13.5	3.3	4.6	2.7	3.1	4.8	9.1	2.3	2.8	7.7	3.7	5.8	2.2
Current E - to $1.00	8	4.9	2.7	2.9	1.9	4.6	5.5	6.9	13	2.9	4.4	2.6	2.9	4.6	8.4	2.2	2.7	7.5	2.7	5.5	2.3
Current E - $1.00 to $2.00	6.7	5	2.8	2.9	1.9	4.7	5.5	7	13	2.8	4.4	2.7	3	4.6	8.8	2.3	2.6	7.2	3.5	5.4	2.2
Current E - $2.00 to $3.00	5.5	5.1	2.8	3	2	4.8	5.6	7	12.8	3	4.4	2.7	3	4.7	8.9	2.3	2.6	7.3	3.6	5.4	2.3
Current E - over $3.00	4.8	5.1	2.9	3	2	4.9	5.7	7.2	13.4	3.1	4.6	2.7	3.1	4.8	9	2.4	2.6	7.4	3.6	5.6	2.3

Figure 2-9. Results of Steps 5 through 9 for Example Study System Illustrated on a Sample Table 2-9

CHAPTER 2 ESTIMATING TRAVEL DEMAND

This interface resulted in two percentage figures, 13.6% and 4.8%. The 13.6% represents the percent of paratransit patrons and individuals with disabilities in the example study system who would prefer Improved System H over all other improved systems. In other words, if Current System A with a $1.50 fare is enhanced to Improved System H, 13.6% of paratransit patrons and individuals with disabilities would prefer Improved System H. The 4.8% represents the percent of paratransit patrons and individuals with disabilities in the example study system who would prefer the current system (in this case, Current System A) over all other improved systems. In other words, if Current System A with a $1.50 fare is enhanced to Improved System H, then 4.8% of paratransit patrons and individuals with disabilities would still prefer the current fixed-route system.

Some paratransit patrons may prefer the original fixed-route system over the "improved" system.

This is an important point to keep in mind when evaluating different alternatives for improving the fixed-route system in order to attract paratransit patrons and individuals with disabilities. In some cases, when changes are made to the fixed-route system, some people may prefer the original system to the improved system. For example, if the improvements chosen result in the example study system best described by Current System A with a $1.50 fare changing to a system best described by Improved System D with no fare, 1.9% of paratransit patrons and individuals with disabilities would prefer Improved System D with no fare while 4.8% would prefer the current fixed-route system. Therefore, the improvements included in Improved System D with no fare may not be most effective in attracting individuals with disabilities to fixed-route services. This is shown in Figure 2-10.

Improved systems may be combined to provide all planned improvements.

If more than one Improved System description includes features which resemble the planned improvements, the percentages shown in Table 2-9 can be combined. For example, if the improvements that are planned are described in both Improved System H and Improved System I, the percentage of people who would prefer both can be added. If all the service features included in both Improved System H and Improved System I are planned for implementation, then, compared to Current System A at a $1.50 fare, the improved system would be preferred by 13.3% (Improved System H) plus 3.2% (Improved System I), for a total of 16.5% who would prefer a system with all the service features of both systems. This is shown in Figure 2-11.

CHAPTER 2 ESTIMATING TRAVEL DEMAND

Percent Who Prefer Each Current or Improved System

CURRENT SYSTEMS	Current Design	IMPROVED SYSTEMS																			
		A	B	C	D	E	F	G	H	I	J	K	L	M	N	O	P	Q	R	S	T
Current A - Free	3.3	5	2.9	2.9	2	4.8	5.7	7.2	13.6	3.3	4.6	2.7	3.1	4.9	9.3	2.3	2.7	7.9	3.8	5.9	2.2
Current A - to $1.00	5.5	4.8	2.4	3	2	4.8	5.7	7.2	13.8	3.3	4.6	2.8	3.1	4.8	8.6	2.3	2.9	8	2.7	5.7	2.2
Current A - $1.00 to $2.00	4.8	5	2.8	3	1.9	4.8	5.7	7.2	13.6	3.1	4.5	2.8	3.1	4.8	8.8	2.3	2.8	7.6	3.7	5.6	2.2
Current A - $2.00 to $3.00	4	5.1	2.9	3.1	2	4.9	5.7	7.2	13.5	3.2	4.5	2.8	3.2	4.9	8.9	2.3	2.8	7.7	3.7	5.5	2.2
Current A - over $3.00	3.3	5.1	2.9	3.1	2	4.9	5.8	7.3	13.8	3.3	4.6	2.8	3.2	4.9	8.7	2.3	2.8	7.5	3.7	5.7	2.2
Current B - Free	2.8	5.1	2.9	3.1	2	4.9	5.8	7.3	13.8	3.3	4.6	2.8	3.2	4.9	9	2.3	2.8	7.7	3.8	5.7	2.2
Current B - to $1.00	5.1	4.8	2.4	3	1.9	4.8	5.8	7.2	13.8	3.3	4.5	2.7	3.2	4.8	8.8	2.1	2.8	8.3	2.8	5.7	2.3
Current B - $1.00 to $2.00	4.6	5	2.8	3	1.9	4.8	5.7	7.1	13.6	3.2	4.5	2.7	3.2	4.8	9	2.2	2.7	7.8	3.8	5.6	2.2
Current B - $2.00 to $3.00	3.7	5.1	2.9	3.1	1.9	4.9	5.7	7.2	13.5	3.3	4.5	2.8	3.2	4.9	9.1	2.2	2.7	7.9	3.8	5.5	2.2
Current B - over $3.00	3.2	5.1	2.9	3.1	1.9	4.9	5.7	7.3	13.8	3.3	4.5	2.8	3.2	4.9	8.9	2.2	2.7	7.9	3.7	5.7	2.2
Current C - Free	2.6	5.1	2.9	3	1.9	4.8	5.8	7.3	13.8	3.3	4.6	2.8	3.2	4.9	9.1	2.2	2.6	8	3.8	5.7	2.2
Current C - to $1.00	3.8	4.8	2.4	3	1.9	4.8	5.8	7.2	14.2	3.3	4.6	2.8	3.2	4.9	8.9	2.3	2.9	8.3	2.9	5.7	2.3
Current C - $1.00 to $2.00	3.4	5	2.9	3	1.9	4.9	5.7	7.2	13.9	3.2	4.5	2.8	3.2	4.9	9.1	2.3	2.7	7.8	3.9	5.7	2.2
Current C - $2.00 to $3.00	2.7	5.2	2.9	3.1	1.9	5	5.7	7.1	13.9	3.3	4.5	2.8	3.2	4.9	9.2	2.3	2.8	7.9	3.9	5.3	2.3
Current C - over $3.00	2.3	5.2	2.9	3.1	1.9	5	5.8	7.2	14.1	3.3	4.6	2.8	3.2	4.9	9	2.3	2.8	7.8	3.9	5.6	2.3
Current D - Free	1.9	5.2	2.9	3.1	2	5	5.8	7.3	14.1	3.3	4.6	2.8	3.2	5	9.2	2.3	2.7	7.9	3.9	5.6	2.2
Current D - to $1.00	6.5	4.6	2.3	2.8	2	4.6	5.6	7	13.4	3.3	4.6	2.6	3	4.7	8.9	2.2	2.9	8.2	2.8	5.9	2.2
Current D - $1.00 to $2.00	5.6	4.8	2.8	2.7	2	4.6	5.6	7	13.3	3.2	4.5	2.7	3	4.8	9.1	2.3	2.7	7.7	3.8	5.8	2.2
Current D - $2.00 to $3.00	4.8	4.9	2.9	2.9	2	4.8	5.6	7	13.1	3.3	4.5	2.7	3	4.8	9.2	2.3	2.7	7.8	3.8	5.7	2.2
Current D - over $3.00	4.1	5	2.9	2.9	2	4.8	5.7	7.1	13.5	3.3	4.6	2.7	3.1	4.8	9.1	2.3	2.8	7.7	3.7	5.7	2.2
Current E - Free	9.7	4.6	2.2	2.8	1.9	4.6	5.5	6.9	13	2.9	4.4	2.6	2.9	4.6	8.4	2.2	2.7	7.5	3.7	5.8	2.2
Current E - to $1.00	8	4.9	2.7	2.9	1.9	4.7	5.5	7	13	2.8	4.4	2.7	3	4.6	8.8	2.3	2.7	7.5	2.7	5.5	2.3
Current E - $1.00 to $2.00	6.7	5	2.8	3	2	4.8	5.6	7	12.8	3	4.4	2.7	3	4.7	8.8	2.3	2.6	7.2	3.5	5.4	2.2
Current E - $2.00 to $3.00	5.5	5.1	2.8	3	2	4.9	5.7	7.2	13.3	3.1	4.5	2.7	3	4.8	8.9	2.3	2.6	7.3	3.6	5.4	2.3
Current E - over $3.00	4.8	5.1	2.9	3	2	4.9	5.7	7.2	13.4	3.1	4.6	2.7	3.1	4.8	9	2.4	2.6	7.4	3.6	5.6	2.3

Note 1.9% for Improved D is significantly less than the 4.8% for the Current A

Figure 2-10. Results of Steps 5 through 9 if Improved System D Was Chosen Instead of Improved System H for the Example Study System as Illustrated on a Sample Table 2-9 Percent Who Prefer Each Current or Improved System

CHAPTER 2 ESTIMATING TRAVEL DEMAND

Percent Who Prefer Each Current or Improved System

CURRENT SYSTEMS	Current Design	IMPROVED SYSTEMS																			
		A	B	C	D	E	F	G	H	I	J	K	L	M	N	O	P	Q	R	S	T
Current A - Free	3.3	5	2.9	2.9	2	4.8	5.7	7.2	13.6	3.3	4.6	2.7	3.1	4.9	9.3	2.3	2.7	7.9	3.8	5.9	2.2
Current A - to $1.00	5.5	4.8	2.4	3	2	4.8	5.7	7.2	13.8	3.3	4.6	2.8	3.1	4.8	8.6	2.3	2.9	8	2.7	5.7	2.2
Current A - $1.00 to $2.00	4.8	5	2.8	3	1.9	4.8	5.7	7.2	13.6	3.1	4.5	2.8	3.1	4.8	8.8	2.3	2.8	7.6	3.7	5.6	2.2
Current A - $2.00 to $3.00	4	5.1	2.9	3.1	2	4.9	5.7	7.2	13.5	3.2	4.5	2.8	3.2	4.9	8.9	2.3	2.8	7.7	3.7	5.5	2.2
Current A - over $3.00	3.3	5.1	2.9	3.1	2	4.9	5.8	7.3	13.8	3.3	4.6	2.8	3.2	4.9	8.7	2.3	2.8	7.5	3.7	5.7	2.2
Current B - Free	2.8	5.1	2.9	3.1	2	4.9	5.8	7.3	13.8	3.3	4.6	2.8	3.2	4.9	9	2.3	2.8	7.7	3.8	5.7	2.2
Current B - to $1.00	5.1	4.8	2.4	3	1.9	4.8	5.8	7.2	13.8	3.3	4.5	2.7	3.2	4.8	8.8	2.1	2.8	8.3	2.8	5.7	2.3
Current B - $1.00 to $2.00	4.6	5	2.8	3	1.9	4.8	5.7	7.1	13.6	3.2	4.5	2.7	3.2	4.8	9	2.2	2.7	7.8	3.8	5.6	2.2
Current B - $2.00 to $3.00	3.7	5.1	2.9	3.1	1.9	4.9	5.7	7.2	13.5	3.3	4.5	2.8	3.2	4.9	9.1	2.2	2.7	7.9	3.8	5.5	2.2
Current B - over $3.00	3.2	5.1	2.9	3.1	1.9	4.9	5.7	7.3	13.8	3.3	4.5	2.8	3.2	4.9	8.9	2.2	2.7	7.9	3.7	5.7	2.2
Current C - Free	2.6	5.1	2.9	3.1	1.9	4.9	5.8	7.3	13.8	3.3	4.6	2.8	3.2	4.9	9.1	2.2	2.6	8	3.8	5.7	2.3
Current C - to $1.00	3.8	4.8	2.4	3	1.9	4.8	5.8	7.2	14.2	3.3	4.6	2.8	3.2	4.9	8.9	2.3	2.9	8.3	2.9	5.7	2.2
Current C - $1.00 to $2.00	3.4	5	2.9	3	1.9	4.9	5.7	7.2	13.9	3.2	4.5	2.8	3.2	4.9	9.1	2.3	2.7	7.8	3.9	5.5	2.2
Current C - $2.00 to $3.00	2.7	5.2	2.9	3.1	1.9	5	5.7	7.1	13.9	3.3	4.5	2.8	3.2	4.9	9.2	2.3	2.8	7.9	3.9	5.3	2.3
Current C - over $3.00	2.3	5.2	2.9	3.1	1.9	5	5.8	7.2	14.1	3.3	4.6	2.8	3.2	4.9	9	2.3	2.8	7.8	3.9	5.6	2.3
Current D - Free	1.9	5.2	2.9	3.1	2	5	5.8	7.3	14.1	3.3	4.6	2.8	3.2	5	9.2	2.3	2.7	7.9	3.9	5.6	2.2
Current D - to $1.00	6.5	4.6	2.3	2.8	2	4.6	5.6	7	13.4	3.3	4.6	2.6	3	4.7	8.9	2.2	2.9	8.2	2.8	5.9	2.2
Current D - $1.00 to $2.00	5.6	4.8	2.8	2.7	2	4.6	5.6	7	13.3	3.2	4.5	2.7	3	4.8	9.1	2.3	2.7	7.7	3.8	5.8	2.2
Current D - $2.00 to $3.00	4.8	4.9	2.9	2.9	2	4.8	5.6	7	13.1	3.3	4.5	2.7	3.1	4.8	9.2	2.3	2.7	7.8	3.8	5.7	2.2
Current D - over $3.00	4.1	5	2.9	2.9	2	4.8	5.7	7.1	13.5	3.3	4.6	2.7	3.1	4.8	9.1	2.3	2.8	7.7	3.7	5.8	2.2
Current E - Free	9.7	4.6	2.2	2.8	1.9	4.6	5.5	6.9	13	2.9	4.4	2.6	2.9	4.6	8.4	2.2	2.7	7.5	2.7	5.5	2.3
Current E - to $1.00	8	4.9	2.7	2.9	1.9	4.7	5.5	7	13	2.8	4.4	2.7	3	4.6	8.8	2.3	2.6	7.2	3.5	5.4	2.2
Current E - $1.00 to $2.00	6.7	5	2.8	3	2	4.8	5.6	7	12.8	3	4.4	2.7	3	4.7	8.9	2.3	2.6	7.3	3.6	5.4	2.3
Current E - $2.00 to $3.00	5.5	5.1	2.8	3	2	4.9	5.7	7.2	13.3	3.1	4.5	2.7	3.1	4.8	8.8	2.3	2.7	7.1	3.4	5.6	2.3
Current E - over $3.00	4.8	5.1	2.9	3	2	4.9	5.7	7.2	13.4	3.1	4.6	2.7	3.1	4.8	9	2.4	2.6	7.4	3.6	5.6	2.3

Note 13.3% + 3.2% = 16.5% for combination of Improved Systems H and I

Figure 2-11. Results of Steps 5 through 9 for Example Study System as Illustrated on a Sample Table 2-9

2-41

CHAPTER 2 ESTIMATING TRAVEL DEMAND

If all service features were implemented, nearly all people would prefer fixed-route services because it would virtually be door-to-door.

This implies that, if all the service features were implemented, nearly 100% of people with disabilities would prefer the new system. If all the service features were implemented, the fixed-route system would be completely secure, extremely convenient, virtually door-to-door, fully accessible to people with disabilities, and comfortable and easy to use. As long as the fare was also low, it is conceivable that all individuals would actually prefer it over other modes of transportation.

If the Improved Systems have a different fare from each other or from the Current System, it is probable that people would prefer the Improved System at a fare up to the highest preferred fare. A higher fare may yield lower percentages. At the same time, if the Current System fare is lower than the Improved System fare, the percent who prefer the Improved System can be anticipated to be maintained if fares are raised to the level shown in the Improved System.

Assume that the example study system has 1,500 ADA-eligible riders or expects 1,500 ADA-eligible riders in 1997. For Step 10, this number of clients is multiplied by the percentage found in Step 9, 13.6%. This results in 204 (1,500 * 13.6% = 204) paratransit patrons who would prefer Improved System H over all other improved systems. This is a potential 204 riders who would switch to a fixed-route system.

TO ESTIMATE BY MARKET SEGMENT

To estimate by market segment, the Current System A with a $1.50 fare row was interfaced with the Improved System H and "current" columns on Tables 2-10 through 2-13. This is shown in Figures 2-12 through 2-15.

CHAPTER 2 ESTIMATING TRAVEL DEMAND

CURRENT SYSTEMS	Current Design	IMPROVED SYSTEMS																			
		A	B	C	D	E	F	G	H	I	J	K	L	M	N	O	P	Q	R	S	T
Current A - Free	6	5.2	3.1	3.5	2	4.7	5.3	7.9	12.5	3.2	4.8	3	3.1	4.8	8.1	2.3	2.5	7	3.7	5.1	2.2
Current A - to $1.00	5.2	5.2	3.1	3.4	2.1	4.7	5.4	7.9	12.6	3.1	4.9	3.1	3.2	5	8.2	2.4	2.6	7	3.8	5.2	2.2
Current A - $1.00 to $2.00	4	5.3	3.2	3.5	2.1	4.8	5.4	7.9	**12.6**	3.2	4.9	3.1	3.2	5	8.3	2.4	2.6	7.1	3.8	5.1	2.3
Current A - $2.00 to $3.00	3.3	5.3	3.2	3.6	2.1	4.9	5.5	8.1	12.9	3.3	5	3.1	3.2	5.1	8.1	2.4	2.6	7	3.7	5.3	2.3
Current A - over $3.00	2.9	5.3	3.2	3.6	2.1	4.9	5.5	8.1	12.9	3.3	5	3.1	3.2	5.1	8.4	2.4	2.6	7.2	3.8	5.3	2.2
Current B - Free	6	5.2	3.1	3.4	2	4.7	5.3	7.8	12.5	3.2	4.8	2.9	3.1	4.8	8.3	2.1	2.4	7.2	3.8	5.1	2.2
Current B - to $1.00	5.4	5.1	3.1	3.4	2	4.6	5.4	7.9	12.5	3.2	4.8	3	3.2	4.9	8.3	2.2	2.4	7.3	3.8	5.2	2.2
Current B - $1.00 to $2.00	4.1	5.3	3.2	3.5	2.1	4.8	5.4	7.9	12.5	3.3	4.8	3.1	3.2	5	8.5	2.3	2.5	7.4	3.9	5.1	2.2
Current B - $2.00 to $3.00	3.5	5.3	3.2	3.5	2.1	4.8	5.5	8	12.8	3.3	4.9	3.1	3.3	5	8.3	2.3	2.5	7.3	3.8	5.3	2.3
Current B - over $3.00	2.9	5.3	3.2	3.5	2.1	4.8	5.5	8.1	12.9	3.3	4.9	3.1	3.3	5.1	8.5	2.3	2.4	7.4	3.9	5.3	2.2
Current C - Free	4.1	5.3	3.2	3.5	2	4.8	5.4	7.9	12.9	3.2	4.9	3	3.2	4.9	8.4	2.3	2.5	7.2	3.9	5.3	2.2
Current C - to $1.00	3.7	5.2	3.1	3.4	2.1	4.8	5.5	7.9	13	3.3	4.9	3.1	3.3	5	8.5	2.4	2.6	7.3	4	5.1	2.2
Current C - $1.00 to $2.00	2.7	5.4	3.2	3.6	2.1	4.9	5.5	7.9	13	3.3	4.9	3.1	3.3	5.1	8.6	2.4	2.6	7.3	4	5	2.3
Current C - $2.00 to $3.00	2.3	5.4	3.2	3.6	2.1	4.9	5.5	8	13.2	3.3	4.9	3.1	3.3	5.1	8.4	2.4	2.6	7.2	4	5.2	2.3
Current C - over $3.00	1.9	5.4	3.2	3.6	2.1	4.9	5.5	8	13.2	3.3	4.9	3.1	3.3	5.1	8.6	2.4	2.5	7.4	4	5.2	2.2
Current D - Free	7.8	4.9	3	3.2	2	4.5	5.2	7.6	12.1	3.2	4.8	2.8	2.9	4.7	8.4	2.2	2.5	7.1	3.8	5.3	2.2
Current D - to $1.00	7	4.8	2.9	3	2.1	4.4	5.3	7.7	12.3	3.2	4.8	2.9	3.1	4.8	8.5	2.3	2.5	7.2	3.8	5.3	2.2
Current D - $1.00 to $2.00	5.6	5.1	3.1	3.3	2.1	4.6	5.3	7.7	12.1	3.3	4.8	3	3.1	4.9	8.6	2.3	2.5	7.2	3.9	5.3	2.2
Current D - $2.00 to $3.00	4.7	5.1	3.1	3.3	2.1	4.6	5.4	7.8	12.5	3.3	4.9	3	3.1	4.9	8.5	2.3	2.5	7.1	3.8	5.4	2.2
Current D - over $3.00	3.8	5.2	3.2	3.3	2.2	4.7	5.4	7.9	12.6	3.3	4.9	3	3.2	5	8.6	2.4	2.5	7.3	3.9	5.5	2.2
Current E - Free	9.4	5	3	3.4	2	4.6	5.2	7.6	11.9	2.9	4.7	2.8	2.9	4.6	8.1	2.3	2.4	6.6	3.5	5	2.2
Current E - to $1.00	8	5	2.9	3.3	2.1	4.6	5.3	7.7	12.1	2.8	4.8	2.9	3.1	4.8	8.2	2.3	2.4	6.7	3.6	5.1	2.2
Current E - $1.00 to $2.00	6.6	5.2	3.1	3.5	2.1	4.7	5.3	7.8	12	3	4.8	3	3.1	4.9	8.3	2.4	2.5	6.8	3.6	5	2.3
Current E - $2.00 to $3.00	5.4	5.3	3.1	3.5	2.1	4.8	5.4	8	12.5	3	4.9	3	3.1	4.9	8.3	2.4	2.5	6.6	3.5	5.2	2.3
Current E - over $3.00	4.6	5.3	3.2	3.5	2.1	4.8	5.4	8	12.5	3.1	4.9	3.1	3.2	4.9	8.4	2.4	2.4	6.9	3.7	5.2	2.3

Figure 2-12. Results of Steps 10 and 11 for Market Segment 1 for the Example Study System as Illustrated on a Sample Table 2-10

CHAPTER 2 ESTIMATING TRAVEL DEMAND

CURRENT SYSTEMS	Current Design	IMPROVED SYSTEMS																				
		A	B	C	D	E	F	G	H	I	J	K	L	M	N	O	P	Q	R	S	T
Current A - Free	5.2	5.2	3	3.2	1.8	5	5.9	7	13.3	3.1	4.5	2.7	2.9	4.8	9	2.2	2.6	7.7	3.5	5.3	2.3
Current A - to $1.00	4.6	5.1	2.9	3.2	1.8	4.9	5.9	7	13.3	3.1	4.5	3	2.9	5	9	2.3	2.5	7.9	3.5	5.4	2.2
Current A - $1.00 to $2.00	3.8	5.3	3	3.3	1.9	5	5.9	7	13.3	3.2	4.5	2.8	3	4.9	9.2	2.3	2.6	7.8	3.6	5.2	2.3
Current A - $2.00 to $3.00	3.1	5.3	3	3.3	1.9	5.1	6	7.2	13.6	3.2	4.6	2.8	3	5	9	2.3	2.6	7.7	3.5	5.4	2.3
Current A - over $3.00	2.7	5.3	3	3.3	1.9	5.1	6	7.2	13.6	3.2	4.6	2.8	3	5	9.2	2.3	2.6	7.9	3.6	5.4	2.3
Current B - Free	4.7	5.2	3	3.2	1.8	5	5.9	7	13.3	3.2	4.5	2.7	3	4.8	9.2	2	2.5	8	3.6	5.3	2.3
Current B - to $1.00	4.4	5.1	2.9	3.2	1.8	4.9	5.9	7	13.3	3.1	4.5	3	3	5	9.2	2.2	2.4	8.2	3.6	5.4	2.2
Current B - $1.00 to $2.00	3.5	5.3	3	3.3	1.8	5	5.9	7	13.3	3.2	4.5	2.8	3	4.9	9.4	2.2	2.5	8.1	3.6	5.2	2.3
Current B - $2.00 to $3.00	3	5.3	3	3.3	1.8	5.1	6	7.1	13.3	3.2	4.6	2.8	3.1	4.9	9.2	2.2	2.5	8	3.6	5.4	2.3
Current B - over $3.00	2.5	5.3	3	3.3	1.9	5.1	6	7.2	13.6	3.2	4.6	2.8	3.1	5	9.4	2.2	2.5	8.1	3.7	5.4	2.3
Current C - Free	3.6	5.3	3	3.3	1.8	5	6	7	13.7	3.2	4.5	2.7	3	4.8	9.3	2.2	2.6	7.9	3.7	5.2	2.3
Current C - to $1.00	3.2	5.2	2.9	3.2	1.8	4.9	6	7	13.6	3.1	4.5	3	3	5.1	9.3	2.3	2.5	8.1	3.7	5.3	2.3
Current C - $1.00 to $2.00	2.6	5.3	3	3.3	1.9	5.1	6	7	13.7	3.2	4.5	2.8	3.1	5	9.4	2.3	2.6	8.1	3.7	5.1	2.3
Current C - $2.00 to $3.00	2.2	5.4	3	3.3	1.9	5.1	6.1	7.1	13.9	3.2	4.6	2.8	3.1	5	9.3	2.3	2.6	7.9	3.7	5.3	2.3
Current C - over $3.00	1.8	5.4	3	3.3	1.9	5.1	6.1	7.1	13.9	3.2	4.6	2.8	3.1	5	9.5	2.3	2.6	8.1	3.7	5.3	2.3
Current D - Free	6.4	5	2.9	3	1.8	4.8	5.8	6.9	12.9	3.1	4.5	2.6	2.8	4.6	9.3	2.1	2.5	7.8	3.5	5.4	2.3
Current D - to $1.00	5.7	4.9	2.9	2.9	1.8	4.7	5.8	6.9	13	3.1	4.5	2.9	2.9	4.9	9.3	2.2	2.5	8	3.5	5.5	2.2
Current D - $1.00 to $2.00	4.8	5.1	3	3.1	1.9	4.9	5.8	6.9	12.8	3.2	4.5	2.7	2.9	4.8	9.4	2.2	2.6	7.9	3.6	5.5	2.3
Current D - $2.00 to $3.00	4	5.1	3	3.1	1.9	4.9	5.9	7	13.3	3.2	4.6	2.7	2.9	4.9	9.3	2.2	2.6	7.8	3.6	5.6	2.3
Current D - over $3.00	3.4	5.2	3	3.1	1.9	4.9	5.9	7.1	13.3	3.2	4.6	2.7	3	4.9	9.5	2.2	2.5	8	3.6	5.6	2.2
Current E - Free	8.9	5	2.8	3.1	1.8	4.8	5.7	6.8	12.6	2.9	4.4	2.6	2.7	4.5	8.9	2.2	2.4	7.2	3.3	5.1	2.3
Current E - to $1.00	7.9	5	2.8	3.1	1.8	4.8	5.7	6.8	12.7	2.8	4.4	2.9	2.8	4.8	8.9	2.3	2.4	7.4	3.3	5.2	2.2
Current E - $1.00 to $2.00	6.6	5.2	2.9	3.2	1.9	4.9	5.8	6.9	12.6	3	4.5	2.7	2.9	4.8	9.2	2.3	2.5	7.4	3.4	5.1	2.4
Current E - $2.00 to $3.00	5.4	5.3	2.9	3.3	1.9	5	6	7.1	13.2	3	4.6	2.7	2.9	4.8	9.1	2.3	2.5	7.2	3.3	5.3	2.4
Current E - over $3.00	4.7	5.3	3	3.3	1.9	5	6	7.1	13.2	3	4.6	2.7	2.9	4.8	9.3	2.3	2.4	7.5	3.4	5.3	2.3

Figure 2-13. Results of Steps 10 and 11 for Market Segment 2 for the Example Study System as Illustrated on a Sample Table 2-11

CHAPTER 2 ESTIMATING TRAVEL DEMAND

CURRENT SYSTEMS	Current Design	IMPROVED SYSTEMS																		
		A	B	C	D	E	F	G	H	I	J	K	L	M	N	O	P	Q	R	S	T
Current A - Free	5	5.4	3.7	2.9	2	6.1	5.3	6.1	15.1	3.7	3.4	2.4	2.9	5.5	8.2	2.8	2.3	6.7	3.7	4.7	2.1
Current A - to $1.00	5	5.4	3.6	2.9	2.1	6	5.3	6.1	15.1	3.6	3.4	2.5	2.9	5.5	8.3	2.8	2.3	6.8	3.7	4.7	2.1
Current A - $1.00 to $2.00	3.5	5.6	3.7	3	2.1	6.2	5.3	6.1	15.1	3.8	3.4	2.5	3	5.6	8.4	2.9	2.4	6.9	3.8	4.6	2.1
Current A - $2.00 to $3.00	3.2	5.9	3.8	3.1	2	6.4	5.4	6.2	15.4	3.9	3.5	2.5	2.9	5.5	8.2	2.9	2.4	6.7	3.7	4.7	2.1
Current A - over $3.00	2.3	5.6	3.7	3	2.1	6.3	5.4	6.2	15.5	3.8	3.5	2.5	3	5.7	8.5	2.9	2.4	6.9	3.8	4.8	2.1
Current B - Free	4.8	5.5	3.6	2.9	2	6.1	5.3	6.1	15.1	3.7	3.4	2.4	3	5.5	8.4	2.6	2.2	7	3.8	4.7	2.1
Current B - to $1.00	4.9	5.4	3.6	2.9	2	6	5.3	6.1	15.1	3.7	3.4	2.4	2.9	5.5	8.4	2.7	2.2	7	3.8	4.7	2.1
Current B - $1.00 to $2.00	3.4	5.6	3.7	3	2	6.2	5.3	6.1	15.1	3.8	3.4	2.5	3	5.6	8.6	2.8	2.3	7.1	3.8	4.6	2.1
Current B - $2.00 to $3.00	3.3	5.8	3.7	3	2	6.4	5.3	6.2	15.3	3.9	3.4	2.4	3	5.5	8.3	2.7	2.3	6.9	3.7	4.7	2.1
Current B - over $3.00	2.3	5.6	3.7	3	2.1	6.3	5.4	6.2	15.5	3.8	3.5	2.5	3	5.7	8.6	2.8	2.2	7.1	3.9	4.8	2.1
Current C - Free	3.5	5.5	3.7	3	2	6.2	5.3	6.1	15.5	3.7	3.4	2.4	3	5.5	8.5	2.7	2.3	7	3.9	4.6	2.1
Current C - to $1.00	3.5	5.5	3.6	2.9	2	6.1	5.3	6.1	15.5	3.6	3.4	2.5	3	5.6	8.5	2.8	2.3	7	3.9	4.6	2.1
Current C - $1.00 to $2.00	2.4	5.6	3.7	3	2.1	6.3	5.3	6.1	15.5	3.8	3.4	2.5	3	5.7	8.7	2.9	2.4	7.1	3.9	4.5	2.2
Current C - $2.00 to $3.00	2.3	5.9	3.8	3.1	2	6.4	5.4	6.1	15.7	3.9	3.4	2.4	3	5.5	8.4	2.8	2.3	6.9	3.9	4.6	2.1
Current C - over $3.00	1.6	5.6	3.8	3	2.1	6.3	5.4	6.2	15.8	3.8	3.5	2.5	3	5.7	8.7	2.9	2.3	7.1	4	4.7	2.1
Current D - Free	6.3	5.3	3.6	2.7	2	5.9	5.2	6	14.7	3.7	3.4	2.3	2.8	5.4	8.5	2.7	2.3	6.8	3.7	4.8	2.1
Current D - to $1.00	6.3	5.1	3.5	2.6	2.1	5.7	5.2	6	14.7	3.6	3.4	2.4	2.8	5.5	8.5	2.8	2.3	6.8	3.8	4.8	2.1
Current D - $1.00 to $2.00	4.7	5.4	3.7	2.8	2.1	6	5.2	6	14.6	3.8	3.4	2.4	2.9	5.6	8.6	2.8	2.3	6.9	3.8	4.8	2.1
Current D - $2.00 to $3.00	4.4	5.6	3.7	2.9	2.1	6.1	5.2	6	15	3.9	3.4	2.4	2.9	5.4	8.5	2.8	2.3	6.7	3.7	4.8	2.1
Current D - over $3.00	3.2	5.4	3.7	2.8	2.1	6.1	5.3	6.1	15.2	3.8	3.5	2.4	2.9	5.6	8.7	2.9	2.3	7	3.9	4.9	2.1
Current E - Free	7.4	5.3	3.5	2.9	2	6	5.2	6	14.5	3.4	3.4	2.4	2.7	5.3	8.3	2.8	2.2	6.4	3.5	4.6	2.1
Current E - to $1.00	7.9	5.2	3.4	2.8	2	5.8	5.2	6	14.4	3.2	3.4	2.4	2.8	5.4	8.3	2.8	2.2	6.5	3.6	4.6	2.1
Current E - $1.00 to $2.00	5.1	5.5	3.6	3	2.1	6.2	5.3	6.1	14.6	3.5	3.4	2.5	2.9	5.5	8.5	2.9	2.3	6.6	3.6	4.6	2.2
Current E - $2.00 to $3.00	4.7	5.8	3.7	3	2.1	6.3	5.3	6.1	14.9	3.6	3.4	2.4	2.9	5.4	8.3	2.9	2.3	6.4	3.5	4.7	2.2
Current E - over $3.00	3.6	5.5	3.7	3	2.1	6.2	5.4	6.2	15.1	3.6	3.5	2.5	2.9	5.6	8.6	2.9	2.2	6.7	3.7	4.8	2.2

Figure 2-14. Results of Steps 10 and 11 for Market Segment 3 for the Example Study System as Illustrated on a Sample Table 2-12

CHAPTER 2 ESTIMATING TRAVEL DEMAND

CURRENT SYSTEMS	Current Design	IMPROVED SYSTEMS																		
		A	B	C	D	E	F	G	H	I	J	K	L	M	N	O	P	Q	R	S	T
Current A - Free	5.6	4.8	2.7	2.8	1.9	4.7	5.6	7	13.6	3.2	4.5	2.7	3.1	4.7	8.8	2.3	2.8	7.6	3.7	5.8	2.1
Current A - to $1.00	4.9	4.8	2.7	2.8	1.9	4.7	5.6	7.1	13.7	3.2	4.5	2.7	3.2	4.8	8.9	2.3	2.9	7.6	3.8	5.8	2.1
Current A - $1.00 to $2.00	4.1	4.9	2.8	2.9	2	4.8	5.6	7.1	13.6	3.3	4.5	2.8	3.2	4.8	9	2.3	2.9	7.7	3.8	5.7	2.2
Current A - $2.00 to $3.00	3.3	5	2.8	2.9	2	4.8	5.7	7.2	14	3.3	4.6	2.8	3.2	4.9	8.8	2.4	2.9	7.6	3.7	5.9	2.2
Current A - over $3.00	2.9	5	2.8	2.9	2	4.8	5.7	7.2	14	3.3	4.6	2.8	3.2	4.9	9	2.4	2.9	7.8	3.8	5.9	2.1
Current B - Free	5.1	4.9	2.7	2.8	1.8	4.7	5.6	7.1	13.7	3.3	4.4	2.6	3.1	4.7	9	2.1	2.7	7.9	3.8	5.8	2.1
Current B - to $1.00	4.6	4.8	2.7	2.8	1.9	4.7	5.6	7.1	13.7	3.2	4.4	2.7	3.2	4.8	9.1	2.2	2.8	7.9	3.8	5.8	2.1
Current B - $1.00 to $2.00	3.8	4.9	2.8	2.9	1.9	4.8	5.6	7.1	13.6	3.3	4.4	2.7	3.2	4.8	9.2	2.2	2.8	8	3.9	5.7	2.2
Current B - $2.00 to $3.00	3.2	5	2.8	2.9	1.9	4.8	5.7	7.2	13.9	3.3	4.5	2.7	3.3	4.8	9	2.2	2.8	7.9	3.8	5.9	2.2
Current B - over $3.00	2.6	5	2.8	2.9	1.9	4.8	5.7	7.2	14	3.3	4.5	2.7	3.3	4.9	9.2	2.3	2.7	8	3.9	5.9	2.1
Current C - Free	3.8	4.9	2.8	2.9	1.9	4.8	5.7	7.1	14	3.3	4.5	2.7	3.2	4.8	9.1	2.2	2.8	7.9	3.9	5.7	2.2
Current C - to $1.00	3.4	4.9	2.8	2.8	1.9	4.7	5.7	7.1	14.1	3.2	4.5	2.7	3.2	4.8	9.2	2.3	2.9	7.9	3.9	5.7	2.2
Current C - $1.00 to $2.00	2.8	5	2.8	2.9	1.9	4.9	5.7	7.1	14.1	3.3	4.5	2.8	3.3	4.9	9.3	2.3	2.9	8	4	5.6	2.2
Current C - $2.00 to $3.00	2	5	2.8	2.9	2	4.9	5.8	7.4	14.3	3.2	4.5	2.8	3.1	5	9	2.4	2.9	7.8	3.8	6	2.3
Current C - over $3.00	2	5	2.8	2.9	1.9	4.9	5.8	7.2	14.3	3.3	4.6	2.8	3.3	4.9	9.3	2.3	2.8	8	4	5.8	2.1
Current D - Free	6.3	4.7	2.7	2.7	1.9	4.5	5.5	6.9	13.3	3.3	4.4	2.5	3	4.6	9.1	2.2	2.8	7.7	3.8	5.9	2.1
Current D - to $1.00	5.3	4.6	2.7	2.6	2	4.5	5.6	7	13.5	3.2	4.5	2.6	3.1	4.7	9.2	2.3	2.8	7.8	3.8	6	2.2
Current D - $1.00 to $2.00	4.7	4.8	2.8	2.7	2	4.6	5.5	6.9	13.2	3.3	4.5	2.7	3.1	4.8	9.3	2.3	2.9	7.9	3.9	6	2.2
Current D - $2.00 to $3.00	3.9	4.8	2.8	2.7	2	4.7	5.6	7.1	13.7	3.3	4.6	2.7	3.1	4.8	9.2	2.3	2.9	7.8	3.8	6.1	2.2
Current D - over $3.00	3.2	4.8	2.8	2.7	2	4.7	5.7	7.1	13.7	3.4	4.6	2.7	3.2	4.8	9.4	2.3	2.8	8	3.9	6.1	2.1
Current E - Free	9.5	4.7	2.6	2.7	1.9	4.6	5.4	6.8	12.9	2.9	4.3	2.5	2.9	4.4	8.7	2.2	2.6	7.1	3.5	5.6	2.1
Current E - to $1.00	8	4.7	2.6	2.7	1.9	4.6	5.5	6.9	13.1	2.8	4.4	2.6	3	4.6	8.8	2.3	2.7	7.2	3.5	5.7	2.2
Current E - $1.00 to $2.00	6.9	4.8	2.7	2.8	1.9	4.7	5.5	6.9	13	3.1	4.4	2.7	3.1	4.7	9	2.3	2.7	7.4	3.6	5.6	2.2
Current E - $2.00 to $3.00	5.6	4.9	2.7	2.9	2	4.8	5.6	7.1	13.5	3.1	4.5	2.7	3.1	4.7	8.9	2.4	2.8	7.2	3.5	5.8	2.2
Current E - over $3.00	4.9	4.9	2.7	2.9	2	4.8	5.7	7.1	13.5	3.1	4.5	2.7	3.1	4.7	9.1	2.4	2.7	7.5	3.7	5.8	2.2

Figure 2-15. Results of Steps 10 and 11 for Market Segment 4 for the Example Study System as Illustrated on a Sample Table 2-13

CHAPTER 2 ESTIMATING TRAVEL DEMAND

A market segment analysis gives the sizes of the four market segments.

Assume the planners for the example study system estimated each market segment size by completing a ridership survey, and market segment populations were determined to be as follows:

- Market Segment 1: 150 persons;
- Market Segment 2: 375 persons;
- Market Segment 3: 75 persons; and
- Market Segment 4: 900 persons.

Table 2-19 illustrates the application of patron-preferred percentages to the total population and market segment population.

Table 2-19. Calculations for Step 14 (Number of Persons Preferring an Improved System by Market Segment) for the Example Study System

Paratransit Patronage	Calculations	Persons Preferring Improved System H
Total Paratransit Patronage and Persons with Disabilities	1500 * 13.6%	204
Market Segment 1	150 * 12.6%	19
Market Segment 2	375 * 13.3%	50
Market Segment 3	75 * 15.1%	11
Market Segment 4	900 * 13.6%	122

For the final step, the number of persons preferring an improved fixed-route system is multiplied by trip generation rates. For the example study system, 204 paratransit patrons and persons with disabilities prefer the Improved System H. Suppose current ridership statistics show that the 1,500 paratransit patrons are making an average of two round-trips per month, or four one-way trips. Thus, the paratransit system supplies about 72,000 trips per year. If statistics such as these are not available, data for the number of ADA-paratransit-eligible persons and trip generation rates may be obtained from the peer systems tables.

Multiplying the 204 persons by a trip rate of 4 trips per month results in 816 trips per month or 9,792 trips per year that may be diverted to fixed-route services if improvements are made which result in a service similar to Improved System H. Assuming a net cost per trip of $2.00 on fixed-route and $15.00 on

CHAPTER 2 ESTIMATING TRAVEL DEMAND

paratransit, this could result in savings of $127,000. (This number does not take into account the capital or operating costs for implementing and maintaining the changes to the fixed-route service. Also, these numbers are simply for illustration. Actual numbers will result when actual operating figures from a local transit system are used.)

PROBABILITY OF PURCHASE

Using the example described in the above steps, 204 people would prefer Improved System H. Improved System H (see Table 2-16) indicates that there is a 75.4% likelihood that people who prefer the system will actually use it. This may mean that, for example: (1) all the people would choose it for 75.4% of their trips; or (2) 75.4% of the people would use it all the time; or (3) there is a 24.6% chance that no one would use it at all. This is shown in Figure 2-16.

In other words, in the first example, (204 people) x (4 trips/month) x (12 months/year) = 9,792 x (.754) = 7,383. In the second example, (204 people) x (.754) = 154 persons x (4 trips/month) x (12 months/year) = 7,392 trips per year.

Similarly, if no changes are made to the current fixed-route system (Current System A with a $1.50 fare), there would be 1,500 people eligible multiplied by 4.8% (Table 2-9) to get 72 people who would prefer the current system. Those 72 people times 4 trips per month times 12 months per year is 3,456 trips per year times 45.2% (Table 2-15) is 1,562 trips. Or, using the second scenario, 72 people times 45.2% is 33 people times 4 trips per month times 12 months per year is 1,584 trips per year. The differences in the results of the two scenarios are due to rounding of figures. A similar analysis can be completed for each market segment by using the proper population totals for each market segment.

CHAPTER 2   ESTIMATING TRAVEL DEMAND

Improved Systems	Market Segments				
	All	1	2	3	4
A	0.588	0.589	0.60	0.646	0.58
B	0.408	0.432	0.455	0.497	0.432
C	0.449	0.464	0.469	0.473	0.437
D	0.326	0.336	0.318	0.372	0.325
E	0.568	0.554	0.579	0.638	0.563
F	0.606	0.584	0.62	0.629	0.604
G	0.658	0.663	0.661	0.657	0.656
H	0.754	0.727	0.758	0.795	0.756
I	0.428	0.424	0.437	0.457	0.425
J	0.568	0.576	0.572	0.527	0.568
K	0.411	0.423	0.417	0.422	0.408
L	0.435	0.431	0.432	0.479	0.435
M	0.561	0.551	0.568	0.587	0.559
N	0.674	0.641	0.688	0.698	0.676
O	0.365	0.353	0.362	0.439	0.367
P	0.387	0.364	0.383	0.382	0.393
Q	0.646	0.604	0.653	0.657	0.65
R	0.393	0.463	0.462	0.474	0.472
S	0.575	0.549	0.572	0.558	0.583
T	0.334	0.326	0.342	0.346	0.33

- Market Segment 1 - People with disabilities who use fixed-route transit
- Market Segment 2 - People with disabilities who use paratransit
- Market Segment 3 - Others who use paratransit
- Market Segment 4 - People with disabilities who normally do not use transit

Figure 2-16. Results of Probability of Purchase Step for the Example Study System as Illustrated on a Sample Table 2-16

CHAPTER 3:

BASIC STEPS

CHAPTER 3 BASIC STEPS

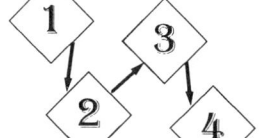

INTRODUCTION

This chapter describes the basic steps for each approach to attract paratransit patrons and people with disabilities to fixed-route services. These steps are as follows:

1. Identify the need;
2. Define funding needs and resources;
3. Conduct public involvement; and
4. Conduct market research.

These steps must be accomplished at the outset of any approach.

These four steps may occur in different orders for various implementations or they may occur nearly simultaneously. In some cases, the steps may occur more than once. For example, it may be useful to conduct additional public involvement after market research is completed. These four steps are very important to start the process and the order discussed here is recommended for most purposes. Specific implementation steps for different approaches are described in the following chapters.

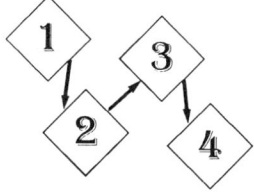

STEP 1: IDENTIFY THE NEED

For any selected method to attract paratransit patrons to fixed-route, different specific approaches may be taken. For example, to decrease the distance a passenger travels to a transit stop, the transit system may choose from several options -- some more feasible and more effective than others. It may increase the number of stops along existing routes if the need exists along core parts of the service area. It may introduce a shuttle service to bring people from outlying areas to stops along the main route, if the need exists in more remote areas. It may erect stops in mall parking lots or at multiple hospital entrances, or at multiple college campus locations if the need relates to specific locations. The need for the improvements must be clearly defined so that the most effective approach can be implemented.

CHAPTER 3 BASIC STEPS

To select the appropriate approach, review the available information and collect additional information as necessary to identify the need for a particular approach. Although each approach may attract people to fixed-route, every transit service area is different and local information is needed to apply the most needed improvements.

Identification of the need may not be an independent step; however, there must be mechanisms to translate input on services to a definition of the appropriate solution.

INFORMATION SOURCES

The transit system needs to be able to learn from available information what is needed to change the service to attract paratransit patrons and people with disabilities. Three sources of information are as follows:

- Ridership and other statistics;
- Paratransit use trends; and
- Public and other input.

Ridership and Service Area Information

The need for specific fixed-route features may be identified from information showing the following:

- Increased traffic congestion in specific locations;
- Changing paratransit eligibility;
- Increased accessibility of the fixed-route fleet; or
- Planned or evolutionary changes in the community leading to a natural service area for specialized services.

Paratransit Use

Collect information on increasing paratransit use to specific locations by doing the following:

- Plotting paratransit origins and destinations on maps;

CHAPTER 3 BASIC STEPS

- Grouping origins and destinations by small geographic areas of the service area;
- Observing common origins and destinations (e.g., hospitals, senior centers, rehabilitation clinics, and shopping destinations) for increasing paratransit traffic; and/or
- Observing vehicle capacity in specific areas and ability to schedule multiple rides to or from specific locations.

From this information, determine the trends of increasing paratransit traffic.

Public and Other Input

It is necessary to be aware of and open to input and suggestions that would define the need for improved fixed-route service. Input may come from such sources as the following:

- Service complaints regarding lack of service or infrequent service;
- Survey results;
- A pattern of complaints regarding specific areas;
- Service complaints related to vehicle accessibility;
- Service complaints related to driver empathy;
- Driver input on passenger needs;
- Discussions with local businesses on related issues, such as parking, future development, customer location, changing demographics, and market opportunities;
- Input from community leaders on key locations that could be better served by accessible fixed-route transit;
- Requests for additional assistance to use transit, such as additional vehicle lifts or securement positions, stop announcements, or travel training; or
- Input from advocacy groups which represent individuals with disabilities.

CHAPTER 3 BASIC STEPS

To review the information from these sources, transit planners must do as follows:

- Review complaints to discern patterns in topics of complaints (driver, service frequency, accessibility, equipment reliability, etc.), location of service, and other patterns;
- Meet with community leaders to discuss the role of transit in their enterprises, particularly with those along proposed routes and along accessible routes;
- Meet with transit system employees, including drivers, paratransit call-takers and schedulers, dispatchers, and supervisor and managerial personnel;
- Meet with advisory committees and consumer representatives; and
- Meet with advocacy groups which represent individuals with disabilities.

Meetings should be designed to receive input on the proposed service features that the transit system is interested in implementing. Before meetings, review with participants the feature types and ask them to be prepared to discuss their preferred ways of implementing the features.

Once the need has been identified, it must be clearly defined so that the necessary resources can also be determined.

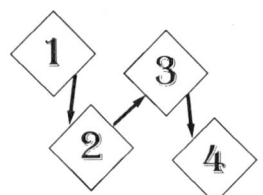

STEP 2: DEFINE FUNDING NEEDS AND RESOURCES

For most systems, the availability of funding will be an important factor in the decision to implement a new service improvement. The accurate identification of funding needs will help in making decisions on priorities and future needs. By carefully calculating the funds needed for approaches, define those which can be most cost-effective in attracting people to the system. Identify those which can be immediately implemented and those which must wait for significant funding allocations. Set up priorities for projects on the basis of costs and anticipated results.

CHAPTER 3 BASIC STEPS

It is important, when embarking on innovative programs to attract riders from paratransit, to explore innovative funding options. Not all approaches will generate revenue to cover investments, but the enhancements to the well-being of the community may prompt unanticipated sources to assist with costs.

The identification of funding needs and resources includes the following three major factors:

1. Identification of the necessary funding levels;
2. Identification of current budget availability and grant, demonstration, or other available future funding; and
3. Identification of other non-traditional revenue sources.

IDENTIFICATION OF NECESSARY FUNDING LEVELS

Make a quick cost estimate.

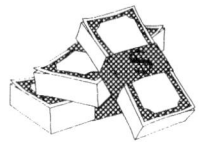

Before being able to define the sources of the necessary funding, identify the level of funding required to start the project. Different amounts of funding are available from different sources, sometimes with restrictions on use. An initial estimate should be made before final decisions on actual service configurations are made.

Consider the types of resources which will be necessary for the project. For example, a new specialized route may require the following:

- New vehicles;
- Additional drivers;
- Marketing and advertising materials;
- Additional driver training;
- Driver uniforms or other special equipment; and
- Fuel, maintenance, and insurance.

Some of these items can come out of existing budgets. Driver training often is part of an existing ongoing training program. Figure 3-1 shows how the costs can be calculated. Figure 3-2 shows the formulas for the spreadsheet developed to calculate the costs. Use local costs and expected mileage to make the estimates realistic.

CHAPTER 3 BASIC STEPS

	A	B	C	D
1	**Vehicles**			
2	Type	Cost	Number Required	Total
3	Modified Van	$35,000	0	$0
4	Low-Floor Small Bus	$65,000	3	$195,000
5	Full-Size Bus	$200,000	0	$0
6	**Drivers**			
7	Number	Hourly Rate*	Annual Hours	Total
8	6	$20	2080	$249,600
9	**Advertising**			
10	Type of Advertising	Development Cost	Distribution/ Reproduction Cost	Total
11	Advertising Agency			$3,000
12	Mailings (200 pieces)	$500	$2	$900
13	Posters (50 posters)	$500	$5	$750
14	Media (5 radio ads)	$1,000	$100	$1,500
15	**Driver Training**			
16	Number of Drivers	Hourly Rate	Training Hours	Total
17	6	$20	24	$2,880
18	**Uniforms or Equipment**			
19	Item	Number	Unit Cost	Total
20	Uniforms	12	$100	$1,200
21	Badges	6	$10	$60
22	Awards	6	$10	$60
23	**Operations**			
24	Item		Unit Cost	Total
25	Fuel	TBD	TBD	TBD
26	Maintenance	TBD	TBD	TBD
27	Insurance	TBD	TBD	TBD
28	**Estimated Total**			$463,050

* Including fringe benefits
TBD = To be determined locally

Figure 3-1. Cost Calculations

CHAPTER 3 BASIC STEPS

	A	B	C	D
1	**Vehicles**			
2	Type	Cost	Number Required	Total
3	Modified Van	35000	0	=B3*C3
4	Low-Floor Small Bus	65000	3	=B4*C4
5	Full-Size Bus	200000	0	=B5*C5
6	**Drivers**			
7	Number	Hourly Rate	Annual Hours	Total
8	6	20	2080	=A8*B8*C8
9	**Advertising**			
10	Type of Advertising	Development Cost	Distribution/ Reproduction Cost	Total
11	Advertising Agency			3000
12	Mailings (200 pieces)	500	2	=B12+(C12*200)
13	Posters (50 posters)	500	5	=B13+(C13*50)
14	Media (5 radio ads)	1000	100	=B14+(C14*100)
15	**Driver Training**			
16	Number of Drivers	Hourly Rate	Training Hours	Total
17	6	20	24	=A17*B17*C17
18	**Uniforms or Equipment**			
19	Item	Number	Unit Cost	Total
20	Uniforms	12	100	=B20*C20
21	Badges	6	10	=B21*C21
22	Awards	6	10	=B22*C22
23	**Operations**			
24	Item	Units	Unit Cost	Total
25	Fuel	TBD	TBD	=B25*C25
26	Maintenance	TBD	TBD	=B26*C26
27	Insurance	TBD	TBD	=B27*C27
28	**Estimated Total**			=SUM(D3:D27)

* Including fringe benefits
TBD = To be determined locally

Figure 3-2. Cost Calculation Formulas

CHAPTER 3 BASIC STEPS

Identify some possible sources.

IDENTIFICATION OF CURRENT BUDGET AVAILABILITY AND FUTURE FUNDING

Although transit systems do not, typically, have extra current and future funding available for new services or programs, it is necessary to review available funding and determine what parts of an innovative program can be funded from existing sources. For example, new vehicles can be procured through a previously approved grant. Additional driver training may fit into the current training budget. Funds for a particular marketing campaign may be diverted to advertise the new service.

Sources of grants and funding at the local, state, and federal level can also be pursued for the new program. Occasionally, special funding is available for new programs, for demonstration programs, or for specific types of programs. A new service feature may fit into one of the categories for which funding is available. It is important to keep in contact with representatives at the state and federal level to remain aware of the status of funding. Contact with government leaders at the local level may also reveal funding availability.

Try some innovative approaches.

IDENTIFICATION OF NON-TRADITIONAL REVENUE SOURCES

In addition to revenue generated through fares and grants, take advantage of non-traditional revenue sources and try to create innovative methods of financing new types of services. Advertisers and private firms may be particularly interested in being associated with and contributing to services which benefit people with disabilities. Some non-traditional revenue-raising techniques are as follows:

- Advertising on vehicles, at stops, on bus shelters, on schedules and brochures, and in newsletters;
- Private-public partnerships with businesses which benefit from the service; and/or
- Private "sponsors" of vehicles or routes.

3-8

CHAPTER 3 BASIC STEPS

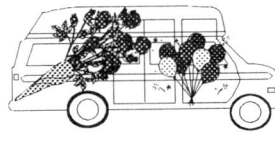

Advertising

Consider the revenue-generating capabilities of advertising on vehicles. Buses have always carried advertisements, but some types of advertisements are more attractive to businesses than others. Advertisements at bus shelters and on vehicle exteriors are more attractive than advertisements on vehicle interiors. Advertising on bus shelters is attractive to businesses because the large advertisements can be seen by a large number of people, not all of whom are current transit riders. Work with potential advertisers on the cost of bus shelter advertisements. Sometimes the advertisers will pay for the construction of the shelter itself or for part of the cost.

Businesses are particularly interested in the wrap-around advertising technique in which the vehicle, windows and all, can be transformed into a moving object advertising the business. Many creative advertisements are moving along city streets, including a giant basketball shoe in Philadelphia, Pennsylvania, and a bus apparently filled with swimming polar bears in Louisville, Kentucky. Advertising can generate significant revenue, and creative ideas can generate additional interest in the transit services provided.

It is important to work with advertisers and advertising agencies to ensure that the advertisements on the vehicles do not clash with the purpose and theme of the routes. This can be particularly important for services directed to historic or tourist attractions. For those services, the attraction of the route may come in part from its compatibility with the environment.

Wrap-around advertising has advantages and disadvantages.

There are advantages and disadvantages to the use of wrap-around advertising. Some advantages are as follows:

- Revenue generation;
- Some reduction in the cost of maintenance (painting);
- Creative advertisements that generate interest in the service; and
- Local advertisements that bring a distinct local and community theme to the service.

CHAPTER 3 BASIC STEPS

Some potential disadvantages are as follows:

- The wrap-around advertisements may mask the identification of the vehicles as part of the circulator service and make them more difficult for passengers to identify.
- Market research has shown that people like to see into the vehicles and be seen from the outside when on the vehicles, largely for security reasons. Advertisements on the windows prevent this. Wrap-around advertisements can also make the vehicle interior darker.
- During hours of outside darkness, the reflection of inside lighting on the inside of the windows prevents riders from being able to see where the bus is at any time.
- Over time, the outside of the vehicle can get dirty and the grime on the wrap-around design can make it more difficult to see through and allow even less light into the vehicle.
- If control cannot be exerted over advertising contents and image, potential problems can arise if the advertisement is inconsistent with local community values. A recent example is the allegedly suggestive theme in a bus advertisement for jeans.
- Unless the advertising contract specifies that the advertiser will pay for the restoration of the bus surface to its original condition at the end of the advertising period, the transit authority will have to absorb the cost of restoration.

Smaller systems for which whole-bus advertising is not feasible can generate revenue through other types of advertisements. Selling placement of posters and cards on buses and at stops are common methods to generate revenue. Other locations for advertisement space are on schedules and brochures distributed by the system. Many transit systems generate newsletters for transit and paratransit riders on which advertisement space can also be sold.

Get ready to sell advertisements all around the system.

To determine where and for how much advertising space can be sold, transit systems need to do the following:

1. **Identify all possible locations (e.g., vehicles, stops, shelters, benches, brochures, schedules, newsletters, and others).** Transit systems need to develop creative

3-10

CHAPTER 3 BASIC STEPS

Find locations, calculate amounts and costs, identify targets, and sell advertising space.

ways to generate advertising revenue. More information on marketing and advertising can be found in Chapter 8.

2. **Determine how much space can be sold in each location (e.g., how many stops and vehicles with how much space, and how much publication space can be sold).** Once all the outlets are determined, define how much of what type of space is available. Determine for newsletters and other publications how much advertising is appropriate and what kinds should be accepted. Newsletters and brochures need to be clearly identifiable with the transit system; however, a balanced distribution of advertisements should cover the publication and distribution costs and also generate additional revenues for service provision.

3. **Determine the cost of advertisements and how much revenue can be and needs to be generated.** Determine costs through comparison with other advertising outlets and calculations of expected circulation.

4. **Define targets for advertisements.** In smaller systems, contact local advertisers as the most likely targets, as well as local franchises and branches of national outlets. In larger systems, national businesses may be interested.

5. **Sell advertisements using dedicated staff, part-time workers, or an outside agency.** An agency can be hired to book advertisement space for a fee. Current staff can also serve in this role, or additional staff may be needed to sell the advertisements on a full- or part-time basis. When new advertising outlets are offered, a skilled sales force can ensure that potential advertisers are contacted.

Private-Public Partnerships

Look for ways to form partnerships with businesses and other private and quasi-public enterprises which benefit from the services fixed-route transit can provide. Partnerships can be developed with the following:

CHAPTER 3 BASIC STEPS

Look for existing connections, and offer something in return.

- Local businesses;
- The chamber of commerce and local branches of national service organizations;
- Educational and training institutions;
- Charitable organizations;
- Employment centers;
- Real estate developments;
- Corporate complexes; and
- Other entities which might exist in the service area.

To develop a partnership with a local private enterprise, it is necessary to offer something in return for the effort. For some businesses and organizations, advertising and the publicity which will accompany the partnership is the reward. Others may be looking for more specialized service considerations for their enterprise. For example, consider offering increased service to a corporate complex, additional stops on a campus, or stops directly in front of downtown stores. The additional costs of such services can be compared to the possible revenue, goodwill, and funding opportunities offered with the partnership.

To effectively involve other organizations, do the following:

- Identify local contacts, such as leaders who live in the service area;
- Identify existing connections, such as corporate or other sponsorship of events; and/or
- Discuss with the organization what they need and determine if the transit system can provide it (e.g., publicity or sales [coupons in newsletters], and/or rides for employees [special routes or stops or reduced fare passes]).

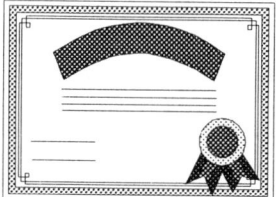

Private Sponsors

Private and quasi-public organizations in the service area may be interested in sponsoring vehicles or routes by providing the funding to operate them. They may also be interested in providing materials, such as printing, for recognition.

3-12

CHAPTER 3 BASIC STEPS

Organizations may also be interested in sponsoring programs with a high level of goodwill associated with them. For example, travel training or transit familiarization training, which is conducted for a great many potential customers, may be a way for a company to generate interest in its services or products. Discuss with private sponsors whether they would be interested in contributing to the costs of printing materials and brochures in order to receive sponsorship recognition. Coupons for the company's services could be offered as part of the training package, along with coupons for transit use.

STEP 3: CONDUCT PUBLIC INVOLVEMENT

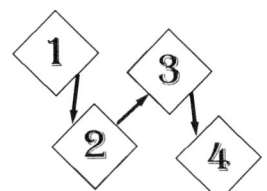

It is important to involve the public early in any new service development, particularly something which may be different from other services already offered. There are numerous methods of public involvement -- some of which are already integrated into the decision-making process. For example, most systems have at least one advisory committee to consult on a variety of issues.

In the development of new service features, conduct at least the following public involvement activities:

To conduct a public involvement program, include at least the following:
- *A task force;*
- *An open workshop; and*
- *An advisory committee.*

- The creation of a task force made up of business and community leaders, riders, and transit staff, which meets until the need and the potential approaches are clearly defined, including funding needs and potential sources;
- At least one open workshop or meeting at which the public is educated on the possible services recommended by the task force and is able to offer input and suggestions; and
- Meetings of all the relevant advisory committees for their input and approval to move forward to implement the service.

TASK FORCE

A task force is a group of people -- representing the interests which would be affected by the program -- who meet over time to discuss approaches and make recommendations. To create a task forced do the following:

3-13

CHAPTER 3 BASIC STEPS

Look to riders, business leaders, community leaders, and representatives of possible destinations.

- Select the interested groups to be invited, who then select their representative;
- Select unaffiliated representatives, as appropriate;
- Set the agenda, the topics for discussion, and the goals of the process;
- Set the overall time frame and schedule and set a completion date for the process, as appropriate;
- Provide technical information and staff to participate in a neutral role at meetings; and
- Provide a neutral facilitator who ensures that all members participate, that the group stays focused on the issues, and that conflicts are addressed and resolved.

The task force should meet serially at its own schedule to discuss the agenda issues and come to a consensus. It may be necessary to provide a meeting room for the group. Provide technical materials and information and a staff person as a technical resource, as well as a meeting facilitator (roles may be shared). At the initial meeting offer a presentation by the transit system staff on the goals and objectives of the program for the task force, including all necessary information for effective decision-making. It is important to be committed to acting on task force recommendations inasmuch as they are feasible and coincide with market and other research findings. The facilitator and transit staff can assist in keeping task force recommendations within budget and other resource limits.

Groups to invite to participate on the task force may include the following:

- Groups representing people with various disabilities, including organizations representing people with vision impairments, people who use wheelchairs, people with hearing impairments, people with developmental and mental disabilities, and other groups;
- Agencies which provide service to older citizens;
- The chamber of commerce and other local business organizations;
- The local tourist bureau or organizations with interests related to particular attractions in the area (historic landmarks; convention center; zoos, parks and recreation areas; etc.);

CHAPTER 3 BASIC STEPS

- Representatives of educational institutions such as trade schools, community colleges, and universities;
- United Way or other charitable organizations; and
- Transportation professionals.

Include a diverse group with a broad range of interests.

It is important to include diverse groups so that the recommendations represent a broad spectrum of interests. It is also important to ensure that the recommendations are not overly influenced by one or two groups. The inclusion of a variety of interests and the work of an effective facilitator can ensure the representation of diverse interests. Learn to provide what the members of the community want. Support for the project from the community can be enhanced by including many local interests early in the decision-making process.

PUBLIC MEETING OR WORKSHOP

Following, or in conjunction with, the work of the task force, schedule at least one open, public meeting or workshop. The purpose of the workshop is to present information on the program and current thinking on its implementation and to receive input from participants. The workshop could be a structured, seminar type of meeting, or it could be a less formal, open house type of gathering.

Advertising the Workshop

Task force members can advertise the workshop.

Be certain that the workshop is well attended by people with diverse interests and stakes in the program. Chapter 8 includes information on effective advertising and marketing techniques for these and other types of activities.

Those who participate on the task force can also suggest ways of reaching the membership of the organizations they represent. Task force members can also take an active role in advertising, distributing information, and encouraging others to attend. Transportation to the meeting may need to be arranged.

Generate community interest in the workshop.

It is important to draw a wide variety of interested parties to the workshop. Some consideration should be given to making the event as attractive as possible. It may need to be held in the

CHAPTER 3 BASIC STEPS

evening to accommodate people's work schedules. It should be advertised as an opportunity to offer opinions on a program that is important to the community, emphasizing that the transit system is interested in people's opinions. Consider creative advertising and other ways to attract different types of participants.

Workshop Format

Provide information, encourage participation, and make staff available to answer questions.

Although the workshop can be structured or informal, include the following basic components:

- Information on the program, the significant issues, and the possible approaches should be distributed to participants. Summary handouts can be supplemented by staff presentations. Graphics, charts, photographs, and other visual aids can be displayed at the workshop.
- All participants should be encouraged to offer their opinions, which should be thoughtfully received. An effective workshop leader or facilitator can ensure that the discussion remains on the topic.
- Transit system and other staff should be available for questions and additional clarification of issues.

Types of Workshops

Ranging from more structured to less, the three basic types of workshops are as follows:

- Seminar;
- Open meeting; and
- Open house.

Seminar Approach

A seminar approach would be structured around staff presentations designed to educate the participants on the program and issues. Informational handouts and visual aids can be very important to clarify complex issues. Questions would be encouraged. Following each educational presentation, a facilitator would lead a discussion of the issues and participants would offer opinions. The purpose of such an approach can be as much to educate participants as to collect input. A seminar approach may last all day, so a structured agenda, with scheduled topics, is important. This type of

CHAPTER 3 BASIC STEPS

workshop may be most appropriate when the issues are complex and there are a great many areas which need discussion. The role of the facilitator is very important in order to address all the complex issues, ensure participation in the discussion, and initiate discussion of a new topic when the current topic is exhausted.

Open Meeting

An open meeting would start with a staff presentation. The discussion is less formal and participants are encouraged to offer opinions and input on the information presented to them and distributed in handouts. Consensus may not necessarily be reached, but a diversity of opinions will be offered. The open meeting is more appropriate when the issues are more straightforward and less education of participants is required from a facilitator or staff member.

Open House

An open house can be designed with various stations (tables staffed with knowledgeable professionals and a variety of print material) on specific, related topics at which staff members distribute information, answer questions, and discuss participants' views. For example, there may be a station with information on the types of vehicle features being considered, with photographs of the vehicles and handouts with vehicle specifications. Another station may show the various routes under consideration for improvement, with blow-up maps on display and handouts with statistics and expected ridership. Another station may include cost and revenue projections and comparisons with other cities. The open house may last a day, with participants arriving throughout the day and remaining until they have collected the information they want. This approach is less effective in formally soliciting opinions, but serves to educate the public on the issues and the service, and their support or opposition can be perceived. It is also a method that appeals to people who are averse to speaking in front of large groups.

ADVISORY COMMITTEE

Most transit systems have one or more advisory committees. The committees are created for specific purposes, such as dealing with accessibility, paratransit, or eligibility issues. They can also be formed to represent specific groups, such as consumers or combinations of consumers, agencies, and

CHAPTER 3 BASIC STEPS

providers.

An advisory committee has the following characteristics :

- Is formed from interest groups within the service area;
- Meets regularly;
- Keeps a record of comments and points of view;
- Seeks consensus on issues, but does not require it; and
- Plays an important role in decision making.

Bring the results of the task force and the workshop to the advisory committee or committees for their recommendations and concurrence. At various important decision points, it is necessary to share the results with the advisory committees at their regular meetings, or at special sessions. It is necessary to keep the advisory committees informed and to gain their support at the necessary junctures. Unrealistic expectations among advisory committee members can be avoided by clearly defining the role of the advisory committee at the outset.

Additional information on involving the public in all aspects of transit can be found in the *ADA Public Participation Handbook.*[1]

STEP 4: CONDUCT MARKET RESEARCH

Different research techniques for different purposes:
- *Telephone survey;*
- *Mail-in survey;*
- *Focus groups.*

Market research is a way to accurately define the market for the particular improvements to the fixed-route system. Market research helps to define the size of the group that will be attracted to the fixed-route and what specific activities will be most effective in attracting them. By defining the size of the group, the transit system can predict what kind of revenue increases may be generated as part of the resource calculation. The market research may also help the transit system identify, on the local level, what particular aspects of a program are going to be most effective. For example, people with disabilities do not like to have to transfer vehicles, but the market research may show that they do not mind transferring at the central transit center because it is well lit and always busy

---

[1] J.N. Balog, A.N. Schwarz, R. Rimmer, M. Hood. *ADA Public Participation Handbook*, KETRON Division of The Bionetics Corporation; Project Action, Easter Seal Society, Washington, DC; September, 1993.

3-18

CHAPTER 3 BASIC STEPS

and they can use almost any route on it. This may lead to more convenient service configurations that frequently use the transit center.

There are a variety of ways to conduct market research. For a large project involving significant investment, it would be necessary to hire a professional firm to conduct the research. For smaller projects, focus groups can be conducted at a relatively low cost. A professional firm may be hired to design a survey and analyze the results, and the surveys themselves could be conducted by in-house staff to conserve costs. However, market research practices do require experienced personnel, if indicative results are desired. The three applicable types of market research are as follows:

- Telephone survey;
- Mail-in survey; and
- Focus groups.

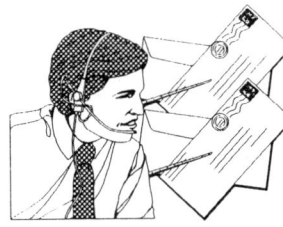

TELEPHONE AND MAIL-IN SURVEYS

For both telephone and mail-in surveys, the purpose is to ask a randomly selected group of respondents to compare service alternatives and indicate which ones they would prefer and which ones they would actually use.

Telephone and mail-in surveys are designed to be asked of a sample of people who represent the varied interests of the community. Two main factors affect the accuracy of the survey results: sample reliability and questionnaire information.

SURVEY SAMPLE

The sample of the population needs to reflect the actual population.

Survey sample reliability depends on working with respondents who accurately represent the target market. If the service is designed to attract people with disabilities, then the survey must be asked of people with disabilities. If the service is designed to attract people who do not normally ride transit, then the survey must be asked of people who do not use transit. In addition, if, for example, 50% of the community does not use transit, then 50% of the respondents should also not be transit riders.

CHAPTER 3 BASIC STEPS

This is not easy to do. It is difficult to know precisely who the target market is and how the market is distributed. Some of the important market segments to consider for new service features may be as follows:

- People with disabilities who work and shop in the target service area;
- Paratransit patrons;
- Older citizens who work and shop in the target service area;
- People who live in outlying areas who work in the target area;
- Tourists and business travelers;
- People who work at restaurants, tourist attractions, and business attractions;
- People who normally drive for various purposes; and
- People who take transit to and from a central location or the target service area.

Random sampling means all people have the same chance of being asked.

There are different ways to select a sample. A random group can be selected from a prepared list, such as those who are registered for paratransit service. If the target market is a broader segment of the community, the sample can be selected using random numbers associated with the telephone directory in order to randomly select a sample of all members of the community. The purpose of random selection is so that each member of the community has an equal chance of being selected. No particular type or group of individuals is more likely to be selected than others and the opinions of the group will not be more heavily represented than others.

Some informational questions on where the respondents live and work and what activities they pursue can be used to ensure that the sample of people asked is appropriately stratified by the size of the important target groups.

Mail-in surveys can be mailed or manually distributed to target population groups.

A mail-in survey can be mailed to a randomly selected mailing list or distributed at key locations. The survey is then completed and mailed back to the transit system. The distribution sites of the survey can target the particular markets. Locations at which to distribute surveys can include the following:

3-20

CHAPTER 3 BASIC STEPS

- The proposed service area at rush hours and during lunch hours;
- Vehicles traveling to and from target service areas;
- Common paratransit origins and destinations;
- Paratransit vehicles;
- Parking garages and lots;
- Transit stops serviced by routes coming into and out of downtown locations;
- Local businesses and restaurants expecting to benefit from the new service;
- Other attractions likely to be served by the new service; and
- Fairs and other gatherings.

Other creative locations can be identified on the basis of local community characteristics.

A mail-in survey can generally produce a return rate of approximately 20 to 25%.

Another method to consider, rather than a mail-in format, is having interviewers at appropriate locations who ask individuals the questions and write down the responses. This can ensure a higher return rate on the surveys, but can require a great deal of staff and cost.

The difficulty with the mail-in, as well as the in-person, survey technique, is that the sample of people who complete the surveys may not be representative of the market population. In mail-in surveys, the rate of return of the completed surveys can be very low and the sample returned may not be randomly distributed. In-person surveys have a higher return rate, but it might not be possible to greatly control the representativeness of who will respond to the questionnaire. Determine the available resources and decide what is the best approach.

CHAPTER 3 BASIC STEPS

Categorical questions identify the sample group and measure sample reliability.

In any survey, some categorical questions need to be included. These are generally placed at the end of the questionnaire and need to be as respectful of privacy as possible. If too intrusive, respondents may not answer them and the information is lost. It is important to put them at the end so that the rest of the survey, the opinion questions which are the purpose of the survey, are completed first.

Figure 3-3 shows some sample categorical questions. They are related to the market segments identified above, but it may also be desirable to collect other information.

SURVEY QUESTIONNAIRE

The difficulty of a survey is that it is all too easy to find out that everyone wants the most extensive and most frequent service at the lowest fare. The questionnaire must also be designed to collect opinions on just what level of service will attract enough people to use it and which added service features are not going to attract additional riders, but only increase the costs.

Below are some tips for developing an effective telephone or mail-in questionnaire.

Make it brief.

⇨ The survey questionnaire should be no longer than absolutely necessary. Most people will not want to spend a lot of time responding to the survey. A long survey instrument will reduce the response rate, and the usefulness of the collected data.

Make it simple.

⇨ Survey questions should be simple, straightforward, and clear without explanation. For mail-in surveys, the respondents will not be interacting with an interviewer. For in-person and telephone questionnaires, the interviewers' explanations could bias the respondents' answers. A pre-test can highlight the difficulties respondents may have. If the pre-test suggests respondents will have difficulty with a question and the wording cannot be changed, specific clarification sentences should be prepared and either included in the question or read by the interviewer.

CHAPTER 3 BASIC STEPS

1. Do you ever use public transit?	___ Yes ___ No
2. Do you use public transit to travel to and from downtown?	___ Yes ___ No
3. About how many times in the past year did you use transit to travel to and from downtown?	_____
4. Where do you live, downtown, this outlying community, that outlying community, or the community far away? *[Transit system would substitute appropriate community names]*	___ downtown ___ this ___ that ___ far away
5. Where do you work, downtown, this outlying community, that outlying community, or the community far away? *[Transit system would substitute appropriate community names]*	___ downtown ___ this ___ that ___ far away
6. How do you normally travel to work? *[More than one mode may be selected]*	___ transit ___ paratransit ___ ride with friend or relative ___ drive ___ walk ___ bike ___ other
7. How would you describe your occupation, manager, executive, professional, hourly, blue collar worker, office worker, retired, or parent at home?	___ manager ___ executive ___ professional ___ hourly ___ blue collar ___ office ___ retired ___ parent
8. Do you have a disability or impairment which makes it difficult for you to use transit?	___ Yes ___ No
9. Would you like to tell me what that is? *[If respondent answers yes to number 8]* _____ _____	
10. Are you over 64 years of age?	___ Yes ___ No
11. Do you work at any retailer or restaurant downtown or at the convention center? *[Transit system would add relevant employment locations]*	___ Yes ___ No

Figure 3-3 Sample Categorical Survey Questions

CHAPTER 3 BASIC STEPS

Test it.

⇨ Pretest and refine the sequence of the questions carefully. If one question asks if a person uses the service, then only those answering yes need to answer the follow-up questions about the quality of service they received. Otherwise, questions should be skipped to relevant locations in the survey instrument.

Avoid ambiguity.

⇨ Questions should seek a single response and not be ambiguous. Be sure the wording does not include multiple questions, double negatives, or non-specific terms. For example, "What is your opinion of the paratransit service provided by the transit authority?" could generate anything from a vague, "Fine," to an elaborate description of a particular trip, neither of which is the information needed.

Be objective.

⇨ Be sure the questions are worded objectively and non-emotionally. Questions such as, "You enjoy riding this service, don't you?" will not generate honest answers from respondents.

Describe the purpose.

⇨ Be sure to include adequate introductory and conclusive information. People like to know the reason for the survey and how the information will be used. They like to know that their responses will be confidential. They should also be thanked for their time. Providing an incentive such as a free pass for one round trip will demonstrate commitment to the respondent.

Use different types of questions.

⇨ Make a distinction among the types of questions asked. There are essentially four types of questions: fact; opinion and attitude; information; and self-perception. Each type of question will collect different kinds of information. Fact questions ask for factual information, such as whether the respondent owns a car. Opinion questions ask their feelings about the service or other issues. Information questions ask about things that the respondent will know, such as their destination. Self-perception questions ask respondents to describe their behavior, such as how often they ride the service.

Think ahead to data needs.

⇨ Consider the data the questions will generate. A question stating, "What do you think of the service?" will generate a great diversity of responses, which would be difficult to categorize and analyze. A question offering alternatives,

3-24

CHAPTER 3 BASIC STEPS

such as, "Do you consider the service to be excellent, good, fair, or poor?" will generate more uniform responses. Rating things from 1 to 10 generates uniform responses while offering more options.

Limit open-ended questions.

⇨ Determine how many and what type of "open-ended" questions there will be, such as "Tell me what you think of this service feature." Open-ended questions are difficult to code and analyze and it can be difficult for an interviewer to record the entire response; therefore the number should be limited. They can be useful in moderation -- if they are worded to keep the response relatively specific and relevant.

Think ahead to analysis needs.

⇨ Try to develop the questions in relation to the types of answers they will generate and how that information can be counted and analyzed. If the question requires too complex a response, it will be difficult to analyze. If the question generates the exact same response from nearly every one (for example, "What city do you live in?"), then the question should be changed or eliminated.

Be careful of using transit terms and jargon.

⇨ Be sure that the words used will be understandable by the respondents. It is not necessary to use complicated words and it is not a good idea to use transit jargon or other terms that the general public might not understand. For example, riders do not usually know the definitions of fixed-route, headway, ADA eligibility, etc. To be sure the survey is free of jargon, pretest it on several people who are not transit professionals.

Be careful when asking potentially intrusive questions.

⇨ Be careful when asking intrusive questions. Many surveys ask about items like income, age, and education level, but the respondents must be very sure about the confidentiality of the survey to respond to such questions. For example, collecting travel log information from riders and asking if their travel times and days are consistent could lead them to be concerned about their safety. When interviewing people with disabilities, some disabilities may be observable and the interviewer would not have to ask about the disabilities. Questions about disabilities need to be carefully worded, with due respect for proper etiquette.

Develop consistent wording.

⇨ Develop the exact wording for each question, each introductory and transitional remark, and all the exact explanations that interviewers may need to give. Using the same words with each respondent ensures consistency. Interviewers need to be trained so that they are consistent in the way they ask the questions and that all respondents receive the same information.

FOCUS GROUPS

Focus groups involve a small group of people who meet together once to discuss their opinions of particular service features, changes to services, training program components, vehicle preferences, or other aspects of a service. A number of groups can meet to express their opinions. The groups can be a mixture of types of members of the community, or stratified by significant types. Each focus group should be led by a professional facilitator who is skilled in encouraging people to speak honestly and to share their views.

Usually, a focus group is formed from a larger group of people who are already familiar with the service. Consider using a professional market research firm to locate particular types of participants, or identify people through in-house means. As with the telephone or mail-in surveys, groups of participants should include the following:

- People with disabilities who work and shop in the target service area;
- Paratransit patrons;
- Older citizens who work and shop in the target service area;
- People who live in outlying areas who work in the target area;
- Tourists and business travelers;
- People who work at restaurants, tourist attractions, and business attractions;
- People who normally drive for various purposes; and
- People who take transit to and from a central location in the target service area.

CHAPTER 3 BASIC STEPS

Target groups may be separated or combined.

The transit system may choose to mix groups or, for example, have one focus group exclusively consisting of paratransit patrons and another focus group consisting of only people who work in the target area -- regardless of how they travel. If a particular group is being targeted, the transit system may form focus groups that are even more specialized, such as a group of people with disabilities who work in the target area, a group of people with disabilities who attend a local university, and a group of people with disabilities who are not employed. People who work in the target area may be divided into executive, middle management, and blue collar workers. Again, a professional market research firm can assist.

More than one focus group meeting may be held.

Limit the issues to ensure detailed discussion.

The focus group sessions typically last 2 hours and address a single issue or a set of issues, so that thorough, detailed discussion can take place. The session usually starts with information from the facilitator about the particular issue, presenting the options to be discussed, or the particular service features that are important to the discussion. The facilitator then asks questions about the group's opinions and guides the discussion.

Focus group facilities provided by professional firms are very useful since the activity is always recorded on audio tape and can be video-taped as well. It is important for all the recording equipment to be hidden or unobtrusive so that people will feel free to express themselves. The proceedings are often observed by transit officials via a one-way see-through mirror. The focus group participants should be told that they are being recorded and observed, but if they do not see the camera they tend to be able to relax.

CHAPTER 3 BASIC STEPS

CONCLUSIONS

Once these four important steps have been accomplished, the specific steps for the approach can be implemented. For different types of approaches, there may be variations on these basic steps. For different transit systems and different communities there may also be variations on the basic steps. It is important to carefully identify the need, define resource needs and sources, conduct public involvement, and do some market research first, before making significant investments and dedicating scarce resources. The secret to successful implementation is to do what will address the need. The secret to efficiently using resources is to only implement services which will benefit people and will be used by them.

CHAPTER 4: LOCATING TRANSIT STOPS CLOSE TO PASSENGERS

CHAPTER 4 LOCATING TRANSIT STOPS CLOSE TO PASSENGERS

INTRODUCTION

This chapter describes the steps to move transit stops closer to passengers through the design of a new operating scheme. Approaches include a route deviation service using low-floor accessible vehicles to bring passengers to where they can transfer to other accessible routes and a circulator service using low-floor accessible vehicles with short headways to quickly travel among frequently used locations.

Both approaches use accessible vehicles to travel to convenient locations so that passengers receive service close to their origins and destinations. The provision of accessible vehicles allows people with disabilities to ride and to benefit from the special training the drivers receive. These approaches are not system-wide, but the availability of the additional services contributes to increased ridership on other, more traditionally designed accessible transit routes.

The steps for locating transit stops close to passengers are as follows:

1. Identify the need;
2. Define funding needs and resources;
3. Conduct public involvement;
4. Conduct market research;
5. Identify approach to address need;
6. Determine personnel and other resource needs;
7. Develop implementation plan;
8. Test the routes;
9. Implement service; and
10. Evaluate the results.

CHAPTER 4 LOCATING TRANSIT STOPS CLOSE TO PASSENGERS

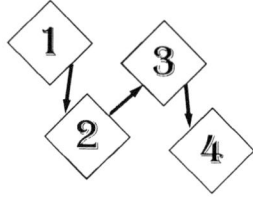

STEP 1: IDENTIFY THE NEED

To locate transit stops close to passengers, learn to identify where the passengers are and where they want to go. Particular areas may be more in need of specialized services for passengers who travel to and from them. Identify those areas with the greatest need.

For a circulator service, identify areas of the service area which have the following characteristics:

- Are relatively compact;
- Contain various attractions, including businesses, entertainment, and tourist sites;
- Attract enough people to make the service popular, whether people currently use transit or not; and
- Include areas which are accessible to people with disabilities, such as places of business and entertainment.

The following locations lend themselves to a circulator service:

- Downtown areas which are served by other routes from outlying areas;
- Historic or tourist areas with multiple attractions which may or may not be within walking distance of each other;
- Shopping and entertainment areas with limited parking or with widespread components; and
- Well-defined communities or subdivisions without regular traditional service whose members may want to travel to local businesses or to stops on main routes.

For a shuttle service, identify areas with the following characteristics:

- Are near the regular routes, but not close enough to be easily accessible to the routes; and
- Include areas where there are people with disabilities and older people who would be interested in using transit.

CHAPTER 4 LOCATING TRANSIT STOPS CLOSE TO PASSENGERS

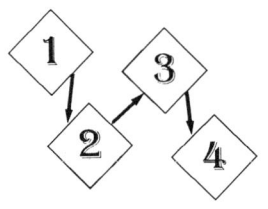

Consider service alternatives and calculate costs.

STEP 2: DEFINE FUNDING NEEDS AND RESOURCES

The funding required for a service that moves stops closer to passengers includes new vehicles and new drivers. The new service may need to be distinguished from other transit in the area, particularly if a goal is to attract people who do not normally use transit. New vehicles (with such features as low floors, lower capacities, and wheelchair securement systems) with distinctive logos and paint schemes can provide identity.

An important feature in attracting people who normally do not use transit can be the operators. Special training for the drivers (including empathy training, assistance training, and training related to the nature of the service) can help attract patrons to a new service. Uniforms which set the drivers apart can be useful, too.

Special marketing can make the service more successful. Marketing and advertising need to target the service area and the customers for the new service.

SERVICE ALTERNATIVES

A circulator service, service routes (that is, routes which make frequent stops throughout a neighborhood and transport people to local destinations and activities), a shuttle service, or other special services can be implemented with different service features. Although each combination provides a certain level of service, each has certain costs. Table 4-1 shows some of the potential features of a special service.

The combinations of service features in Table 4-1 provide different levels of service. The first row may be considered the highest level of service because it is free, runs frequently, and runs all week for extended hours. It covers a wide service area and represents a significant investment and operating costs. The bottom row, a more limited service, has lower operating costs; it may or may not represent less of a capital investment.

CHAPTER 4 LOCATING TRANSIT STOPS CLOSE TO PASSENGERS

Table 4-1. Potential Alternative Service Features

Service Area	Routes	Vehicle Size	Vehicle Type	Service Frequency	Days & Hours	Fares
Wide Area	8	Small Bus/Van	Low-Floor Bus	5 Minutes	7 Days, All Hours	Free
Specific Areas	6	Small Bus/Van	Accessible Van	10 Minutes	5 Days All Hours, Short Weekend Hours	$0.50
Downtown Only	4	30' Bus	Accessible Bus	15 Minutes	5 Days All Hours	$1.00
One Area	2	40' Bus	Accessible Bus	20 Minutes	5 Days Peaks Only	$2.00

COST CALCULATIONS

Routes and Vehicles

To calculate the funding needs, identify the service components and estimate the costs. Tables 4-2 through 4-5 show the results of a method for calculating the annual service costs using a spreadsheet. The cost values are for illustrative purposes only and may not represent actual industry-wide or local costs. Establish the values within local, actual parameters and substitute them into the method tables. Table 4-2 is for a single part of the service area served by two routes. Table 4-3 is for a downtown service area served by four routes. Table 4-4 is for a broader area served by six routes and Table 4-5 is for a wide area served by eight routes. Table 4-6 shows the spreadsheet formulas for arriving at the cost calculations. The number of vehicles per route assumes that the route or loop can be completed in approximately 20 minutes. For a 20-min headway, only one vehicle would be required. To reduce the headways to 5 min, four vehicles would be required for each route. These estimates can be adjusted according to the actual proposed routes and the time required to complete them.

CHAPTER 4 LOCATING TRANSIT STOPS CLOSE TO PASSENGERS

Vehicle Costs

Estimates for each type of vehicle are included. The cost assumes, as shown in Table 4-6, full financing of the vehicle at a 10% rate over 5 years. Costs for three types of vehicles are shown, with formulas for estimated costs. The initial cost for an accessible body-on-chassis small bus is estimated at $60,000. The initial cost for a low-floor bus is estimated at $120,000. The initial cost for a 30-ft bus is estimated at $180,000. These initial costs can vary for individual systems, depending on the included features, the number purchased, and the manufacturer. Research the local environment to estimate the costs to use in the calculations. The annual costs reflect the annual payments to pay the principal and interest on the purchase loan. These costs would be very different if the vehicles were acquired through federal grants and only 20% of the costs would need to be provided.

Driver Costs

The number of drivers per route is based on the estimated number of shifts. This could vary somewhat for different systems, depending on their policies for driver shifts. The driver costs assume a $20.00 rate, including fringe benefits. This is a representative rate, based on the Top Hourly Wage Rate Summary, published by the American Public Transit Association. Services may experience peak ridership at, for example, the morning, lunch, and evening rush hours. Split shifts and differential vehicle allocation may be required. This can increase the number of drivers and the driver costs. Evaluate the local conditions in order to allocate the appropriate number of drivers and driver shifts.

Operations Costs

The annual operations cost includes the driver and vehicle costs. The annual operations cost would include all costs for fuel and fluid, maintenance, insurance, administration, and other needs. This $5.69 per mile reflects the 1993 Section 15 data provided by transit operators. The estimate may vary greatly for different systems. An estimate can be made by calculating total annual costs for the existing system and dividing by the annual service miles. Table 4-6 assumes an average speed of 10 miles an hour, multiplied by the number of service hours a year. This can be calculated for actual average speed by calculating total vehicle miles and dividing by the total service hours.

CHAPTER 4 LOCATING TRANSIT STOPS CLOSE TO PASSENGERS

Table 4-2. Cost Calculations for Service with Two Routes

	A	B	C	D	E	F	G	H	I
1	Number of Routes	Service Frequency (minutes)	Number of Vehicles/ Route	Vehicle Type	Annual Vehicle Cost	Service Hours/ Week	Number of Drivers	Annual Driver Cost	Annual Operations Cost ($5.69/mi)
2	2	5	4	Small Bus	$126,624	126	25	$1,040,000	$2,982,470
3	2	5	4	Low Floor	$253,248	126	25	$1,040,000	$2,982,470
4	2	5	4	30'	$379,872	126	25	$1,040,000	$2,982,470
5	2	10	3	Small Bus	$94,968	106	16	$665,600	$1,881,797
6	2	10	3	Low Floor	$189,936	106	16	$665,600	$1,881,797
7	2	10	3	30'	$284,904	106	16	$665,600	$1,881,797
8	2	15	2	Small Bus	$63,312	90	9	$374,400	$1,065,168
9	2	15	2	Low Floor	$126,624	90	9	$374,400	$1,065,168
10	2	15	2	30'	$189,936	90	9	$374,400	$1,065,168
11	2	20	1	Small Bus	$31,656	70	4	$166,400	$414,232
12	2	20	1	Low Floor	$63,312	70	4	$166,400	$414,232
13	2	20	1	30'	$94,968	70	4	$166,400	$414,232

CHAPTER 4 LOCATING TRANSIT STOPS CLOSE TO PASSENGERS

Table 4-3. Cost Calculations for Service with Four Routes

	A	B	C	D	E	F	G	H	I
1	Number of Routes	Service Frequency (minutes)	Number of Vehicles/ Route	Vehicle Type	Annual Vehicle Cost	Service Hours/ Week	Number of Drivers	Annual Driver Cost	Annual Operations Cost ($5.69/mi)
2	4	5	4	Small Bus	$253,248	126	50	$2,080,000	$5,964,941
3	4	5	4	Low Floor	$506,496	126	50	$2,080,000	$5,964,941
4	4	5	4	30'	$759,744	126	50	$2,080,000	$5,964,941
5	4	10	3	Small Bus	$189,936	106	32	$1,331,200	$3,763,594
6	4	10	3	Low Floor	$379,872	106	32	$1,331,200	$3,763,594
7	4	10	3	30'	$569,808	106	32	$1,331,200	$3,763,594
8	4	15	2	Small Bus	$126,624	90	18	$748,800	$2,130,336
9	4	15	2	Low Floor	$253,248	90	18	$748,800	$2,130,336
10	4	15	2	30'	$379,872	90	18	$748,800	$2,130,336
11	4	20	1	Small Bus	$63,312	70	7	$291,200	$828,464
12	4	20	1	Low Floor	$126,624	70	7	$291,200	$828,464
13	4	20	1	30'	$189,936	70	7	$291,200	$828,464

CHAPTER 4 LOCATING TRANSIT STOPS CLOSE TO PASSENGERS

Table 4-4. Cost Calculations for Service with Six Routes

	A	B	C	D	E	F	G	H	I
1	Number of Routes	Service Frequency (minutes)	Number of Vehicles/ Route	Vehicle Type	Annual Vehicle Cost	Service Hours/ Week	Number of Drivers	Annual Driver Cost	Annual Operations Cost ($5.69/mi)
2	6	5	4	Small Bus	$379,872	126	76	$3,161,600	$8,947,411
3	6	5	4	Low Floor	$759,744	126	76	$3,161,600	$8,947,411
4	6	5	4	30'	$1,139,616	126	76	$3,161,600	$8,947,411
5	6	10	3	Small Bus	$284,904	106	48	$1,996,800	$5,645,390
6	6	10	3	Low Floor	$569,808	106	48	$1,996,800	$5,645,390
7	6	10	3	30'	$854,712	106	48	$1,996,800	$5,645,390
8	6	15	2	Small Bus	$189,936	90	27	$1,123,200	$3,195,504
9	6	15	2	Low Floor	$379,872	90	27	$1,123,200	$3,195,504
10	6	15	2	30'	$569,808	90	27	$1,123,200	$3,195,504
11	6	20	1	Small Bus	$94,968	70	11	$457,600	$1,242,696
12	6	20	1	Low Floor	$189,936	70	11	$457,600	$1,242,696
13	6	20	1	30'	$284,904	70	11	$457,600	$1,242,696

CHAPTER 4 LOCATING TRANSIT STOPS CLOSE TO PASSENGERS

Table 4-5. Cost Calculations for Service with Eight Routes

	A	B	C	D	E	F	G	H	I
1	Number of Routes	Service Frequency (minutes)	Number of Vehicles/ Route	Vehicle Type	Annual Vehicle Cost	Service Hours/ Week	Number of Drivers	Annual Driver Cost	Annual Operations Cost ($5.69/mi)
2	8	5	4	Small Bus	$506,496	126	101	$4,201,600	$11,929,882
3	8	5	4	Low Floor	$1,012,992	126	101	$4,201,600	$11,929,882
4	8	5	4	30'	$1,519,488	126	101	$4,201,600	$11,929,882
5	8	10	3	Small Bus	$379,872	106	64	$2,662,400	$7,527,187
6	8	10	3	Low Floor	$759,744	106	64	$2,662,400	$7,527,187
7	8	10	3	30'	$1,139,616	106	64	$2,662,400	$7,527,187
8	8	15	2	Small Bus	$253,248	90	36	$1,497,600	$4,260,672
9	8	15	2	Low Floor	$506,496	90	36	$1,497,600	$4,260,672
10	8	15	2	30'	$759,744	90	36	$1,497,600	$4,260,672
11	8	20	1	Small Bus	$126,624	70	14	$582,400	$1,656,928
12	8	20	1	Low Floor	$253,248	70	14	$582,400	$1,656,928
13	8	20	1	30'	$379,872	70	14	$582,400	$1,656,928

CHAPTER 4 LOCATING TRANSIT STOPS CLOSE TO PASSENGERS

Table 4-6. Cost Calculation Formulas

	A	B	C	D	E
1	Number of Routes	Service Frequency (minutes)	Number of Vehicles/ Route	Vehicle Type	Annual Vehicle Cost
2	2	5	4	Small Bus	=A2*C2$15828[1]
3	2	5	4	Low Floor	=A3*C3$31656
4	2	5	4	30'	=A4*C4$47484
5	2	10	3	Small Bus	=A5*C5$15828
6	2	10	3	Low Floor	=A6*C6$31656
7	2	10	3	30'	=A7*C7$47484
8	2	15	2	Small Bus	=A8*C8$15828
9	2	15	2	Low Floor	=A9*C9$31656
10	2	15	2	30'	=A10*C10$47484
11	2	20	1	Small Bus	=A11*C11$15828
12	2	20	1	Low Floor	=A12*C12$31656
13	2	20	1	30'	=A13*C13$47484

Table 4-6. Cost Calculation Formulas (Concluded)

	F	G	H	I
1	Service Hours/ Week	Number of Drivers	Annual Driver Cost	Annual Operations Cost ($0.50/mi)
2	126	=ROUND(A2*C2*(F2/40),0)	=A2*G2*2080*20	=A2*C2*126*10*52*5.69
3	126	=ROUND(A3*C3*(F3/40),0)	=A3*G3*2080*20	=A3*C3*126*10*52*5.69
4	126	=ROUND(A4*C4*(F4/40),0)	=A4*G4*2080*20	=A4*C4*126*10*52*5.69
5	106	=ROUND(A5*C5*(F5/40),0)	=A5*G5*2080*20	=A5*C5*106*10*52*5.69
6	106	=ROUND(A6*C6*(F6/40),0)	=A6*G6*2080*20	=A6*C6*106*10*52*5.69
7	106	=ROUND(A7*C7*(F7/40),0)	=A7*G7*2080*20	=A7*C7*106*10*52*5.69
8	90	=ROUND(A8*C8*(F8/40),0)	=A8*G8*2080*20	=A8*C8*90*10*52*5.69
9	90	=ROUND(A9*C9*(F9/40),0)	=A9*G9*2080*20	=A9*C9*90*10*52*5.69
10	90	=ROUND(A10*C10*(F10/40),0)	=A10*G10*2080*20	=A10*C10*90*10*52*5.69
11	70	=ROUND(A11*C11*(F11/40),0)	=A11*G11*2080*20	=A11*C11*70*10*52*5.69
12	70	=ROUND(A12*C12*(F12/40),0)	=A12*G12*2080*20	=A12*C12*70*10*52*5.69
13	70	=ROUND(A13*C13*(F13/40),0)	=A13*G13*2080*20	=A13*C13*70*10*52*5.69

---

[1] These annual payments are calculated based on a 5-year loan at a 10% annual interest rate. These payment amounts can be found in any standard mathematics or finance text or in selected computer programs. For example, the annual cost of a $60K vehicle is $15,828.

CHAPTER 4 LOCATING TRANSIT STOPS CLOSE TO PASSENGERS

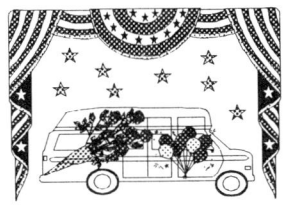

Additional costs -- one-time or ongoing -- may be incurred. Start-up costs may include the following:

- Initial driver training,
- Initial program advertising,
- Start-up promotions,
- Special vehicle painting or decorations, and/or
- Distinctive signs or bus stop markers.

Ongoing costs may include the following:

- Ongoing driver training;
- Driver uniforms;
- Promotional literature, schedules, and brochures;
- Advertising sales; and/or
- Marketing campaigns.

STEP 3: CONDUCT PUBLIC INVOLVEMENT

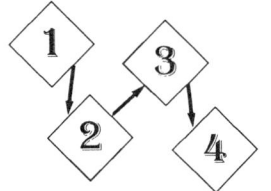

In addition to task forces, public meetings, and advisory committees, meet with target groups -- consumers and community businesses.

In addition to using task forces, public meetings, and advisory committees, consider other public involvement approaches which may attract interest in the service and ideas on cost containment and revenue generation strategies. For services which bring stops closer to passengers, the most important groups to involve during early planning stages are as follows:

- People with disabilities and older residents in specific locations to be targeted by the service, as well as groups which represent them, and
- Businesses and retail establishments in the target areas.

Consider holding separate meetings with each group to obtain preliminary opinions. Then, hold a joint meeting with specific issues on the agenda. The issues should include the following:

- Any areas where there are substantial differences of opinion and
- Funding and revenue issues.

CHAPTER 4 LOCATING TRANSIT STOPS CLOSE TO PASSENGERS

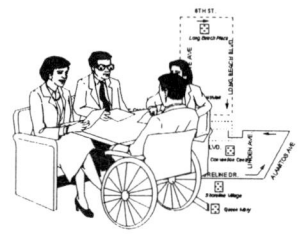

Provide the following kinds of backup information to meeting participants:

- Proposed service routes and configurations;
- Service interests of the two groups and how they can and cannot be met;
- Cost estimates, funding estimates, and potential deficit estimates; and
- Proposals for increased service with increased revenues.

Learn to identify target groups and individuals in the community.

In all public involvement, it is important for participants to be involved in solving problems as well as identifying them. Consumers who want more convenient services need to understand the costs involved and participate in the identification of funding sources. Businesses interested in customers being transported to their locations should participate in revenue generation through sponsorship and partnership programs.

It may be necessary to identify regional organizations to assist. State or regional offices of groups may be able to participate more fully than representatives at the local level. A regional or general headquarters may be more involved than a single branch of a business. Become familiar with the service users in the community.

STEP 4: CONDUCT MARKET RESEARCH

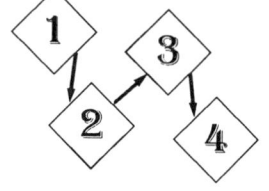

A new service can have a variety of characteristics. Each characteristic must be considered and evaluated through market research and public evaluation. Focus groups, surveys, and conjoint analysis are useful market research methods. Refer to Chapter 3 for additional information on market research.

Use focus groups, surveys, and conjoint analysis to conduct market research.

The vehicles for the new service may be very different from others in the system. There may be special fares. The particular areas served by the service must be carefully chosen. The routes and destinations of the service must also be carefully selected. The scope, duration, and cost of the system must be considered in terms of the available budget.

CHAPTER 4 LOCATING TRANSIT STOPS CLOSE TO PASSENGERS

FOCUS GROUPS

Use of focus groups as a market research tool was discussed in Chapter 3. Detailed discussion of how Long Beach Transit used focus groups is provided in the following paragraphs.

LONG BEACH TRANSIT

When Long Beach Transit began to develop its downtown circulator, they held focus groups to determine the most attractive type of service to offer to people who work in the downtown area. It was believed that people would be more likely to eat lunch in a restaurant or run errands in the downtown area if they could get around quickly and return to work within their lunch hour. The transit system also believed that people who typically take their cars to work would choose transit if they could get around during the work day.

Three focus groups were held on the same day in Long Beach. The first group consisted of executives from businesses in the downtown Long Beach area who worked with employee benefits or services for their companies. The second and third groups were employees of downtown businesses.

The members of each group were asked about their current transit use and their opinions on the following:

- The concept of a circulator;
- Their potential usage patterns;
- Design elements of the vehicles;
- Fares;
- Potential routes;
- A time schedule for the routes; and
- Names for the service.

The focus group participants seemed to endorse the concept of a circulator service. They thought that the design of the vehicle should be attractive and not resemble the regular buses, which were perceived to be dirty and unpleasant. They preferred a vehicle with a light, airy feeling.

CHAPTER 4 LOCATING TRANSIT STOPS CLOSE TO PASSENGERS

The participants wanted routes to areas where parking is difficult, for example, to restaurants, businesses, and travel centers.

Most of the people in the second and third groups indicated they would use such a service. The executives largely perceived it to be for other people.

Other opinions included the following:

Vehicles Other Than Buses
- People were not comfortable riding a bus. Buses were associated with other types of people ("indigents, criminals"), so the vehicle could not be like a bus. Rail did not have an image problem, and certain types of upscale vehicles were acceptable.

Low-floor Vehicles
- Participants particularly liked the low-floor vehicles. To the groups they appeared fast and efficient, not old and chunky.

Able to See Through Windows
- People did not like darkened windows. They were concerned about security and wanted to be sure people could see into the vehicle in case there was a problem inside. They also wanted to be able to see inside the vehicle before they got on board.

Two Doors
- They preferred two doors. In case of a problem on the vehicle, they wanted to be able to get off from more than one exit.

Closed Vehicle
- They did not want an open vehicle. The target riders were people who commute into downtown and go out at lunch time. Workers did not want to have their hair blown or become otherwise disarrayed on their way to and from lunch.

Frequent Service
- Frequent service was important. A 10-min wait was too long, but 5-min was acceptable.

CHAPTER 4 LOCATING TRANSIT STOPS CLOSE TO PASSENGERS

SURVEYS

Some service features are more attractive than others, but not all are affordable. The difficulty of a survey is that it is all too easy to find out that everyone wants the most extensive and most frequent service at the lowest cost. The survey must be designed to collect opinions on just what level of service will attract enough people to use it and which added service features will increase costs without attracting additional riders.

The survey should ask respondents to compare and contrast service features in likely combinations. The survey should also ask respondents to project how likely they are to actually use the service. Respondents may indicate that a certain service configuration would be very attractive and a good idea, but they would never use it because they use personal vehicles throughout the day.

Figure 4-1 illustrates some questions for a survey based on the service configurations shown in Table 4-1.

CHAPTER 4 LOCATING TRANSIT STOPS CLOSE TO PASSENGERS

Please rate the likelihood of your using the described service on a scale of 1 to 10, in which a 1 means you would not use it at all and a 10 means you would use it every day.	
1. On a scale of 1 to 10, how likely are you to use a bus service in the *[name of one part of the service area]* only that runs Monday through Friday 6 am to midnight and weekends 8 am to 4 pm with buses every 10 minutes? How likely are you to ride it if the fare is Free? 50 cents? $1.00? $2.00?	*[Interviewer Circle Response]* 1 2 3 4 5 6 7 8 9 10 1 2 3 4 5 6 7 8 9 10 1 2 3 4 5 6 7 8 9 10 1 2 3 4 5 6 7 8 9 10 1 2 3 4 5 6 7 8 9 10
2. On a scale of 1 to 10, how likely are you to use a bus service in the *[name of one part of the service area]* only that runs Monday through Friday 6 am to 8 pm with buses every 20 minutes? How likely are you to ride it if the fare is Free? 50 cents? $1.00? $2.00?	1 2 3 4 5 6 7 8 9 10 1 2 3 4 5 6 7 8 9 10 1 2 3 4 5 6 7 8 9 10 1 2 3 4 5 6 7 8 9 10 1 2 3 4 5 6 7 8 9 10
3. On a scale of 1 to 10, how likely are you to use a bus service in the *[name of one part of the service area]* only that runs Monday through Friday 6 am to midnight with buses every 15 minutes? How likely are you to ride it if the fare is Free? 50 cents? $1.00? $2.00?	1 2 3 4 5 6 7 8 9 10 1 2 3 4 5 6 7 8 9 10 1 2 3 4 5 6 7 8 9 10 1 2 3 4 5 6 7 8 9 10 1 2 3 4 5 6 7 8 9 10

Figure 4-1. Survey Questions On Service Configurations

CHAPTER 4 LOCATING TRANSIT STOPS CLOSE TO PASSENGERS

CONJOINT ANALYSIS

To obtain a more sophisticated evaluation of potential rider service preferences, transit systems can employ professional firms that use computer programs to conduct conjoint analysis of survey responses. The technique asks respondents to rank service features and rate the importance of the features to them. Then the surveys offer respondents pairs of various service configurations, of which the respondents choose one. On the basis of pair-comparisons, a utility value is assigned to the service feature level (5-minute headways, 10-minute headways, $1.00 fare, etc.) for each respondent. The utility value represents the value of that feature to the respondent. The computer program then adds the various utility values for all respondents to determine the particular combinations which will be used by the most people. The analysis emulates real-life decisions, in that, for all product choices, people select a group of services according to what is available, what they can afford, and what most appeals to them. (For example, patrons may prefer on-demand, door-to-door service and all new vehicles, but not be willing to pay the $15.00 a ride that it would cost; however, they may be willing to forgo some convenience for a reasonable cost.)

STEP 5: IDENTIFY APPROACH TO ADDRESS NEED

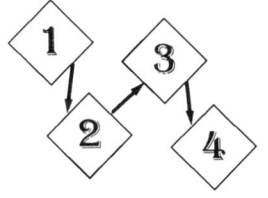

Determine service area routes, vehicles, fares, and service features.

The next step is to select the approach that will be taken, including routes, destinations, vehicles, and other characteristics of the system. Determine the important factors for the new system and decide how to address each factor given the available resources. At a minimum, the following are relevant:

- Service area;
- Specific routes and destinations;
- Vehicle size and type;
- Service features, such as frequency of service, hours and days of service, and peak and off-peak service;
- Fares;
- Any special features, such as additional driver training, special policies or procedures, or a theme or distinctive

4-17

CHAPTER 4 LOCATING TRANSIT STOPS CLOSE TO PASSENGERS

identity for the service; and
- The scope and duration of the program.

These interrelated factors can be combined in different ways depending on available funding and potential revenues. A larger service area but with relatively infrequent service could be implemented for a particular cost, or a smaller service area could be served with more frequent service for a similar cost. If the fare is low, the service may be limited to a few routes and destinations. If the fare is a little higher, more stops may be included.

Look at the possibilities and select the feasible service approaches. Table 4-1 showed some potential alternatives. The best service, a combination of the features at the top of the table, is probably the most expensive service to provide. The features at the bottom of the table offer the least amount of service. Although such a service may be less expensive to provide, it may not attract many patrons.

SERVICE CONFIGURATION COMPARISONS

Tables 4-7 through 4-11 show comparisons of different service configurations. These comparisons can be used in determining whether to implement a circulator service. Each table shows system configurations with similar annual costs, based on the calculations made in Table 4-6.

Table 4-7. Service Configurations with Approximately $400,000 in Annual Costs

Service Area	Routes	Vehicle Size	Vehicle Type	Service Frequency	Days & Hours
One Area	2	Small Bus	Accessible Bus	20 Minutes	5 Days, Peaks Only
One Area	2	Small Bus	Low-Floor Bus	20 Minutes	5 Days, Peaks Only
One Area	2	30' Bus	Accessible Bus	20 Minutes	5 Days, Peaks Only

CHAPTER 4 LOCATING TRANSIT STOPS CLOSE TO PASSENGERS

Table 4-8. Service Configurations with Approximately $800,000 in Annual Costs

Service Area	Routes	Vehicle Size	Vehicle Type	Service Frequency	Days & Hours
One Area	2	Small Bus	Accessible Bus	20 Minutes	5 Days, Peak Only
One Area	2	Low-Floor Bus	Accessible Bus	20 Minutes	5 Days, Peak Only
One Area	2	30' Bus	Accessible Bus	20 Minutes	5 Days, Peak Only

Table 4-9. Service Configurations with Approximately $1,100,000 in Annual Costs

Service Area	Routes	Vehicle Size	Vehicle Type	Service Frequency	Days & Hours
Specific Areas	6	Small Bus	Accessible Bus	20 Minutes	5 Days, Peak Only
One Area	2	Small Bus	Accessible Bus	15 Minutes	5 Days, All Hours

Table 4-10. Service Configurations with Approximately $2,100,000 in Annual Costs

Service Area	Routes	Vehicle Size	Vehicle Type	Service Frequency	Days & Hours
One Area	2	30' Bus	Accessible Bus	5 Minutes	7 Days, All Hours
Downtown Only	4	30' Bus	Accessible Bus	15 Minutes	5 Days, All Hours

CHAPTER 4 LOCATING TRANSIT STOPS CLOSE TO PASSENGERS

Table 4-11. Service Configurations with Approximately $7,500,000 in Annual Costs

Service Area	Routes	Vehicle Size	Vehicle Type	Service Frequency	Days & Hours
Wide Area	8	Small Bus	Accessible Bus	10 Minutes	5 Days, All Hours; Short Weekend Hours
Wide Area	8	Low-Floor Bus	Accessible Bus	10 Minutes	5 Days, All Hours; Short Weekend Hours
Wide Area	8	30' Bus	Accessible Bus	10 Minutes	5 Days, All Hours; Short Weekend Hours

LONG BEACH TRANSIT

Figure 4-2 depicts the route for the downtown circulator in Long Beach, California. This route was selected as a result of the market research program using focus groups described previously. The route runs through the major business corridors, Ocean Boulevard (East-West) and Pine Avenue (North-South), and travels to the major business, transit, and tourist locations downtown. Shoreline Village, the Queen Mary, and Catalina Island are major tourist destinations. The World Trade Center and Convention Center are important business locations, for local business as well as business travelers. Pine Avenue and Ocean Boulevard are the major corridors for local businesses, restaurants, and services. At the Transit Mall patrons can transfer to other transit, including the Los Angeles Metro Blue Line to downtown Los Angeles. The inclusion of all the major downtown destinations makes the circulator a popular mode for a variety of passengers. Three distinct "loops" serve the downtown area.

CHAPTER 4 LOCATING TRANSIT STOPS CLOSE TO PASSENGERS

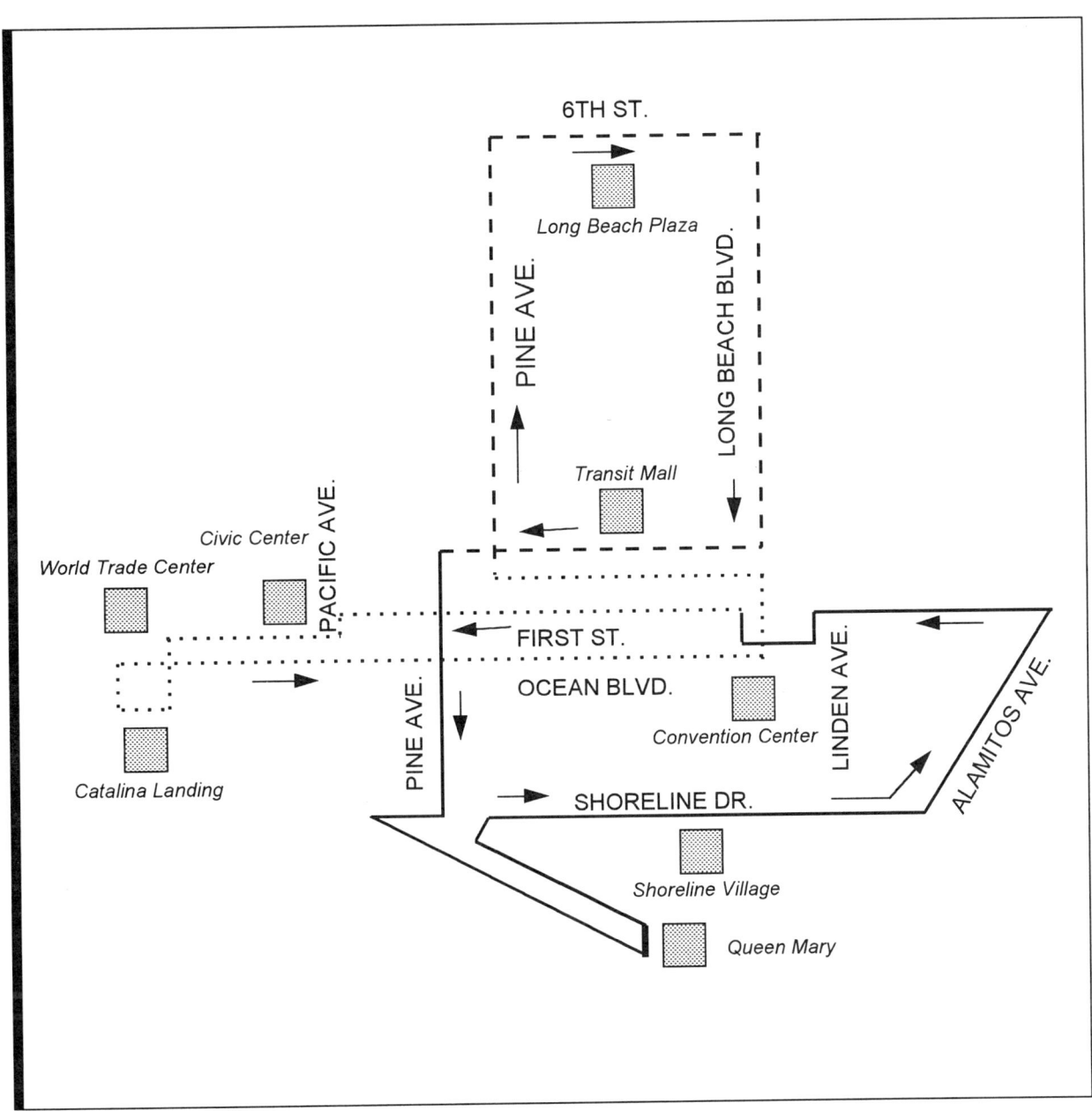

Figure 4-2. Long Beach Downtown Circulator Route

CHAPTER 4 LOCATING TRANSIT STOPS CLOSE TO PASSENGERS

LEHIGH AND NORTHHAMPTON TRANSPORTATION AUTHORITY

Figure 4-3 shows the route deviation configuration for the Lehigh and Northampton Transit Authority's (LANTA, Allentown, Pennsylvania) Evening Starlight service.

The LANTA daytime shuttles were conceived as an efficient method for providing suburb-to-suburb trips and for providing core-city-to-suburb and suburb-to-core-city trips. The daytime shuttles primarily link residential and employment centers. The evening shuttles cover much the same service areas as the daytime shuttles; however, the runs are optimized for shopping services and other evening recreational uses.

As shown in Figure 4-3, there are five evening shuttle routes. Routes 1, 2, and 5 are designed as loops -- vehicles use different roads going out and coming back. The vehicle on Route 3 uses the same roads going out and coming back, so the route is not a loop. Route 4 uses the same roads going out to Easton (South Side) and returning, but makes a loop within South Side. The routes interconnect at three Metro Transit Centers (MTCs). The MTCs are major bus stops which allow for timed transfers between several Metro bus routes.

With the advent of the ADA-complementary paratransit rule, LANTA recognized the evening routes were an opportunity to provide an efficient demand-responsive alternative to conventional fixed-route services. Also, designing the evening shuttle routes as demand-responsive routes meant that a paratransit complement would not be required.

CHAPTER 4 LOCATING TRANSIT STOPS CLOSE TO PASSENGERS

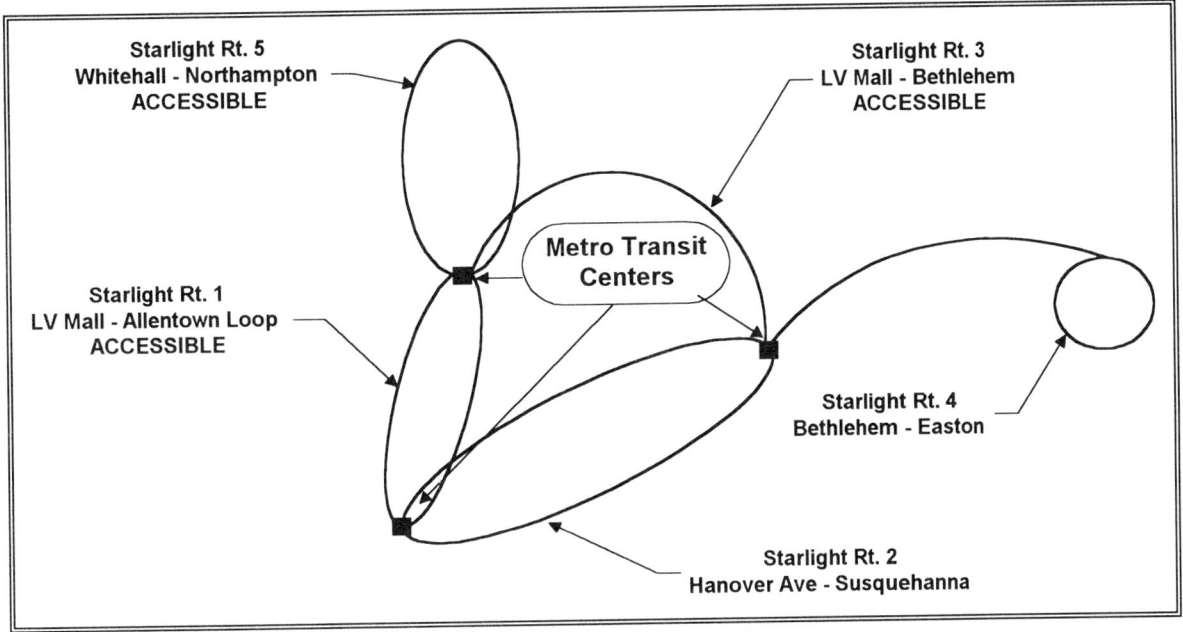

Figure 4-3. LANTA Evening Starlight Routes

Final review by interested groups, staff, and board members.

It may be useful for the transit system to collect opinions on the recommended service configurations from staff members other than those closely involved with the service planning. Internal meetings can be held to discuss the feasible approaches and some of the implementation issues. It might also be useful to present the final list of approaches to the advisory committee, subcommittee, or task force, and solicit their input. They may have additional ideas or suggestions, and it is important to ensure that the process and decisions are still in line with their earlier input.

CHAPTER 4 LOCATING TRANSIT STOPS CLOSE TO PASSENGERS

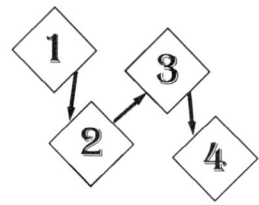

STEP 6: DETERMINE PERSONNEL AND MAINTENANCE NEEDS

PERSONNEL

After a service approach has been selected, determine the level of staffing necessary for the program. Addition of drivers, creation of separate dispatch functions, hiring of driver supervisors, determining whether separate management is required, and other office and maintenance staffing should be evaluated.

Questions to be answered are as follows:

- **How many new drivers are needed and should they come from the current roster or be hired separately?**

Drivers

The number of drivers needed depends on the number of routes and the number of shifts. Hiring of the drivers depends on specific characteristics of the transit system. For many systems, union rules will describe the applicable hiring practices. In other systems, the definition of the service itself will define what type of hiring may be done. Systems without unions will have to examine the number of extra board drivers available, the level of staffing on other routes, and overall driver staff levels, and existing driver skill levels to determine the sources of drivers.

- **Will the service be large enough or different enough to require separate dispatch functions?**

Dispatch

Most new services can probably use existing dispatchers; others may require a separate dispatcher. If the system concentrates on services for older riders and people with disabilities, then separate dispatching may be necessary to ensure that problems, such as inoperable lifts, insufficient vacant wheelchair securement positions, or medical emergencies, can be handled efficiently by properly trained dispatchers.

CHAPTER 4 LOCATING TRANSIT STOPS CLOSE TO PASSENGERS

Supervisors

- **Will enough drivers and staff be involved to require separate supervisory or management staff?**

This largely depends on the size of the system, the size of the new service, and the level of new staffing in comparison to current personnel.

- **Will additional office staff or maintenance personnel be required?**

Office

For many systems, office functions and vehicle maintenance for the new service can be handled within existing resources. Office functions should be minimal. However, if new types of vehicles are procured for the service, additional maintenance considerations may include hiring mechanics trained in maintaining the new vehicles or additional training for mechanics.

OTHER RESOURCE NEEDS

Maintenance

Different types of vehicles may require different parts, types of tools, equipment (for example, lifts), and maintenance personnel skills. Different requirements for skills may lead to different mechanic grades and training and salary requirements. For systems which contract out maintenance work, these issues need to be explored with the contractor. The vehicle manufacturer may be able to provide preventive maintenance schedules and training requirements.

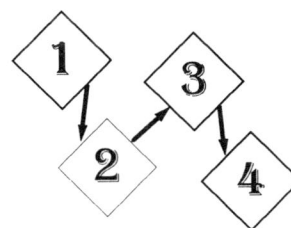

STEP 7: DEVELOP IMPLEMENTATION PLAN

In order to smoothly implement the service, develop a fully detailed implementation plan. Figure 4-4 shows the possible components of an implementation plan. Not all components will apply to all services, and some services may have additional components. Transit systems should identify all components of implementation to ensure that implementation occurs in the appropriate sequence and that potential problems are identified and solved as soon as possible.

CHAPTER 4 LOCATING TRANSIT STOPS CLOSE TO PASSENGERS

Figure 4-5 shows a possible Gantt chart for the implementation plan. Some components are start-up activities and some are ongoing, but require early decisions. None of the activities can be accomplished instantaneously. Allow adequate time, especially for time-consuming activities such as vehicle procurement.

1. **Vehicle procurement**
   A. Grant application
   B. Grant approval
   C. Vehicle specifications determination
   D. Release of RFP
   E. Receipt of proposals
   F. Evaluation of proposals
   G. Selection of vendor
   H. Negotiations with vendor
   I. Vehicle delivery
   J. Vehicle acceptance
2. **Drivers**
   A. Driver hiring and/or selection
   B. Driver training
3. **Revenue generation plan**
   A. Advertising sales plan
   B. Private partners plan
   C. Other plans
4. **Marketing plan**
   A. Marketing budget decisions
   B. Selection of advertising firm or development of advertising in house
   C. If selecting a firm, release of an RFP
   D. If selecting a firm, receipt and evaluation of proposals and selection of a firm
   E. If using an outside firm, working with the firm to develop a marketing campaign
5. **Personnel assignments**
   A. Overall program responsibility
   B. Oversight and management positions
   C. Reporting hierarchy
   D. Troubleshooting responsibilities
   E. Emergency responsibilities
   F. Driver/supervisor responsibilities
   G. Vehicle dispatch responsibilities
   H. Vehicle maintenance responsibilities
   I. Service complaint resolution responsibilities
   J. Program evaluation responsibilities
6. **Program evaluation**

Figure 4-4. Possible Components of an Implementation Plan

CHAPTER 4 LOCATING TRANSIT STOPS CLOSE TO PASSENGERS

Implementation Element	Year 1												Year 2									
	1	2	3	4	5	6	7	8	9	10	11	12	1	2	3	4	5	6	7	8	9	10
Procure Vehicles																						
Grant Approval	◁																					
Vehicle Specifications		◁			◁																	
Release of Vehicle RFP						◁																
Receipt of Vehicle Proposals							◁	◁														
Evaluation of Proposals								◁	◁													
Selection of Vendor									◁	◁												
Negotiations with Vendor															◁							
Vehicle Delivery																◁						
Vehicle Acceptance															◁	◁	◁					
Hire and Train Drivers																						
Driver Hiring/Selection															◁	◁						
Driver Training																◁	◁					
Generate Revenue																						↑
Advertising Sales										◁		◁										↑
Partnership Development										◁	◁											↑
Implement Marketing Plan										◁												↑
Determine Budget																						
Release RFP*												◁										
Select Firm												◁										
Develop and Conduct Marketing																						↑
Assign Personnel																						
Program Responsibilities	◁											◁										
Specific Responsibilities																	◁					
Evaluate Program																			◁			↑

START UP

* If conducting marketing campaign in house, no firm needs to be selected

Figure 4-5. Implementation Gantt Chart

4-21

CHAPTER 4 LOCATING TRANSIT STOPS CLOSE TO PASSENGERS

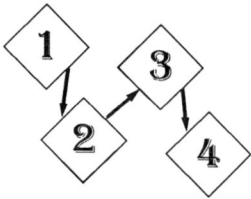

STEP 8: TEST THE ROUTES

Before the new service start-up, test the routes by operating the vehicles along all parts at various times of the day. This testing achieves such goals as the following:

- Enables personnel to determine the estimated time between stops under different traffic conditions,

- Ensures that the vehicles are maneuverable on all the streets and all the corners,

- Assesses the abilities of drivers to maneuver the vehicles,

- Allows the drivers to practice the routes and familiarize themselves with all their features, and

- Ensures that there are no unforeseen obstacles along the routes (such as low-hanging branches or structures) or obstacles close to curbs or stops that the vehicles would hit.

Operate the vehicles over the routes repeatedly, carefully timing the runs and the stop times. Include dwell time at each stop with additional dwell time at some stops to emulate the boarding and securement of wheelchairs on the vehicles.

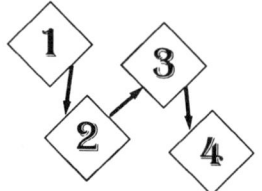

STEP 9: IMPLEMENT SERVICE

Start-up of the new service should be well advertised and include festivities. Effective methods of publicizing the start-up include the following:

Start up the service with celebrations and publicity.

- An opening ceremony with local celebrities and government officials;
- Media coverage before and during the opening service day, including newspaper articles, local television and radio news coverage, and other media involvement;
  Significant, market-focused advertisement leading to the opening day;

4-28

CHAPTER 4 LOCATING TRANSIT STOPS CLOSE TO PASSENGERS

- Special events, such as a transportation fair, to exhibit the new vehicles, meet the drivers, distribute flyers and schedules, and so forth;
- Free fares for the first week of service; and
- Special giveaways or drawings, in conjunction with the new service, to increase public awareness and interest.

With significant publicity and advertisement regarding the opening day, it is especially important that the opening go off smoothly and on time. If problems are anticipated, it is probably better to schedule the start-up for later than to have to delay it once has been publicized.

STEP 10: EVALUATE THE RESULTS

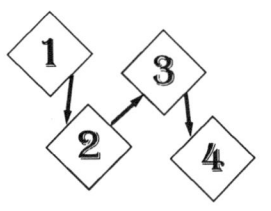

Evaluate service by measuring ridership, customer satisfaction, and revenues.

The transit system should collect baseline data before service changes; then, a month or two after the service is running smoothly, the system should evaluate the success of the service. Important measures of success include the following:

- High and growing levels of ridership,
- High customer satisfaction,
- High levels of ridership by people with disabilities,
- Increased ridership on other services which come into the target service areas,
- Frequent requests for information on the service and distribution of schedules and brochures,
- Increasing fare revenues, and
- Advertiser satisfaction with the visibility and effectiveness of advertisements.

Be prepared to evaluate success by having data collection and analysis procedures in place shortly after implementation of the service. Some methods of data collection are as follows:

- Ridership data can be collected on board the vehicles, either through fare revenues or through manual counting methods. Rather than count all riders all the time, operators can count riders for sample days or weeks, which can be used to calculate estimated ridership. Peak and off-peak ridership can be counted as well. Manual

4-29

CHAPTER 4 LOCATING TRANSIT STOPS CLOSE TO PASSENGERS

Evaluate success by gathering data on ridership levels, customer satisfaction, and requests for information.

counts of riders with disabilities can also be made for sample time periods or on an ongoing basis.

- Customer satisfaction can be measured through on-board surveys conducted periodically by transit system staff. The number and nature of service complaints can also be used to judge the level of satisfaction with the service. Surveys and complaint reviews can indicate where adjustments are necessary to improve service delivery.

- Advertiser satisfaction can be gauged through formal or informal surveys. Increasing advertising revenue and a growing list of clients are also measures of advertiser satisfaction.

- Keeping track of information requests and the number of brochures or schedules requested on an ongoing basis can indicate success and the level of demand.

One of the best ways to evaluate the success of the system is to have transit system staff ride the service, observe the drivers, and talk with the riders.

CHAPTER 5:

TRAINING DRIVERS

CHAPTER 5 TRAINING DRIVERS

This chapter describes implementation of a driver empathy training program and development of an in-house training video.

INTRODUCTION

Fixed-route operators receive a great deal of training before they provide transit service. For many fixed-route systems, assisting people with disabilities is a new component of the service. Training on how to provide appropriate service to people with disabilities helps operators to improve their skills and enhances their awareness of the needs of people with disabilities. Such training (variously known as sensitivity training, rider or passenger assistance training, or empathy training) is designed to enable operators to assist passengers with disabilities, communicate with them, and offer services necessary for people to use public transit.

This chapter describes how to implement an effective driver empathy training program and emphasizes the development of an in-house video for use in training. A video using current drivers and actual passengers will be significantly more effective than one which is less applicable to the system. The video is only one component of a broader driver empathy training program, but can be an important feature. As with all operator training, it must persuade operators to follow training policies -- even when unsupervised. A relevant, effective program is more likely to convince operators to follow the training policies and to always offer courteous and helpful service to people with disabilities.

This chapter discusses the nine steps necessary for the training of drivers:

1. Identify the need;
2. Define funding needs and resources;
3. Conduct a public involvement program;
4. Conduct market research;
5. Determine training contents;
6. Establish a development team;
7. Develop and produce materials;
8. Distribute the video; and
9. Evaluate the results.

CHAPTER 5 TRAINING DRIVERS

Training may be necessary for specific topics.

STEP 1: IDENTIFY THE NEED

The need for driver empathy training is often revealed through public participation and through information received from passengers and employees. Indications of the need for driver empathy training may include the following:

- Increasing complaints related to driver performance;
- Increasing complaints from passengers with disabilities;
- Complaints related to the operation of accessibility equipment on the vehicles;
- Input from advisory committees, task forces, or public meetings on driver training issues;
- Comments on surveys related to driver empathy and communication with people with disabilities;
- Input from the drivers themselves;
- Increasing accessibility of the vehicle fleet; or
- Reevaluation of the current training curriculum.

There may be a need for training on very specific topics. For example, the New York Metropolitan Transit Authority Long Island Bus Division developed a video to train drivers to announce stops. The Cambria County Transit Authority in Johnstown, Pennsylvania, developed a video (with a Project ACTION grant) about disabilities that are "hidden" and which may be difficult for drivers to recognize (for example, epilepsy, deafness, and dementia). Training may be required in other specific areas, such as the following:

- Operation of the lift, including assisting standees;
- Operation of the wheelchair securement system;
- Securement of various types of mobility devices, such as three-wheeled scooters or unconventional wheelchairs;
- New fare issues or policies;
- Other new policies and procedures, such as identifying service animals, allowing personal care attendants onto the system for special fares, or meeting the needs of riders with travel trainers;
- Policies and procedures regarding bus stop announcements;
- Communication issues; and/or
- General courtesy and etiquette for working with people with disabilities.

CHAPTER 5 TRAINING DRIVERS

Meet with drivers, advisory committees, consumer representatives, and employees who serve the public, to discuss the need for driver empathy training or an improved course.

STEP 2: DEFINE FUNDING NEEDS AND RESOURCES

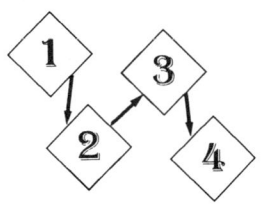

For the most part, empathy training can be added to existing driver training; additional costs, however, related to the development of new materials and the acquisition of materials developed by other systems and organizations, may be necessary.

Funding needs are tied to available in-house expertise and time.

Professional firms may be hired to train trainers in particular topics. Training programs and videos are available from public and private sources.

If there is no full-time trainer on the staff, staff time will need to be devoted to developing a curriculum and acquiring materials.

Look for community resources and in-kind contributions.

For the development of a video, determine the availability of in-house resources for working on the video, including staff members with experience, local editing facilities, and contacts in the community for adding titles and graphics.

When the San Mateo County Transit District in California developed a video for driver training, they hired a production firm through a competitive bidding process for a cost of $35,000. That is a recent price, but may not be indicative of possible costs -- other training films by professional production firms have cost as much as $100,000.

When the Metropolitan Transit Authority Long Island Bus Division in New York developed its video, the work was completed in house. The script was written by the Department of Customer Services and the Safety and Training Department. The editing was accomplished by a local university through an employee contact. The only direct charge was for duplicating the video.

Look for in-kind contributions from organizations and firms in the community, use actual drivers and passengers, and borrow available video and other equipment in order to minimize costs.

CHAPTER 5 TRAINING DRIVERS

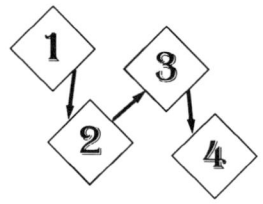

Create a task force that reflects diverse opinions. Include drivers, people with disabilities, and other passengers.

STEP 3: CONDUCT PUBLIC INVOLVEMENT

A task force will be a major component of the development of a driver empathy training program or a video. Include a variety of participants, as well as transit system staff members. Members could include the following:

- Transit passengers with disabilities,
- Interested advisory committee members,
- Driver trainers,
- Driver supervisors,
- Drivers,
- Customer service staff members or supervisors,
- Individuals who have contacted the transit system regarding driver training issues, and
- Representatives of agencies that provide services to older passengers and passengers with disabilities.

Involve drivers in planning and developing the training and video because it will be directed at them. Their participation can ensure that the final product is relevant and that the drivers can enthusiastically use the training in their jobs. Driver trainers and supervisors should assist in integrating the training with other driver training elements and job components.

The San Mateo County Transit District works with a group of people with disabilities in its driver training program. The group conducts training and participates in all training sessions. This group helped identify the need for a new driver training video and worked with the firm hired to produce the video on all aspects of production.

Invite potential task force members to participate in development of training materials. Specify their role and the goals of the process. Activities in which the task force members may participate are as follows:

- Initial conceptualization of the program;
- Identification of available resources;
- Input on training contents, scripts, and other materials;
- Direct participation in development;
- Review of draft materials;

CHAPTER 5 TRAINING DRIVERS

- Final review of developed videos and materials; and
- Direct participation in training activities.

STEP 4: CONDUCT MARKET RESEARCH

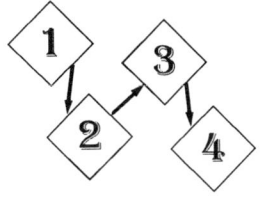

Use a survey to target the appropriate level of training in assistance and understanding of passengers with disabilities.

To accurately target training needs, it is necessary to understand what passengers are seeking from drivers when they need assistance. Drivers cannot provide all the assistance that some passengers may want, but additional help from drivers can encourage people to use the fixed-route system. To target people who ride paratransit and to determine the appropriate level of understanding and assistance, survey people who use paratransit and ask them, specifically, what assistance and understanding operators could provide to make it easier to use the fixed-route system. Figure 5-1 shows some questions that could be included in a survey. The survey may be taken over the telephone to a sample of those who are registered for paratransit. It may also be undertaken on board paratransit and transit vehicles. Chapter 3 provides additional information regarding surveys.

Ask respondents about policies, procedures, and possible new skills that should be included in training. Open-ended questions may lead to responses which are too general for analysis or to the expectations of policies that the transit system cannot implement. However, one open-ended question at the end of the survey (such as, "Do you have any other comments?") may produce valuable information. Determine possible topics by working with the task force, attendees at public meetings, and advisory committees. If there is some controversy over the contents of the survey, consider using focus groups to arrive at possible training components. Focus groups are discussed in Chapter 3.

CHAPTER 5 TRAINING DRIVERS

1. Have you ever ridden *[name of fixed-route service]*?	____Yes ____No
2. When was the last time you rode *[name of fixed-route service]*?	_____
3. Why don't you ride it now? _____ _____	
4. Do you need to board a van or bus using the wheelchair lift?	____Yes ____No
5. (If Yes to Question 4) If the driver helped you board on the wheelchair lift, would you be able to use *[name of fixed-route service]*?	____Yes ____No
6. (If Yes to Question 5) On a scale of 1 to 10, where 1 is not at all likely and 10 is very likely, how likely do you think you would be to ride *[name of fixed-route service]*?	1 2 3 4 5 6 7 8 9 10
If the drivers announced all the major stops on the route, would you be able to use *[name of fixed-route service]*?	____Yes ____No
On a scale of 1 to 10, where 1 is not at all likely and 10 is very likely, how likely do you think you would be to ride *[name of fixed-route service]* if the drivers announced all the major stops on the route?	1 2 3 4 5 6 7 8 9 10
If drivers were able to communicate with you on the bus, would you be able to use *[name of fixed-route service]*?	____Yes ____No
On a scale of 1 to 10, where 1 is not at all likely and 10 is very likely, how likely do you think you would be to ride *[name of fixed-route service]* if drivers were able to communicate with you on the bus?	1 2 3 4 5 6 7 8 9 10
Do you have any comments or anything you would like to tell us about our service? _____ _____ _____ Thank you!	

Figure 5-1. Sample Survey Questions on Driver Assistance

CHAPTER 5 TRAINING DRIVERS

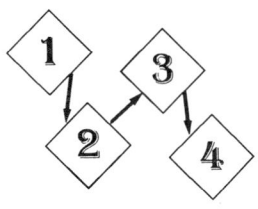

Use a variety of media to convey key training elements.

STEP 5: DETERMINE TRAINING CONTENTS

Training conducted by only using videos will not be as effective as training which incorporates other approaches and techniques. The most effective training uses different media to convey the same information, such as lecture, discussion, videos, handout materials, graphic and visual displays, hands-on activities, and written activities. Training programs, including training videos, need to include certain key elements. These elements should reflect the transit system's specific problem areas and issues. Below are descriptions of key elements to include in videos and training programs on specific topics: training on lift operation, training on wheelchair securement, training on stop announcements, and training on specific disabilities. Consider these outlines and decide how a training video can be integrated with other training techniques to most effectively train drivers.

TRAINING ON LIFT OPERATION

A training program on lift operation should include the following elements:

- Description of the components of the lift;
- Description of policies for lift use, including when wheelchair securement positions are full, and for standees;
- Description of policies in the event the lift is inoperable;
- Instructions for proper use of the lift;
- Instructions for proper placement of the mobility device on the lift; and
- Instructions for assisting passengers onto and off the lift, according to policies.

Use slides and lecture to describe lift usage and designate policies. A video program can also show the components of the lift. Use a video program to demonstrate the operation of the lift. Conduct a hands-on practice to allow drivers to practice the techniques and become familiar with the equipment. At a minimum, provide handouts listing reference materials related to the lift and a troubleshooting guide for use on the road.

CHAPTER 5 TRAINING DRIVERS

TRAINING ON WHEELCHAIR SECUREMENT

A training program on wheelchair securement should include the following elements:

- An overview of the types of securement systems in use in the service;
- Information on the advantages and disadvantages of each type of system;
- Information on policies related to securement assistance;
- Step-by-step instructions on using each type of system;
- Instructions for securing unconventional mobility devices;
- Instructions on safely storing the system components on the vehicles;
- Techniques to increase efficiency; and
- Techniques to assist passengers who resist using or are reluctant to use the system.

Consider a lecture format to describe the securement systems, their advantages and disadvantages, and the policies related to securement. The lecture should be accompanied by a slide presentation or handouts. Use a video to show the systems with step-by-step instructions on their use, storage instructions, and efficiency techniques. Create hands-on practice activities with the system and role-play with mock passengers to increase learning.

TRAINING ON STOP ANNOUNCEMENTS

A training program on announcing bus stops should include the following:

- An overview of the reasons for the requirement to announce stops,
- A good demonstration of how to make the announcements,
- Information about the equipment on the vehicles and how to use it (for example, microphones, enunciators, and "talking bus" technology),
- What to do if equipment is not working, and
- Information about the importance of the stop announcements to passengers who need them.

CHAPTER 5 TRAINING DRIVERS

A video can convey this information, if accompanied by a lecture and group discussion activities. In the video, include proper techniques demonstrated by an actual driver. The Long Island Bus Division also included in its video a segment where there is no narration, only the sounds of the bus. The viewers are asked, "Do you know where you are?" Facilitate an interactive discussion of drivers' experiences on the bus when passengers do not know where they are on the route.

TRAINING ON SPECIFIC DISABILITIES

A training program on specific disabilities should include the following:

- Information on how to recognize a disability, especially those that are hidden;
- Information on how to communicate with and assist the passenger; and
- Information on characteristics of the disability which can have an impact on the bus trip, such as safety or health concerns.

Convey this information using a video tape, in conjunction with lectures and group discussion of the topic. Work with local medical, rehabilitation, and independent living facilities to develop accurate contents.

STEP 6: ESTABLISH A DEVELOPMENT TEAM

There are two basic approaches to developing the training components: in-house development or hiring of an outside firm with the appropriate expertise.

IN-HOUSE DEVELOPMENT

To develop a video in house, select a group of people who have the necessary skills and understanding to create the appropriate materials. Participants in the development process must understand the following:

- The needs and abilities of passengers with disabilities;
- The local and federal requirements related to accessibility for people with disabilities, including the Americans with

Select the development team from in house or hire a firm through a competitive process.

CHAPTER 5 TRAINING DRIVERS

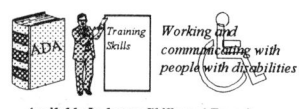

Available In-house Skills and Experience

Disabilities Act;
- The accessibility features of the vehicle fleet;
- Skills necessary for training drivers;
- Skills necessary to develop the training components; and
- Methods to communicate and work with people with disabilities.

In addition, those working on the video will need some understanding of the production skills necessary to complete the project, including the following:

- Writing an appropriate, believable script;
- Interviewing drivers and passengers to record information and audio portions of the video;
- Operating video equipment;
- Staging of video sequences, including use of appropriate backgrounds and elimination of distracting elements;
- Video editing;
- Use of cleared (public domain) music;
- Securement of a signed release for persons appearing in the video; and
- Audio and title dubbing.

Some of these skills may be available locally, through university film departments or other facilities, and friends and relatives of employees may also have such skills, but avoid amateur production. Consider mixing employee capabilities and available outside resources to achieve the desired results within the available budget. For example, someone who has worked in marketing services may be good at writing the script; someone who has a good background in amateur video may do the filming; and the local university may agree to do the editing and dubbing, or, the editing capabilities may be purchased once the video is filmed in house.

OUTSIDE FIRM

An outside firm is selected through an RFP process.

If an outside firm will be selected to produce a video, a Request for Proposals (RFP) process is the most effective method to acquire the services. A competitive bidding process is necessary, but the quality of the services rendered is more significant than acquiring the services at the lowest cost. With an RFP, consideration of the qualifications of the competing firms is possible, so the firm with the most experience and best ideas is selected.

CHAPTER 5 TRAINING DRIVERS

Request for Proposals

The San Mateo County Transit District released an RFP which included the following elements:

- A general description of the video to be developed;
- A list of the services to be provided by the successful proposer;
- A schedule for completion of the video;
- A list of specific elements to include in the proposal, including a demonstration video; and
- The cost of the project.

The RFP also included the various legal, procurement, and insurance requirements.

RFP components, related specifically to the procurement of services to provide a training video, are described in the following paragraphs.

Description of the Video

The RFP included a description of the video to be produced. Figure 5-2 shows a sample description.

List of Services

Carefully describe the services that the successful proposer must provide. This will lessen the likelihood of disputes over the expectations of the contract. For a video production, considerable preparations are necessary before actual shooting begins. The quality of the video depends on the quality of the preparations. The quality of the production relies on the accomplishment of various editing and review steps. Figure 5-3 shows a sample list of services for a video production company.

> The scope of the services shall consist of the creation of a video program that will help bus operators understand and accommodate people with disabilities and people who are elderly on transit system vehicles. The objectives of the video are as follows:
>
> 1. To teach bus operators about the transportation needs of people with disabilities and people who are elderly;
>
> 2. To help bus operators empathize with people with disabilities and people who are elderly by demonstrating their needs;
>
> 3. To educate operators about transportation requirements of the Americans with Disabilities Act; and
>
> 4. To train operators in the specific methods of serving these customers.
>
> The video will primarily be shown during bus operator training. The transit system may also show the video to community groups of people with disabilities and people who are elderly or to groups that serve this population.
>
> The video should be about 20 to 25 minutes long and should be realistic, informative, and interesting. Although the material lends itself to documentary format, the transit system is open to other approaches. The transit system would also encourage the use of music when appropriate, images and graphics, and other special effects.
>
> The Proposer will work in conjunction with transit system staff and at least one representative of people with disabilities, selected by the transit district, in the production of the video.

Figure 5-2. Sample Video Description

CHAPTER 5 TRAINING DRIVERS

The specific services to be provided shall be as follows:

1. Meet with transit system staff and representative(s) of people with disabilities to develop the concept and to understand the important elements of the video.

2. On the basis of input from transit system staff and representatives of people with disabilities, write a script.

3. Deliver the script in accessible formats as required. For this project, all scripts must also be delivered in print form of letters at least 30 points in size:

This is 30 point type.

4. With input from transit system staff, decide on locations and scheduling of staff and equipment.

5. With input from transit system staff, select talent.

6. If necessary, develop storyboards of specific scenes.

7. Incorporate appropriate images, graphics, and special effects in the video.

8. Incorporate appropriate cleared music in the video.

9. Produce a fine-cut edited master on betacam SP, 1 inch, or D2 videotape, incorporating the elements described above.

10. Deliver one (1) Protection Master (betacam SP) and four (4) VHS copies of the video made from the edited master.

11. Deliver one (1) master copy of the video in open-captioned format.

Figure 5-3. Sample List of Services

Schedule for Completion

Include a schedule in the proposal, even though it may be adjusted to accommodate the actual production of the video. It is important to outline the expectations at the outset, so that proposers are aware of the time constraints and can plan to produce the video within the anticipated time frame. With so many preliminary preparations and requirements for input from the transit district and members of the community with disabilities, delays are possible. However, the proposer can promise to maintain the schedule in the proposal and the subsequent contract, which can minimize delays. Figure 5-4 shows a sample schedule from an RFP.

Proposal Elements

As with all RFPs, it is a good idea to outline the required elements of the proposal. In this way, the proposals all include the necessary elements and are relatively uniform in content. This makes them easier to compare and easier to review. Figure 5-5 shows a sample list of proposal elements.

Project Cost

Including the cost allows evaluation for quality and ensures all proposals are within available budget.

For a project of this type, include the overall budget of the project in the RFP. If the available budget is fixed and is already known, including it in the RFP has two distinct advantages.

First, it allows proposers to offer exactly what they can accomplish within the budget. They will not offer something too elaborate and too expensive for the budget. This avoids the situation where all the proposals offer something beyond the available budget and none can be selected.

The second advantage is that, since all the proposals will have similar costs, the evaluation of the proposals can rely on the quality of the proposal and the likely quality of the resulting product. For projects where the quality of the result is very important, something can be lost if the lowest bid must be accepted, even if the quality is not as good. When evaluating proposals, select the firm that appears to offer the most for the expected cost.

CHAPTER 5 TRAINING DRIVERS

> The project shall be completed in the following stages.
>
> 1. Within 21 calendar days after receipt of the Notice to Proceed, Proposer shall submit the first draft of the script for transit system approval.
>
> 2. Within 10 calendar days of receipt of the transit system's comments regarding the first draft of the script, Proposer shall submit a second draft of the script for transit system approval.
>
> 3. Within 6 calendar days of receipt of the transit system's comments regarding the second draft of the script, Proposer shall submit a final draft of the script for transit system approval.
>
> 4. Within 10 calendar days of receipt of the transit system's approval of the final draft of the script, Proposer will meet with staff and representative(s) of people with disabilities and decide on locations and scheduling of staff and equipment.
>
> 5. Within 5 calendar days of decisions regarding locations and scheduling of staff and equipment, Proposer shall submit talent selection for transit system approval.
>
> 6. Within 10 calendar days of the transit system's approval of talent selection, Proposer shall submit any storyboards of specific scenes for transit system approval.
>
> 7. Within 30 calendar days of receipt of the transit system's comments regarding any storyboards, Proposer shall submit the off-line edit for transit system approval.
>
> 8. Within 15 calendar days of receipt of the transit system's approval of the off-line edit, Proposer shall submit the final on-line edit for transit system approval.
>
> 9. Within 5 calendar days of receipt of the transit system's approval of the fine-cut edited master, Proposer shall submit four (4) VHS copies and one (1) Protection Master (betacam SP) of the video to the transit system.
>
> 10. Within 30 days of receipt of the transit system's approval of the fine-cut edited master, Proposer shall submit one (1) Master of the video in open-captioned format.
>
> The transit system shall issue its approval for each stage of the Project described above within a reasonable period of time from submission of the designated product. If the period for the transit system's review, comment, and approval of any one stage exceeds ten (10) calendar days, such time in excess of ten (10) calendar days shall be added to the time of completion.

Figure 5-4. Completion Schedule from RFP

CHAPTER 5 TRAINING DRIVERS

Proposals shall include the following sections.

A. <u>Demonstration Tape</u>

Proposer must submit a recent VHS video that it produced.

B. <u>General Experience and Qualifications</u>

Proposer should include as an appendix to the proposal a brief description of its qualifications for this project. Proposer should demonstrate proven capability and experience in creating a video on similar or related projects.

C. <u>Specific Experience and Qualifications</u>

Proposer should include, as an appendix to the proposal, previous experience on similar or related projects. Project descriptions should include a summary of work performed and the name, address, and telephone number of three (3) present or former clients for which Proposer has performed comparable services. These clients will be contacted as references.

D. <u>Project Understanding</u>

Proposer shall demonstrate its understanding of the proposed project and the various subtasks.

E. <u>Technical Approach/Treatment of Project</u>

Proposer shall describe its technical work plan for performing the Scope of Services. This should include a brief narrative describing the creative approach, a work program outlining proposed tasks, and the number of personnel required. Proposer shall also address its approach to coordination between transit system staff, representative(s) of people with disabilities, and Proposer's staff.

F. <u>Management Plan</u>

Proposer shall describe how it will staff and manage this Project. Project team members are to be identified by name, field of expertise, and specific responsibilities on the Project. The organizational structure for the project team must be detailed in the proposal. Individual resumes must be included for all Project team members.

G. <u>Organization and Background</u>

The Proposal shall include a brief summary of the overall organization and background of the Proposer's firm, including areas of practice and its internal quality control program. The Proposer's background resources and capabilities in relevant areas must be described.

H. <u>Project Cost</u>

The Proposal shall include a total fixed-price quotation for completion of the Project described herein. The sum shall include all labor, materials, taxes, insurance, subcontractor costs, and all other expenses necessary to complete the Project in full accordance with the specified requirement.

The transit system has a budget of $35,000 for production of the empathy training video and four (4) copies.

Figure 5-5 Sample List of Proposal Elements

CHAPTER 5 TRAINING DRIVERS

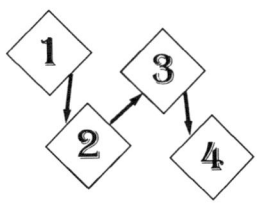

Follow a schedule that includes script approvals, enough time for filming, and reviews and approval of the video.

STEP 7: DEVELOP AND PRODUCE MATERIALS

Although the RFP may include a schedule, this schedule should serve only as a guideline, depending on the most efficient process for completing the project. The production company may have procedures which work best for them, so, in order to complete the project in the most efficient way, work with the production company to develop a schedule that meets the need to review the materials and suits the requirements for the production. Figure 5-6 shows a video production schedule submitted by a production company during the course of the project. Include a penalty for late delivery of final product to avoid extensive delays.

6/24	Second Draft Script Delivered
6/27 - 7/8	Transit System Review/Approval of Second Draft Script
7/11 - 7/14	Script Changes Incorporated
7/25, 26 & 28	Remote Production
8/1 - 8/4	Transcriptions
8/5 - 8/8	Selection of Interview Clips and Insertion into Script, Revision of Narration as Necessary
8/8	Final Draft Script Delivered
8/9 - 8/23	Transit System Approval of Final Draft
8/25	Voice-over Recording
8/26 - 8/29	Off-line Edit
8/30 - 9/13	Transit System Review/Approval of Off-line Edit
9/14 - 9/15	On-line Edit
9/16	Evaluation Dub Delivered

Figure 5-6. Empathy Training Video Production Schedule Submitted by Production Company

Interviews

Review and Approval of Draft Scripts

The development and production process should be as follows:

- Conduct interviews with transit staff, drivers, and passengers;
- Submit first draft of the script for transit system approval;
- Submit second draft of the script for transit system approval;
- Transit system reviews/approves second draft script;
- Script changes incorporated;
- Meet with staff and representative(s) of people with disabilities and decide on locations and scheduling of staff and equipment;

CHAPTER 5 TRAINING DRIVERS

Location, Talent, and Equipment Selection

Remote Production

Final Script From Interview Clips

Final Editing and Approval

Submission of Open-Captioned Version

- Submit talent selection for transit system approval;
- Submit any storyboards of specific scenes for transit system approval;
- Remote production;
- Transcriptions;
- Select interview clips and insert into script, revise narration as necessary;
- Final draft script delivered;
- Transit system approves final draft;
- Voice-over recording;
- Off-line edit;
- Transit system reviews/approves off-line edit;
- On-line edit;
- Evaluation dub delivered;
- Submit four (4) VHS copies and one (1) Protection Master (betacam SP) of the video to the District; and
- Submit one (1) Master copy of the video in open-captioned format.

INTERVIEWS

Interviews provide background information for the contents of the video. Drivers, other transit staff, and passengers should be interviewed. Interviews with drivers can provide information about situations they face and the training they feel they need and tips and techniques to include in the video. Interviews with staff provide information on the policies which need to be included in the video. The interviews can also help personnel to structure the goals and objectives of the training.

Interviews with passengers provide information on riding the transit system and using the accessibility equipment. Understanding the perspective of passengers is crucial to providing appropriate service and to being empathetic to passengers. Passengers can describe the specific parts of their transit trips which are difficult as well as the assistance they have received and the attitudes they have experienced which have made their travel more enjoyable.

CHAPTER 5 TRAINING DRIVERS

Interviews may be conducted in house or by a production company. Tape-record the interviews. The voices of those interviewed can be added to the video narration to enhance the immediacy of their comments. Get releases from anyone whose image or voice may be considered for inclusion in the video. Everyone should be asked to sign a release at the outset. In exchange for the release, each should be paid $1.00.

SCRIPT REVIEW AND APPROVAL

If a task force has been developed, involve the members in all script reviews and approvals. If there are members of the task force who have vision impairments, it may be necessary for the script to be delivered on audio tape or in large print or to make those versions after it has been delivered. It is easier to require the contractor to deliver the scripts in the required formats. Work with the members of the task force and those reviewing any scripts to determine what format is required and include it in the RFP and the contract.

Have a diverse group of people review the scripts from various points of view. For example, drivers need to review it to make sure that the policies and procedures conform to their normal practices and do not conflict with other policies that they routinely follow. Maintenance personnel should review the scripts to ensure that they reflect what the equipment can actually do in the circumstances.

Have people with disabilities review the script to ensure that the information is accurate and appropriate. It is useful if there is someone who is very active among people with disabilities who can also review the script for the proper, non-discriminatory attitudes and language.

Management staff and supervisory personnel should review the scripts to be sure that the policies and procedures described conform to system policies and with the local, state, and federal regulations.

Select a member of the staff to compile reviewer comments and direct the production company in making the appropriate changes. If there are conflicting review comments, the staff person can work out a compromise with the reviewers.

TALENT, LOCATION, AND EQUIPMENT SELECTION

Often, the most effective video will use actual transit system drivers, vehicles, and passengers; however, professional actors can be used. The selection of talent needs to be made jointly by the production company, the transit system, and the members of the task force. Remember, when selecting transit staff to perform in a video, some will consider it a form of recognition and those not selected may be upset. Using transit system staff offers the following advantages:

- The message is more immediate and relevant to the trainees,
- Costs are limited because people are already on the payroll,
- Employees can participate in developing and learning about the video,
- Interest about the final product and an enthusiasm among employees to effectively implement it are generated, and
- The applicability of the subject to the intended audience is increased.

Transit system employees can be used as "extras" (for example, as other passengers on the vehicles, people waiting at stops, and other people in the scenes). This involves more of the employees and makes the production even more localized. In this way, all sorts of employees become aware of the message of the training and feel a part of the message.

The location selection and the use of the vehicles are very important as well. Choose scenic locations. Select sites, such as bus stops, that are well maintained and satisfy the requirements for accessibility. Use vehicles and other equipment that are in good repair. Check for such items as operating headlights, accurate destination signs, and operating lifts, doors, and windows. Check items on the day of filming, to prevent or reduce shooting delays. Look into corners and all areas of the shoot for things that do not fit or are not correct. Even if the script and the actors are impeccable, visual incongruities will distract the viewers and detract from the message of the video.

CHAPTER 5 TRAINING DRIVERS

STORYBOARDS

Storyboards are visual and text presentations of the flow of a particular scene. These can be very important if it is not clear from the script what points are being conveyed in the scene. Storyboards can also be useful if there is some controversy regarding the policies or procedures and how they are presented. Use the storyboards to clarify the message of the video for those participating in reviews of the materials. Not all scenes need to be depicted in storyboards prior to shooting.

REMOTE PRODUCTION

Remote production, the actual filming of the video sequences at locations in the service area, is the most expensive and complicated step of the production. Compress the time of the production schedule as much as possible to reduce the disruption to normal working and the number of people involved, both from the transit authority and from the production company. In order to minimize the time and financial impacts of the remote production, plan carefully and tightly coordinate all resources. Planning and coordination tips follow.

Select locations in advance.

⇨ Select all locations in advance and prepare a schedule with the production company of when shooting will take place at each location. Determine who will be in the scenes at each location and arrange for them to be transported at the appropriate times.

Assign one person to coordinate.

⇨ Consider assigning one person to provide information, and coordination. This can alleviate confusion from conflicting information from different sources. On the filming days, crews will be in various locations of the service area and may need information and assistance.

Check equipment to anticipate production delays.

⇨ Try to anticipate problems which could delay the remote production schedule. Make sure that all equipment that will be used is in good working order. Check the lifts and other operating equipment before shooting to make sure they will work when the time comes. Make sure that all necessary equipment is on board, such as all the

CHAPTER 5 TRAINING DRIVERS

Be clear with the production company about costs of schedule changes.
⇨ components of the securement system. Shooting delays cost time and money.

⇨ Be clear with the production company about who is responsible for the costs incurred if shooting cannot be done on the day scheduled by the production staff. For example, if it rains the day that shooting is scheduled, the production people will need to be paid and the schedule change will affect other shooting schedules of the company. Be clear about who pays the additional cost. If possible, a mix of indoor and outdoor shooting locations can help minimize the impact of unpredictable weather.

Use vehicles in the scene to transport talent.
⇨ It is probably most efficient to have the vehicles which will be used in the filming transport passengers and extras to each scene location.

Maintain communication.
⇨ Maintain communication between the remote production sites and the garage or property in order to update the schedule and have the talent on site at the appropriate times.

Arrange for employee volunteers.
⇨ Arrange for transit employees to volunteer to appear in the video. Be prepared to rearrange schedules so that volunteers can be available for the shooting. Many people may be involved in the shooting for 2 or 3 days or longer.

Consider weekend shooting.
⇨ Determine whether weekend shooting is feasible and desirable. This depends on the availability of employees over the weekend and whether the route schedules are lighter than the weekdays, making vehicles and personnel more available.

Anticipate the impact on regular service.
⇨ Anticipate how shooting will affect regular service through blocked bus stops, the creation of traffic delays, or other problems. Be prepared to block traffic and communicate with vehicles on the routes to alert them of any impacts from the filming.

View daily video footage.
⇨ Consider having staff members view the daily raw footage to be certain that what is filmed is usable in terms of the

visual accuracy and the consistency of what is shown. For example, if something was filmed but not noticed during the day, it might be possible to reshoot the material the following day as an addition to the regular schedule. It is usually too expensive to go back to remote shooting, days or weeks after it is completed. For example, those present might not have noticed a shot of a vehicle with a non-working headlight or with "Out of Service" on the destination sign or a performer having a change in clothes (such as removing a jacket) which can be a problem when the scenes are edited.

Shoot still photographs.

⇨ Shoot still photographs of key scenes and people for later use in brochures and other print media in support of the video.

INTERVIEW CLIPS AND FINAL SCRIPT

An effective method for conveying information is to use the actual voices of passengers and drivers as part of the video. These can be recorded during interviews. From the original draft script, select important points and ask people about them in the interviews. These interviews can be conducted by the production company.

When the filming is done and the tape edited, add the most appropriate clips from interviews to the tape to provide part of the narration. When selecting narrative clips from interviews, whether done by the production company or in house, some important considerations include the following:

- The clarity of the voice and the quality of the sound, so that the words can be clearly understood;
- The appropriateness of the language used, so that discriminatory language is not inadvertently included in the training video;
- The applicability of the content of the clip, so that the words match the accompanying video images; and
- The conformance of the clip with the overall tone of the video, which should be helpful, supportive, hopeful and positive in all aspects.

The final script prepared by the production company should include the actual wording of the selected clips, along with other narration and voice-over.

OPEN-CAPTIONED VERSION

Be sure to make a version that is captioned for people with hearing impairments. This is important for review and for use of the video by people with disabilities. Choose whether to make two versions, one captioned and one without captions, or to just make the captioned version.

REVIEWS OF EDITED VIDEO

When the video is nearly complete, review it carefully. Any inaccuracies, inconsistencies, or quality problems need to be identified. Work with the production company to determine what can be done about them and the impact on the costs. Some things may not be correctable within the budget and may have to be tolerated or eliminated. It is important to identify those changes which are necessary and those which can be easily accomplished. Other changes may need to be negotiated.

Those reviewing the video should be the same as those who reviewed the earlier draft scripts. Be sure to allow adequate time for proper review and a meeting among the reviewers if necessary.

Review the video again after changes are made to ensure that it is satisfactory.

Production companies resist changes to their products unless adequate funding has been allocated from the beginning. It is very expensive to change things once the production is final. Sequential approval of scripts and other materials are considered by production companies to be carved in stone. The transit system will have to make all decisions with due diligence.

CHAPTER 5 TRAINING DRIVERS

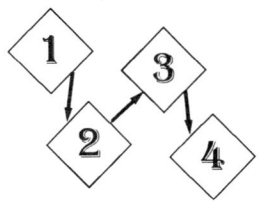

STEP 8: DISTRIBUTE THE VIDEO

There are two aspects of the distribution of the video. The most important is in training to improve the skills of the drivers. The second is advertising its completion in the community and making the community aware of improved driver capabilities.

Distribute the video through driver training, but also let the community know about it. Recognize those who participated.

DRIVER TRAINING CURRICULUM

Typically, after being hired, drivers are trained in a broad range of topics; annually, on a selection of important topics; after incidents; and as part of discipline on specific topics. Empathy training is a significant component of all training schedules. Initial empathy training can be included in a training program in passenger relations and passenger assistance methods. Although an empathy training video is not sufficient in itself for initial or annual empathy training, the video can be an important component of the curriculum, and a locally developed video can emphasize the importance of the topic and encourage drivers to provide exemplary service.

At least a full day of empathy training for initial training and annual training for all drivers, in small groups of 10 to 15 students per instructor, is necessary. The video can be accompanied by lecture, informal discussions, and hands-on activities. Driver empathy training tips follow.

Involve people with disabilities in training.

⇨ Involve people with disabilities in developing empathy training materials and in conducting training. Some members of the community may be experienced in training and can conduct sessions. Others may be more interested in being present to answer questions and present their views on the role of the driver in transporting people with disabilities.

Use training to encourage drivers to use the information they have.

⇨ Use lectures and examples to encourage drivers to provide the necessary service and to make the required efforts to communicate and assist passengers. Many drivers, particularly those receiving annual training, have the information and skills, but do not understand the importance of all the service components — from announcing stops to operating the lift to communicating with people with sensory impairments.

CHAPTER 5 TRAINING DRIVERS

Emphasize the importance of assisting passengers.

⇨ Emphasize, within company policy, the importance of assisting people with disabilities by describing discipline procedures for violations. Review the complaint process, the street supervisor role, and whether "undercover" passengers ride the service to observe drivers. Passenger assistance and empathy need to be just as important as other activities for which drivers can be disciplined.

Use hands-on activities.

⇨ Use hands-on activities to allow drivers to understand for themselves some of the limitations of people's impairments and the importance of the assistance and courtesy a driver can provide. The San Mateo County Transit District devotes most of an afternoon to an exercise in which each driver selects a disability and uses equipment to emulate it. Drivers sit in wheelchairs, wear earplugs, wear blindfolds, etc., to emulate a particular impairment. They then ride on a transit district bus to a local shopping mall, where they go inside to the food court and order and eat. They finish the trip by riding the bus back to the transit property. Similar activities can be undertaken on a smaller scale at the system by having drivers use the equipment, then complete tasks related to riding the bus and locating destinations. This temporary impairment does not begin to simulate for drivers how people with disabilities live, but it allows them to come to their own conclusions regarding how much they can help people when they have the right attitude and provide the appropriate service and assistance.

ADVERTISING IN THE COMMUNITY

After completion of the video, make the community and the transit employees aware of its availability and its inclusion in the driver training curriculum. Public efforts to recognize the achievements of the drivers and other employees makes the video a component of the transit property culture and engenders enthusiasm for the principles it espouses.

Advertising possibilities are as follows:

- If a newsletter is published for transit and/or paratransit riders, describe the video and the training curriculum in the video.

CHAPTER 5 TRAINING DRIVERS

- Work with the local media to cover the new training, including information about the people who appear in the video and how it will be used in training.
- Submit information about the video to the transit trade publications.
- At public meetings and at public board meetings, include the new video and training on the agenda.
- Provide recognition for participants, through awards and certificates. Present the awards at a public meeting or board meeting. Alert the local media so they can cover it. Participation of people with disabilities and with local groups in the video can lead to coverage by television stations as well as newspapers.
- Try to incorporate still photographs taken during the video shoot in brochures, schedules, advertisements, mailings and other print materials. Clips from the video may also be used for television advertising or public service announcements. Be sure to obtain releases from those who participate to allow the use of their images and voices in all applications.

STEP 9: EVALUATE THE RESULTS

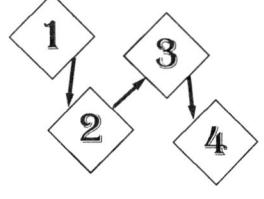

There are two main measures of the success of a driver empathy training program: changes in the drivers' attitudes and changes in the passengers' attitudes. Changes in drivers' attitudes can be measured through surveys of the drivers or can be observed in service. Changes in the passengers' attitudes can be measured through surveys or can be inferred from increased ridership by people with disabilities on the fixed-route services.

DRIVER ATTITUDES

Driver Surveys

Driver attitudes to passengers with disabilities can be measured through surveys taken anonymously. If the information is collected anonymously, drivers may be more honest regarding their attitudes. This can be important in determining if the empathy training is causing unforeseen problems for the drivers. For example, requirements for assistance can be causing drivers undue concern regarding schedule adherence. There may also be difficulties with particular passengers that the drivers can identify. These new issues can be incorporated into additional training.

CHAPTER 5 TRAINING DRIVERS

Meetings With Drivers | Meetings with drivers, either individually or in groups, can also provide a forum for measuring attitudes and service provision. If drivers can identify particular problem areas, these can be addressed in policy adjustments or in additions to the training program. If meetings are held, be sure that drivers understand that they will not be disciplined for what they reveal or discuss. This technique can be used effectively in many applications related to driver activities.

PASSENGER ATTITUDES

Passenger Surveys | Measure passenger attitudes using a survey. Surveys can be distributed in newsletters so that passengers can mail them back. Staff members can ride on vehicles and conduct on-board surveys, or surveys can be taken over the phone, with a randomly selected sample of members of the community. These techniques are discussed in detail in Chapter 3.

Track Survey Responses Over Time | Track the survey responses over time to see if there are changes. Also include questions on the survey form so that respondents can indicate what routes they use. Particular problems can be identified, whether they are related to traffic congestion, overcrowded vehicles, vehicle or stop accessibility, or driver attitudes.

Measure the Ridership of People With Disabilities | Another way to measure passenger attitudes is to count the number of times that people with disabilities board the fixed-route system. As more people become aware of increased driver skills, they will be more likely to use fixed-route. If people are satisfied with the fixed-route service they receive, they are more likely to use it more frequently. Increasing use of the fixed-route by people with disabilities over time is indicative of a successful program.

CHAPTER 6: PROGRAMMING ACCESSIBLE BUS STOP IMPROVEMENTS

CHAPTER 6 PROGRAMMING ACCESSIBLE BUS STOP IMPROVEMENTS

INTRODUCTION

Design and construct new transit facilities to be fully accessible to people with disabilities.

This chapter describes how transit systems can plan and conduct programs to improve bus stop accessibility. The chapter also presents important elements to consider when designing accessible transit facilities.

Design and construct new transit facilities to be readily accessible to and usable by people with disabilities, including people who use wheelchairs. Public transit design standards are found in the *ADA Accessibility Guidelines* (ADAAG), Appendix A to 49 CFR Part 37. These accessibility guidelines cover new construction and renovation. An illustrated handbook to the ADAAG guidelines, which addressed the applications to transit facilities, was developed by the Volpe National Transportation Systems Center and the Federal Transit Administration. The document contains special information on how to best make transit facilities accessible.[1]

Provide accessibility enhancements when facilities are upgraded or when new facilities are constructed.

In addition to new construction of accessible facilities, transit systems may desire to upgrade their bus stops to enhance accessibility. Accessible facilities and bus stops are important features for making a transit system accessible to and usable by people with disabilities.

As with bus stop enhancements, transit facility access may be an integral part of a new construction project, or it may be associated with a program to renovate an existing facility.

Accessibility design in new construction requires innovative thought and design assistance from individuals with disabilities and the organizations with which they are associated. The requirement to design for accessibility must be a goal from the beginning.

---

[1] J.N. Balog, D. Chia, A.N. Schwarz, and R. B. Gribbon, *Accessibility Handbook for Transit Facilities*, KETRON Division of the Bionetics Corporation; Volpe National Transportation Systems Center; Federal Transit Administration, DOT-VNTSC-FTA-92-4 (1992).

CHAPTER 6 PROGRAMMING ACCESSIBLE BUS STOP IMPROVEMENTS

Accessibility enhancements can benefit everyone.

In contrast, accessibility design as part of a rehabilitation project may require an innovative architectural approach in addition to a willingness to overcome institutional barriers. Many rehabilitation initiatives are designed to replace a shabby edifice with a more acceptable one. Often there is a desire to take only minimal corrective action. However, one must recognize that the budget for appropriate accessibility features often equals or exceeds the budget for basic remedial measures.

Instituting steps to maximize accessibility benefits all riders. Everyone benefits from large, easy-to-read signs. Everyone benefits from direct, clearly marked walkways in parking lots. Everyone benefits from clear, audible public address systems. Everyone benefits from ticket counters, telephones, and vending devices that are easy to find and reach.[2]

This chapter describes seven steps for programming accessible bus stop improvements. These steps are as follows:

1. Identify the need;
2. Define funding needs and resources;
3. Conduct public involvement;
4. Conduct market research;
5. Select target stops;
6. Determine improvements; and
7. Evaluate enhancements.

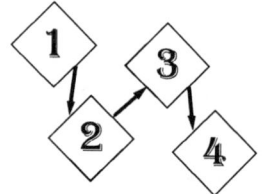

Catalog stops and rate accessibility.

STEP 1: IDENTIFY THE NEED

Bus stop and transit facility improvements which promote accessibility, safety, and usability will assist in attracting individuals with disabilities to the fixed-route system.

Well-established, quantitative methods for documenting the need for new transit facilities, including central terminals, transfer centers, and park-n-ride lots, are regularly used by transit systems. In contrast, there are no established quantitative methods for documenting the need to enhance

---

[2] *Ibid*, p. 2-1

CHAPTER 6 PROGRAMMING ACCESSIBLE BUS STOP IMPROVEMENTS

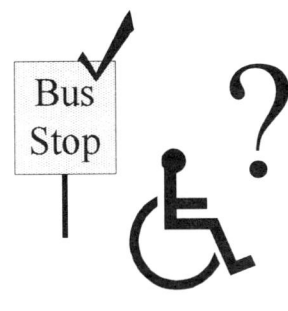

overall bus stop accessibility. This chapter provides a systematic approach to improving the accessibility of bus stops within a transit system. As used in this chapter, "Identifying the need" goes beyond recognizing a generalized need to do something -- it encompasses a transit system's performing the following activities:

- Developing a catalog of all (or some) of the bus stops,
- Rating the current accessibility of each stop in the catalog, and
- Estimating the degree of difficulty in making each stop in the catalog accessible.

Every transit system acknowledges the need to increase the number of accessible bus stops. This chapter discusses ways to quantify the need and plan a systematic, proactive response.

DEVELOP A CATALOG OF BUS STOPS

To develop a catalog of bus stops requiring accessibility improvements, collect information from riders, drivers, and others about bus stops, through public outreach and market research. Then, review planned capital projects for required accessibility improvements.

Passenger and Operator Reports

Transit systems often rely on anecdotal reports from passengers and operators to identify bus stops requiring enhancements to improve accessibility. Passengers may call to request that specific bus stops be made accessible. An advisory committee, if asked to prioritize routes for the introduction of accessible buses, will often identify important bus stops for accessibility enhancements. Operators may radio dispatchers that there are passengers who want or need to use the lift who are waiting at stops where it would be dangerous or difficult to deploy the lift.

6-3

CHAPTER 6 PROGRAMMING ACCESSIBLE BUS STOP IMPROVEMENTS

Such reports are important and indicative. Unfortunately, some transit systems often rely exclusively on these anecdotal reports to identify transit stops for improvement. Tallying sporadic reports from users will not provide a systematic approach to bus stop enhancements. Such reports identify problems, but do not indicate the overall level of need.

Better techniques to systematically identify and upgrade bus stops are needed. Following a plan for bus stop upgrades and accessible facility design will maximize the attractive impact of the accessibility improvements for persons with disabilities and general users.

Planned Capital Projects

The need to upgrade bus stops may arise because of a capital improvement project planned by a transit system, community, or regional planning agency. Typical capital improvements might involve rehabilitation of an existing transit facility, the systematic upgrading of neighborhood sidewalks and roadways, or the replacement of dilapidated signage. ADA accessibility issues are intertwined with all capital improvement projects. If a capital project is in the planning stage, the object is not to determine whether something needs to be done, but what to do and how to best do it.

In summary, the need to improve transit stop or transit facility accessibility may be identified through carefully solicited customer input or as part of a capital improvement project. In either case, there are systematic methods for assessing the need; involving consumers in the planning process; developing, reviewing, and evaluating the improvement plan; and using this feedback to adjust the ongoing schedule for improvements.

CHAPTER 6 PROGRAMMING ACCESSIBLE BUS STOP IMPROVEMENTS

RATE THE CURRENT ACCESSIBILITY OF STOPS

Develop a bus stop database which includes an estimate of current and potential accessibility. If there are many stops in a transit system, developing a bus stop database may seem daunting; however, there are several efficient methods to prepare a database. Some of these methods are described in the following subsections. Select the method best suited to the local environment. Use volunteers or students to reduce personnel costs.

Video Tape Bus Stops

Use video tape to record and evaluate bus stop accessibility.

The City of Tucson Transit Department pioneered an effective video tape method to catalog bus stops from inside a moving bus running its regular route. The process they used can be described as follows:

- Assign a technician (or hire a college student during the summer) to collect the information;
- Have the driver alert the technician as each stop is approached;
- Through the bus window, the technician video tapes the bus stop and approximately 15 feet on either side of the stop, including the curb cut, sidewalk, and/or hard-packed surface if present.
- The technician speaks into the video camera's microphone to identify the bus stop and rate the bus stop's current and potential accessibility.
- Add other brief comments as needed.
- At the office, view the video tape and input the data into a bus stop database. Some elements to include in the database are as follows:

    - Location of the stop;
    - Routes served by the stop;
    - Amenities at the stop, such as a shelter, roof, or benches;

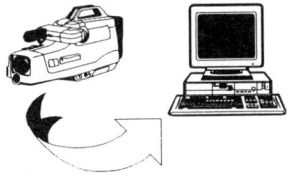

CHAPTER 6 PROGRAMMING ACCESSIBLE BUS STOP IMPROVEMENTS

- Location of the nearest curb cut;
- Availability of an accessible path to the stop (for example, sidewalks or curb cuts leading to the stop or the entrance to the shelter);
- Availability of clear space for a lift pad (96 inches long by 60 inches wide);
- Availability of a location for posting schedules;
- Slope and surface considerations; and
- Other relevant considerations.

- Design this database to accept graphic data. Use a computer with plenty of free disk space and the ability to capture video frames so that a photograph of each bus stop can be retained in the database.
- Retain the videotape as a permanent record.

For estimation purposes, an individual can generally ride two bus routes and enter the bus stop data into the computer each day.

Use Paper and Pencil

The Indianapolis Public Transportation Corporation used a more labor-intensive pencil and paper method to catalog bus stops. The process they used can be described as follows:

Collaborate with the city engineering department.

- Have service planning personnel work jointly with staff from the city engineering department;
- Visit and assess each stop separately; and
- Develop a work plan for each stop.

INTERFACE WITH GLOBAL POSITIONING SYSTEM

Use volunteers deployed in the field to complete a different but related project.

The Regional Transit District of Denver, Colorado, cataloged its bus stops and evaluated their accessibility in conjunction with a program to calibrate its new Global Positioning System (GPS). Within 3 months, 12 graduate students visited each bus stop with a GPS receiver and a form for evaluating bus stop accessibility. The process they used can be described as follows:

CHAPTER 6 PROGRAMMING ACCESSIBLE BUS STOP IMPROVEMENTS

- Transmit the latitude and longitude of each stop back to base.
- While waiting for confirmation from the GPS receiving unit, complete the form to evaluate the stop's current accessibility. At the same time, prepare a description of improvements and enhancements needed to achieve full ADA-compliance.
- Once GPS and accessibility data are collected, add accessibility data to the geocoded database.
- From the geocoded database, prepare bus stop accessibility reports as needed.

DEVELOP AN ESTIMATE OF THE DIFFICULTY OF ACHIEVING ACCESSIBILITY

Appendix A of the ADA regulations includes the requirements of accessible facilities.[3] Part 10 of that appendix has specific requirements for transit facilities. *The Accessibility Handbook for Transit Facilities* fully explains all the guidelines related to transit facilities.[4] The *Handbook* also contains a complete set of ADA-design checklists in its appendixes. Figure 6-1, drawn from one of the appendixes, can be used in determining the accessibility of current bus stops.

---

[3] U.S. Department of Transportation, 49 CFR Part 37, Transportation for Individuals With Disabilities; Final Rule, September 6, 1991.
[4] Balog, et al., *op. cit.*, Appendix

CHAPTER 6 PROGRAMMING ACCESSIBLE BUS STOP IMPROVEMENTS

YES	NO	BUS STOPS AND SHELTERS	Regulation 49 CFR 37: Appendix A, Section
☐	☐	Are all new bus stops and bus shelters designed to accommodate people using wheelchairs and to permit full deployment of lifts?	10.1
☐	☐	Do accessible bus stop pads provide a minimum clear length of 96 inches, measured from the curb or the roadway edge?	10.2.1
☐	☐	Do accessible bus stop pads provide a minimum clear width of 60 inches, measured parallel to the roadway?	10.2.1
☐	☐	Do all bus stop pads have a firm, stable surface with a slope the same as the roadway itself, measured parallel to the road?	10.2.2
☐	☐	Do all bus stop pads have a maximum slope of 1:50 (for water drainage) measured perpendicular to the roadway?	10.2.2
☐	☐	Do all accessible bus shelters allow individuals using wheelchairs to enter from the public way and reach a location within the shelter?	10.2.1
☐	☐	Do all accessible bus stop shelters provide a minimum clear floor space of 30 x 48 inches, completely included within the shelter?	10.2.1
☐	☐	Are all accessible bus stop shelters connected by an accessible path to the bus boarding area?	10.2.1
☐	☐	Are all accessible bus stop shelters connected by an accessible curb cut with the roadway?	4.7 & 4.29
☐	☐	Are all bus route identification signs accessible in terms of character size, finish and contrast?	4.30.3 & 4.30.5

Figure 6-1. Bus Stop Accessibility Checklist

The regulations require a bus pad with a clear footprint of at least 96 inches deep by 60 inches wide, to accommodate the deployment of the wheelchair lift. This pad must be connected to any shelters by an accessible path. The surface of the pad needs to be stable and should be of the same slope as the roadway, to ease boarding and alighting.

A shelter must have a clear floor space of at least 30 inches by 48 inches, completely located within it. These dimensions allow a person in a typical wheelchair to be inside the shelter. Any other items in the shelter, such as benches, shelves or poles, must be positioned to allow for this clear space.

CHAPTER 6 PROGRAMMING ACCESSIBLE BUS STOP IMPROVEMENTS

As used at Tucson, a working definition of an accessible bus stop is one at which an individual using a wheelchair can do the following:

- Travel up the curb cut,
- Continue along a hard-packed surface to the stop, and
- Wait on a hard-packed surface where ghe bus' lift can operate freely.

Even using this broad definition, the Tucson Transit Department determined that only 18% of its bus stops satisfied all three criteria; 52% met at least one criterion; and 30% met none of the criteria[5].

The Indianapolis Public Transportation Corporation (IPTC) involved the city construction division in the resolution of the bus stop accessibility problem, starting with the earliest stages of assessment. IPTC realized that its fixed-route service planners and the city construction engineers would bring different perspectives to the catalog and work write-up. Transit service planners would be more interested in defining the enhancements that would make the stop more usable by bus drivers and patrons. City engineers would be more interested in determining the feasibility and cost of making those improvements.

Involve city engineers early.

The on-site collaboration between transit and city personnel resulted in an individual work write-up and accessibility plan developed in the field for each bus stop. Initially, this was a more laborious process than Tucson's; however, this collaboration resulted in an agreed-upon work plan for each bus stop. IPTC feels that the early involvement of city engineers was critical in gaining support from the city and for ensuring that the bus stop upgrade program was implemented.

---

[5] G.S. Synder, *Tuscon Transit Stop Inventory and Capital Improvement Plan: Final Report* (June, 1994).

CHAPTER 6 PROGRAMMING ACCESSIBLE BUS STOP IMPROVEMENTS

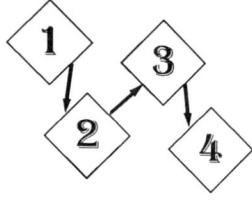

STEP 2: DEFINE FUNDING NEEDS AND RESOURCES

If the need for accessibility is defined through anecdotal reports of passengers and operators, address each problem as it is raised. In this case, there is no compelling need to develop a cost estimate for remedying the complete problem in a systematic manner. By knowing the budget for miscellaneous improvements, it can be consumed on an item-by-item basis.

Another approach is to address the overall problem as thoroughly as the budget and staffing allow. Make a preliminary estimate of costs and staffing required, and survey the available sources of funding and personnel. Develop a concept for the scope of work and the resources that will be required.

In preparation, determine the origin and scope of the problem, as well as the type of response necessary. Determine how much and what level of consumer involvement is needed for problem identification and resolution. Make a preliminary determination of whether the solution necessitates a formal bidding and contracting process, or whether less formal, more flexible remedies are feasible.

Figure 6-2 illustrates the types of issues to be resolved with the consumer advisory body at this stage of the planning. These issues determine the preliminary scope of work and initial budget. (The scope of work and budget can be reassessed later in light of new or changed information; however, the initial approach to the problem should be defined at this point.)

Determine what research and development are needed to arrive at the optimal solution -- localized problems may be addressed with limited research; systemic problems may require implementation of a formal research and development effort.

CHAPTER 6 PROGRAMMING ACCESSIBLE BUS STOP IMPROVEMENTS

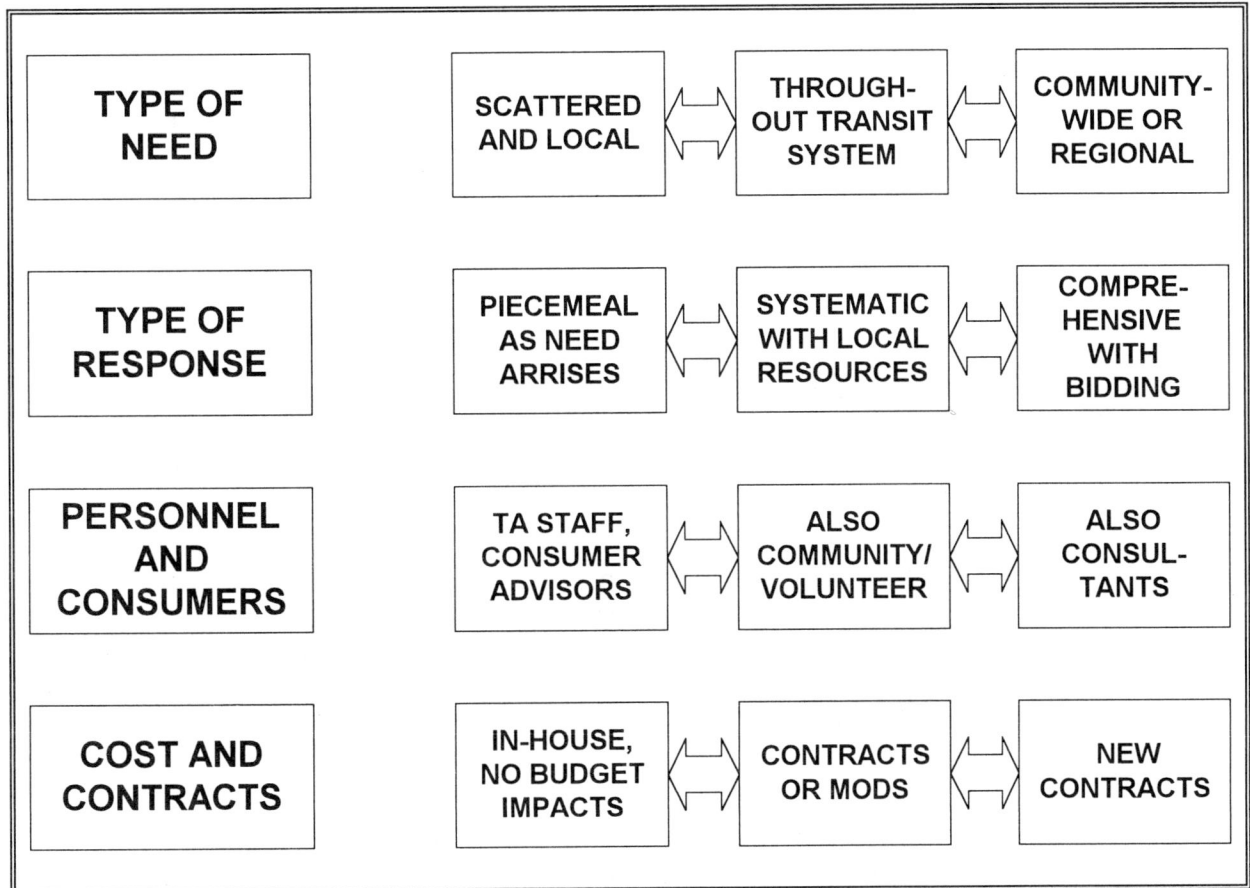

Figure 6-2. Planning and Budget Issues

Deciding to systematically improve the accessibility of bus stops requires development of a cost estimate for that work. Developing quick cost estimates of accessibility enhancements is the second step after creation of the bus stop database.

Three estimate methods:
- *Unique cost*
- *Typical costs, and*
- *Bids.*

The three methods for developing these estimates are as follows:

- Estimate the unique cost for each bus stop on the basis of individual work plans for each stop;
- Assign typical costs to accessibility factors in the bus stop database and aggregate those costs to achieve a statistical estimate of the total cost of improvements; or
- Put the project (or parts of the project) out for bid and use the responses to estimate the cost of all portions of the work.

6-11

CHAPTER 6 PROGRAMMING ACCESSIBLE BUS STOP IMPROVEMENTS

ESTIMATE UNIQUE COSTS

Indianapolis approached the cost estimation problem pragmatically. Each stop had been evaluated by the transit system service planner and by the city engineer. A stop-by-stop work plan had been developed. The team was readily able to develop a list of stops where it was feasible to achieve accessibility.

ASSIGN TYPICAL COSTS

Tucson approached the cost estimation problem systematically. It developed an extensive multi-dimensional database of its bus stops. The current accessibility of the site was evaluated using a multi-dimensional model. Typical costs were estimated for each of a variety of possible accessibility improvements and site enhancements. The range of costs and treatments were recorded in the database. An estimate of the total cost of improvements was developed for the whole bid, a roster of 100 bus stops.

Biggest problems: Bus stop pad size and Slope.

Each stop had a unique situation. Some solutions required much planning. Some stops could not be made accessible -- usually because there was not enough right of way to provide an adequate landing pad with the lift down or enough room to provide a safe egress for individuals with disabilities. The regulations require that the pad be at least 60 inches wide by 96 inches deep. The regulations also require that the pad slope be no more than 1:50. Unless the solution or improvement was fairly simple (e.g., installation of a sign or shelter or placing a known quantity of concrete), there were no cookbook cost estimates.

Indianapolis' intention was to do as much as it could quickly within a limited budget. Dollars could be maximized and time minimized by having the work done through change orders to existing street contracts. Therefore, IPTC personnel actually correlated three factors in determining which stops to improve: 1) feasibility of the improvements; 2) potential for attracting paratransit patrons; and 3) whether there were city street repair contracts ongoing in the area.

CHAPTER 6 PROGRAMMING ACCESSIBLE BUS STOP IMPROVEMENTS

When these factors came together, IPTC generally negotiated with the city project engineer who asked the contractor for an estimate. The work was approved and completed through a minor change order. Even though they were feeling their way through the project, IPTC staff felt this approach resulted in piecemeal small projects being accomplished cost-effectively and efficiently.

USE BID RESPONSE TO ESTIMATE COSTS

The determining factor is the approach selected to conduct the program of improvements. To bid a defined set of improvements for a roster of bus stops, develop a master cost estimate for the project -- the master estimate may not be exactly correct for any given bus stop, but it will be reasonably correct overall for the project. If working within available funds, obtain a firm and exact unit price for each bus stop. Carefully describe the work to be done at each stop and seek quotes for the improvements on an individual or a few-at-a-time basis.

In the first instance, the project will not proceed until an acceptable bid is received; however, the project will have a firm total price, an established level of work quality, and a projected completion date. In the second instance, the piecemeal nature of the project allows work to start as soon as funds are available, but there is no assurance that work can be completed within the available budget. Moreover, it is probably more difficult under the piecemeal approach to ensure a uniform quality of workmanship than under a bid approach.

The comprehensive approach means more time in planning and less in implementation.

The piecemeal approach means less time in planning and more in implementation.

In the bid situation, more transit authority staff time initially will be required while the specifications and cost estimate are being prepared and the project brought through the bid process. However, there are relatively fewer staff time requirements after the contract has been awarded. In contrast, there is probably less of an initial personnel time requirement if the entity receives quotes and conducts the project piecemeal; but, there is a greater responsibility for the direct supervision of the project and for quality assurance.

6-13

CHAPTER 6 PROGRAMMING ACCESSIBLE BUS STOP IMPROVEMENTS

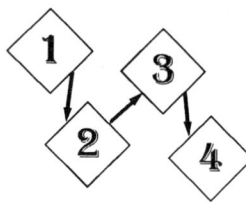

STEP 3: CONDUCT A PUBLIC INVOLVEMENT PROGRAM

PUBLIC INVOLVEMENT INTEGRATED IN PLANNING

Figure 6-3 shows how the public can be integrated into the planning of bus stop accessibility improvements. Public involvement in the planning process helps to ensure that the plans will be implemented. Plans developed with public involvement and approval are more visible, have more support, and are much more difficult to shelve than plans developed in private.

In Figure 6-3, the left side of the diagram presents the five steps for developing a prioritized work plan for bus stop upgrades. The right side of the diagram presents the complementary input of the consumer advisory body. Important aspects are as follows:

- **Develop a bus stop accessibility database.** During the earliest planning stage, prepare a catalog of the existing accessibility of the bus stops. Ask the advisory body to recommend which bus routes should be evaluated first, and make a list of stops known to have accessibility problems.
- **Develop a cost estimation methodology.** Develop a method for estimating the complexity and cost of upgrading the bus stops. Ask consumers to contribute insights about the relationship of accessibility features and attractiveness, to assist by reviewing the costing methodology, and/or to develop a methodology for determining the difficulty of upgrading stops.
- **Integrate data on bus stop utilization.** Add information about the current frequency of utilization of bus stops. Ask consumer advisors to provide information on which stops people with disabilities use most heavily or might use most heavily in the future.

CHAPTER 6 PROGRAMMING ACCESSIBLE BUS STOP IMPROVEMENTS

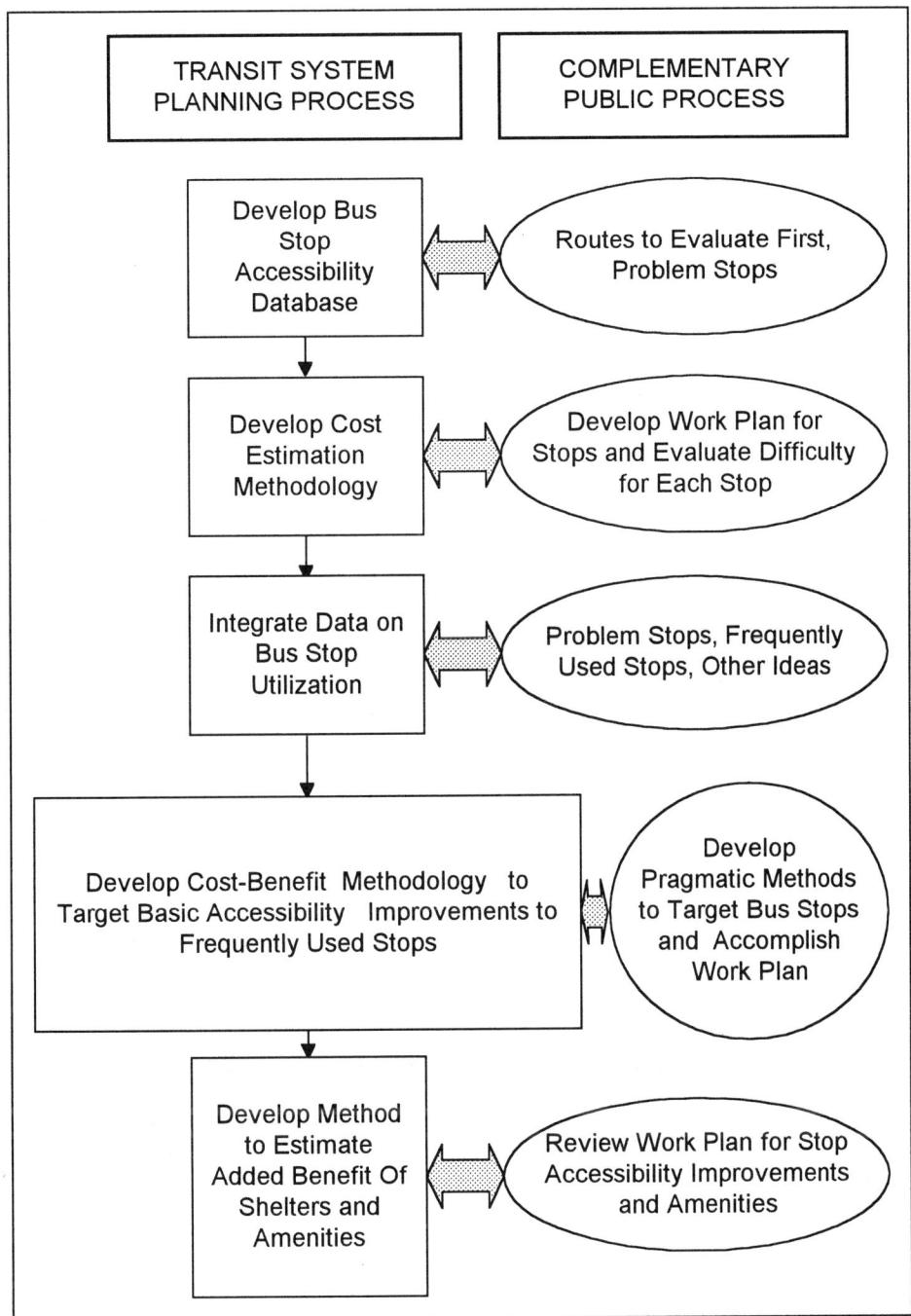

Figure 6-3. Integrated Consumer Involvement in Accessibility Improvements Planning

CHAPTER 6 PROGRAMMING ACCESSIBLE BUS STOP IMPROVEMENTS

- **Develop a cost-benefit methodology to target basic accessibility improvements to frequently used stops.** Work with consumers to establish a method for prioritizing the list of bus stops to be improved.

- **Develop a method to estimate the added benefit of shelters and amenities.** Work with consumers to develop a method for deciding which stops should receive enhanced amenities because they will be key stops in the accessible transit system.

ROLE OF CONSUMER ADVISORS

Ask consumer advisory committees to survey individuals with disabilities who use paratransit in order to make a list of frequently used bus boarding locations. Ask consumers to identify locations at which they would enter and exit the bus system if it were accessible. Ask consumer advisory committees to provide input on the most important bus routes from the point of view of users with disabilities. Work with city planners and consumers to attempt to identify sites where new housing, medical or work complexes are likely to become frequent trip generators.

Figure 6-4 shows a possible questionnaire for advisory committee members for them to answer and share with coworkers who have disabilities.

CONSUMER ADVISORY COMMITTEE

Do not rely exclusively on the numerical values that result from the prioritization process. Consumer advisors should participate extensively in the review of the priority scores. Authorize them to deliberate the outcome of the process, to visit prospective bus stop locations or view them on tape, and to suggest alternative sites for a higher priority level.

CHAPTER 6 PROGRAMMING ACCESSIBLE BUS STOP IMPROVEMENTS

> We are working to decide what transit stops to make accessible to people with disabilities. Some of the improvements for stops might include larger shelters, room for a wheelchair lift on the ground, and curb cuts and other access. Please answer the questions below to help us decide which stops to improve.
>
> 1. Where is the bus stop closest to your house?
>   _____
>
> 2. Have you ever taken the bus from that stop?
>
>   ❑ Yes ❑ No
>
> 3. Do you know what routes stop there?
>
>   ❑ Yes. Which ones? _____
>   ❑ No
>
> 4. Would you use the stop if it were accessible to people with disabilities?
>
>   ❑ Yes ❑ No
>
> 5. Please think about the place you travel to the most each week. Do you know the bus stop nearest to it?
>   ❑ Yes. Please write in the location.
>   _____
>
>   ❑ No. Please write in the intersecting streets nearest to where you travel to the most each week.
>   _____
>
> 6. Have you ever taken the bus to that location?
>
>   ❑ Yes ❑ No
>
> 7. Would you use a stop at this location if it were accessible to people with disabilities?
>
>   ❑ Yes ❑ No
>
> Thank you very much for your help. Your answers will help us provide better service for all our riders.

Figure 6-4. Questionnaire for Use by Advisory Committee Members

CHAPTER 6 PROGRAMMING ACCESSIBLE BUS STOP IMPROVEMENTS

Consumer advisor input can be helpful because it reflects experience; can prevent costly, inefficient decisions; and gives the public a greater stake in the success of the program.

Conduct early, significant, and ongoing planning meetings with a consumer advisory committee to target bus stop improvements. Otherwise, locations where improvements are most needed may be overlooked.

In one system, the bus stop committee met (and continues to meet) monthly or bimonthly. The committee includes one individual who uses a wheelchair as a representative of individuals with disabilities. The mandate of the committee is to improve bus stops for all riders, including those with disabilities. Transit system planners, transit system service personnel, and city engineers assist the committee.

Before the transit system and city engineering teams go into the field, have the bus stop subcommittee discuss and decide which routes should be analyzed first. Record such decisions to prevent revisiting the same subject. Begin each meeting with a review of the preceding meeting and a discussion of progress made by the city and the transit system in the intervening period. Over the course of several meetings, have the committee discuss and decide upon the criteria to be used for determining bus stop accessibility[6]. Also ask the committee to identify known problem stops and known high-volume transit stops. An open, interactive public participation process is important throughout the bus stop improvement program.

PUBLIC INVOLVEMENT TO IDENTIFY STOPS FOR IMPROVEMENT

Use the public involvement program, in conjunction with market research, to identify the stops to make accessible and to determine priorities for which stops to make accessible first. From

---

[6]In determining accessibility, IPTC's staff and committee largely relied upon *Bus Stop Accessibility: A Guide for Virginia Transit Systems for Complying with the Americans With Disabilities Act of 1990*: Virginia Department of Rail and Public Transportation (July, 1992).

CHAPTER 6 PROGRAMMING ACCESSIBLE BUS STOP IMPROVEMENTS

the public involvement perspective, emphasize outreach to agencies that serve people with disabilities and at public meetings to discuss priorities and finalize decisions.

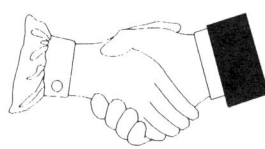

Outreach to Agencies

Following the development of an inventory of bus stops and needed accessibility improvements, work with the entities in the service area which provide services to people with disabilities, such as human service agencies, hospitals, clinics, nutrition sites, senior centers, and others, to determine which bus stops are nearest to them and provide access to their location.

The outreach can be in the form of a letter to each agency asking for information about bus stops near their locations. One-on-one meetings may also be held. Consider holding meetings with one or more agencies which have locations in the same general part of the service area, to discuss which stops, if made accessible, would serve clients of more than one agency.

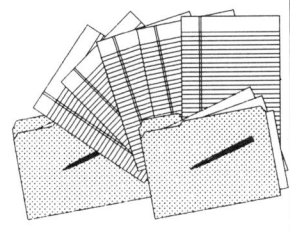

Considerations to discuss include the following:

- The comparative level of effort and expense required to make different stops accessible;
- The definition of accessibility and what is required to make stops ADA-accessible;
- Which stops may not be useful to clients even if they are accessible, because of barriers between the stops and the agency location (for example, steps, hills, and major roads);
- The likelihood that clients of the agency would or could use fixed-route, even with accessible stops;
- The conjunction of accessible stops with travel training and other education programs aimed at agency clients and clients' caregivers;
- The availability and deployment of accessible vehicles;
- Which improvements are most applicable for their clients; and/or
- Services provided on the vehicles, such as stop announcements and assistance with lifts and securement.

CHAPTER 6 PROGRAMMING ACCESSIBLE BUS STOP IMPROVEMENTS

Work with agencies to determine the appropriateness of making stops near their locations accessible and prioritize the placement of individual stops. Work with them to establish a feasible schedule for improvements and to schedule other educational activities. Also work with the agencies to promote attendance at public meetings to discuss bus stop accessibility.

Public Meetings

Before deciding which stops to make accessible, hold public meetings. Publicize the meetings through newsletters, mailings, and newspaper advertisements. They may also be targeted to the clients of agencies, with publicity handled through the agencies and the meetings taking place at their sites.

At the public meetings, discuss the list of bus stop improvements and priorities, as defined through the outreach activities and market research. Describe the justifications for the improvements and the priorities. Establish priorities according to such factors as the following:

- Stops which can be made accessible the soonest and for the least cost, such as those which are nearly accessible, or have sufficient room for expansion;
- Stops which will serve the largest number of people with disabilities, based on overall ridership at the stops or potential ridership by people with disabilities;
- Stops served by routes with accessible vehicles; or
- Interests of agency representatives.

Listen to participants at the meetings and make adjustments to the priorities. Be clear regarding the costs of improvements and the available resources for such improvements.

Public involvement and market research regarding identification of stops to improve for accessibility will often occur simultaneously. Public meetings are best scheduled after other

CHAPTER 6 PROGRAMMING ACCESSIBLE BUS STOP IMPROVEMENTS

forms of public involvement and research are completed, because then justification for the decisions will be clear and can be readily explained to public participants. Figure 6-5 shows the interaction of the public involvement and market research processes.

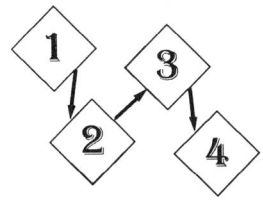

STEP 4: CONDUCT MARKET RESEARCH

Develop an estimate of the probable use of newly accessible bus stops by people with disabilities. This estimate is critical in establishing the sequence of the work. Use the measure of current and expected ridership to prioritize the sequence of bus stop improvements.

In deciding which bus stops to improve earliest, work with consumer advisors to estimate probable increased future utilization.

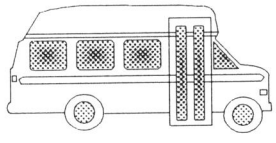

INFORMATION FROM THE PARATRANSIT SYSTEM

Ask the local complementary paratransit service to identify locations where people with disabilities travel. A list of frequently used paratransit origins and destinations can identify potential accessible bus stop locations on the fixed-routes. If the paratransit system has an automated trip booking and scheduling database, it should be able to develop a list of frequent paratransit pickup and drop-off sites. Compare this list against the bus stop accessibility inventory to identify bus stops close to frequent paratransit patron origins and destinations.

Deciding how to attract persons to use the fixed-route system by upgrading bus stops that are likely to be used by current paratransit patrons is a major step in prioritizing the sequence in which the stops will be improved.

Along with correlating current paratransit use and bus stop accessibility, the transit system and consumers should use direct market research to prioritize the improvements.

CHAPTER 6 PROGRAMMING ACCESSIBLE BUS STOP IMPROVEMENTS

Figure 6-5. Public Involvement and Market Research to Identify Stops

DIRECT MARKET RESEARCH

Conduct direct market research of riders and other members of the community through questionnaires distributed to transit and paratransit riders, newsletters with mail-back forms, and newspaper advertisements with clip-out coupons to indicate preferences.

CHAPTER 6 PROGRAMMING ACCESSIBLE BUS STOP IMPROVEMENTS

Questionnaires Distributed to Riders

To learn about preferences for bus stop accessibility, distribute questionnaires to paratransit and fixed-route riders. Distribute questionnaires to paratransit riders on the paratransit vehicles, at common origins and destinations, and through mail inserts when other information or eligibility applications are mailed. On the paratransit vehicles and at common sites, provide a box where respondents can drop completed forms. Paratransit drivers can return the box to the transit system. Include a return address so respondents can mail the forms back.

Distribute questionnaires to fixed-route riders on the fixed-route vehicles, at transit centers, at ticket vending locations, and through general mailings, such as inserts in utility bills. Provide a mail-back address on the questionnaire. On vehicles and at transit locations, provide a box to return the questionnaires.

Figure 6-6 shows a sample questionnaire to send to riders.

Newsletters with Mail-Back Form

Many transit systems mail or otherwise distribute newsletters to paratransit and fixed-route riders. The newsletters can include a brief questionnaire to be dropped in a box or mailed back to the transit system. Highlight the questionnaire with a box which can be clipped and sent back to the transit system.

CHAPTER 6 PROGRAMMING ACCESSIBLE BUS STOP IMPROVEMENTS

We are deciding what transit stops to make accessible to people with disabilities. Some of the improvements for stops might include larger shelters, room for a wheelchair lift on the ground, and curb cuts and other access. Please answer the questions below to help us decide which stops to improve.

1. Where is the bus stop you use the most?
   _____

2. Do you think that stop could be used by people with disabilities? ❏ Yes ❏ No

3. Do you think people with disabilities would use the stop if it were improved to make it more accessible? ❏ Yes ❏ No

4. Please indicate, on a scale of 1 to 10, how high a priority should that stop have for improvements (where a 1 means it should have very low priority and 10 means it should be improved right away)?

   ❏ 1 ❏ 2 ❏ 3 ❏ 4 ❏ 5 ❏ 6 ❏ 7 ❏ 8 ❏ 9 ❏ 10

5. On a scale of 1 to 10 (where 1 means it would not change your riding habits at all and a 10 means you would definitely ride more often), how likely are you to use the transit system more often if the stop were improved?

   ❏ 1 ❏ 2 ❏ 3 ❏ 4 ❏ 5 ❏ 6 ❏ 7 ❏ 8 ❏ 9 ❏ 10

6. Is there another stop which you think should be made accessible?

   ❏ Yes. Where is it? _____ ❏ No

7. On a scale of 1 to 10, how high a priority should that stop have for improvements (where a 1 means it should have very low priority and 10 means it should be improved right away)?

   ❏ 1 ❏ 2 ❏ 3 ❏ 4 ❏ 5 ❏ 6 ❏ 7 ❏ 8 ❏ 9 ❏ 10

8. On a scale of 1 to 10 (where 1 means it would not change your riding habits at all and a 10 means you would definitely ride more often), how likely are you to use the transit system more often if the stop were improved?

   ❏ 1 ❏ 2 ❏ 3 ❏ 4 ❏ 5 ❏ 6 ❏ 7 ❏ 8 ❏ 9 ❏ 10

9. Is there another stop which you think should be made accessible?

   ❏ Yes. Which one _____ ❏ No

10. On a scale of 1 to 10, how high a priority should that stop have for improvements (where a 1 means it should have very low priority and 10 means it should be improved right away)?

    ❏ 1 ❏ 2 ❏ 3 ❏ 4 ❏ 5 ❏ 6 ❏ 7 ❏ 8 ❏ 9 ❏ 10

11. On a scale of 1 to 10 (where 1 means it would not change your riding habits at all and a 10 means you would definitely ride more often), how likely are you to use the transit system more often if the stop were improved?

    ❏ 1 ❏ 2 ❏ 3 ❏ 4 ❏ 5 ❏ 6 ❏ 7 ❏ 8 ❏ 9 ❏ 10

Thank you very much for your help. Your answers will help us provide better service for all our riders.

Please drop this questionnaire in the box or return it to: Mr. Accessibility Planner
Your Transit Authority
123 Main Street
Thistown, MA 02134

Figure 6-6. Sample Questionnaire to Send to Riders

CHAPTER 6 PROGRAMMING ACCESSIBLE BUS STOP IMPROVEMENTS

Newspaper Advertisements

When placing advertisements regarding accessibility or other topics, include a clip-out coupon with questions about what stops to make accessible. Coupons could offer cents off a transit ride. When the drivers collect the coupons and return them to the transit system, the information can be collected. Figure 6-7 shows an example of an advertisement with a clip-out coupon with questions.

UTILIZATION BY GENERAL PASSENGERS

Target improvements to bus stops that are frequently used by general passengers or might be frequently used if a stop were present. Use Section 15 passenger counts to provide bus-stop-by-bus-stop boarding and alighting data. Also utilize information on plans for new commercial or residential developments.

The current degree of utilization of each bus stop by people with disabilities would generally be expected to correlate with utilization by general passengers; however, some locations may generate or receive many trips by people with disabilities, but rather few trips by general passengers. These locations should receive special consideration for accessibility improvements and amenities targeted at general passengers.

CHAPTER 6 PROGRAMMING ACCESSIBLE BUS STOP IMPROVEMENTS

Your Transit System

We Have New Buses!

Come see our new buses -- fully accessible, clean, and quiet. The new buses are on routes:

> A (Baker Street)
> D (South Main)
> 14 (North City)
> 24 (River Drive)
> 23 (South Side)

Picture of a bus here.

COME RIDE WITH US

Clip here

We are also going to improve bus stops to make them more accessible (larger shelters, room for a wheelchair lift on the ground, and/or curb cuts and other access). Which stops should we improve first?

Return this coupon with your choices the next time you ride and **take 25¢ off the cost of your trip.**

Write the location (such as, corner of 1st Ave. and Main Street, etc.) of the three bus stops you think should be changed first.

1. _____

2. _____

3. _____

Figure 6-7. Sample Advertisement with a Clip-out Coupon with Questions

CHAPTER 6 PROGRAMMING ACCESSIBLE BUS STOP IMPROVEMENTS

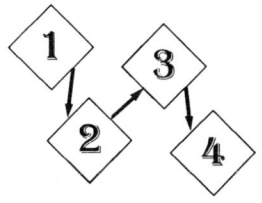

Three elements:
- *Bus stop catalog,*
- *Cost estimate, and*
- *Frequency of use.*

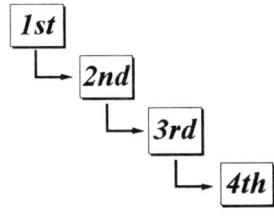

STEP 5: SELECT TARGET STOPS

Develop a methodology for selecting target stops by using consumer input gained throughout the project or rely on analyzing information in the database. The optimal method combines qualitative inputs from consumer advisors with quantitative inputs from the accessibility database; however, as will be seen in Steps 6 and 7, available funding and the method that will be used to administer the work will substantially influence the final selection of stops to be enhanced and the sequence of the work.

SETTING PRIORITIES

At this point in the planning, the transit system should have a catalog of bus stops, a cost estimate and work plan for achieving ADA accessibility for each stop, and an index of the frequency of use of each stop. These products of the planning process should have been developed in cooperation with consumer advisors.

Prioritize the stop list by using a numerical formula and by involving consumers in developing the formula and in review of the resulting prioritized list.

Tucson developed a plan for prioritizing accessibility improvements by evaluating the bus stop list against the following goals:

- All new capital improvements should adhere to ADA requirements and increase the accessibility of the transit system.
- Sites selected for enhancement should be as close as possible to boarding or disembarking locations which are more heavily used by the current paratransit riders. Operationally, this means selecting bus stops nearest to the top 25% of frequently used paratransit trip generators or destinations.
- Selected sites should contribute to a network of accessible sites no more than 1/4 mile distant from one another.
- Selected sites should be those most heavily used by the general transit ridership. Stops selected for enhancement

CHAPTER 6 PROGRAMMING ACCESSIBLE BUS STOP IMPROVEMENTS

should meet the market needs of the general public, current paratransit riders, and other individuals who are most likely to require accessible access to the fixed-route system.

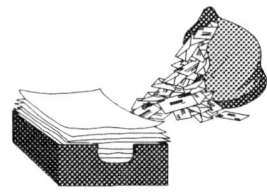

INPUT FROM PUBLIC INVOLVEMENT PROGRAM AND MARKET RESEARCH

From the questionnaires completed by those contacted by the members of the consumer advisory committee and the questionnaires completed by paratransit and fixed-route riders, generate a list of the stops most frequently mentioned. If questions are asked regarding whether the improvements would increase ridership, include this information in the list. Develop a database of stops mentioned and use the information to set priorities. On the basis of the questions in Figures 6-4 and 6-6, some of the database items would be as follows:

- Bus stop location, along with transit system designation for the stop;
- Number of times it was mentioned by paratransit riders;
- Number of times it was mentioned by fixed-route riders;
- Number of times it was mentioned as being near a home or most frequently used stop;
- Average score for priority; and
- Average score for likelihood of use if improved.

From this information, determine which stops have the highest priority.

PRAGMATIC CONSIDERATIONS

There may be compelling reasons to select target stops from a more operational perspective. For instance, expedite the program of bus stop improvements by piggy-backing them on existing contracts for city street work. This process tends to favor bus stop improvements made near street improvements.

CHAPTER 6 PROGRAMMING ACCESSIBLE BUS STOP IMPROVEMENTS

Bolster the deliberations of a citizens' committee with hard data. Prioritize the bus stop list by conducting a computerized benefit-cost analysis on information contained in the bus stop database. Prioritize stops for improvement by using the computerized selection process and taking into account the following:

- Current and probable future general population ridership;
- The potential and likelihood for utilization by persons with disabilities; and
- The complexity and cost of the desired improvements.

The outcome of the deliberations on site selections should be a systematic, sequenced, proactive, cost-estimated plan for bus stop enhancements. It is likely to be a multi-year plan or a phased plan, with the highest priority stops rehabilitated in the early phases. Revisit and revise such a plan in the out years to incorporate new information about frequently utilized stops or desired bus stop accessibility features.

STEP 6: DETERMINE IMPROVEMENTS
SELECTING STOP AMENITIES

Most of the improvements to achieve accessibility will be basic, consisting of installing curb cuts and 60 inch-by-96 inch pads. If there are sidewalks, they should be integrated with the bus stop. In addition to basic improvements, include bus stop amenities whenever feasible. As used here, bus stop amenities range from benches to shelters, with shade plantings and/or extra security considerations.

Lighted, large, covered shelters are important to transit users with disabilities.

The research, upon which this guidebook is based, determined that persons with disabilities considered amenities to be very important. For example, people with disabilities who use fixed-route transit assigned the attribute, "Lighted Shelters," the highest utility value of any attribute ranked. They also rated "Large, Covered Shelters" as their sixth most important attribute. The research also revealed that people who use wheelchairs and the fixed-route system like having benches at bus stops.

6-29

CHAPTER 6 PROGRAMMING ACCESSIBLE BUS STOP IMPROVEMENTS

Therefore, having determined the sequence for bus stop improvements and having cost-estimated the plan to include accessibility, consider, with consumer groups, all possible approaches to including bus stop amenities such as shelters and lighting.

Locating a bus stop under a street light is a smart use of resources.

Work with consumer groups to determine which high-frequency stops have enough land for a bus pad, a bench, a shelter, and lighting. Any bench, shelter, bus stop sign, or lighting fixture should be placed so as not to impede the deployment of the bus lift or the use of the accessible path by people with disabilities.

Whenever possible, locate new bus stops near illumination by a street lamp. Conversely, encourage the installation of street lighting at existing bus stop locations, whether accessible or not.

TRANSIT CENTER DESIGN ELEMENTS

Tucson, Arizona's Tohono Tadai transit facility was the first transit facility in the country to be designed and constructed in full accordance with the ADA guidelines. The facility includes items which can attract people with disabilities to use the fixed-route, such as announcement of stops and routes; large, covered shelters; lighted shelters; accessible seating; and wheelchair locations.

Through a design review process, Tucson incorporated and built on the travel experiences of many people with disabilities in achieving the final architectural design of Tohono Tadai. The finished facility is a model of accessible, usable architecture. Some accessibility features are as follows:

- Signage in Grade #2 Braille;
- Speakers at each bus bay to announce arrivals, routes, and departures;
- Flashing red lights to attract attention to the digital sign boards;
- A two-way amplified speaker system at the information booth;
- Accessible public phones, vending machines, and counter heights;

CHAPTER 6 PROGRAMMING ACCESSIBLE BUS STOP IMPROVEMENTS

- Motion-sensor toilets and lavatories;
- Rounded edges on benches, counters, and all protruding surfaces; and
- An accessible tot lot.[7]

Open Space Clearance

Locating the columns in relation to the benches and setback between the columns and the edge of the curb so as to open up the clearances was particularly important to persons with mobility disabilities.

Rounded Corners

Rounding corners on all structural elements and amenities, benches, and columns, to eliminate protrusions which could cause injuries was particularly important for persons with visual impairments.

Visibility and Design of Signs

Several items were important to people with vision and hearing impairments. Among the items were highly visible signage set at the correct height and incorporating Grade #2 Braille, flashing lights and buzzers; a color and lighting scheme that would make the signs easy to read; signs with a modern appearance; and signs that were bright and easy to see. Solutions included a flashing light and other annunciators at each bus bay to alert individuals with hearing impairments to the bus arrival. Another light flashes if there is a schedule change.

Location of Air Ducts

The Tucson transit centers are not enclosed or air-conditioned. Small shelters and trees provide shade, but the only enclosed area is the customer service booth. Cool air is provided at the benches through an evaporative cooling system. This system pipes cool air from ducts from just behind the benches. In meetings, the advisory committee members requested that special care be taken so that the air would also blow out over the wheelchair spaces adjoining the benches and that the duct work would not obstruct the clearance.

---

[7] Project ACTION, "Tucson's Tohono Tadai Transit Center," *Project ACTION Update*, Summer, 1995, p. 11.

CHAPTER 6 PROGRAMMING ACCESSIBLE BUS STOP IMPROVEMENTS

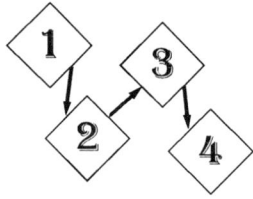

STEP 7: EVALUATE ENHANCEMENTS

Evaluate the outcomes of a bus stop enhancement program using one of the following methods.

- Solicit opinions from the consumer advisory group on the value of the outcome, as well as from the bus operators having routes with enhanced accessibility. Review comments from the general public.
- Directly count bus boardings by people with disabilities and lift deployments.
- Monitor, over time, the decrease in paratransit use by people who live near newly accessible fixed-route stops and who previously were frequent paratransit riders.

Whatever method is chosen, keep the advisory committee involved in continued planning and aware of ongoing successes.

CHAPTER 7:
TEACHING PASSENGERS TO USE THE FIXED-ROUTE SYSTEM -- TRAVEL TRAINING

CHAPTER 7 TEACHING PASSENGERS TO USE THE FIXED-ROUTE SYSTEM -- TRAVEL TRAINING

INTRODUCTION

Transit systems are continually challenged to provide to all people, including those with disabilities, transit services that provide full access to all opportunities afforded by a community. To this end, transit systems must provide complementary paratransit to all people who cannot use fixed-route buses. Many people with disabilities, however, can use fixed-route buses for their travel needs, rather than complementary paratransit, if they receive travel training.

There are essentially four kinds of travel training -- informational presentations, tailored travel training, peer model training, and general travel training. Informational presentations are given to groups of people likely to use paratransit or fixed-route services. With tailored travel training, a person with a disability is matched with a program of travel training specifically designed to satisfy the individual's travel needs. In peer model training, a person with a type of disability similar to that of the person being trained coaches that individual. In general travel training, the transit system provides general presentations, open to anyone in a community, that describe the transit system and how to use fixed-route transit.

This chapter details the steps needed to develop an effective travel training program. These steps are as follows:

1. Identify the need;
2. Define funding needs and resources;
3. Conduct public involvement;
4. Conduct market research;
5. Select training model and approach;
6. Develop travel training materials;
7. Implement approach; and
8. Evaluate the program.

CHAPTER 7 TEACHING PASSENGERS TO USE THE FIXED-ROUTE SYSTEM -- TRAVEL TRAINING

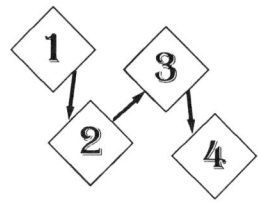

STEP 1: IDENTIFY THE NEED

The first step is to identify the need for a travel training program. There are a number of sources of information, such as the ADA eligibility determination process, requests for information, and outreach activities.

ADA ELIGIBILITY PROCESS

Use the ADA paratransit eligibility process to identify the need for travel training and send information about travel training to potential candidates. Travel training information can be sent to all who apply for paratransit eligibility when blank applications are mailed to them. Receipt of travel training information can be a means of self-screening for the need for training.

Look at ADA paratransit eligibility applications for potential travel training candidates.

Applications for ADA complementary paratransit service can include a clear explanation of travel training, a question about whether the applicant would be interested in it, and information about fixed-route service. Be sure to note that an interest in travel training will not affect whether or not the applicant is eligible for ADA complementary paratransit service.

Include travel training information in the notification of eligibility determination, whether or not the applicant is eligible for paratransit. In the early planning stages, the information may describe various travel training options and ask the applicant to indicate his or her preference.

Look at requests for training and information.

Those people who are ineligible for ADA paratransit are potential travel training candidates. The eligibility determination process can be designed to also identify people who are not eligible for complementary ADA paratransit, but would be good candidates for travel training. Review these files to determine what type of travel training program can be established, and if the current program satisfies training needs.

CHAPTER 7 TEACHING PASSENGERS TO USE THE FIXED-ROUTE SYSTEM -- TRAVEL TRAINING

The type of travel training needed can also be obtained by reviewing ADA eligibility applications. If most of the people are older, an informational presentation may be most appropriate. If most of the people in this database have vision impairments, travel training tailored to an individual may be most appropriate. If people come from an area of the city, where general knowledge of the transit system is limited, general travel training may be required. As the database of people ineligible for ADA paratransit expands, note demographic and location data that can be employed later.

INFORMATION REQUESTS

Determine how many times people with disabilities ask different types of questions about the system.

Requests for training, transit information, or travel planning assistance constitute another source of information. Categorize the types of questions asked by callers by working with those who receive information calls, on both paratransit and transit systems. Interviews with or surveys of call-takers can reveal trends in information requests.

Consider establishing procedures for keeping track of the reasons for calls. A simple form for checking question types can be used by call-takers. Figure 7-1 shows a possible form. Identify the most important questions related to possible travel training. Review the agendas and include them on the form. Call-takers simply check the form each time a question is asked. Review the forms at the end of a week or month to determine which questions are asked most frequently.

Establish a way to identify people with disabilities when they call.

If particular questions are asked regularly, or with increasing frequency, it may signal the need for a particular type of travel training. Review the topics of the questions callers ask to be sure they are adequately covered in any travel training program. Consider establishing a way to identify callers with disabilities. It is not appropriate to ask people directly, and many will not answer accurately if asked directly, but the information may be revealed in conversation. The call-taker can also ask if the person needs a lift-equipped vehicle, which may indirectly identify riders who use wheelchairs.

7-3

CHAPTER 7 TEACHING PASSENGERS TO USE THE FIXED-ROUTE SYSTEM -- TRAVEL TRAINING

Call-Taker Name:	Date:	
Question	Check (✓) each time the question is asked	Count
How much is the fare?		
How do transfers work?		
What should I do to signal a bus?		
What is the procedure for boarding and disembarking in a wheelchair?		
How do I pay the fare, if I use a wheelchair lift in the back of the bus?		
How do I read a system map?		
How do I read a bus schedule?		
What types of discount fares are available for people with disabilities?		
Could someone help me plan a specific bus trip?		
Other questions:		

Figure 7-1. Call-Taker Question Form

OUTREACH ACTIVITIES

If schedules and transit information are mailed to people who request it over the telephone, a brief insert can be included describing planned or existing travel training. If the insert will be mailed to all people who request information, it can be general in nature. Figure 7-2 shows some possible wording for a travel training informational insert.

CHAPTER 7 TEACHING PASSENGERS TO USE THE FIXED-ROUTE SYSTEM -- TRAVEL TRAINING

Consider sending a brief insert with information mailings.

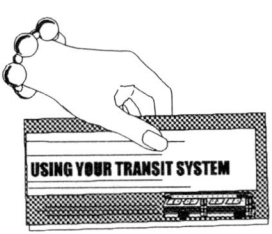

> **TRAVEL TRAINING FOR THE BUS**
>
> If you or someone you know has difficulty using the bus, because of
> - a disability,
> - advanced age,
> - illness, or
> - other reasons,
>
> training is available at no cost to make using the bus easier.
>
> Training will provide general information about the bus system, schedules and assistance in reading the schedules, trip planning information and tips, and information about the system's policies and procedures.
>
> Specialized training for people with specific disabilities is also available.
>
> For additional information, contact:
>
> Ms. _____
> Training Coordinator
> City Transit System
> 123 Main Street
> Righthere, WI   53000
> Phone:_____
> Fax:_____
> TDD:_____
> Thank you for riding the bus!

Figure 7-2. Possible Travel Training Informational Insert

In addition, assess information from other internal sources, such as bus operators and other transit professionals who come into contact with people with disabilities. Information may also be collected at meetings, in individual interviews, or through surveys. This information might consist of requests for information, indications that a new center for people with disabilities is about to be opened, or an indication that many similar questions are being

CHAPTER 7 TEACHING PASSENGERS TO USE THE FIXED-ROUTE SYSTEM -- TRAVEL TRAINING

asked of transit personnel. This information can help identify the need for a travel training program and the model that should be used.

Another approach is to develop a team of operators, call-takers, supervisors, and others, who can work to address several travel training issues. These issues may include whether travel training is needed, what types of training are needed, where the training should occur, and who should do the training. Gathering all of the transit system's experts in one room for a short time can produce excellent insights into these issues.

Explore forums (such as advisory committees, task forces, and public hearings and meetings) that enable the public to participate in decision-making. The various citizens' advisory committees can be a source of valuable information about how people in the broader community identify the need for travel training. Task forces may be organized to address particular service problems or the general travel needs of specific geographic areas. Elicit their opinions about a proposed travel training program. Add travel training to the agenda at public hearings, workshops, and consultation meetings.

Assess the value for travel training by evaluating progress in making the transit fleet accessible. Also assess the process of the city in installing physical improvements so fixed-route buses can be a viable alternative for people with disabilities. As the transit system becomes more accessible, travel training needs will change.

As an area becomes more accessible, more people will be able to get to their destinations by fixed-route rather than only paratransit. By strictly interpreting ADA paratransit eligibility, a transit system can create a large market for travel training, particularly if accessibility of various locations is used in the eligibility determination process.

From all of these sources, determine the absolute amount and type of travel training required. The next step involves an assessment of funding needs and resources.

CHAPTER 7 TEACHING PASSENGERS TO USE THE FIXED-ROUTE SYSTEM -- TRAVEL TRAINING

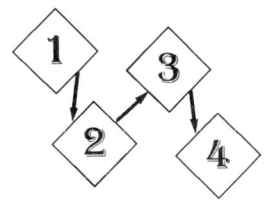

STEP 2: DEFINE FUNDING NEEDS AND RESOURCES

TRAINING MODEL ALTERNATIVES

The four basic training models (informational presentations, tailored training, peer model training, and general travel training) each require different resources. Selecting the most appropriate model depends on various factors, including the extent of community and transit agency resources.

Informational Presentations

Informational presentations about the system and how to use it are made to groups in the community. Conduct presentations at sites where there are numerous potential patrons who may need information before they use the system. Possible locations include senior citizen residences, apartment complexes in which numerous people with disabilities reside, and activity centers frequented by senior citizens and people with disabilities. This general approach provides some training for participants, but does not address individual needs. The advantage is that information can be distributed widely, without requiring highly trained staff, particularly if a video is used as part of the presentation.

To determine the costs for an informational presentation approach, identify who will develop and make the presentations. Estimate how many presentations will be made and the amount of staff time involved. Volunteers from the community may be able to make some of the presentations, but staff time will be needed to identify trainees and sites and to schedule the presentations. Table 7-1 shows some of the components of a cost estimate. Chapter 5 of this Guidebook includes information on the development of a training video, much of which can be applicable to the development of an informational video for travel training.

CHAPTER 7 TEACHING PASSENGERS TO USE THE FIXED-ROUTE SYSTEM -- TRAVEL TRAINING

Table 7-1. Informational Presentations Approach: Cost Components

Staff Time			
Presentation Development	Number of Hours	Hourly Cost	Total Cost
Identification and Scheduling	Number of Hours	Hourly Cost	Total Cost
Presentations	Number of Hours	Hourly Cost	Total Cost
Handouts			
Development	Number of Hours	Hourly Cost	Total Cost
Copying	Number of Copies	Cost per Copy	Total Cost
Travel Costs			
	Number of trips	Cost per Trip (bus fare, mileage rate, parking, taxi fare, etc.)	Total Cost
Audiovisual Materials			
Video Development	Development Time and Cost	Production Cost	Total Cost
Audiovisual Cassette Development	Development Time and Cost	Production Cost	Total Cost
Slide Presentation Development	Development Time and Cost	Production Cost	Total Cost
Total Cost of Informational Presentations			

CHAPTER 7 TEACHING PASSENGERS TO USE THE FIXED-ROUTE SYSTEM -- TRAVEL TRAINING

Tailored Travel Training

Tailored travel training is usually performed by an agency specializing in training people with disabilities in independent living skills.

In the second training model, a person with a disability is matched with a program of travel training specifically tailored to his or her travel needs. This work is usually performed by an agency specializing in training people with disabilities in the skills needed to live independently. Travel training is thus an outgrowth of an extensive intake process.

The components of a comprehensive, customer-oriented intake process are as follows:

- Determining the person's specific travel needs;
- Determining how much the person knows about the transit system;
- Determining if there are any specific disabilities that hinder the person's ability to travel; and
- Determining how independent the person is and how quickly he or she adjusts to new experiences.

The cost components of this model must be thoroughly examined. First, contact the local agencies and determine what resources they have available for use in travel training. Second, determine what resources are available for free as part of their current mission and how much additional services will cost if they are required by a transit training program. Third, assess the status of volunteers in coaching independent living skills. Determine how much staff coordination time will be required if this model is implemented. (Staff time may be required to publicize a travel training program, refer people to an outside agency, monitor the effectiveness of the agency, and/or provide a continuing resource to people who have been travel trained).

CHAPTER 7 TEACHING PASSENGERS TO USE THE FIXED-ROUTE SYSTEM -- TRAVEL TRAINING

Peer Model Training

The third technique is peer model training. In this technique, a person with a disability similar to that of the person being travel trained does the training. The peer performs most of the training and indicates how he or she personally deals with traveling by fixed-route transit. This training usually includes the peer accompanying the patron on a trip to ensure that the new patron is comfortable with the new situation.

In order to obtain the cost of a peer model training alternative, determine the availability of volunteers to do this training. Work with an oversight committee to determine the number of volunteers needed and to identify them. After sufficient volunteers are identified, determine whether the basic program should be developed in house, by a group of people with disabilities, or by some outside agency. Even if outside individuals develop and implement the program, someone on staff will spend some time coordinating travel training.

Develop formal arrangements with outside individuals involved in training. If a group of people with disabilities or an outside agency develops and implements peer model training, make specific arrangements or enter into a contract to establish what the group will do for the transit system and to allocate costs for the various components of the program.

General Travel Training

The fourth alternative is general travel training. Often, travel training for the general population is valuable and may be critical in communities where there are many new people or where there is a sizable transient population, such as college towns. New people may be good candidates for transit but may not know how to use the system. Distribute fare schedules or a system map at meetings for those who need basic information about using the system.

CHAPTER 7 TEACHING PASSENGERS TO USE THE FIXED-ROUTE SYSTEM -- TRAVEL TRAINING

The general travel training alternative can be the least costly of the models. Costs include developing a presentation and handouts, advertising the meetings, and providing presentations.

AVAILABLE RESOURCES

Review all potential resources in a community.

Review all potential resources available in the community, including centers for independent living, services for people with visual impairments, paralyzed veterans organizations, rehabilitation hospitals, clinics, and organizations associated with particular diseases. Service organizations, such as the Kiwanis, Rotarians, Shriners, or Knights of Columbus, may be resources. These organizations may have existing programs into which travel training can be integrated and may be able to provide funding or volunteers for particular aspects of the training. With a complete inventory of potential community resources, and a set of understandings with different agencies, a program may be implemented for a modest sum.

Explore the availability of grants from state agencies and private sponsors. Determine whether the state departments of transportation, health, or social services have grants available to fund travel training. Private sponsors may be interested in helping underwrite the cost on a one-time or continuing basis. Such organizations as HMOs, insurance companies, or foundations might be approached as possible resources.

The final resource is monies allocated by the transit system itself. While there will be some costs for travel training, they may be partially or totally off set by the fact that more people will be able to use lower-cost fixed-route transit, rather than paratransit, to travel in a community.

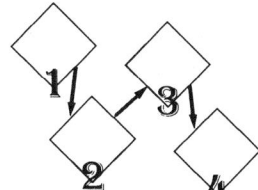

STEP 3: CONDUCT PUBLIC INVOLVEMENT

In addition to other public involvement activities, establish an oversight committee. This group will be absolutely necessary to learn the specific travel training needs of people with disabilities in the community. This group may also provide volunteers to perform some of the training and develop some of the materials.

7-11

CHAPTER 7 TEACHING PASSENGERS TO USE THE FIXED-ROUTE SYSTEM -- TRAVEL TRAINING

OVERSIGHT COMMITTEE MEMBERS

Consider encouraging the following people to serve on an oversight committee:

- Transit users with disabilities;
- Bus operators, including bus operator trainers;
- Transit planners involved in disability issues;
- Agency professionals with knowledge of disabilities and their implications for bus travel;
- Mobility trainers for people with visual impairments;
- People who are geographically distributed throughout the transit service area; and
- People with disabilities who attend local universities.

Develop a citizens' oversight committee to help develop materials and implement the program.

This mix of transit providers and customers can provide the skills and awareness needed to develop a travel training program. In addition, working together will greatly increase understanding among the groups. Responsibilities may include project oversight, boarding time studies, surveys, field studies, bus demonstrations, public presentations, and evaluation of the program.

THE ROLE OF THE OVERSIGHT COMMITTEE

In any approach to travel training, continuing communication with the oversight committee is important. Have discussions with as many people with disabilities as possible -- If only a few people with disabilities are involved, the needs of others may not be adequately expressed.

Good communication is essential.

Involve the community as much as possible. For example, good communication with members of the community can assist in the following:

- Identifying peer trainers;
- Identifying locations for informational presentations;
- Identifying trainers for training tailored to individuals; and

7-12

CHAPTER 7 TEACHING PASSENGERS TO USE THE FIXED-ROUTE SYSTEM -- TRAVEL TRAINING

- Contacting groups and individuals who would benefit from peer or transit system presentations.

Over time, community resources will become apparent, but make the initial contacts to start the process -- it takes time to become aware of all the available services and people.

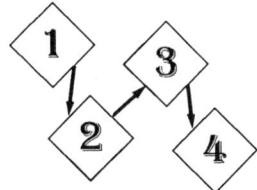

STEP 4: CONDUCT MARKET RESEARCH

After developing a method to involve the public in the design and implementation of a travel training program, augment the program by conducting market research to support the training models being considered for the transit system. If an informational presentation approach is used, market research may be necessary to either verify or correct impressions that people with disabilities may have about transit. If an independent living approach is being considered, interview people working for an independent living center. Ask them to identify the types of travel training a transit system can provide to assist the independent living agency in doing its work. If a general travel training approach is being considered, survey potential patrons to determine what topics should be addressed and when training should occur.

The approach requiring the greatest amount of market research is the informational presentation. In this technique, efforts are made to correct impressions about fixed-route transit that may prevent people with disabilities from using it.

Determine the factors which prevent people with disabilities from using fixed-route transit. Communicate with the oversight committee and anyone else identified by the committee who can provide information about the transportation needs and feelings of people with disabilities.

The major topics that will be brought up in these discussions are likely to focus on the following:

- Attitudes of passengers;
- Attitudes of bus operators; and
- Boarding time for a person using a wheelchair.

CHAPTER 7 TEACHING PASSENGERS TO USE THE FIXED-ROUTE SYSTEM -- TRAVEL TRAINING

Perform those types of market research required by the prospective travel training alternative.

The following market research approaches help identify whether the assumptions people with disabilities have regarding these issues are supported by research.

PASSENGER ATTITUDE SURVEY

To measure passenger attitudes, administer a short survey at some major transit stops, or mail the survey to a sample of transit users. At transit stops, make every effort to distribute it throughout the service day to ensure that a representative group of respondents is contacted. The survey should also be distributed in an organized fashion (for example, either given to everyone or to every second, third, fourth, or fifth individual waiting at the bus stop).

A survey can also be administered through the mail. Mailing lists might be available from monthly pass lists, from lists of names and addresses supplied in previous surveys, or from a list of people attending previous public hearings and meetings.

Questions that could be used in a survey to find out if transit patrons are concerned about the boarding times required by people who use wheelchairs are shown in Figure 7-3.

CHAPTER 7 TEACHING PASSENGERS TO USE THE FIXED-ROUTE SYSTEM -- TRAVEL TRAINING

Passengers are more likely to respond to a short survey.

```
1. Have you ever observed a person in a wheelchair boarding a bus?
      ___ YES  ___ NO

2. If YES, how long do you think the boarding took?

      ___ Less than 1 Minute
      ___ Between 1 and 2 Minutes
      ___ Between 2 and 3 Minutes
      ___ Between 3 and 4 Minutes
      ___ Longer than 4 Minutes

3. How would you rate your concern about the use of wheelchair lifts delaying
   bus schedules and operations?

      ___ Not Concerned
      ___ Somewhat Concerned
      ___ Very Concerned

4. Have you ever given up your seat to a person with a disability or an elderly
   person?

      ___ YES
      ___ NO

5. If you answered YES to question 4, how did you feel about being displaced?

      ___ Helpful
      ___ Awkward
      ___ Resentful
      ___ Angry
      ___ Does not apply-Have not had to give up my seat
      ___ Other_____
              (Please Indicate)
```

Figure 7-3 Passenger Attitude Survey Questions

Distribute the passenger attitude survey to as many people as possible.

Make an effort to distribute this survey to as many people as possible, so an accurate measure can be taken of how the transit patrons feel. If the survey is to be mailed back, be sure to follow up to ensure adequate response.

CHAPTER 7 TEACHING PASSENGERS TO USE THE FIXED-ROUTE SYSTEM -- TRAVEL TRAINING

BUS OPERATOR ATTITUDE SURVEY

A bus operator attitude survey should be conducted as part of an operator sensitivity program.

Measure operator sensitivity through a survey administered prior to sensitivity training. This will help the instructors gauge the degree to which sensitivity training is necessary. A survey done prior to sensitivity training is likely to provide a better indication of sensitivity than a survey done afterward. After training, people may answer the questionnaire in a manner that management seeks, even though answers may not mirror the respondents' thoughts.

Doing a survey too close in time to a sensitivity class may produce false statements. Doing a survey at another time, such as mailing it out to all drivers or leaving it in their assignment boxes may solicit more honest responses. If people are not paid for the time they take to answer the survey, the response rate may be low. It is likely that drivers who have serious sensitivity problems will not answer the survey. Thus, it is probably best to administer a survey immediately prior to a compulsory sensitivity program, when they will be paid to answer the survey.

Some of the questions which could be asked by a survey of bus operators are in Figure 7-4.

Use survey results to find areas for additional training and to advertise driver skills.

Using the responses to the survey, determine whether particular areas require additional driver sensitivity training. Conduct surveys on a continuing basis, in order to assess whether or not additional sensitivity training is required. Share the survey results with the bus operators to impress upon them the importance of sensitivity to people with disabilities.

If the survey indicates a high degree of operator sensitivity and awareness, consider a publicity campaign, directed at people with disabilities, to advertise operator skills. This can be combined with other positive market research results.

CHAPTER 7 TEACHING PASSENGERS TO USE THE FIXED-ROUTE SYSTEM -- TRAVEL TRAINING

1. Do you personally know anyone with a disability?

    __Yes
    __No
    __Not sure

2. How often do you have contact with people with disabilities?

    ___Daily
    ___At least once a month
    ___Less than once a month
    ___Not sure

3. Is there any person with a disability whom you can call a close friend or relative?

    ___Yes
    ___No
    ___Not sure

4. Thinking about jobs, housing, transportation, and access to public places, how much discrimination do you think there is against people with disabilities overall?

    ___A great deal
    ___Some
    ___Not too much
    ___None at all
    ___Not sure

5a. Place an X next to anyone you know with a disability.
    (Mark all that apply.)

    ___ A coworker, supervisor, or employee
    ___ A patron who rides your bus
    ___ A neighbor
    ___ An employee in a local store, restaurant, or business
    ___ A friend
    ___ A child in the neighborhood
    ___ A member of your household
    ___.A relative in your household
    ___ Another relative (outside your immediate household)

Figure 7-4 Bus Operator Survey Questions

CHAPTER 7 TEACHING PASSENGERS TO USE THE FIXED-ROUTE SYSTEM -- TRAVEL TRAINING

> 5b. For each person you know with a disability, indicate whether you feel the relationship is generally pleasant and easy or is strained and uncomfortable due to his or her disability.
>
> | Pleasant and Easy | Strained and Uncomfortable | |
> |---|---|---|
> | ___ | ___ | A coworker, supervisor, or employee |
> | ___ | ___ | A patron who rides your bus |
> | ___ | ___ | A neighbor |
> | ___ | ___ | An employee in a local store, restaurant, or business |
> | ___ | ___ | A friend |
> | ___ | ___ | A child in the neighborhood |
> | ___ | ___ | A member of your household |
> | ___ | ___ | A relative in your household |
> | ___ | ___ | Another relative (outside your immediate household) |
>
> 6. Many parking lots have spaces for drivers with disabilities. Do you think there are too many of these spaces, too few, or about the right number?
> ___Too many
> ___Too few
> ___About right
> ___Not sure
>
> 7. Do you feel people with disabilities are discriminated against in the following circumstances?
>
> | Yes | No | |
> |---|---|---|
> | ___ | ___ | Equal pay for equal work |
> | ___ | ___ | Equal opportunity in employment |
> | ___ | ___ | Equal access to education |
> | ___ | ___ | Equal access to public transportation |
> | ___ | ___ | Equal access to public places like stores, restaurants, and places of worship |
> | ___ | ___ | Equal access to theaters and sports events |

Figure 7-4 Bus Operator Survey Questions (Continued)

CHAPTER 7 TEACHING PASSENGERS TO USE THE FIXED-ROUTE SYSTEM -- TRAVEL TRAINING

8. Do you think there is more or less discrimination against people with disabilities than there was 10 years ago?

    ___More
    ___Less
    ___Same
    ___Not sure

9. How long do you think it takes a wheelchair to board a bus?

    ___Less than 1 minute
    ___Between 1 and 2 minutes
    ___Between 2 and 3 minutes
    ___Between 3 and 4 minutes
    ___Between 4 and 6 minutes
    ___Between 6 and 8 minutes
    ___Between 8 and 10 minutes
    ___More than 10 minutes

10. When you encounter a person with a severe disability, how often do you feel the following emotions?

Often	Occasionally	Never	
___	___	___	Anger, because they cause inconvenience
___	___	___	Fear, because you feel what's happened to them might happen to you
___	___	___	Awkwardness or embarrassment, because you don't know how to behave with them
___	___	___	Resentment, because they get special privileges
___	___	___	Pity, because of their situation
___	___	___	Lack of concern, because they can manage okay
___	___	___	Admiration, because they overcome so much

Figure 7-4- Bus Operator Survey Questions (Continued)

CHAPTER 7 TEACHING PASSENGERS TO USE THE FIXED-ROUTE SYSTEM -- TRAVEL TRAINING

---

11. How do you feel when you're assigned a lift-equipped bus? (Check as many as is appropriate.)

    ___ <u>Angry</u>, because operating the lift is a hassle
    ___ <u>Fearful</u>, because you don't know how to deal with people with disabilities
    ___ <u>Awkward</u>, because you're not familiar with lift operation
    ___ <u>Stressful</u>, because you think a wheelchair boarding will put you behind schedule
    ___ <u>Neutral</u>, because you're used to dealing with people with disabilities

12. Do you feel embarrassed or awkward because you don't know whether or not people with disabilities want you to help them?

    ___ Yes
    ___ No
    ___ Not sure

Figure 7-4. Bus Operator Survey Questions (Concluded)

WHEELCHAIR BOARDING TIME STUDIES

An important issue, as people with disabilities increase their use of fixed-route transit, is the time it takes to board using a wheelchair and the impact on the schedule. Conduct research to measure the time it takes to board. This is particularly important after accessible vehicles have been in use for a period of time and when active efforts are being made to attract people with disabilities to fixed-route services. Follow the steps below for a boarding time study:

1. Select a set of bus routes where people using wheelchairs frequently board. This can generally be identified by collecting information from regular driver counts or through a brief survey of bus drivers.

2. Organize a group of volunteers or others to conduct the survey. The survey teams should include a person using a wheelchair and a person not using a wheelchair. Seek

CHAPTER 7 TEACHING PASSENGERS TO USE THE FIXED-ROUTE SYSTEM -- TRAVEL TRAINING

volunteers from the travel training oversight committee, other advisory committees, staff, or particular client groups. Seek volunteers from among those using manual and powered wheelchairs and 3-wheel scooters.

3. Assign the survey teams to particular segments of the chosen bus route during specific trips, boarding at specific locations. The tests should be conducted at peak and at non-peak times.

4. Issue each team a stopwatch to time boarding and deboarding times for people using wheelchairs. Boarding times should begin when the bus operator begins deploying the lift and should end when the operator returns to his or her seat after the wheelchair has been secured. Deboarding times should begin when the operator begins to undo the wheelchair securing straps/hooks and should end when the person is on the sidewalk.

5. Record the entire time required to negotiate the allotted route segment. While they are doing this, perform boarding and alighting tests of persons using wheelchairs and record them on a form similar to the one displayed in Figure 7-5. Note on the form any circumstances that might hinder people boarding in wheelchairs. The more common comments might be summarized numerically as in Figure 7-5.

6. During the same day of the week, during approximately the same weather conditions, record times over the same route segment to indicate how long it takes a bus to negotiate the route segment without wheelchair boardings or deboardings.

Perform analyses, using any standard statistical package to compute such information as the average boarding and deboarding times and the standard deviation. Two thirds of the boarding and deboarding times should be within one standard deviation. This information will determine the actual time that people using wheelchairs take to board fixed-route transit buses.

CHAPTER 7 TEACHING PASSENGERS TO USE THE FIXED-ROUTE SYSTEM -- TRAVEL TRAINING

BOARDING TIME SURVEY

SURVEYING TEAM _____

Route and Segment # _____

DATE _____

Trip Number	Bus Type	Boarding Location	Dir. (N,S, E,W)	Due to Arrive	Arrival Time	Board Time	Depart Time	Alighting Location	Due to Arrive	Arrival Time	Alight Time	Depart Time	Comments

COMMENTS

1. Two wheelchair users boarded.
2. Two wheelchair users alighted.
3. Lift jammed at boarding location.
4. Lift jammed at alighting location.
5. Driver did not apply securement system.
6. Bus type was not as indicated.
7. Bus awaited transfer enroute.
8. Unusual stop enroute (explain)

Figure 7-5. Boarding Time Survey

CHAPTER 7 TEACHING PASSENGERS TO USE THE FIXED-ROUTE SYSTEM -- TRAVEL TRAINING

The preceding studies are by no means exclusive, but they do demonstrate the types of market research that can be used as a foundation for a travel training program. The research results will be particularly useful in the informational presentation or general travel training models. The information can help convince people that using fixed-route transportation is a viable transit alternative.

STEP 5: SELECT A TRAINING MODEL AND APPROACH

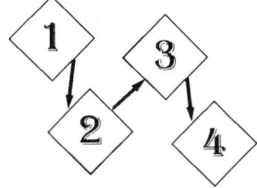

Select the travel training model and approach with as much input as possible from the oversight committee -- their involvement is critical for the success of a travel training program, no matter what model is chosen.

Earlier discussion identified the basic travel training model alternatives available. These are as follows:

- Informational presentations;
- Training tailored to an individual;
- Peer model training; and
- General travel training.

Determining which model to use in travel training is a function of the needs of a community; the amount of market research work required; the availability of expertise, time, and funding at the transit system; and the availability of expertise, time, and funding in the community at large. Figure 7-6 summarizes the characteristics of the four travel training alternatives. Based upon the needs identified and the resources available to do travel training, identify a model. Then identify an approach for performing this model.

CHAPTER 7 TEACHING PASSENGERS TO USE THE FIXED-ROUTE SYSTEM -- TRAVEL TRAINING

Make a final determination of the travel training model alternative to be used in the community.

CHARACTERISTICS	TRAVEL TRAINING MODEL ALTERNATIVES			
	Informational Presentation	Tailored Travel Training	Peer Model Training	General Travel Training
Needs met	People with Disabilities, Elderly	People with Disabilities	People with Disabilities	People with Disabilities, Elderly, General Public
Amount of market research required	High	Low	Low	Low
Amount of transit system expertise required	Low	Low-High	Medium	Low
Amount of transit system time required	Low	Low-High	Low	Low
Amount of transit system funding required	Low	High	Low	Low
Amount of community expertise required	Low	High (Low, if program is already present)	Medium	Low
Amount of community time required	Low	High	Low	Low
Amount of community funding required	Low	High (Low if program is already present)	Low	Low

Figure 7-6. **Characteristics of Travel Training Models**

7-24

CHAPTER 7 TEACHING PASSENGERS TO USE THE FIXED-ROUTE SYSTEM -- TRAVEL TRAINING

Essentially four approaches can be used in travel training. The four are as follows:

- In house training;
- Referral system;
- Outside firm; and
- Peer-to-peer training.

Table 7-2 shows the most appropriate approaches for each of the training model alternatives. Informational presentations can be made by in-house staff, or members of the community can conduct them for their peers. Although in-house expertise may exist, training tailored to an individual is often best approached through an outside firm or organization, either through a contractual arrangement or on a referral basis. The peer model can be best implemented through referral to groups in the community and by special arrangements with them or through a peer-to-peer approach. General travel training can be conducted in house or through members of the community.

Table 7-2. Most Appropriate Approaches For Training Model Alternatives

Approaches	Informational Presentations	Tailored Travel Training	Peer Model	General Travel Training
In-House Training	✓			✓
Referral System		✓	✓	
Outside Firm		✓		
Peer-to-Peer Training	✓		✓	✓

To do effective travel training, an organization should have expertise in some areas of the health and social sciences.

To accomplish effective travel training, an organization should have expertise in those portions of physical therapy, occupational therapy, and psychology which affect a person's decision to use one method of travel over another. While a few major transit systems may have hired people with this expertise to do ADA paratransit certification or other duties, they are not always present in house at most systems.

CHAPTER 7 TEACHING PASSENGERS TO USE THE FIXED-ROUTE SYSTEM -- TRAVEL TRAINING

Organizations that are part of the travel training oversight committee may have the needed expertise. They may supply training that can be integrated into a program. If this is the case, the transit system's role might be to organize a program to use these resources.

In deciding upon a travel training approach, determine the role of volunteers.

In deciding which travel training approach will be used, determine how volunteers can provide some of the resources needed by the program. In communities with a significant pool of volunteers, much of the travel training can be accomplished by them. This can save a transit system money. In communities without a ready pool of volunteers, an approach requiring significant personal interaction may be expensive.

The availability of funding and staff resources is important. Money may be available from internal transit system resources or from some type of external grant source. The amount of money will determine what type of program can be funded. Similarly, the staff resources that can be committed to a training program affect what type of program can be implemented. There may be expertise on hand to do travel training; however, consider how the commitment of staff time will affect other work areas.

IN-HOUSE TRAINING

To do travel training in house, identify staffing requirements. Develop presentations on general information about the transit system and the features buses have that can assist people with disabilities. General training should encompass how much the fare is, how to obtain transit timetables, how to read timetables, how to use the system map, and how and why one requests transfers when boarding buses.

If travel training is conducted in house, responsibilities for each of the training models vary. For informational presentations and general travel training, responsibilities include the following:

CHAPTER 7 TEACHING PASSENGERS TO USE THE FIXED-ROUTE SYSTEM -- TRAVEL TRAINING

For travel training done in house, transit system responsibilities will vary depending on the travel training model chosen.

- Development of materials;
- Production of materials, including handouts and audio-visual items;
- Identification of presentation sites;
- Scheduling and coordination of presentations;
- Identification and assignment of staff time for presentations and other tasks;
- Advertising; and
- Notification of presenters.

For training tailored to an individual, responsibilities include the following:

- Development of a tailored program, which may or may not be based on a standard program;
- Varying levels of coordination with outside agencies;
- Staff training and education;
- Identification and dedication of professional staff time;
- Identification of trainees;
- Scheduling and coordination of trainees and trainers; and
- Distribution of fare media or vouchers for training rides.

For peer model training, responsibilities include the following:

- Identification of an adequate pool of peers for training needs;
- Contractual, in-kind, or volunteer arrangements with peers;
- Identification of trainees;
- Scheduling and coordination of trainees and trainers; and
- Distribution of fare media or vouchers for training rides.

Determine, on the basis of available in house resources and staff, whether in-house training is the best approach. Conducting training in house offers control of the level, amount, and type of training provided. If the training provides considerable benefits -- by moving people onto fixed-route services, by improving community relations, or by expanding the role and responsibilities of people with disabilities within the transit agency -- the program may be expanded as resources allow.

CHAPTER 7 TEACHING PASSENGERS TO USE THE FIXED-ROUTE SYSTEM -- TRAVEL TRAINING

If travel training presentations are made at outlying locations, look for places that are convenient for trainees.

Some systems require all people who are determined eligible for ADA paratransit to go through a short course in using fixed-route. The purpose is to make everyone aware of the availability of fixed-route transit. Even if paratransit is the preferred method of travel, there may be occasions when fixed-route transit is an option. For example, when a person is traveling with a companion, fixed-route transit service may be preferred because of lower cost or greater convenience.

Be careful in selecting travel training presentation sites. Often, the easiest place for a presentation is on site. Unfortunately, transit terminals and even the transit system's general offices are sometimes difficult to reach.

Presentations made in outlying areas should be convenient for trainees. Travel training should also occur at convenient times and days of the week. Often a good option is Saturday morning or afternoon. Be sure the presentation site (particularly the rest rooms, entrances, stairwells, and elevators) is accessible to people with disabilities. The site should also be in a safe area.

REFERRAL SYSTEM

Another approach to travel training is the referral system. In this approach, system personnel do not do any training themselves, but refer candidates to experts in the community who perform travel training. Identify trainers who are experts in various areas, based on passenger disabilities and training requirements. Organizations which provide services to people with disabilities may identify trainers (for example, their staff members, people with disabilities with whom they work, or others in the community with whom they have contact). An organization for people with vision impairments, for example, may be equipped to train people in transit travel. Contact community organizations to identify training which already takes place and the sources of expertise. Arrange for referrals from the paratransit eligibility process or other procedures to the organizations that can provide training.

Develop a database with all of the gathered information to set up the referral system. The database should include any

CHAPTER 7 TEACHING PASSENGERS TO USE THE FIXED-ROUTE SYSTEM -- TRAVEL TRAINING

A database is an essential element of a referral system.

community resources that can assist a person desiring travel training. This database should include the following:

- The name of the agency,
- Areas of expertise (travel training skills),
- The names of the people the agency will serve,
- The names of contact people,
- Geographic area, and
- Date of information.

This information is typically available from large umbrella organizations such as the United Way. Telephone the various appropriate agencies to identify points of contact and willingness to cooperate with a transit agency in a program of travel training. The oversight committee is also a valuable resource. Members should be consulted to obtain referral information prior to any major data-gathering activity.

Although this approach does not require much involvement of in-house transit system staff, it is still necessary for someone sensitive to the needs of people with disabilities to make the referrals at the transit system. This person should understand and be able to take the initiative to acquire additional resources if a special need arises.

OUTSIDE FIRM

To hire an outside firm to do travel training, develop an RFP. Set up a committee, to develop the RFP, composed of transit system staff members and people with disabilities. While the RFP should include all of the basic contractual RFP components, include these additional items:

- Discussion of the definition of travel training;
- An indication of the types of disabilities that will require travel training;
- An indication of the type and amount of effort that will be required to do travel training;
- A requirement that the proposers indicate their approach to travel training;
- A requirement for a clear statement indicating the expertise the proposer has to do travel training;

CHAPTER 7 TEACHING PASSENGERS TO USE THE FIXED-ROUTE SYSTEM -- TRAVEL TRAINING

- An indication of what the relationship of the transit system and travel training firm will be after the firm has been chosen;
- A requirement for the firm to indicate the types of reports it will make regularly on its expenditure of funds;
- The transit system's measures to monitor the performance of the contract;
- The process to be used if the proposers wish to develop joint venture proposals; and
- The method of payment to the selected contractor.

Decide the criteria which will be used to evaluate the RFP.

Before the RFP is circulated, work with members of the selection committee to develop criteria for evaluating proposals. Some possible criteria might include the following items:

- The experience of the proposing firm in doing training for people with disabilities;
- The experience of the people identified in the proposal in training people with disabilities;
- The quality of the approach suggested by the proposing firm;
- The cost of the service being provided;
- The degree to which the proposal provides a comprehensive approach to travel training for all people with disabilities;
- The degree to which the proposed services will interface with other services for people with disabilities;
- Financial viability of the proposer; and
- Adequacy of services and equipment.

A strict set of criteria must be established before the proposals are evaluated, so everyone knows exactly what they are. Attach numerical weights to the evaluation criteria, so that the reviewers can assign specific scores in each category.

To determine who should receive the RFP, conduct an inventory of potential travel training providers. Probably the best potential providers are local social service agencies who know the problems encountered by people with disabilities and know how to address them (either internally or by referral to other agencies). If an organization can draw upon national experts when required, it is a definite advantage.

CHAPTER 7 TEACHING PASSENGERS TO USE THE FIXED-ROUTE SYSTEM -- TRAVEL TRAINING

If any travel training work is done by outside agencies, develop a monitoring method.

While it is probably best to have this work done by a local agency, in some cases the level of expertise may not be present to do effective travel training. If this is the case, send the RFP to national companies that specialize in travel training, or the state or regional offices of national groups. If in doubt about whom to send RFPs to, contact local agencies for their input.

If any travel training work is contracted to outside agencies, develop a method to ensure that the contractor is providing a continuously high-quality product. The RFP should include reporting requirements, follow-up studies, trainee surveys, training program evaluation forms completed by trainees and caregivers, and other mechanisms to monitor the quality of the services.

PEER-TO-PEER TRAINING

One of the lowest cost and most productive methods of travel training is peer-to-peer training. This approach can either be used by itself or with other travel training approaches. It involves a person with a disability serving as a coach for another person who has a disability. The coach travels with the trainee and shows the trainee exactly what he or she must do to use the transit system effectively.

The coach can show the trainee how to do the following:

- Select a transit route;
- Determine the fare (types and amount of fare payment);
- Hail a bus;
- Use a wheelchair lift; and
- Pay the fare.

The coach can also show the trainee what the bus operator will do for the patron.

This approach requires the identification of individuals who will act as trainers for travel training. One ready source of volunteers may be members of the oversight committee or people they know.

CHAPTER 7 TEACHING PASSENGERS TO USE THE FIXED-ROUTE SYSTEM -- TRAVEL TRAINING

These volunteers may require instruction in some aspects of travel training. The instruction for coaches should include training in the following topics:

- An overview of public transit in the community;
- Reviews of all bus routes in a system and the major points of interest near them;
- The transit system's fares;
- The process used to determine ADA paratransit eligibility;
- The process used to apply for a reduced fare identification card for people with disabilities;
- The process used to hail a bus, particularly for those with vision impairments;
- The process of boarding, securing, and alighting a person in a wheelchair; and
- The process for registering a complaint or offering a suggestion.

In the class for instructors, convey tips that can be used by students to make travel by fixed-route transit easier. Include what subjects should be brought up, what types of training approaches can be used, and tips for travel training.

After the trainers have been trained, assign candidates for travel training to those who will be most compatible with them. Some traits that should be considered in assigning peer coaches to students include the following:

- Similar demographic background;
- Similar outside interests;
- The pace of learning the student seems to prefer;
- Similarity of disabilities; and
- Similarity of outlook on life.

CHAPTER 7 TEACHING PASSENGERS TO USE THE FIXED-ROUTE SYSTEM -- TRAVEL TRAINING

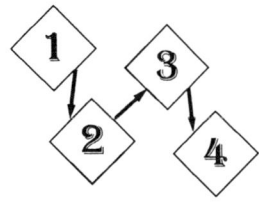

STEP 6: DEVELOP TRAVEL TRAINING MATERIALS

A travel training program is a good opportunity to assess whether information for the general public and for people with disabilities is adequately informing people about transit services.

Examine the schedules to see if they are easy to read. Ask the travel training oversight committee to review the format of schedules to ensure that they are readable by people with disabilities. Ensure that no color is used on the schedule that cannot be detected by people with limited vision or color blindness. Develop an approach for providing schedule information to people with visual impairments.

Clearly present all fare information on one panel of the schedule or brochure. The availability of reduced fares for older riders and people with disabilities during off-peak hours must be indicated on the schedule. Note in the schedule that a transit rider must present a Medicare card or some other type of identification when they board the bus to be eligible for the discounted fare. Be sure that people can find and read the fare information.

The introduction of a travel training program is an opportunity to review those materials that describe the transit system and how to use it.

If the transit system is not fully accessible, indicate accessible bus routes. Provide clear directions for times when a wheelchair-lift-equipped bus is not scheduled. These directions should indicate whether there is a fixed-route accessible bus demand program or how a person can secure complementary ADA paratransit.

Examine the system map to make sure that it shows all bus routes in the system through graphic techniques that make the map easy to use for all people. On the system map, identify basic information about fare programs for people with disabilities and other programs, such as the travel training program, that are oriented to patrons with disabilities.

CHAPTER 7 TEACHING PASSENGERS TO USE THE FIXED-ROUTE SYSTEM -- TRAVEL TRAINING

Develop an article about fixed-route services available for people with disabilities.

Develop an article about fixed-route transit services available to people with disabilities. Indicate basic information regarding how to use a bus; transit fares; how to obtain materials in accessible format; and boarding, securing, and disembarking passengers using wheelchairs. Figure 7-7 illustrates such an article.

Consider developing specific materials for travel training use, such as an article that debunks some of the myths about riding fixed-route buses. Some of the myths that arise and the ways to discredit them are shown in Figure 7-8.

Another article could describe efforts to address the needs of people with disabilities, to encourage people to use transit, and to offer travel training to people who wish it. While most of the materials will be required for travel training itself, some materials will be for home reference. Travel trainers should have copies of all timetables and system maps to help people identify which transit services to use.

Develop home reference materials.

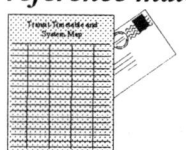

To develop new materials that are easy to use, refer to schedules and brochures developed by other transit systems.

Travel trainers may develop a small, pocket-sized information card to distribute with all important information about using fixed-route buses, including phone numbers to call in an emergency. An example card is shown as Figure 7-9.

CHAPTER 7 TEACHING PASSENGERS TO USE THE
FIXED-ROUTE SYSTEM -- TRAVEL TRAINING

HOW BUSES CAN SERVE YOU	**What to Do First** _____ _____ **How to Get Transit Information** _____ _____ **Fares Information** _____ _____ **How to Get Bus Schedules** _____ _____ **How to Identify Your Bus** _____ _____	**Programs for People with Disabilities** -Off-peak reduced fare program for people with disabilities -On-call, accessible fixed-route buses -Completely accessible routes -Signaling devices for those with vision impairments -Travel training programs **Telephone Number for Additional Transit Info. For People with Disabilities**	**Procedures for Boarding People Using Wheelchairs** -Hailing the Bus _____ -Using the Wheelchair Lift _____ -Being Secured in the Bus _____ -Paying the Fare _____ -Deboarding the Bus _____ **Compliments or Complaints General Transit Information Telephone Number**

Figure 7-7. Sample Information Article

CHAPTER 7 TEACHING PASSENGERS TO USE THE FIXED-ROUTE SYSTEM -- TRAVEL TRAINING

Myth	Method for Discrediting Myth
➣ Boarding a person in a wheelchair takes too much time.	➣ Boarding time studies.
➣ People with disabilities are likely to be the victims of criminals if they use fixed-route transit.	➣ Security program--crime statistics.
➣ Bus operators are unfriendly and not sensitive to the needs of people with disabilities.	➣ Bus operator attitude surveys. ➣ Training programs.
➣ Fixed-route buses are unreliable.	➣ On-time statistics from a transit agency.
➣ Wheelchair lifts are unreliable.	➣ Procedures and training for maintaining lifts. ➣ Statistics on lift reliability.
➣ Fixed-route buses are always getting into accidents.	➣ Transit agency safety program. ➣ Accident statistics.

Figure 7-8. Myths and Methods to Discredit Them

The Super Transit Authority			Telephone Number
➣ Number of general transit travel information			555-1000
➣ Number for customer complaints			555-2000
➣ Number of ADA paratransit provider			555-3000
➣ Number to call if problems occur after the customer complaint office closes			555-4000
➣ People at transit agency who can be notified if problems occur			
Name:	Terry Transit	Tel.	555-5555
Name:	Barry Bus	Tel.	555-5556
Name:	Sharon Schedule	Tel.	555-5557

Figure 7-9. Travel Training Information Card

CHAPTER 7 TEACHING PASSENGERS TO USE THE FIXED-ROUTE SYSTEM -- TRAVEL TRAINING

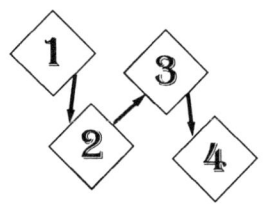

STEP 7: IMPLEMENT THE APPROACH

The following discussion identifies some of the issues that should be raised in implementing a travel training program.

DEFINE THE TRAINING AUDIENCE

Define the audience adequately.

Define the target audience for travel training adequately. People with different types of disabilities have profoundly different training needs. People who use wheelchairs will want to know about the procedures for hailing a transit bus, boarding while using a wheelchair, securing a wheelchair and passenger, and deboarding in a wheelchair. People with visual impairments may be more concerned with the specifics of a journey from their house to some of their most common destinations, including work, school, or shopping. People with hearing impairments may be concerned about how a driver can respond to questions and how they can indicate that their bus stop is coming up.

When developing a program, allow enough variation to address any possible needs of people with disabilities.

DEFINE TRAINING OBJECTIVES AND TOPICS

Be clear about what will be accomplished with a travel training program and which topics will be discussed to accomplish these objectives. A travel training program might have the overall objective of making the use of fixed-route buses the mode of choice. To this end, a set of topics might include the information shown in Figure 7-10.

Develop a set of training objectives and topics that will address those needs as identified in conversations with advisory groups and in any market research work that is done.

CHAPTER 7 TEACHING PASSENGERS TO USE THE FIXED-ROUTE SYSTEM -- TRAVEL TRAINING

> 1. How to use a bus--
>   a) bus schedules,
>   b) system maps, and
>   c) paying your fares;
>
> 2. Discrediting popular myths about bus riding --
>   a) attitudes of drivers and
>   b) attitudes of passengers who do not have a disability; and
>
> 3. Training people in riding a bus --
>   a) summoning the bus,
>   b) boarding a bus using a wheelchair,
>   c) securing a wheelchair and passenger in a bus, and
>   d) deboarding a bus.

Figure 7-10. Training Objectives and Topics

IDENTIFY TRIP GENERATORS

Use the oversight committee to help identify major trip generators that are either trip origins or trip destinations for people with disabilities. Some possible sites are the following:

- Large apartment complexes;
- Large employers;
- Shopping centers;
- Hospitals;
- Educational facilities;
- Houses of worship;
- Community centers; and
- Rehabilitation centers.

In addition to data that can be acquired from members of the oversight committee about the local trip generators, use a list of the most common origins and destinations served by the ADA complementary paratransit service. This list will be valuable in a number of ways. Plot destinations on a map to check the distribution of accessible fixed-route buses to see if they can be adjusted to better serve the origins and destinations of people with disabilities. If informational presentations are given, use this list as a starting point of sites for general presentations about travel training or as an actual travel training program.

CHAPTER 7 TEACHING PASSENGERS TO USE THE FIXED-ROUTE SYSTEM -- TRAVEL TRAINING

TRAINING BUS

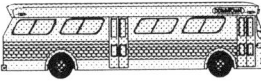

An important tool for travel training is an actual bus that people would encounter as they travel by fixed-route. Because many of those being trained have never been on a transit bus before, it is necessary to demonstrate how to signal to be picked up by a bus, how a wheelchair lift works, how a wheelchair and passenger are secured, how a fare is paid, and how a patron indicates to a driver that he or she wishes to get off a bus.

If there are different types of transit buses, with different wheelchair lift locations or securement positions, have examples of these different types of buses at travel training sessions. This is particularly important if some of the buses in the transit system's fleet have rear-door-mounted wheelchair lifts, while others have front-door-mounted lifts.

Consider having small groups ride together on the system.

As part of the training, consider having small groups ride together on the system, make transfers, and encounter as many circumstances as possible. To make the training most effective, do the following:

- Break large groups into groups of three to five people and have each small group ride with a trainer;
- Ride during off-peak hours to avoid crowds, but not if the headways would be too long;
- Plan transfers at stops with a number of routes, so the trainer can teach trainees about identifying routes;
- Provide regular fare media to trainees, such as tickets or tokens, but train them on how and where to purchase their own; and
- Be sure operators are notified that travel training may occur on their vehicles at any time, with dispatchers providing current information.

CHAPTER 7 TEACHING PASSENGERS TO USE THE FIXED-ROUTE SYSTEM -- TRAVEL TRAINING

SLIDE PRESENTATIONS

Another tool to use for travel training is an audiovisual display. The least expensive and most flexible is a slide show illustrating how a person with a disability can utilize fixed-route transit. While this technique can be used, it depends upon the presentation skills of the person doing the training. A more expensive display than a slide show is a video. A video can provide a uniform presentation (which can be critiqued by an oversight committee) and can provide a consistent explanation of all major points covered in a travel training program.

SELECTING TRAINERS

Three types of trainers can be used in a travel training program: representatives from the transit system; other paid professionals; and volunteers.

Transit System Representatives

Three types of individuals can engage in travel training from a transit system. These are highly skilled professionals who are familiar with the transportation concerns of people with disabilities, other professionals, and bus operators.

Highly skilled professionals, sensitive to the needs of people with disabilities, are generally involved in providing ADA complementary paratransit. While their talents can be used for any of the travel training model alternatives, they are most needed if a program of travel training tailored to the individual is chosen. They might be involved in the initial determination that a person is not eligible for ADA complementary paratransit, but would benefit from travel training. These people may be engaged in some of the individualized instruction that is part of travel training. If travel training is done by an outside entity, this person would be the logical choice to monitor the contractor's performance.

CHAPTER 7 TEACHING PASSENGERS TO USE THE FIXED-ROUTE SYSTEM -- TRAVEL TRAINING

Other professionals at the transit system can be involved in making informational presentations about travel training and in providing general travel training. Included in this group may be individuals from the travel information center who can give travel planning assistance with general travel planning sessions.

Bus operators also can assist with travel training. They are often the most knowledgeable, experienced, and empathetic of all transit employees. If a decision is made to employ a training bus as part of an informational presentation, an operator or qualified staff person must be assigned to drive the bus to a site and operate the wheelchair lift. This person must also be aware of the needs of people with disabilities. Select an operator who is particularly friendly with passengers, talkative, well informed about the system and the service area, and skilled in the use of accessibility equipment. The appearance of a friendly, competent operator will encourage people to trust the transit system to transport them.

Other Professionals

Develop a cooperative relationship with community agencies that can assist in travel training.

In addition to transit system personnel, involve other paid professionals in travel training, particularly training tailored to an individual. The inventory of community resources will reveal programs offered by other agencies which can be used by those being travel trained. Developing a cooperative relationship with these agencies can result in high-quality training, through referrals, at a very low cost. Consider working with community agencies to jointly develop training programs that can then be administered by transit system professionals. Combine transit expertise with expertise on the capabilities of people with disabilities to develop an effective program.

The second set of outside professionals involved in travel training may include people or organizations contracted by the transit system. Employ outside professionals if there are insufficient internal transit system and local agency resources, there is a commitment by the transit system to do individualized travel training, and the funds exist to accomplish this goal.

CHAPTER 7 TEACHING PASSENGERS TO USE THE FIXED-ROUTE SYSTEM -- TRAVEL TRAINING

Volunteers

Volunteers can be recruited from the oversight committee or on their recommendation. Volunteers with disabilities have firsthand experience of some of the challenges in using fixed-route buses. A person being travel trained may be more comfortable asking questions of a person with a similar disability.

ADVERTISING

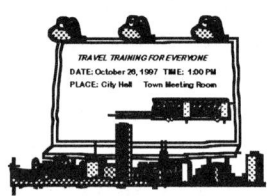

After a travel training program has been developed, advertise its availability to all who might want to avail themselves of it.

Review the list of trip generators and identify those where travel training could assist many people. These locations should be contacted and, optimally, they can serve as sites for training. If they agree to be sites or agree to cooperate, post notices about training at these locations or at nearby sites, distribute brochures describing the program, insert information in newsletters or local newspapers for these locations, and make presentations at meetings held at these locations.

Other sources of travel training candidates are organizations that are advocates for the needs of people with disabilities. A notice in these organizations' newsletters can be very effective publicity.

Send notices to any people who are using ADA paratransit who might be candidates for travel training to see if they are interested in the service.

Develop a campaign that encourages family members to participate.

Develop a campaign that encourages people to urge relatives with disabilities to be travel trained. This may involve the development of a short article that explains what training is, debunks some myths about travel training, and indicates some of travel training's benefits.

CHAPTER 7 TEACHING PASSENGERS TO USE THE FIXED-ROUTE SYSTEM -- TRAVEL TRAINING

Churches, synagogues, and mosques can often be used to heighten awareness of travel training and services. Make efforts to contact places of worship.

Contact local newspapers, particularly neighborhood papers, so they can write an article about the new training. Provide them with information and try to include a photograph of training taking place at a scenic location or a landmark.

The process of developing and implementing a travel training program is ongoing. Be alert to modifications to improve the training. Be aware of additional locations and organizations which might be enlisted to facilitate future travel training efforts. Once the first round of training is completed, do not assume the work is done. Travel training programs must be continually improved if they are to attract new riders.

ASSESS PARTICIPANTS' SKILL LEVELS

Assess the different skill levels of people in order to determine what kinds of travel training are appropriate.

In order to assess what types of travel training are appropriate for each individual, evaluate each candidate's abilities. This assessment may be as simple as taking all necessary information from the initial application form and making a decision.

The application for travel training should be a direct result of the outreach and paratransit eligibility determination process. As efforts are made to publicize training, applications should be distributed by transit agency personnel at various meetings they attend and mailed to anyone requesting them. An application form might include the information as shown in Figure 7-11.

CHAPTER 7 TEACHING PASSENGERS TO USE THE FIXED-ROUTE SYSTEM -- TRAVEL TRAINING

```
                Travel Training Application Form
Name
                                    _____

Address
                                    _____
                                    _____
                                    _____

Telephone Number                    _____
Age_____       Sex         _____M _____F

Do any of these conditions
apply to you:
➢ use a wheelchair                  _____Y _____N
➢ have difficulty seeing in
  daylight                          _____Y _____N
➢ have difficulty seeing
  during the nighttime              _____Y _____N
➢ require some type of
  mobility aid                      _____Y _____N
➢ have difficulty hearing           _____Y _____N
➢ other                             _____
                                    _____
                                    _____

Are you eligible for ADA paratransit?
_____ Yes         _____ No         _____ Don't know

What types of things would you like us to cover in a travel
training session?
                    _____
                    _____
                    _____

FOR ADDITIONAL INFORMATION CALL TRANSIT SYSTEM A
AT _____.
```

Figure 7-11. Travel Training Application Form

CHAPTER 7 TEACHING PASSENGERS TO USE THE FIXED-ROUTE SYSTEM -- TRAVEL TRAINING

The evaluation should be checked by telephone if there are any questions or if a reviewer cannot determine what type of travel training is appropriate from the application.

PERFORM TRAVEL TRAINING

A program should be developed which is tailored to the person or group being travel trained.

After all the preparatory work, travel training can begin. Tailor a program to the individual or group of people being travel trained. Information gathered on the travel training application form will indicate those specific skills requested by applicants. Instructors can emphasize and elaborate on these sections in the program. The program should address the topics as shown in Figure 7-12.

---

1. Discussion of the community's transit system
2. Reassurances
    a) Explain findings of market research involving the attitude of fellow passengers
    b) Explain market research concerning the attitude of drivers
3. Discussion of the materials needed to ride a fixed-route bus (schedules and route maps)
4. Transit fares
    a) Reduced fares
    b) Transfers
    c) Zone charges
    d) Other items as appropriate
5. Discussion of a bus
    a) Place to pay fare
    b) Place to get information
    c) Typical questions drivers can answer
    d) How to notify driver of the need to leave the bus
6. Wheelchair procedures (if needed)
    a) Boarding a bus using a lift
    b) Having a wheelchair and passenger secured in a bus
    c) Deboarding a bus
7. Explanations of incentives
    a) Free fares for an introductory number of trips or for all ADA-eligible trips
    b) Guaranteed ride program
8. Real-world practice
    a) Using the transit system with a travel trainer or companion
    b) Using the transit system individually
9. Resources available for future reference or assistance

Figure 7-12. Suggested Topics for Travel Training Program

CHAPTER 7 TEACHING PASSENGERS TO USE THE FIXED-ROUTE SYSTEM -- TRAVEL TRAINING

LISTS OF TRAVEL COMPANIONS AND TRAVEL TRAINERS

As part of travel training, consider matching riders with peer companions to travel with them on their first trips. For people with a low level of impairment, such assistance may be all that is necessary. For people with more significant impairments, a structured companion program may be necessary. Work with local agencies to develop the program. In general, companions can travel regularly with the rider, providing less and less assistance over time. By the end of the program, the companion travels separately from the rider and observes as the trips are completed independently.

Work with the project's oversight committee to compile a list of peer companions and qualified travel trainers who can accompany the newly trained individuals on trips.

STEP 8: EVALUATE THE PROGRAM

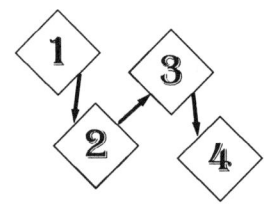

To determine if a travel training program has been a success, and warrants continuing support, measure the effectiveness of the program. Ways to evaluate a travel training program are discussed in the following subsections.

OBJECTIVE EVALUATION MEASURES

Use a number of objective measures to evaluate the program.

One objective evaluation method is to count the number of people who have participated in such travel training activities as informational presentations, training sessions, and surveys. The number of brochures distributed, the number of articles in various publications, and the number of interviews with reporters concerning the program could also be used to objectively measure the success of the program.

Another evaluation measure consists of counting the number of accessible bus boardings starting with a 4-year average. A 4-year average should be used initially because the number of boardings or persons using wheelchairs is generally so low in the absence of a serious program to increase the use of accessible fixed-routes that wide variations from year to year are likely.

7-46

CHAPTER 7 TEACHING PASSENGERS TO USE THE FIXED-ROUTE SYSTEM -- TRAVEL TRAINING

After travel training has occurred, survey those who received the training to determine whether their attitudes toward riding buses have changed and whether this change resulted in increased use of fixed-route buses by people with disabilities.

SUBJECTIVE EVALUATION MEASURES

Track the number of people who attend public hearings.

An indirect measure of whether or not the program is effective is to track the number of people with disabilities who attend public hearings. The number and type of complaints by people with disabilities also can help determine if some aspects of a travel training program should be changed.

Have the project formally or informally evaluated by members of the project oversight committee and by any general advisory committee of people with disabilities who assist the transit system.

CONCLUSIONS

Effective travel training is affected by Sensitivity training, equipment reliability and ADA paratransit determination system.

In this chapter, a series of steps have been presented that, if followed, can result in a valuable travel training program. These steps involve identifying a need for travel training, defining funding needs and resources, conducting public involvement, conducting market research, selecting a training model and approach, developing travel training materials, implementing the program, and evaluating the program.

While the previous discussions itemized the fundamental components of a travel training program, the following items (not intrinsically part of a program) can have a major effect on it:

- Proper sensitivity training, emergency response training, and training in recognizing people with hidden disabilities for all bus operators. If the operators are not adequately trained in these areas initially, and continually given refresher training, the best travel training can have little effect.

7-47

CHAPTER 7 TEACHING PASSENGERS TO USE THE FIXED-ROUTE SYSTEM -- TRAVEL TRAINING

- Equipment reliability. People who are travel trained have to feel confident that if they choose to use fixed-route transit, all equipment related to the wheelchair lift and securement hardware will be present and in good working order.

- A thorough review of a transit system's ADA paratransit eligibility determination system. In the absence of accessible bus services and a travel training program, many transit systems interpret the rules regarding functional disability very liberally. Tightening the interpretation of these rules becomes more feasible with a program of travel training in place. Reevaluation of the ADA paratransit eligibility determination process can result in many people, who are currently using ADA complementary paratransit, using fixed-route buses.

The intent of the ADA is to encourage people with disabilities to use mainstream community services, with complementary paratransit used only when their needs cannot be satisfied by accessible fixed-route service. Merely having a disability, physical or mental, is not sufficient for exclusive use of paratransit. Ideally, a single, non-biased third party should be involved in assessing eligibility for paratransit services. By rigorously enforcing the ADA paratransit eligibility requirements and offering a comprehensive travel training program for a quality fixed-route service, many current paratransit riders can become satisfied fixed-route transit riders.

CHAPTER 8: MARKETING FIXED-ROUTE SERVICES

CHAPTER 8 MARKETING FIXED-ROUTE SERVICES

INTRODUCTION

The purpose of a marketing campaign is to influence the behavior of people in a way that results in a willing exchange between the fixed-route system and the customer. The system exchanges a service for the time, money, or involvement of customers.

Historically, marketing was concerned with large groups of people -- the mass market. Consumers were treated as a more or less homogenous group, with similar needs, desires, and expectations. But recently, marketing has focused on defining groups of people more precisely into market segments or target markets or niche markets. Markets are segmented on the basis of several criteria (income, marital status, age, address, occupation, education, hobbies, buying patterns, etc.), that can be used in various combinations so that the fixed-route system is marketing services to a narrowly defined group of consumers.

Target markets, correctly defined, are exclusive yet exhaustive. They define a particular group of people and the definition can be applied to everyone in the group. Paratransit patrons form one such market segment. On the basis of transportation choice, they can be differentiated from fixed-route riders, from people who travel in a single occupant vehicle, and from people who walk to their destination. However, successful marketing to paratransit patrons requires that this group be further defined into ever smaller, niche markets. A rider with a vision impairment has needs, desires, and expectations of transportation that a rider with a cognitive disability does not. Marketing campaigns that treat paratransit patrons as an undifferentiated mass will fail. The great challenge of marketing to paratransit patrons is to identify the market segments that exist within that larger group, decide on the approach that will result in a willing exchange, and conduct the campaign. Marketing to paratransit patrons is a definitive example of niche marketing.

Paratransit riders are a market segment that proves an old Chinese proverb, "Tell me and I'll forget, show me and I may remember, involve me and I'll understand."[1] Paratransit riders, as a group, often do not or sometimes cannot respond to standard marketing efforts of telling and/or demonstrating, for

---

[1] Quoted in Menchin, Robert S. *The Mature Market*. Probus Publishing Co., Chicago, Illinois. 1989. p. 71.

CHAPTER 8 MARKETING FIXED-ROUTE SERVICES

example, how to ride a bus. They often need to be involved on a more personal, one-to-one basis, so that they are active participants in learning about transportation choices. To identify their transportation choice needs and expectations, use focus groups, advocacy committees, and trusted representatives. Individual contact should occur and is important. Without feelings of trust and confidence in the safety, reliability, and security of fixed-route service, paratransit riders will not be interested in learning how to ride the bus.

MARKETING

Expectations and costs of fixed-route

Marketing is more than advertising. It is "... the analysis, planning, implementation, and control of programs designed to create, build, and maintain beneficial exchange relationships with target audiences for the purpose of achieving the marketer's objectives." [2] Unlike education or public relations, marketing is action-oriented and seeks to educate and to change attitudes in order to induce people to take desired action. Marketing is an approach or philosophy that an organization embraces in order to meet the expectations of present and future customers.

Marketing depends on a willing exchange between marketer and customer. Each has something the other wants. The transit system provides transportation; the passenger provides a fare, and, in the focus of this guidebook, rides fixed-route instead of paratransit service. Each benefit involves costs. An exchange results " ... whenever the target customer perceives the benefits of the behavior the marketer seeks to exceed the costs or sacrifices the behavior entails and this ratio of benefits to costs is better than that achieved by 'spending' the costs in any other conceivable way."[3] Generally, benefits to the customer are costs to the marketer.

---

[2] Phillip Kotler and Alan Andreasen. *Strategic Marketing for Nonprofit Organizations*, 4th ed. Englewood Cliffs, New Jersey: Prentice Hall. 1991. p. 38.

[3] *Ibid* p. 125.

CHAPTER 8 MARKETING FIXED-ROUTE SERVICES

While the exchange of money for a product or service is an overt exchange, it often represents the culmination of a series of more covert exchanges between marketer and customer. Unless the covert exchanges take place, and continue to occur every time the customer and the marketer interact, no money will be exchanged and the relationship between customer and marketer breaks down.

Convenience
Safety
Risk

For example, regarding covert exchanges, there are several exchanges that take place when a person who is frail and elderly rides a fixed-route bus. These exchanges involve safety, convenience, and risk, which are all covert costs. The passenger must meet the bus' schedule, may have to walk a good distance to the stop, and may have to wait for extended periods of time in inclement weather. Once the bus arrives, this passenger must board, pay the fare, find a seat, and sit down before the driver pulls out. On the bus, this passenger must interact closely with strangers and a possibly discourteous driver and undergo a possibly uncomfortable ride, while worrying if he or she is on the right bus, what to do if the bus breaks down, and if the bus will keep to its schedule. For this passenger, the fare is just one of many costs. The marketing task of the transit system is to discover these costs, recognize their validity, and design systems and procedures that reduce these costs to minimally acceptable levels.

These costs are not limited to paratransit riders. They are costs that all mass transit riders pay, although general public passengers do not have to overcome certain obstacles in paying them. All passengers expect the following characteristics in a transit ride:

Expectations of a transit ride:
- *Safe*
- *Clean*
- *Easy-to-use*
- *Predictable*
- *Enjoyable*
- *Priced right*

- Safety (free from physical injury, the threat of physical injury, and negative feelings),
- Cleanliness (clean vehicles, stops, and terminals; drivers in presentable uniforms),
- User-friendliness (easy-to-read-and-understand instructions posted at stops and terminals; courteous drivers who take the time to explain),
- Predictability (a realistic schedule; well-maintained vehicles so as to avoid breakdowns; if an accident or breakdown occurs, the system has an effective contingency plan,

CHAPTER 8 MARKETING FIXED-ROUTE SERVICES

- Enjoyability (friendly drivers who try to know their regular passengers and offer pleasant, smooth rides), and
- Value (inexpensive in terms of risk, safety, and convenience).[4]

Changing to fixed-route involves a high degree of personal involvement.

Marketing fixed-route service to paratransit riders is asking a group of riders to change their behavior in ways that will definitely increase their costs without always increasing their benefits. The decision to change to fixed-route requires a high degree of personal involvement on the part of riders. With little or no previous experience in riding fixed-route service upon which to draw, riders must make a transportation choice that does the following:

- Involves elemental aspects of one's self-image;
- Involves personal or economic sacrifices;
- Risks major personal or social costs if the wrong choice is made; and
- Involves considerable peer pressure for or against.[5]

These are all high costs. For people with disabilities and older riders, they can be particularly high. If the costs to the customers are greater than the benefits, then no exchange will occur. Therefore, transit systems must find ways to reduce these costs to acceptable levels so that an exchange will take place. The marketing process provides the structure that enables exchanges to take place.

THE MARKETING PROCESS

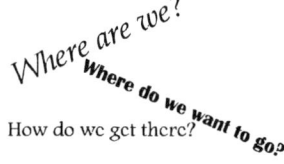

The marketing process systematically provides information, sets marketing goals and objectives, designs the marketing mix, implements plans, and then evaluates the results. The process answers three basic questions about the organization: Where are we? Where do we want to go? How do we get there? This is shown in Figure 8-1.

---

[4] Peter M. Schauer, *Marketers in Transit Workbook*. Boonville, Missouri.

[5] Kotler. p. 130.

CHAPTER 8 MARKETING FIXED-ROUTE SERVICES

Figure 8-1. The Marketing Process

Each element of a marketing plan reinforces and augments the strengths of the other components. A great promotional campaign cannot compensate for a product or service that does not meet the needs of customers. The immediate response by customers to a promotion's free trial period offer or witty advertising slogan may be encouraging but repeat customers will be few as people realize that the service was not what they expected and did not help them simplify or improve their lives. On the other hand, a well-designed service cannot achieve anticipated levels of success unless potential customers know it exists and how it can benefit them.

RESEARCH

Where are we?

Research is perhaps the most important element in the marketing process. It answers the first question -- Where are we? Research does not have to be formal, expensive, or done only for major decisions. A mixture of formal and informal methods provides a more complete picture than just using one method. Whatever form it takes, research is essential to discovering what paratransit riders need, desire, and expect from transit, as well as their anxieties and fears. Guesswork and assumptions are neither accurate nor adequate and often reflect wishful thinking. (See Chapters 4 and 6 for more information on market research).

CHAPTER 8 MARKETING FIXED-ROUTE SERVICES

Less formal, more personal research methods are useful.

With paratransit riders, less formal, more personal methods that allow an exchange of views will gain information and increase involvement with the transit system. Focus groups are excellent, as are interviews with people who are elderly and people with disabilities on board fixed-route and paratransit vehicles. Conduct presentations with question and answer sessions to clubs, organizations, and advocacy groups in order to gather information. Be sure that the transit system representative giving the presentation is calm, knowledgeable, trustworthy, and interested in helping the audience solve their transportation problems.

PLANNING

Where do we want to go?

On the basis of the research results, design the marketing campaign so that it reflects where the organization wants to go. Setting goals and objectives provides direction and motivation to staff, tells the outside world what the organization thinks is important and where it is going, and provides criteria for measuring success or failure. To succeed, goals and objectives must be as follows:

Goals and objectives must be practical, realistic, measurable, part of the organizational culture, and unique.

- Practical (the organization must have the necessary facilities, personnel, funds, and equipment);
- Realistic (the political and social climate of the community must be in accord with what the organization wants to achieve);
- Measurable (goals that cannot be measured in quantitative and qualitative ways are not useful);
- Part of the organizational culture (goals and objectives will fail unless employees know that top management supports them and rewards progress toward achieving them [hidden agendas and unspoken rules tend to undermine overt plans, particularly those that require fundamental changes]); and
- Unique (in fulfilling its goals and objectives, the organization will offer its customers something that no one else can).

STRATEGY

How do we get there?

After the goals and objectives are set, develop strategies that will allow the organization to answer question 3 - how do we get there? These strategies must address the issue of market segmentation and the 5 Ps of marketing -- product, placement, price, promotion, and people. Market segmentation is the division of a large market into smaller, target or niche markets that share certain

CHAPTER 8 MARKETING FIXED-ROUTE SERVICES

characteristics. Design and deliver services that satisfy the needs, desires, and expectations of the niche markets. Concentrate offerings and do not waste resources by trying to please everyone.

Market segmentation depends on the following criteria:

- Exclusivity (the group is separable from other segments),
- Exhaustiveness (every potential target group member can be included in some group),
- Measurability (the market segment can be easily identified and its needs and desires can be measured),
- Accessibility (the market segment can be reached and served),
- Substantiality (the segment is large enough to be worth pursuit by a marketing campaign), and
- Differential responsiveness (each segment responds differently to marketing campaigns).[6]

Markets can be defined on the basis of many criteria -- income, age, marital status, employment, transportation choice, and/or physical characteristics. Paratransit patrons form a market segment, but need to be further defined to be reached successfully. Each general group -- people who are elderly, people with developmental disabilities, people with hearing disabilities, and people with vision disabilities - needs to be treated as a discrete niche with materials and approaches tailored to that niche. If populations are large enough to meet the substantiality criteria, then the four general groups can themselves be further segmented as shown in Figure 8-2.

Because people who are elderly and people with disabilities need high involvement in choosing transportation modes, small groups are more appropriate for marketing approaches than are larger, more impersonal ones. A niche market may be defined as a group home or a workplace that employs one or two people with developmental disabilities.

---

[6] *Ibid.* pp. 169-170.

CHAPTER 8 MARKETING FIXED-ROUTE SERVICES

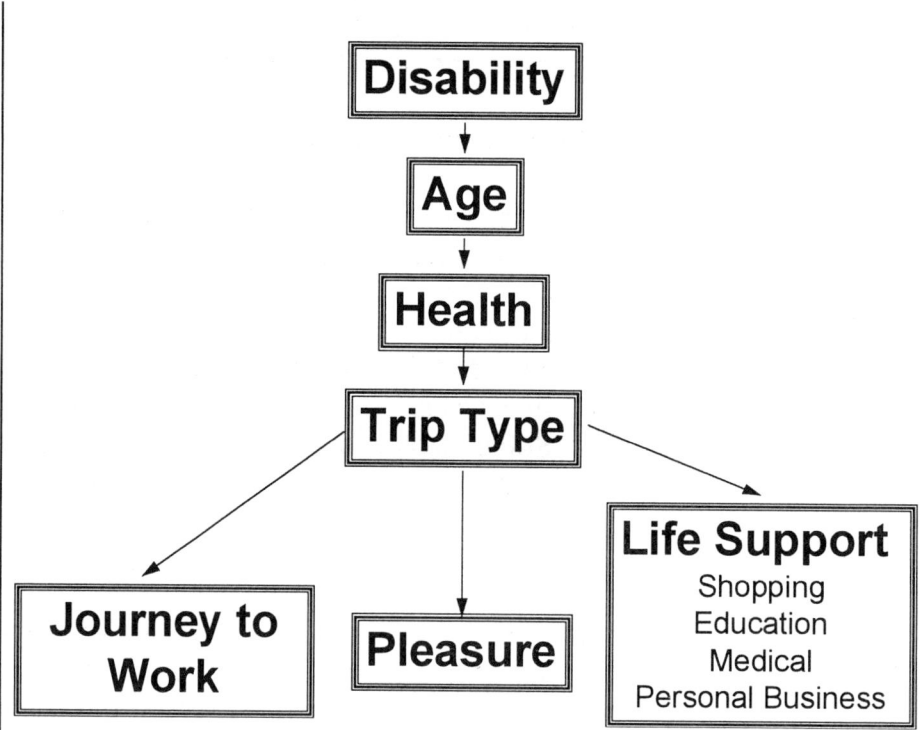

Figure 8-2. Further Segmentation of Market Niches

Marketers should recognize that the transit system serves direct customers and indirect customers. Direct customers are the people who actually ride the bus. Indirect customers are the people who support and assist the direct customers, people with disabilities, and other riders. Direct and indirect customers are shown in Figure 8-3. Indirect customers, through the communication feedback loop, significantly influence direct customers (that is, riders).

CHAPTER 8 MARKETING FIXED-ROUTE SERVICES

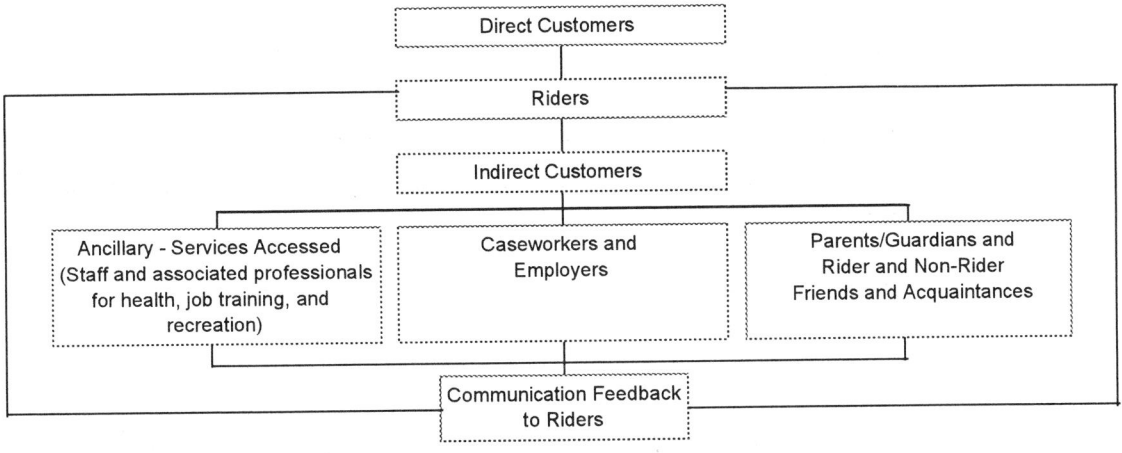

Figure 8-3. Direct and Indirect Customers

People who provide support and assistance are niche markets in themselves.

People who provide support and assistance are niche markets in themselves and are important targets in efforts to influence the behavior of direct customers. They help people who are elderly and people with disabilities decide about transportation. Employer involvement is also crucial in determining whether a person with a disability can use fixed-route to get to work if, for example, the bus gets the person to work 10 minutes late.

Once the niche markets are defined, use the 5 Ps of marketing to form the marketing campaign. The 5 Ps are product, placement, price, promotion, and people.

5 Ps of Marketing

Product
Placement
Price
Promotion
People

Product

The product is the service.

Product is the service that the transit system is offering to its customers, in this case, fixed-route service instead of paratransit service. The product will likely have to be redesigned to accommodate the needs, desires, and expectations of people who have been riding paratransit and who cannot use fixed-route vehicles in the same way as the general population.

CHAPTER 8 MARKETING FIXED-ROUTE SERVICES

Placement

Placement is access to the service.

Placement is the location at which the customer accesses the service. Bus stops, routes, schedules, and vehicle availability determine if, for example, a rider who uses a wheelchair will be able to ride the bus to and from work everyday or if he or she must continue to rely on paratransit or private transportation.

Price

Price is also reduction of risk and inconvenience.

Price is the recognition and acceptance of the utility costs (that is; risk, convenience, safety, high involvement of self, and change) of riding fixed-route instead of paratransit.

Promotion

Promotion consists of introductions, special offers, and advertising.

Promotion involves service introductions, special offers, and advertising that is usually mistaken for marketing. Make promotions to these niche markets personal, individual, and in formats that take into account the disabilities associated with the people within a market segment. For people who are elderly and people with disabilities, direct techniques and one-on-one promotions are most effective. Radio, TV, and the newspapers usually do not work well; however, riders who are elderly have a tradition of newspaper reading, so newspapers are an effective tool in reaching them. Promotions always must be tailored to niche market characteristics.

People

Transit personnel, especially drivers, must be seen as trustworthy.

People are essential in marketing to riders with disabilities who are elderly. The enhancement of their lives through mobility is the reason for the marketing activities. Transit system personnel, particularly drivers, are the key to delivering courteous, helpful service that is competent and timely and delivered while minimizing fears and anxieties.

This is a niche market, even at times focusing on the individual person. A marketing campaign that succeeds with people with developmental disabilities will fail to reach people who are elderly. On the other hand, a campaign that is successful with people who are elderly will often reach people with disabilities as well. (People who are elderly typically do not consider themselves as having a disability.) A bus schedule printed in Braille and a speaking bus will

CHAPTER 8 MARKETING FIXED-ROUTE SERVICES

not be useful to a person with a hearing disability. There is no mass market approach; however, by focusing on the 5 Ps, a unique approach for the market can be found.

IMPLEMENTATION

Changing to fixed-route is a big step -- allow 9 to 12 months.

Implementation of the marketing process is a critical step. A long time frame in which to implement a new service, or an established service that has been redesigned for new customers, is necessary. Set aside at least 9 months to a year for initial implementation. Because changing to fixed-route from paratransit is a major change, allow adequate time for individuals to make up their minds and to try the new service. Make management plans flexible enough to allow for adjustments to the process as it develops. Premature closure of the marketing program will prevent it from reaching potential passengers and will create distrust in current riders.

EVALUATION

Make formal and informal evaluations.

The final part of the marketing process is evaluation. Determine what succeeded and what failed. Similar to research, conduct evaluations on an individual or small group basis, with ample opportunities for discussion and opinions from customers. Use a mixture of formal and informal evaluations to form a more complete picture. Evaluation is actually the beginning of the next marketing cycle, with the lessons of the previous effort incorporated into the next. As such, marketing is a continuous, strategic process.

While the process may appear daunting, taking it step by step and allowing enough time will result in a successful program. The following section explains how marketers can reach their target markets.

MARKETING TO PARATRANSIT RIDERS

There are five important components for marketing to paratransit riders. First, riders are looking for consistency and reliability of services. Second, travel training encourages switching to the fixed-route services. Third, particular promotional formats are most effective. Fourth are the ten cardinal rules for marketing to people with disabilities. The fifth component is the difference among marketing to the four primary paratransit market niches.

CHAPTER 8 MARKETING FIXED-ROUTE SERVICES

CONSISTENCY AND RELIABILITY

Qualities that work on a mass market basis are qualities that niche markets would also like to enjoy, only tailored in ways that are accessible. Riders who are elderly and people with disabilities need, desire, and expect the same excellent service that the general public wants and expects in public transportation. This excellent service is based on a consistent product that is delivered with a uniform look, feel, and sound. Frequent changes and inconsistent service are confusing to all riders, but are particularly disturbing to paratransit riders who are trying to negotiate fixed-route service.

Mark vehicles in a consistent pattern that instantly makes them recognizable as one of the system and makes access to information an act that does not require hunting and searching. Place route numbers and names on the same place on all vehicles. Develop a strong, obvious color scheme to appear on all the vehicles in service. Doors that are painted a contrasting color to the body of the bus help those with vision and orientation problems locate entries and exits more quickly. Display a recognizable logo on all sides of the bus to help people recognize it without having to read.

Replace words with pictographs whenever possible. This helps people who have cognitive disabilities, those who are illiterate, and people for whom English is a foreign language.

Make the appearance of the drivers as consistent and obvious as the vehicles. Distinctive uniforms, complete with properly worn hats, make them recognizable as part of the transit system and give them greater authority. People with disabilities and riders who are elderly have to rely on the assistance of the driver and need to feel confident in his or her ability to help them. A uniform helps build confidence in both the driver and the passengers.

Attributes that build brand awareness for the general public are more than just aids to people with disabilities and riders who are elderly. Consistent appearance signals to customers that they will get the same satisfactory service every time. For example, the benchmark of this concept is McDonald's restaurants. The golden arches symbolize a type of value and level of service that is the same in Moscow, Tokyo, Paris, and Boonville, Missouri. There is never any doubt about the procedures -- where a person orders, pays, receives, and consumes the products. The "how to go about

CHAPTER 8 MARKETING FIXED-ROUTE SERVICES

People learn landmarks, shapes and colors. Avoid unnecessary changes.

it" is clear and requires little effort on the part of consumers. Transit managers need to strive for the same levels of predictability to persuade riders to use fixed-route transit.

Predictability and consistency are important because some riders travel by rote. Having learned the route, bus, and driver, they do not look for any other information, such as route numbers, bus numbers, or street addresses. They travel using landmarks of building shapes, colors, and other distinguishing characteristics in the surroundings that have significance to them. While true of some general public riders, this behavior is more prevalent in people with cognitive disabilities or literacy problems that prevent them from reading, processing, and retaining information presented in writing. To assist these riders to use fixed-route, predictable, service is necessary. A route change or delay, problems with the bus, or a construction detour are not only sources of anxiety but may cause riders to become disoriented and incapable of locating themselves. They will not know where they are and will not have the tools to find out. Fixed-route operators need to do the following:

If there are changes the transit system should give notice, contact riders, increase driver responsibility, and contact sites.

- Avoid changes unless absolutely necessary,
- Give plenty of notice so that rote travelers can adjust to any required change,
- Make personal contact with riders likely to have difficulty adjusting to the changes (volunteers, advocacy groups, caseworkers, employers, and family members can be involved in this task),
- Increase the driver's responsibilities as guide and assistant, so that he or she is identifying and helping passengers at risk of becoming confused by the change, and
- Establish a telephone tree for sources of information used by rote travelers (that is, worksites, schools, social services, and family).

TRAVEL TRAINING

Travel training is a proven method of helping paratransit riders switch to fixed-route. Conducted on a one-to-one basis or in very small groups, travel training can build the skills and confidence necessary to ride fixed-route. Peer instructors can demonstrate how difficulties are best handled -- the best way to board the lift, what the driver is expected to do, and what to expect from other passengers. Travel training can also prepare travelers who memorize their trips, the rote travelers, on what to do if the route changes or if there is an

CHAPTER 8 MARKETING FIXED-ROUTE SERVICES

emergency. Drivers participate in travel training as well by providing day-to-day reinforcement of how to ride the bus and by acting responsibly and courteously when someone needs help.

Travel training is an educational, outreach effort that covers three areas of transit travel, as shown in Figure 8-4.

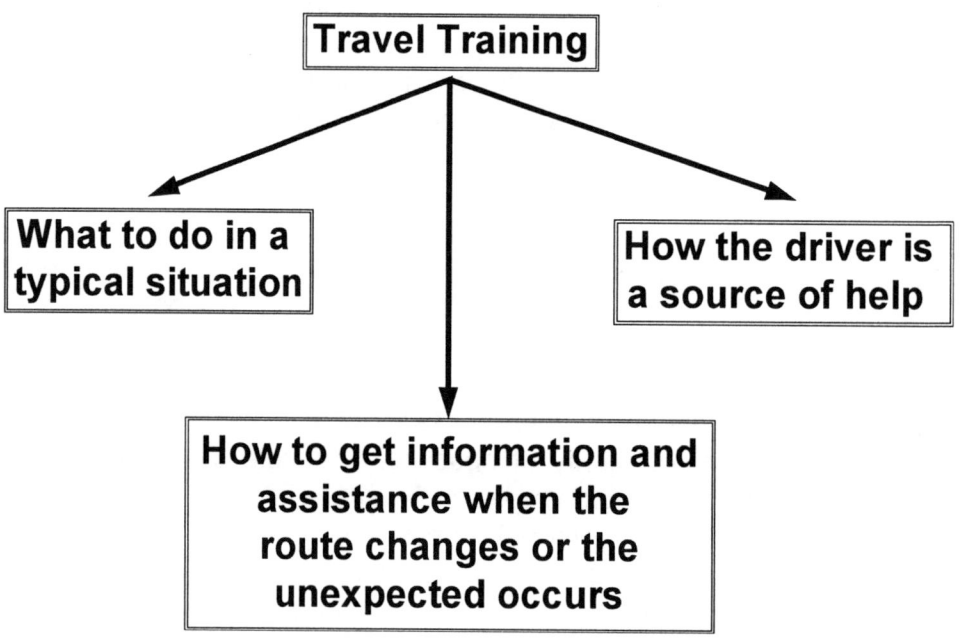

Figure 8-4. Three Areas of Transit Travel Training

There are four critical times for riders with cognitive disabilities.

People with cognitive disabilities or with developmental disabilities can ride fixed-route, but need help to do so. Travel training can help riders cope with the critical times. These critical times and appropriate transit system response are as follows:

1. The initial ride with the trainer -- The trainer should alert the driver that the person in training is going to be riding the bus at these times and will probably need some extra attention at first.
2. The first ride alone -- The driver should be courteous and reassuring, without being patronizing.

8-14

CHAPTER 8 MARKETING FIXED-ROUTE SERVICES

3. Expected changes -- The transit system should offer sessions with travel trainers and/or ask for volunteers from the social service network (for example, group homes and independent living groups) to help their clients adjust to the change.
4. Unexpected changes -- During travel training, trainees should receive maps and how-to cards, which use pictographs instead of text that show how to get help.

PROMOTIONAL FORMATS

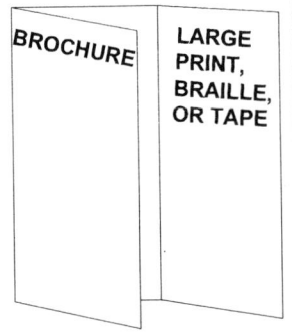

Promotions are communications with niche markets in languages, formats, and contexts that individuals in the market understand and with which they feel comfortable. Particularly in the paratransit field, creative thinking and new perspectives are needed to ensure that the marketing message is understood. For people with visual disabilities, brochures, schedules, and other printed materials should be available in large print, Braille, or audio tape. In communities with sizable populations for whom English is a second language, information should also be available in a multilingual format. Using pictographs instead of words will help reach people who are illiterate, residents and visitors who cannot read English, and persons with cognitive disabilities.

Pictures and Symbols

Pictographs are often used in maps and brochures for tourist destinations that attract people from all over the world. Maps of San Francisco or Disney World provide many clues to help people orient themselves. Shapes and colors of buildings are depicted to give the map depth. Distinguishing landmarks and multicolored lines depicting transportation routes are more helpful than maps covered with text and numbers. People have different cognitive abilities so printed material should offer as many clues as possible to enable people to orient themselves.

Newspapers

Newspapers are not suitable for all paratransit patrons, but are useful for reaching riders who are elderly who retain the newspaper-reading habit. Such riders can be reached through newspaper ads and special tabloid-type inserts that come out annually or at times of special promotions (for example, Christmas shopping or special events). The text can be extensive, as long as the print is large and the ad is uncluttered. To create a uniform appearance, use the same typeface used for other transit texts and prominently display the logo. If colors are used, they should be the same as those on the vehicles. A uniform organizational image is the key to projecting a secure, reliable image for the transit system.

Classic layouts work well because customers who are elderly are accustomed to them and know what to expect. Always feature a follow-up mechanism such as the system's telephone number and address. The ad should also be a call to action: a coupon to clip and mail in for a free bus pass or 50¢ off a beverage at participating restaurants upon presentation of a monthly bus pass are some potential response mechanisms. Figure 8-5 shows a classic layout.

Figure 8-5. Classic Advertisement Layout

CHAPTER 8 MARKETING FIXED-ROUTE SERVICES

Color

Color offers a strong visual cue to riders that the bus, ad, or bus stop, is part of the bus system. Color can also enhance safety. Highway departments use strongly contrasting colors (such as yellow or orange backgrounds with black lettering) which are easy to recognize and read. Other strong combinations are as follows:

- White on green;
- White on blue;
- White on brown; and
- Black on white.

Avoid low contrasts -- they are difficult to read. Generally, strong, primary colors are exciting, while pastels are soothing. Many systems throughout the country use white buses because of maintenance costs; however, white buses are more difficult to see on the street or when approaching a bus stop. Strong colors will make the vehicles easier to see from a distance and heighten awareness of the transit system's existence.

Photographs

Photographs should be in black and white or in full color, clear, and crisp and should show people engaged in desirable behavior. Focus on people's faces and never show a bus without passengers.

Basic Components

Whatever format is chosen, promotions should tell paratransit riders the following same basic information:

- Routes - places to go on each route;
- Schedules - times that riders can get to their destinations and hours and frequencies of service;
- How to ride or how to get travel training;
- Cost to passengers in terms of fares; and
- Availability of accessible buses and helpful, courteous, professional drivers.

*Basic Information --
Routes,
Schedules,
How to Ride,
Cost, and
Accessibility*

CHAPTER 8 MARKETING FIXED-ROUTE SERVICES

All promotions and materials directed at paratransit target markets should also include, frequently and prominently, the following three international symbols as appropriate:

1. The international symbol of accessibility;

2. The international symbol for TDD communications; and

3. The international symbol for information.

These symbols are the best tool currently available for "mass marketing" to the paratransit rider.

TEN CARDINAL RULES FOR MARKETING TO PEOPLE WITH DISABILITIES

Figure 8-6 lists rules to follow when designing a marketing campaign and promotional materials.

CHAPTER 8 MARKETING FIXED-ROUTE SERVICES

①	Segment the market into niches. Paratransit riders are in themselves a niche market compared with transit ridership as a whole; however, within the niche, there are distinct groups with separate needs, desires, and expectations of transit. People who are elderly do not consider themselves as having a disability and will not respond to marketing programs that address them as having a disability.
②	Research the formats and methods needed to communicate with each niche and, with further research, the needs of each individual paratransit rider.
③	There is no mass approach with which to target these markets. When possible, each paratransit niche will derive a general impression of the service from the system's general marketing program, but to get niche patrons to ride fixed-route will require one-on-one communication and demonstration.
④	Refine the marketing message to make it clear and empathetic without being patronizing.
⑤	When use of print media is appropriate, use large print and an uncluttered layout with lots of white space.
⑥	When using color, remember to use colors with high contrasts -- black on yellow, black on orange, or white on black -- that will stand out and be easy to read. Use the same colors throughout the system -- from the buses to the bus stop signs to logos and stationary. A consistent appearance increases patron confidence.
⑦	Use alternatives to text and script -- pictographs, logos, and cartoons -- to clarify the message and cue behavior without the customer having to read text.
⑧	Avoid a contrived look when using photographs. Keep the design of the ad or brochure simple and uncomplicated. Do not let the materials look as if they are striving for a "big effect."
⑨	Develop a familiar theme, approach, and look. Pretest it using focus groups and personal interviews with members of the target market, make adjustments, and then stick with it.
⑩	Evaluate the marketing program "on the fly" and at designated intervals. Based on the evaluation, make changes when they are necessary.

Figure 8-6. Ten Cardinal Rules for Marketing to People with Disabilities

MARKETING TO PARATRANSIT NICHE MARKETS

There are four distinct paratransit niche markets, each with its own characteristics: people who are elderly; people who use wheelchairs; people with visual impairments; and people with hearing impairments. Figures 8-7 through 8-10 provide tips on marketing to these niches.

CHAPTER 8 MARKETING FIXED-ROUTE SERVICES

Riders who are elderly do not consider themselves as having a disability -- ensure that marketing reflects this.
Riders who are elderly consist of the "young" old, who view themselves as active individuals capable of independent action, and the "frail" old, who need assistance. The size of both these groups is increasing as the population ages and medical advances prolong life.
Riders who are elderly respond best to advertisements in which the subjects appear to be slightly younger than themselves. The advertising campaign for Oldsmobile, "It's not your father's Oldsmobile," while aimed at younger consumers, worked well with the young old who felt that they were not driving an "old man's car."
More than half of all women 65 years and older live by themselves.[7] While, wanting to be independent, they cannot provide all their own transportation, so in some ways are captive riders -- but are not always captives of fixed-route.
Riders who are elderly have higher expectations of retirement than did their parents. Riders who are elderly and have a higher income and higher living standards than those previously the norm, have greater service expectations. Riders who are elderly are not simply grateful for a ride -- they expect a quality ride too. This trend will increase as Baby Boomers age and expect to be able to continue an active life into retirement.

Figure 8-7. Tips on Marketing to Older Riders

Put the person first, not the disability. Treat each person as an individual and work hard to address his or her personal needs with high-quality service in a comfortable environment.
Avoid language that condescends. Avoid terms like handicapped, wheelchair-bound, and physically challenged.
Remove obstructions and barriers to transit use, such as insufficient numbers of accessible vehicles on routes (particularly at rush hour), lifts that malfunction, bus stops that do not accommodate wheelchairs, bus stops located across busy streets or in locations without sidewalks, drivers who stop too far from the curb, and drivers who do not assist with the lift or securement.
Feature clear pictures of people in wheelchairs using fixed-route service in advertisements and brochures.

Figure 8-8. Tips on Marketing to People Who Use Wheelchairs

---

[7] Robert Leventhal. "The Aging Consumer: What's all the Fuss about Anyway?" *Journal of Consumer Marketing.* Vol. 8 No.1. Winter 1990. p. 29.

CHAPTER 8 MARKETING FIXED-ROUTE SERVICES

Do not rely on Braille, although materials should be provided in this format, if requested. Only 5% to 10% of people who are blind can read Braille. Large print and audio formats should also be available.
Drivers should announce stops and speak to passengers as they board the vehicle. Drivers should remember that there is no reason to raise their voices for people with visual impairments.
Devices that indicate with sound where the exit is -- beepers or some sort of tone -- will help people who lack visual cues to locate the door.
Use contrasting colors on bus doors so that they stand out. Use bright, contrasting colors for brochures and schedules, bus stops, and terminals. They help people recognize the bus system. Use lighter colors on top and darker colors below (to resemble wainscoting) in vehicles and facilities to help people orient themselves.
Maintain well-lit buses and facilities. Do not locate stops in dark, poorly lit locations.

Figure 8-9. Tips on Marketing to People with Visual Impairments

Have telecommunications devices for people with hearing impairments (TDD) and print the number prominently on all literature and materials.
In facilities, install smoke alarms and other devices that signal with a flashing light as well as a siren.
Realize that even accomplished lip readers can only understand about 65% of all that is said to them. Speak slowly and look directly at the person's face when talking. Provide training for drivers.
Have a person fluent in sign language available whenever the bus system is operating and make sure people know that this service is available. Realize that there are two forms of sign language -- signed English and American Sign Language -- and that an interpreter in one is useless in the other.
Use a one-to-one approach when marketing transit service to people with a hearing impairment. This community has diverse communication needs.

Figure 8-10. Tips on Marketing to People with Hearing Impairments

CHAPTER 8 MARKETING FIXED-ROUTE SERVICES

WHAT CHANGES TO THE TRANSIT SYSTEM WOULD ENCOURAGE YOU TO RIDE IT?

When survey respondents were asked, "What changes to the transit system would encourage you to ride it?" responses ranged from "no change" to specific changes like "no coffee breaks on the bus" and "change the disinfectant used on the buses." The two most frequently mentioned changes were "bus stop closer to home" and "reliable schedules." In general, changes mentioned by respondents fell into the following three broad categories:

- Changes to facilities (such as bus stops, shelters, sidewalks, and vehicles),
- Changes to services (including schedules, travel training, and education programs for other passengers), and
- Changes to driver performance and behavior.

CHANGES TO FACILITIES AND VEHICLES

Changes respondents would like to see made to transit facilities and vehicles included the following:

- Facilities
    - Bus stop closer to home,
    - Stops not located across busy streets,
    - Sidewalks on the way to the bus stop,
    - Sidewalks kept clear of snow,
    - Curb cuts,
    - Benches at stops,
    - Ventilated bus shelters, and
    - Increased safety at bus terminal; and
- Vehicles
    - Beeping doors to signal exit,
    - Bigger route numbers on buses,
    - Route numbers on the left side and rear of bus,
    - More comfortable seating,
    - Bars to hold onto and pull oneself up with,
    - Access for walker/scooters,
    - Reserved seats for people unable to stand,
    - Lower steps and smaller steps (with less rise per step), and
    - Lowering steps.

CHAPTER 8 MARKETING FIXED-ROUTE SERVICES

Changes should be considered for the entire trip -- not just the bus.

Some of the changes listed indicate that the respondents are thinking in terms of the entire trip they are making, not just the bus ride. Not only are they worried about getting on the bus (bars to pull oneself up with, lower steps, and access for walker/scooter), they are concerned about being able to reach a bus stop (stops closer to home, stops not located across busy streets, curb cuts, sidewalks, snow removed from sidewalks), being able to wait for the bus (benches at stops, ventilated bus shelters), getting on the right bus (more and larger route numbers on buses), having a place to sit (reserved seating area), getting off the bus (beeping doors to indicate exit), and being safe when they arrive (increased safety at bus terminal).

Enhance reliability, frequency, and destinations.

CHANGES TO SERVICE

Service changes mentioned reflect some common complaints about mass transit service and some that need to be made to accommodate riders with disabilities:

- Reliable schedules;
- More frequent schedules;
- Extended service hours;
- Consistent schedules;
- Expansion of service area;
- Elimination of the need to transfer;
- Routes to senior centers, VA hospitals, etc.;
- Travel training;
- Education program for other passengers; and
- Longer term passes.

Drivers should help riders.

CHANGES TO DRIVER PERFORMANCE

A third general area of concern was the performance of bus drivers. Respondents felt that drivers should be their allies in negotiating fixed-route service. Several respondents indicated that the driver should function as an active intermediary between passengers with disabilities and passengers who might be discourteous, impatient, or disruptive. Responses in this area included the following:

- Assistance getting on and off;
- Time to get on and off;
- Buses come to a complete stop;
- Drivers announce stops;

CHAPTER 8 MARKETING FIXED-ROUTE SERVICES

- Drivers trained to use wheelchair stations, lifts, and other equipment;
- Stop closer to curb;
- More polite bus drivers;
- Smoother rides;
- No speeding; and
- No coffee breaks on bus.

Bus drivers must perform a complex job. Not only do they have to drive safely and keep to a schedule, they must function as representatives of the transit system as a whole. For most passengers and non-passengers, bus drivers <u>are</u> the transit system, and their performance of their jobs helps determine public opinion about transit. This is particularly true for paratransit riders who necessarily interact more with drivers than do other riders.

[P]roduct
[P]lacement
[P]rice
[P]romotion
[P]eople

THE 5 Ps AND SURVEY RESPONSES

Using survey responses as a base determination of what paratransit riders need and expect from fixed-route service, formulate a marketing plan. "The marketing approach implies specification of a product to be engineered in a manner so as to resolve some problem facing target consumers."[8] The 5 Ps of marketing -- product (in the case of transit -- service), placement, price, promotion, and people -- provide the framework around which a plan is built.

PRODUCT AND SERVICE

In common with general public passengers, paratransit riders want fixed-route service to operate safely, to be on time, to have well-maintained vehicles and shelters, and to have convenient stops near the places they most often frequent. For people who have mobility difficulties, these service goals are even more important. Standing in the hot sun waiting for a bus is inconvenient and annoying for general public passengers, but for an elderly person who cannot stand for long periods of time, it may be impossible.

---

[8] Seymour H. Fine *The Marketing of Ideas and Social Issues*. New York: Praeger Series in Public and on profit Sector Marketing. CBS Educational and Professional Publishing. 1981, p. 21.

CHAPTER 8 MARKETING FIXED-ROUTE SERVICES

Several survey respondents indicated that paratransit riders wanted fixed-route service to function as paratransit service. Doorstop service, being able to arrive and depart when you want, direct travel to a destination, and always having a seat or position are features that people who ride paratransit and people who never ride any form of transit want on fixed-route service. Fixed-route service cannot deliver this level of service but it can offer more flexibility for paratransit riders by eliminating the need to reserve a ride in advance. This flexibility can be further enhanced by improvements to schedules, routes, stops and shelters, vehicles, and service.

Schedules: Provide enough service and enough time to serve.

Schedules

Schedule improvements include the following:

- Reviewing and redesigning schedules so that drivers have enough time to assist those who need help and still keep to the schedule,
- Reviewing and redesigning schedules to better serve riders with disabilities so that destinations most often visited (that is, clinics, hospitals, employment sites, and shopping areas) are served by transit at the correct times,
- Sufficient numbers of vehicles during peak times on busy routes so that persons in wheelchairs or with other equipment can board, and
- Offering more evening and weekend service.

Routes: Have commonly visited destinations and reduce transfers.

Routes

Route improvements may include the following:

- Reviewing and redesigning routes to better serve riders with disabilities so that destinations most often visited (that is, clinics, hospitals, employment sites, and shopping areas) are served by transit and
- Reviewing and redesigning routes to reduce the number of transfers that most paratransit riders would need to make.

CHAPTER 8 MARKETING FIXED-ROUTE SERVICES

Stops: Provide good placement and quality.

Stops and Shelters

Improvements to stops and shelters may include the following:

- Placement of stops so that passengers do not have to cross busy streets;
- Installation of bus shelters that have benches and enough room for persons using wheelchairs;
- Cooperative efforts with city government to install curb cuts and sidewalks near bus shelters and terminals;
- Bus schedules and general information about the transit system posted in bus shelters;
- Adequate and routine maintenance of bus shelters; and
- Safety precautions for bus shelters, including good visibility, shelter from the elements, and routine patrols by security.

Vehicles: Provide accessibility, identification, visibility, and usability.

Vehicles

Improvements to vehicles may include the following:

- Making all fixed-route vehicles accessible;
- Development of a reserved seating system for riders who are elderly or riders with disabilities;
- Printing of route and vehicle numbers in large numerals and posting them on the front, on the sides near the doors, and on the back of the vehicle;
- Interior and exterior paint schemes that are highly visible and assist with rider orientation;
- Grab bars near stairs and handholds near waist-level height; and
- Beeping devices to indicate entrances and exits.

Service: Ensure good customer relations and provide travel training.

Service

Service improvements may include the following:

- Establishment of a customer relations department staffed by experienced transit officials to handle liaison with riders with disabilities;
- Establishment of an advisory committee of paratransit riders, representatives of the disabled community, and interested agencies; and
- Establishment of a travel training program for riders.

CHAPTER 8 MARKETING FIXED-ROUTE SERVICES

PLACEMENT

The placement of fixed-route transit is implicit in its name. At certain stops along a specified route at certain times of certain days, consumers and transit service intersect. That place is not at the door of a rider's home or at the door of the destination, but somewhere along the fixed-route that the vehicle travels at regular intervals on particular days.

Consistent performance is an attribute that riders with cognitive disabilities count on because bus travel becomes a pattern that can be repeated without variation or frequent need for learning new skills. For such riders, unexpected changes in routes or significant schedule delays are cause for anxiety.

Transit systems must ensure consistent service and adherence to schedules. Consistent service requires the following:

- Realistic schedules that allow time for passengers who take more time than average to board and exit vehicles and time for drivers to assist passengers and operate lifts and secure wheelchairs without having to speed or operate vehicles in an unsafe manner;
- A maintenance schedule that keeps vehicles and lifts in service;
- Sufficient numbers of vehicles to serve paratransit riders during peak times so that waits for available wheelchair positions are not excessive; and
- An adequate plan to handle vehicle breakdowns and other emergencies.

Fixed-route transit needs to appear at the bus stop according to schedule. This is important for any passenger but for people with mobility problems unexpected delays or problems can be much more difficult and disruptive.

PRICE

"The real price of everything ... is the toil and trouble of acquiring it."

In marketing, price refers to more than the actual dollar amount that passengers pay to ride the bus. Virtually every purchase, whether tangible or intangible, involves some mixture of financial and social costs. In fact, Adam Smith attached greater significance to the latter: "The real price of everything, what everything really costs to the man who wants to acquire it, is the toil and trouble of acquiring

CHAPTER 8 MARKETING FIXED-ROUTE SERVICES

it."[9] Price refers to the indirect costs of time, inconvenience, social costs, and risks that riders must undertake when riding the fixed-route system. The survey indicated that respondents want to pay either no more than $1.00 (cost to $1.00) or no more than $2.00 (cost $1.00 to $2.00). However, respondents were also interested in the indirect costs involved in riding fixed-route. Many of the service features they want to see in fixed-route reduce risks and increase safety.

Paratransit riders are concerned about courtesy and patience from bus drivers and from other passengers. To some passengers with disabilities, the potential social costs, resulting from discourtesy and lack of understanding by other passengers, are high. Professional, courteous performance of passenger assistance by drivers can help reduce social costs for riders and set examples for other riders. Drivers who announce stops, competently handle lifts and wheelchair stations, clearly answer questions, operate the bus safely and smoothly, and allow time for passengers to get on, sit down, and then exit, will go far in relieving the anxieties that paratransit riders have about using fixed-route.

While the direct costs transit passengers pay for riding the bus are always at the forefront, the indirect costs cannot be ignored. Riders must consider the entire trip they are making, of which the bus ride is just one portion. Survey respondents emphasized the importance of safe, accessible, comfortable bus stops and shelters so that waiting for the bus does not pose too high a price to pay in terms of security, exposure to inclement weather, and the physical demands of waiting.

PROMOTION

Promotion is the aspect of marketing that people think of when they talk about "marketing." Promotion is seen as a solution for falling ridership, poor service, or the need to attract new riders. However, promotion will fail unless service lives up to the promises, either implicit or explicit, made in promotional efforts. If transit services hope to attract paratransit riders and keep them on fixed-route service, a long-term effort is required.

---

[9] *Ibid.* p. 83.

CHAPTER 8 MARKETING FIXED-ROUTE SERVICES

Promotion can include trial periods, free travel days, money-back guarantees, assistants-ride-free programs, and introductory rides.

Promotion lets target riders (paratransit riders) know that fixed-route service is now available to them and that the transit service stands ready to help them make the transition from paratransit to fixed-route travel. Trial periods, free travel days or hours, warranties or money-back guarantees, assistants-ride-free programs, and introductory rides with a transit-provided guide are ways to introduce paratransit riders to fixed-route. To keep them on fixed-route, good, courteous service is necessary. Promotional campaigns need to run for a sufficiently long time -- at least 9 months -- so that people will have time to make up their minds to respond.

Promotion to people with disabilities may require other formats in addition to newspaper ads, brochures, pamphlets, posters, and radio and TV ads. Word of mouth among current paratransit riders, while riding paratransit, would be an avenue of inexpensively reaching potential riders. Information would have to be correct (make sure the paratransit driver knows about fixed-route service or at least how riders can get information) because inaccurate information can set back any promotion.

Communication with the Transit System

In response to the question, "If you wanted to learn about fixed-route, where would you get information?" most people answered "call the bus company." Present-day communications offer several ways to "call the bus company." To ensure good communication, the bus company should be equipped with TDD (telecommunications devices for people with hearing impairments) numbers as well as voice numbers. Fax and e-mail numbers can be distributed as routinely as voice numbers. For people with visual disabilities, brochures, schedules, and other printed materials should be available in large print, and sometimes in Braille, or audio tape. In communities with sizable populations for whom English is a second language, information should also be available in a multilingual format. Using pictographs instead of words will help reach people who are illiterate, residents and visitors who cannot read English, and persons with cognitive disabilities.

Good Service

PEOPLE

In making sure transit has all the necessary equipment and facilities and is operating smoothly on efficient routes and schedules, systems sometimes forget that transit is a service delivered to people by people and that poor service delivered by discourteous, poorly trained people will negate any advantages brought by

CHAPTER 8 MARKETING FIXED-ROUTE SERVICES

excellent equipment and facilities. There is no substitute for good service, competently and cheerfully delivered by employees who are interested in helping people ride the bus.

Drivers and Other Riders

Paratransit riders able to ride fixed-route service are concerned about two groups of people -- drivers and other passengers. Passengers with disabilities, to a greater or lesser degree, must rely on the driver for assistance. Driver training programs need to include sensitivity sessions, role playing, and information on when and how to help as well as how to operate equipment and lifts. Passengers with disabilities should participate in the training.

Drivers and other employees can better communicate with passengers with disabilities by remembering the following:

- Avoid terms like "handicap," "cripple," and "invalid";
- Put the person first, the disability second;
- Focus on abilities and let people do as much for themselves as they can;
- Do not use euphemisms like "mentally challenged" or "special abilities";
- Do not worry about using common expressions like "see here" to a blind person or "listen up" to a person with a hearing impairment; and
- Do not be embarrassed for yourself or the persons with disabilities.[10]

One of the keys to providing service is to remember that passengers are individuals. Of course, competent, courteous treatment is to be given to each passenger, but some passengers need a little extra attention. Examples are discussed below.

Older Passengers

Passengers who are elderly may crave a little conversation and a courteous comment meant just for them. For senior riders who regularly ride the same route, a continuing conversation with "their" regular driver frequently develops. If the driver is going on vacation or transferring to another route, the driver should tell his "regulars" and let them know that the new driver also will look after them.

---

[10] Reedy, 1993, p. 36.

CHAPTER 8 MARKETING FIXED-ROUTE SERVICES

Positive Attitude

A positive attitude to passengers is important. Paratransit riders who make the change to fixed-route service might appreciate verbal recognition from the driver that they are doing OK. Of course, driver comments should not be false, condescending, or demeaning and should be sincerely meant.

Negative Passengers

Negative attitudes of passengers need to be addressed. Drivers need to be firm, courteous, and positive.

Angry and Upset Passengers

Demanding, angry, and upset passengers also need to be handled. A detached, professional attitude and patience are virtues in handling upset passengers. Drivers should do the following:

- Speak in a normal to quiet tone of voice so that the passenger has to lower his or her voice to hear what the driver is saying;
- Listen carefully to what the person is saying, ignoring inflammatory phrases and rhetoric;
- Decipher what the real problem is (maybe the driver and the transit provider are being used as scapegoats for what is really bothering the passenger);
- Inform the passenger about the complaint system and provide forms for complaints; and
- Resolve the situation within the transit provider's guidelines and procedures.

Anxious Passengers

Anxious passengers need to be reassured. Drivers and all transit personnel should be aware that it is common for people, particularly passengers with cognitive disabilities, to treat transit travel, once learned through travel training or by trial and error, as a habit that is done by rote. Unexpected changes are extremely upsetting to these passengers. If the bus breaks down or has to deviate from its normal route, the driver should take steps to reassure anxious passengers by explaining what is happening and that the situation is being resolved.

Impatient Passengers

Impatient passengers need to be calmed. A driver, through prompt, yet unhurried, assistance to those who need it, can act as an intermediary between former paratransit riders who now ride fixed-route (perhaps taking a little more time to maneuver on and off the bus) and impatient passengers.[11]

---

[11] Elaine Novak, *Developing Policies and Procedures for the Paratransit Operation Complaint System,* p. 13.

CHAPTER 8 MARKETING FIXED-ROUTE SERVICES

Interaction between passengers with disabilities and the general public is more difficult to control. Unless schedules are designed to allow time for passengers with disabilities, delays will be inevitable. These delays can be stressful to other passengers. An area of concern for passengers who are elderly or passengers with disabilities (who cannot stand for long periods or who have difficulty maintaining their balance in a moving bus) is having a place to sit. Reserved seating arrangements can cause resentment by general public passengers who are forced to stand. Requiring the bus driver to ask people to give up their seats for passengers with disabilities could place the driver in a difficult, if not impossible, situation.

A marketing campaign directed at general public passengers will not erase problems of social interaction, but it can alert everyone to the difficulties people with disabilities face when using fixed-route transit and provide some pointers on how to help. This kind of social marketing is challenging because people are being asked to change their behavior (that is, give up a seat or wait for the lift) without any direct benefit to them. In the case of giving up a seat, people are also being asked to act individually and spontaneously in a group situation. However, the bus driver and the transit system can set the example by courteous service and by demonstrating a strong commitment to helping passengers with disabilities ride fixed-route.

DRIVER TRAINING

Driver training should be developed in partnership with community advocacy groups for people with disabilities. Communication techniques, sensitivity sessions, and recognition of the various types of disabilities and how the driver can help with each one should be stressed. Areas to be covered are listed in Figure 8-11.

CHAPTER 8 MARKETING FIXED-ROUTE SERVICES

I. Introduction
    A. Objectives
    B. ADA and integrating paratransit riders into fixed-route
II. Disabilities
    A. Sensory
        1. Visual
        2. Hearing
    B. Physical
        1. Wheelchair
        2. Other
    C. Cognitive
        1. Mental retardation
        2. Autism
        3. Traumatic brain disorder
        4. Learning disabilities
        5. Alzheimer's
    D. Health
III. How to communicate
    A. Listening techniques
    B. Adjust style to fit the person
    C. Verification techniques
IV. Sensitivity sessions
    A. Issues involved
    B. Role playing
    C. Small group exercises
    D. Knowing when and how to help
V. Driver test and evaluations

Figure 8-11. Topics for Driver Training

TRAVEL TRAINING

Travel training can also be developed in cooperation with community advocacy groups for people with disabilities. Transit personnel or adequately supervised and trained volunteers (preferably with a similar disability as the person being trained) should ride by appointment and on a one-to-one basis with people who are uncertain how to use fixed-route vehicles. Introductory rides should be free and participants should be given maps, schedules, and how-to-ride guides in appropriate formats.

CHAPTER 8 MARKETING FIXED-ROUTE SERVICES

COMMUNITY RELATIONS

General public riders are informed of the difficulties passengers with disabilities face when using fixed-route service, why transit should be accessible, and what they can do to help. Newspaper ads; advertising placards on the bus, at stops, and at terminals; radio and television public service announcements; and newspaper stories about accessible transit service can let people know that fixed-route service is for everyone. Passengers should be assured that they will not experience delays or be late for their destinations because of assistance given to passengers with wheelchairs or passengers who take a little more time to board.

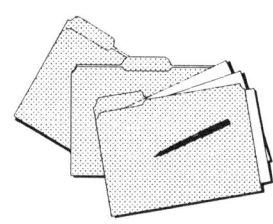

COMPLAINT SYSTEM

The change from paratransit to fixed-route can be difficult. The complaint system should be adapted to communicate in new formats and with people who might have difficulty communicating. The most competent people in the transit system should handle complaints quickly and directly. Passengers need to know the complaint procedures. Prepare separate brochures or include details in system maps or schedules in large print or Braille or on computer disk or electronic bulletin board and on audio tape. A standard complaint system should have the characteristics listed in Figure 8-12.

A. Passenger contacts transit system
  1. Listen to complaint
  2. Repeat the complaint back to verify information
  3. Apologize to the passenger
  4. Acknowledge the passenger's feelings
  5. Let the passenger know that action will be taken
  6. Thank the passenger
B. Write down complaint on designated form. Serious complaints should be submitted by passenger in writing if that is possible. Create a paper trail for complaint and write down every action taken in regard to complaint.
C. Forward complaint to supervisor or manager.
D. Investigate complaint, listening to everyone involved.
E. Resolve situation and communicate resolution to the passenger.[12]

Figure 8-12. Example of a Standard Complaint System

---

[12] *Ibid.*

CHAPTER 8 MARKETING FIXED-ROUTE SERVICES

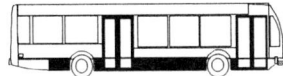

VEHICLE MODIFICATIONS

Adopt color schemes that will increase visibility of buses and make them easier to ride. Three color schemes can help passengers orient themselves to the bus and its motion. These are as follows:

1. Follow the example of NASA. To help astronauts orient themselves in the weightless conditions of space, surfaces that are "down" are painted in dark colors, while surfaces that are "up" are painted in light colors.
2. Paint bus doors a contrasting color so that passengers can easily discern where the entrances and exits are.
3. Paint or apply to the interior of vehicles broad vertical stripes. The stripes help people, particularly passengers who are elderly or those with vision or spatial orientation problems, to maintain their sense of balance and reduce their risk of falling as the vehicle moves, slows, and stops.[13]

How to Ride

HOW-TO-RIDE GUIDE FOR FIXED-ROUTE SERVICE

Prepare brochures in various formats (for example, large print, Braille, appropriate languages, audio tape, computer disk and e-mail) that let paratransit riders know that fixed-route service is available and that there are training opportunities to help them. Distribute brochures on paratransit services; through social service agencies; and at senior centers, public libraries, city and county offices, and medical offices. Any eligibility standards for fixed-route that the transit system has should be included in the brochure, as well as route maps and descriptions for accessible routes. Information presented in the brochure should include the following items:

- Who can use fixed-route service,
- Which buses are accessible,
- Who can use the lifts and with what equipment,
- When people with disabilities or wheelchair users ride,
- What kinds of wheelchairs are allowed on the bus,
- How wheelchairs are secured,
- How to get on and off the bus,
- How much it costs,

---

[13] S.U. Park, B.J. Gilmore, and D.A. Streit. *User-Friendly Bus Interior Design: Reducing Falls Through Improved Visual Environment*. University Park, Pennsylvania: The Pennsylvania State University. 1994.

CHAPTER 8 MARKETING FIXED-ROUTE SERVICES

- What happens if there are problems,
- What sort of seating arrangements there are for people who cannot stand,
- That the ride is safe, and
- How the driver can help.

"For Further Information" numbers (for example, voice, fax, telecommunications devices for people who are hearing impaired, and e-mail) and information about travel training should be prominent. Separate brochures should be prepared for particular target markets such as persons using wheelchairs, senior citizens, or people with hearing impairments.

Changing Definition of the Niche Market

RIDERS WHO ARE ELDERLY

As more people age, the definition of senior citizen is changing. More people are working longer, through necessity or choice, and do not consider themselves as "old." More accurate definitions of senior citizens are the "young" old and the "frail" old. The young old do not feel comfortable with the label old and do not usually participate to the same degree in senior citizen center activities as senior citizens have in previous years. The young old can be attracted by images of fun, youthful attitudes and activities and a sense of adventure. Images showing youthful-looking senior citizens riding the fixed-route to the ballpark or on a shopping expedition downtown would appeal to this group. In contrast, the frail old are more interested in safety, assistance from the driver, having a place to sit, having time to get on and off the bus, and no harassment from other passengers. Brochures, placards, bus cards, posters, and newspaper ads can show a competent, authoritative driver helping an elderly woman onto the bus.

INTRODUCTORY RIDES

Free Rides!

Implement an introductory trial offer of 1 week of free rides for paratransit riders who try fixed-route. If riders decide to stay on fixed-route, a half-price monthly pass can be offered. This program should be instituted on a continuing basis with periodic spurts of more publicity and advertisements to remind people that the offer is still in place.

A variation would be guaranteed satisfaction to new riders who have switched from paratransit to fixed-route. If passengers are not satisfied with the service they have received on fixed-route, their next five rides on fixed-route would be free.

During the introductory trial period, for people who travel with assistants, assistants should ride free as well as the person with a disability. After the trial period, assistants should be able to buy reduced price passes.

CONCLUSIONS

Marketing is more than advertising. In order to attract and then keep people riding fixed-route, all five elements of the marketing mix need to be in place and mutually supportive so as to give passengers the level of service they expect from fixed-route service. The exchange relationship between marketer and customer must be mutually beneficial, with costs to the passenger reduced as much as possible. Marketers need to treat customers as individuals and segment the paratransit market into niche markets. This is not a quick, overnight task, but one that, once accomplished, can provide quality service for all passengers. Quality service, cheerfully and professionally delivered, is the most powerful marketing tool transit systems possess.

CHAPTER 9: EVALUATING SUCCESS

CHAPTER 9 EVALUATING SUCCESS

INTRODUCTION

This chapter describes methods to evaluate the success of programs implemented to attract paratransit patrons to fixed-route services. Chapters 4 through 8 described the following five specific approaches to attracting paratransit patrons to fixed-route services:

- Locating transit stops close to passengers;
- Training drivers;
- Programming accessible bus stop improvements;
- Teaching passengers to use the fixed-route system -- travel training; and
- Marketing fixed-route services.

This chapter includes basic steps to evaluate the success of all of the approaches. In addition, for each approach described in the Guidebook, there are specific methods for evaluation. The criteria for success are also described.

BASIC STEPS

For each of the approaches to attract paratransit patrons to fixed-route services, the three basic evaluation steps are as follows:

- Passenger counts,
- Surveys, and
- Observation of service.

Not all riders pay full fare.

For many transit systems, obtaining accurate passenger counts can be difficult. Fares and revenue are carefully counted and accounted for, but, with the variety of fare media in use in most systems, it is not always possible to translate revenue into numbers of passengers. Some passengers pay full fare; others use passes; and still others pay discounted fares for multiple purchases. Older passengers and passengers with disabilities pay discounted fares; students pay discounted fares; and there are sometimes other programs in place for varying fares. So, it is not easy to determine from revenue how many people are riding. Even if the farebox counts the number of fares

CHAPTER 9 EVALUATING SUCCESS

deposited, people using daily, weekly, monthly, or school term passes do not deposit fares.

Not all riders with disabilities use the lift.

To evaluate a program to attract people with disabilities, the counting can be complicated by the fact that not all passengers with disabilities use the lift and many have disabilities which are not obvious.

It may be desirable to look at numbers of passengers who use particular routes or stops, depending on what type of approach was implemented to attract passengers with disabilities. This kind of information cannot be calculated from general revenues.

Evaluate current passenger counting capabilities.

Put programs in place to count passengers and to count passengers with disabilities. To determine the appropriate programs, define the capabilities which exist within the farebox and the fare purchase systems. Explore the possibilities within existing capabilities. Some possibilities are as follows:

- If the farebox counts the number of fares deposited, use that to measure the number of some types of passengers. Make comparisons over time to determine how ridership changes.
- If reports are available on the amount of fare media (tokens, passes, etc.) sold by location (main office, transit centers, fare machines, other locations, etc.), compare them over time to determine if more people are riding in different parts of the service area.
- If farebox revenue reports are available by route, compare them over time to determine if more fares are being collected on specific routes. Select routes such as those targeted for particular programs or with newly accessible vehicles or with newly accessible stops.
- If farebox revenue reports are available by vehicle, compare the revenue on accessible vehicles to revenue on non-accessible vehicles. The appropriate comparison can be made between vehicles on the same route, vehicles on routes in the same parts of the service area, or routes that typically experience similar revenue levels.

CHAPTER 9 EVALUATING SUCCESS

Implement a manual counting system, if necessary.

COUNTING ALL PASSENGERS

If no mechanism is in place to count the number of passengers who board, implement a program to conduct the counts manually. Counts can be done by drivers or by other employees on the vehicles. Other employees could be regular employees or temporary employees, such as students, hired to count passengers.

The easiest way to count passengers is through a sample, rather than a continuous count throughout the system. A sample allows the count to be conducted over a short time and can reduce the employee time required to complete it. If employees or temporary employees are used, then their time can be concentrated during the sample period. If the count will be conducted by drivers, then a sample minimizes the change in their routine. It is difficult for drivers to start doing something new while they are picking up passengers, but it is possible for them to conduct the counts for a brief time.

There are several ways that a sample can be selected. For the most part, it is preferable to conduct all the samples at the same time, whether it is over a day, a week, or a month. The results will then be comparable, without potential changes due to seasonal or other ridership changes. Some possible sample selections are as follows:

- **To sample ridership at particular times of the day**. On particular routes or on all routes, have drivers or other employees count the number of riders who board during the specified hours. The purpose may be to count the number of riders during the morning or evening rush hours; or to count the number of riders in the off-peak hours, such as 10:00 am to 2:00 pm; or to count the number of riders during the night hours.
- **To sample ridership for particular destinations.** Determine which routes serve the particular destinations and count the riders that board at those stops or disembark at those stops. For example, there may be considerable traffic to and from shopping centers, hospitals, business or industrial parks, or other locations. The sample can be taken for an entire week or day and compared over time for changes. For example, a sample may be taken on one

Monday each month and compared to determine if there is an increase in ridership over the months. Or the sample may be taken for a week each quarter to determine if there is a change. Be aware of possible causes for ridership fluctuations. For example, shift workers may not ride every weekday, so it is necessary to count on the same day each week to compare similar situations. The last day of the month or Fridays may generate additional ridership to locations with banks. Senior discounts at grocery or department stores on a specific day each week may generate additional ridership. Certainly the first weekday after Social Security checks are received can have significantly higher ridership as individuals make their way to the bank and to stores.

- **To sample ridership on particular routes.** Identify the route to measure ridership and count the riders on that route for an entire sample day, week, or month. Compare the ridership over time to determine if there are changes. The route may be selected because of approaches which target it. For example, accessible vehicles may have been added or accessible bus stops may have been installed. The route may serve common destinations for the paratransit service.
- **To sample ridership for specific stops.** If a new transit center or accessible stops have been added to the system, count the number of people who board or disembark at the particular stops. Employees could count the passengers at the stops rather than on the vehicles. The different routes served by the stop can be counted at the same time.

COUNTING PASSENGERS WITH DISABILITIES

Most systems have a method to count the number of times that the lift is used on the fixed-route. Typically, drivers report on lift usage at the end of the day or shift. For passengers with other types of disabilities, methods need to be implemented to count how often they board.

If passengers with disabilities are eligible for reduced fares on the transit system with an ID card, then the number of people who use the ID can be counted.

CHAPTER 9 EVALUATING SUCCESS

In order to be able to accurately count the number of people with disabilities who board the vehicle, set up the discount fare system within the following guidelines:

- The ID card must be distinguishable from other discount passes, such as for elderly people, students, or others.
- Consider the policies for the use of the ID cards to purchase discount tickets or tokens, in comparison to discount cash fares on the vehicle. Counting the purchase of discount tickets provides a good estimate over time of the number of rides people with disabilities take on the system, but does not allow an estimate by route, service area, or transit stop. Actual counts of the use of discounted tickets and passes for cash fares may be more difficult for the drivers to conduct, but they can be more targeted and specific.
- Consider the use of contrasting types of passes to distinguish among passengers with disabilities to determine the effectiveness of particular programs. For example, different discount ID cards for people who are paratransit eligible and for people eligible for a fixed-route discount would allow counts of people who moved from paratransit to fixed-route.
- Implement a very simple method for drivers to count passengers. Fareboxes can be equipped with manually operated counters so that drivers indicate which type of fare is collected. Other hand-held or mounted manual counters can be distributed on sample days. Avoid methods that require too much time or procedures which are too complex.

If ID cards are not used for people with disabilities, it can be difficult to identify many of the people with disabilities who use the service. However, the next section on surveys describes a way to count persons with disabilities.

SURVEYS

Surveys of riders, drivers, and the general public can be very useful to measure the success of a program implemented to attract people with disabilities to the fixed-route services. Survey suggestions are as follows:

- Survey riders to determine if people with disabilities are using the system more frequently.

CHAPTER 9 EVALUATING SUCCESS

- Survey to determine people's attitudes toward the system or if they perceive improvements in the service provided.
- Survey riders to determine if focused efforts, such as accessibility of bus stops or vehicles, are achieving the intended objectives.
- Survey the general public to determine the effectiveness of public relations campaigns, marketing efforts, driver performance and attitudes, and the growth of the number of people with disabilities riding the fixed-route services.

Surveys of Riders with Disabilities

Survey riders over the telephone, through the mail, or on board the vehicles. Some considerations for the most appropriate type of survey to conduct are as follows:

How many people with disabilities ride fixed-route?

How many people with disabilities ride both fixed-route and paratransit?

How effective are programs targeted to specific routes?

How effective are public relations?

How is driver performance?

How often do people with disabilities use the fixed-route service?

- Interview people on board the vehicles or at stops to determine how often people with disabilities are using the service.
- Conduct telephone or mail-in surveys of those registered for paratransit to determine how many people with disabilities ride paratransit and also use the fixed-route.
- Conduct telephone surveys of riders who are not registered for paratransit through a random sample (from the telephone book or other list) and screening questions to determine if the person rides transit.
- Conduct surveys on board target route vehicles to measure particular, focused efforts, or conduct surveys at stops on the routes.
- Survey the general public over the telephone or through the mail to determine the effectiveness of public relations, marketing, and information campaigns.
- Survey riders over the telephone, on board vehicles, or through a mail-in survey distributed on vehicles or at stops to evaluate driver performance and attitudes. In on-board surveys, people may be reluctant to answer about the drivers who would be present.
- Survey riders over the telephone, on board vehicles, or through a mail-in survey distributed on vehicles or at stops to evaluate the frequency of use by people with disabilities. In on-board surveys, people may be reluctant to answer about people with disabilities, some of whom may be riding at the time.

CHAPTER 9 EVALUATING SUCCESS

Table 9-1 shows some of the advantages and disadvantages of telephone, on-board, and mail-in surveys.

Different types of surveys can be developed to achieve the targeted results. Figures 9-1 through 9-3 show sample surveys of people with disabilities to evaluate the success of programs to attract paratransit patrons to fixed-route services.

Table 9-1. Advantages and Disadvantages of Telephone, On-Board, and Mail-in Surveys

Survey Feature	In-House Telephone Survey	Professional Telephone Survey	On-Board Survey	Mail-In Survey
Response Rate	Response rate ensured through personal contact with adequate follow-up	Response rate ensured through personal contact with adequate follow-up	Response rate ensured through personal contact, but no chance to follow-up	Response rate usually is low
Cost	Costly, but duration control can keep costs down	Professional services can be costly	Duration control can keep costs down	Low cost of printing and mailing
Personnel Training	Personnel training necessary	Training part of professional service	Personnel training necessary	Little training required
Reliability of Results	Reliability based on instrument, personnel quality	Professionals ensure reliability	Reliability based on instrument, personnel quality	Reliability based on instrument and response rate
Sample Reliability	Respondents chosen at random	Professionals ensure reliability	Reliability guided by transit system	Bias if inadequate response rate
Comprehensiveness of Instrument	10-12 minutes ≈ 25 questions	15-20 minutes > 25 questions	5-10 minutes < 25 questions	2 minutes 8 questions

CHAPTER 9 EVALUATING SUCCESS

Date:	Time:	Interviewer:
Vehicle #:	Tour #:	Survey #: (on vehicle today)

Hello, my name is _____ and [*name of transit authority*] is conducting a survey to ask people about their use of the service. May I ask you a few questions while we're riding?

1. First, we want to talk to people from all over town, so do you live [*description of part of service area*]?
   ❑ Yes ❑ No

2. Do you live [*description of part of service area*]?[1]
   ❑ Yes ❑ No

3. What kind of place are you traveling to now? (Read list if necessary)
   ❑ Home
   ❑ Work
   ❑ School
   ❑ Doctor
   ❑ Clinic
   ❑ Store
   ❑ Friend/Relative's House
   ❑ Other (write in)
   _____

4. Approximately how many times each week do you ride the bus? (Is that *how many* round-trips?)
   _____

5. How many times did you ride in the past week?
   ❑ once, or one round-trip
   ❑ 2-3 round-trips
   ❑ 4-5 round-trips
   ❑ 6 or more round-trips

6. What was the purpose of *those* trips? (Write in number of trips, to total answer in #5)
   ___ Home
   ___ Work
   ___ School
   ___ Doctor
   ___ Clinic
   ___ Store
   ___ Friend/Relative's House
   ___ Other
   _____

7. Have you ever ridden on [*name of paratransit service*]?
   ❑ Yes ❑ No

Thank you very much for your time and thank you for using [*Transit Authority Name*].

Figure 9-1. Example of On-Board Survey of Riders With Disabilities to Evaluate Frequency of Fixed-Route Use

---

[1] Description of part of the service area may be something that divides the area into parts, such as north or south of a major street and east and west of another major street. Respondents could be asked what neighborhood or section they live in, if that is a good identifier. Zip codes may be useful in a large service area. Telephone exchanges can be combined with specific questions related to that part of the service area. It is too intrusive to ask a person's actual address, which they will be reluctant to give--they may then be reluctant to respond to the survey.

CHAPTER 9 EVALUATING SUCCESS

Call 1	Date:	Time:	Interviewer:	Result:
Call 2	Date:	Time:	Interviewer:	Result:
Call 3	Date:	Time:	Interviewer:	Result:

Hello, my name is _____ and [*name of transit authority*] is conducting a survey to ask people about their use of the service. May I ask you a few questions about [*name of transit authority*]?

1. First, we want to talk to people from all over town, so do you live [*description of part of service area*]? ❏ Yes ❏ No

2. Do you live [*description of part of service area*]? ❏ Yes ❏ No

3. Have you ever ridden on [*name of transit authority*]? ❏ Yes ❏ No

4. [*If yes to Question 3*] When was the last time that you rode on [*name of transit authority*]? _____

5. [*If yes to Question 3*] What kind of place do you travel to on [*name of transit authority*]? (Read list if necessary)
   ❏ Home
   ❏ Work
   ❏ School
   ❏ Doctor
   ❏ Clinic
   ❏ Store
   ❏ Friend/Relative's House
   ❏ Other (write in) _____

6. Approximately how many times each week do you ride the bus? (Is that *how many* round-trips?) _____

7. [*If Answer to Question 6 is 1 or more* times] How many times did you ride in the past week?
   ❏ once, or one round-trip
   ❏ 2-3 round-trips
   ❏ 4-5 round-trips
   ❏ 6 or more round-trips

8. What was the purpose of your trips? (write in number of trips, to total answer in #7)
   ___ Home
   ___ Work
   ___ School
   ___ Doctor
   ___ Clinic
   ___ Store
   ___ Friend/Relative's House
   ___ Other
   _____

Thank you very much for your time and thank you for using [*Transit Authority Name*].

Figure 9-2. Telephone Survey of Paratransit Riders to Evaluate Frequency of Fixed-Route Use

CHAPTER 9 EVALUATING SUCCESS

Call 1	Date:	Time:	Interviewer:	Result:
Call 2	Date:	Time:	Interviewer:	Result:
Call 3	Date:	Time:	Interviewer:	Result:

Hello, my name is _____ and I'm calling for [*Transit Authority Name*]. In order to understand how many people with disabilities use fixed-route services, we are conducting a brief survey of people in the community. Your telephone number was selected at random to represent people in your area and we would appreciate your help. May I speak to the head of the household? [*If head of household is not available, ask to speak to any member of the household 16 years of age or older.*]

1. Does anyone in your household, 16 years of age or older, have difficulty using regular public transportation due to a physical, mental or other health condition?
   - ❏ Yes [*go to question #2*]
   - ❏ No [*terminate - using closing statement below in Figure 9-5*]

2. Which members of your household have difficulty using regular public transportation? [*List below - accept name or relationship to respondent*]

3. Is this person (Are these people) able to travel outside of your home? [*Record responses below*]

	Name or relationship	Able to travel
1.		❏ Yes ❏ No
2.		❏ Yes ❏ No
3.		❏ Yes ❏ No
4.		❏ Yes ❏ No

[*If all persons listed above are unable to travel, terminate using closing statement below in Figure 9-5.*]

Total # of people with a disability who are able to travel	

4. [*If not speaking with person #1 in Question 3*] May I please speak with [*name or relationship for first person in # 3. If he or she is unable to respond, ask for care giver.*]

[*Complete a separate questionnaire for each person.*]

5. Which of the following conditions make it difficult for you to use public transportation. Please answer yes or no after each condition I mention. [*Read list and record responses below.*]

Difficulty walking, standing, sitting, or going up and down stairs	❏ Yes ❏ No
Difficulty using hands or arms	❏ Yes ❏ No
Difficulty seeing (even with glasses)	❏ Yes ❏ No
Difficulty hearing (even with a hearing aid)	❏ Yes ❏ No
Difficulty understanding or interacting with people	❏ Yes ❏ No

Figure 9-3. Telephone Survey Screening Questions

CHAPTER 9 EVALUATING SUCCESS

Any other condition which makes it difficult to travel unassisted. Please describe. _____ _____	❏ Yes ❏ No
6. Have you had this condition for 6 months or longer?	❏ Yes ❏ No
7. Do you have these difficulties year round or only during winter months due to cold weather or snow?	❏ Yes ❏ No
8. Do you need the assistance of another person to travel?	❏ Yes ❏ No
9. Do you need any special equipment or assistance to travel such as a cane, braces, or a service animal? If yes, what is it you need?	❏ Wheelchair ❏ Cane, crutches, or walker ❏ Braces ❏ Artificial limb ❏ Service animal ❏ Scooter ❏ Other _____ ❏ No special equipment

I would like to ask you some questions about [*Transit Authority Name*]. Your answers and any information which would permit identification of you or your household will be regarded as strictly confidential.

[*At this point continue with full set of survey questions with screened respondents.*]

Figure 9-3. Telephone Survey Screening Questions (Concluded)

SURVEYS OF THE GENERAL PUBLIC

The opinions of general public riders are also important to evaluate the success of a program. Use surveys to evaluate the visibility and impact of a mass marketing campaign. The success of a driver training program can be observed by any riders on the vehicle. Measure the perceptions of driver performance through surveys of riders over the telephone or on board the vehicles. All riders should be able to observe that riders with disabilities receive the assistance and courtesy they require to use fixed-route.

Figure 9-4 shows sample questions for a telephone survey of the general public regarding the effectiveness of a marketing campaign. Figure 9-5 shows sample questions for a telephone survey of the general public regarding the effectiveness of driver training. Figure 9-6 shows sample questions for an on-board survey of the general public to evaluate services for people with disabilities.

CHAPTER 9 EVALUATING SUCCESS

Call 1	Date:	Time:	Interviewer:	Result:
Call 2	Date:	Time:	Interviewer:	Result:
Call 3	Date:	Time:	Interviewer:	Result:

Hello, my name is _____ and [name of transit authority] is conducting a survey to ask people about their use of the service. May I ask you a few questions about [name of transit authority]?

1. First, we want to talk to people from all over town, so do you live [description of part of service area]? ❏ Yes ❏ No

2. Do you live [description of part of service area]? ❏ Yes ❏ No

3. Have you ever ridden on [name of transit authority]? ❏ Yes ❏ No

4. [If yes to Question 3] When was the last time you rode on [name of transit authority]? _____

5. Approximately how many times each week do you ride the bus? (Is that how many round-trips?) _____ round-trips

6. Have you seen or heard our new advertising campaign, [Description of the new campaign or slogan] ❏ Yes ❏ No

7. Where did you see or hear it? [Check all that are mentioned]
   - ❏ Television
   - ❏ Radio
   - ❏ Newspaper
   - ❏ Billboards
   - ❏ Bus and bus shelter ads
   - ❏ Other _____

8. On a scale of 1 to 10, with 10 being excellent and 1 being poor, how memorable would you say the campaign is? [Write in response] _____

9. On a scale of 1 to 10, how well do you think the campaign encourages people to ride [name of transit authority]? [Write in response] _____

10. On a scale of 1 to 10, how well do you think the campaign portrays [name of transit authority] as an enjoyable way to travel? [Write in response] _____

11. Please name the one thing that you remember most about the advertisements you saw or heard? [Write in response]
    _____
    _____

Thank you very much for your time and thank you for using [Transit Authority Name].

Figure 9-4. Telephone Survey of General Public to Evaluate Marketing Campaign

CHAPTER 9 EVALUATING SUCCESS

Call 1	Date:	Time:	Interviewer:	Result:
Call 2	Date:	Time:	Interviewer:	Result:
Call 3	Date:	Time:	Interviewer:	Result:

Hello, my name is _____ and [name of transit authority] is conducting a survey to ask people about their use of the service. May I ask you a few questions about [name of transit authority]?

1. First, we want to talk to people from all over town, so do you live [description of part of service area]? ❏ Yes ❏ No

2. Do you live [description of part of service area]? ❏ Yes ❏ No

3. Have you ever ridden on [name of transit authority]? ❏ Yes ❏ No

4. [If yes to Question 3] When was the last time that you rode on [name of transit authority]? _____

5. Approximately how many times each week do you ride the bus? (Is that how many round trips?) _____

I would like you to tell me whether you strongly agree, agree, disagree, or strongly disagree with the following statements.

6. Drivers are courteous and friendly. [Read responses, if necessary.]
   - ❏ Strongly agree
   - ❏ Agree
   - ❏ Disagree
   - ❏ Strongly disagree

7. Drivers drive safely.
   - ❏ Strongly agree
   - ❏ Agree
   - ❏ Disagree
   - ❏ Strongly disagree

8. Drivers understand the needs of people with disabilities.
   - ❏ Strongly agree
   - ❏ Agree
   - ❏ Disagree
   - ❏ Strongly disagree

9. Drivers do not complain when they provide assistance to people with disabilities.
   - ❏ Strongly agree
   - ❏ Agree
   - ❏ Disagree
   - ❏ Strongly disagree

10. Drivers announce stops on the bus routes throughout the trip.
    - ❏ Strongly agree
    - ❏ Agree
    - ❏ Disagree
    - ❏ Strongly disagree

Thank you very much for your time and thank you for using [Transit Authority Name].

Figure 9-5. Telephone Survey of General Public to Evaluate Driver Training Program

CHAPTER 9 EVALUATING SUCCESS

Date:	Time:	Interviewer:
Vehicle #:	Tour #:	Survey #: (on vehicle today)

Hello, my name is _____ and [*name of transit authority*] is conducting a survey to ask people about their use of the service. May I ask you a few questions while we're riding?

1. First, we want to talk to people from all over town, so do you live [*description of part of service area*]?   ❏ Yes ❏ No
2. Do you live [*description of part of service area*]?   ❏ Yes ❏ No
3. What kind of place are you traveling to now? [*Read list if necessary*]
   - ❏ Home
   - ❏ Work
   - ❏ School
   - ❏ Doctor
   - ❏ Clinic
   - ❏ Store
   - ❏ Friend/Relative's House
   - ❏ Other (write in) _____

4. Approximately how many times each week do you ride the bus? (Is that how many round-trips?)   _____ round-trips

5. When you ride, have you ever seen a person with a disability boarding the bus?   ❏ Yes ❏ No
6. [*If yes to Question 5*] Thinking of the last time a person with a disability boarded the bus, did the driver assist the rider?   ❏ Yes ❏ No
7. What kind of assistance did the driver provide? [*Write in response*]
   _____
   _____

8. On a scale of 1 to 10, with 10 being excellent and 1 being poor, how well would you say the driver assisted the rider? [*Write in response*]   _____

9. On a scale of 1 to 10, how much easier do you think the driver made the trip for the rider? [*Write in response*]   _____

Thank you very much for your time and thank you for using [*Transit Authority Name*].

Figure 9-6. On-Board Survey of General Public to Evaluate Service for People With Disabilities

Sample Size

Select the size of the sample, or the number of responses that are required, in relation to the entire target group, carefully. The sample needs to be large enough so that the responses can be considered representative of the opinions of all the members of the target group or population. The larger the sample size, the more likely the sample is representative. Sample size should be as large as possible and large enough to ensure accuracy. The more diverse the population is, in terms of sex, race, income, age, etc., the larger the sample should be. This is particularly true if the research is going to make conclusions about the subgroups through stratification.

If the population is very uniform, then a large sample size is not as important. If the results of the survey are going to be the basis of a high-risk decision, then the accuracy is very important and the sample needs to be as large as possible. If, on the other hand, the results are related to lower risk decisions, or will be one component of a large amount of information, then a large sample size is not as important.

Table 9-2 shows some recommendations for sample sizes, depending on the target population size and how reliable the data will be. Figure 9-7 provides an explanation of how to determine sample size using Table 9-2.

SERVICE OBSERVATION

The third method to measure a program's success is to observe service being delivered and determine whether the objectives of the program are being achieved. This is most appropriate for programs in driver training and passenger (travel) training. However, some aspects of system accessibility, transit stop location, and system marketing can be measured through service observation.

Table 9-2. Recommendations for Sample Sizes

SAMPLING PARAMETERS	SIZE OF POPULATION					
Estimate, Accuracy, Reliability	500	1,000	2,500	5,000	50,000	500,000
Est 1.0%, Acc ± 1.0%, Rel 90%	174	211	242	254	266	268
Est 1.0%, Acc ± 1.0%, Rel 95%	216	276	330	353	377	380
Est 2.5%, Acc ± 1.0%, Rel 90%	284	397	522	583	651	689
Est 2.5%, Acc ± 1.0%, Rel 95%	326	484	381	798	919	935
Est 10%, Acc ± 3.5%, Rel 90%	142	166	184	191	198	199
Est 10%, Acc ± 3.5%, Rel 95%	180	220	254	267	281	282
Est 10%, Acc ± 5.0%, Rel 90%	82	89	94	96	97	97
Est 10%, Acc ± 5.0%, Rel 95%	108	121	131	135	138	138
Est 35%, Acc ± 3.5%, Rel 90%	251	334	418	457	498	502
Est 35%, Acc ± 3.5%, Rel 95%	294	416	555	624	703	712
Est 35%, Acc ± 5.0%, Rel 90%	165	198	224	235	245	246
Est 35%, Acc ± 5.0%, Rel 95%	206	259	307	327	347	349
Est 35%, Acc ± 10%, Rel 90%	55	58	60	61	61	62
Est 35%, Acc ± 10%, Rel 95%	74	80	84	86	87	87
Est 45%, Acc ± 3.5%, Rel 90%	261	353	449	493	541	546
Est 45%, Acc ± 3.5%, Rel 95%	304	437	592	672	764	775
Est 45%, Acc ± 5.0%, Rel 90%	174	211	242	254	266	268
Est 45%, Acc ± 5.0%, Rel 95%	216	276	330	353	377	380
Est 45%, Acc ± 10%, Rel 90%	59	63	65	66	67	67
Est 45%, Acc ± 10%, Rel 95%	80	87	92	93	93	95

CHAPTER 9 EVALUATING SUCCESS

DETERMINING THE SAMPLE SIZE FOR A SURVEY

Suppose that your agency thinks that 35% of the population of your community rides public transit more than once a week. You desire to sample the community to determine the actual percentage of the community which travels on the bus. You need to determine a sample size for the survey. You live in a community of 50,000 persons. You want to come up with an answer through sampling that should be within ± 5% of the "real" answer with a reliability of 95%.

Size of population	50,000
Frequency estimate	35%
Desired accuracy	± 5% (Margin of error)
Reliability	95%

Table 9-2 indicates that you should complete 347 surveys from persons randomly selected from the population to achieve this level of accuracy and reliability.

INTERPOLATING FROM THE TABLE

Suppose you complete the survey, and the results indicate that 44% of the population ride the bus. You are in a bit of a quandary because you expected an answer in the range of 35% ± 5%, i.e. in the range 30% to 40%. This response is out of the expected range. You wonder whether your expected range was too conservative and there are actually more riders than you anticipated.

Checking Table 9-2 again, you see that if 377 surveys (rather than 347) had been conducted, and an answer of 44% had resulted, you could have concluded that the "real" answer was in the range of 45% ± 5%, with **95%** certainty. You also see that if you had conducted only 266 surveys (rather than 347), and an answer of 44% had been obtained, you could have stated that the "real" answer was in the range of 45% ± 5%, with **90%** certainty.

With these facts in mind, you might decide to continue the surveying effort until you complete 377 surveys and are again within a known range of reliability. Alternatively, you might decide to **interpolate** to estimate the reliability value for this sample, which lies somewhere between 90% and 95%. A **linear** interpolation yields the answer of 93.6% certainty, which conservatively should be viewed as a 93% certainty level.

This example illustrates that it is possible to interpolate within the values in Table 9-2 to arrive at the desired sample size. When the estimate, accuracy, and reliability are known, you may interpolate across a horizontal row to determine the sample size for any intermediate population size. Likewise, when the population size is known, you may interpolate down any vertical column to determine the sample size for intermediate values of estimate, accuracy, or reliability.

Figure 9-7. Determining the Sample Size for a Survey.

The three basic steps to implementing a service observation program are to define the program objectives to be measured, develop observation procedures and observe service, and analyze the observations.

Define Objectives to Be Measured

Depending on which program is being evaluated, define the objectives that will be measured through the observation of service.

Possible objectives for a driver training program include the following:
- Improved driver courtesy,
- Positive driver attitude toward people with disabilities,
- Increased driver ability to assist passengers with disabilities,
- Frequent stop announcements,
- Effective driver efforts to communicate, and
- Efficient driver use of securement systems.

Possible objectives for a travel training program include the following:
- Increased passenger familiarity with service procedures,
- Improved passenger capabilities with lift and securement,
- Observed high passenger comfort level, and
- Increased use of discount fares and passes.

For a stop location program, a transit system may want to examine changes in patterns of boarding and deboarding.

For a system accessibility program, a transit system may want to achieve more frequent use of accessibility equipment.

For each objective, determine the observable aspects that can be measured. For example, for driver courtesy, observe drivers when passengers board, to be sure drivers are following the procedures for proper courtesy. In the same way, observe driver responses to the assistance needs of people with disabilities. Determine the stops and cross streets that drivers are required to announce and observe to be sure the drivers are following the proper procedures.

CHAPTER 9 EVALUATING SUCCESS

Forms help ensure that observations are consistent.

Develop Observation Procedures

Procedures for observing service include methods and forms for recording observations, methods to achieve an appropriate sample, and methods to ensure anonymous observation of actual service.

Methods and Forms for Recording Observations

To accurately analyze any service observations and to come to appropriate conclusions, institute procedures so that each observer, whether a volunteer or a staff person, is looking for the same types of behaviors and can recognize them. Determine distinct standards for the program to be measured, define how they can be observed, and provide each observer with a standardized tool for recording the observations.

Figure 9-8 shows a sample form for evaluating some specific components of a driver training program.

Appropriate Sample

To obtain an appropriate sample, be sure to observe on a variety of routes that represent the types of services provided across the service area. If there is a combination of commuter service and other types of service, be sure to observe on commuter routes as well as other routes. Observe service during the peak and off-peak hours. Include observations during the evening service hours as well.

If not all routes include accessible vehicles, concentrate on those routes that are accessible or partially accessible. Include observations on boardings from accessible bus stops and bus stops that have not been upgraded.

An efficient procedure is to have observers ride on the route and get off at various stops, then board the next bus to observe the driver on the next vehicle. This works well if the headways are not overly long. The time waiting for the next vehicle can be devoted to recording additional observations and organizing forms and procedures for the next route segment.

CHAPTER 9 EVALUATING SUCCESS

Segment #:	End Time:	Route #:
Date:	Start Stop:	Driver:
Start Time:	End Stop:	Vehicle #:

Use a separate form for each route segment observed.

Observation of rider #1

Time a person with a disability boarded the vehicle.   _____

Did the rider use the lift?   ❒ Yes ❒ No
1. Describe observed impairment.

_____

2. Describe observed driver attitude.

_____

Rank the driver according to the scale below on the following items.

1	2	3	4	5	6	7	8	9	10
Poor		Fair		Average		Good		Excellent	

3. How courteous was the driver to the rider?   _____
   ❒ Not applicable

4. How well was the driver able to assist the passenger with a disability?   _____
   ❒ Not applicable

5. How well did the driver make all the required stop announcements (refer to route list)?   _____
   ❒ Not applicable

6. How well did the driver make efforts to communicate with the passenger with a disability?   _____
   ❒ Not applicable

7. How efficient was the driver in working with the securement system?   _____
   ❒ Not applicable

Figure 9-8. Evaluation Form for Service Observation to Evaluate Driver Training Program

CHAPTER 9 EVALUATING SUCCESS

Methods to Ensure Anonymity

If observers board the vehicle and begin questioning the driver, the driver will know that he or she is being observed and evaluated and may behave differently than at other times. Drivers must not know that they are being observed. Some procedures to ensure observer anonymity are as follows:

- Use observers from outside the agency, including volunteers and regular riders. Driver supervisors, trainers, and management staff will most likely be recognizable to drivers and may affect their behavior.
- Develop procedures that make it less obvious that the observers are evaluating. Avoid coming on board with a clipboard and writing down everything the driver does.
- Condense observation recording forms onto index cards or other forms that make it easier to record observations without being obvious.
- Record observations on a dictation-size tape recorder. The driver would be unlikely to be able to hear the comments and the observer may appear to be a professional working while riding the bus.
- Devote some thought to the appearance of the observers. Transit system logos on clothes may be noticed by the drivers. It is best if observers fit in among the other riders -- they should be dressed for the office on commuter routes, dressed as tourists on the weekends, and so forth.
- Observers should try to sit near the driver so they can evaluate without moving around, but they should not be so near as to be obvious.

Analyze the Results

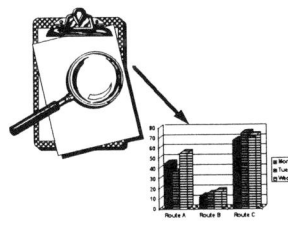

Analyze the results to determine how well the objectives have been met, particularly for target-specific areas. There may be specific topics of driver training which require more attention. There may be specific routes or parts of the service area in which drivers are less able to work with people with disabilities, perhaps because fewer people with disabilities ride those routes. Specific drivers or vehicles may pose difficulties for people with disabilities. Problems may occur more frequently during certain times of the day, due to peak capacity or due to an increased number of people with disabilities on the vehicles for whatever reasons.

Cross-tabulate the results to answer specific research questions. Based on the form shown in Figure 9-8, Table 9-3 shows how different cross-tabulations of results can answer research questions. Figure 9-9 shows the results of a cross-tabulation from fictional data showing different results by time of day. From the figure, it appears that courtesy, stop announcements, and communication efforts decrease during the peak hours. An evaluation of the analysis may show that the drivers become very busy at those times and find it difficult to keep up with all the requirements. Additional training may be required.

SPECIFIC STEPS FOR EACH APPROACH

For each of the five approaches (locating stops close to passengers, training drivers, making the system accessible, teaching passengers to use the system - travel training, and marketing fixed-route services), there are specific steps that would most effectively measure the success of the program. Steps for each approach are described below.

LOCATING STOPS CLOSE TO PASSENGERS

To measure the success of a program to locate stops close to passengers, through a circulator service or shuttle service, the success of the program can be measured through passenger counts and surveys of riders.

CHAPTER 9 EVALUATING SUCCESS

Table 9-3. Using Cross-Tabulations to Answer Research Questions

Cross-Tabulation	Research Questions Addressed
By Date	Are there differences in service by day of the week?
	Are there differences in service between weekday and weekend service?
By Time of Day	Are there differences by time of day?
	Are there differences between peak and off-peak service?
	Are there differences among shifts?
By Bus Stop	Are there differences between route segments?
By Route	Are there differences between routes?
	Are there differences between accessible and non-accessible routes?
By Driver	Are there specific driver training needs?
	Who are drivers with good skills and attitudes?
By Vehicle	Are there difficulties with particular vehicles, such as older vehicles or vehicles with different types of equipment?
By Lift Use	Are there differences in attitudes toward people who need to board on the lift and people with other types of impairments?
By Observed Impairment	Are there differences in driver attitudes to people with different types of disabilities?

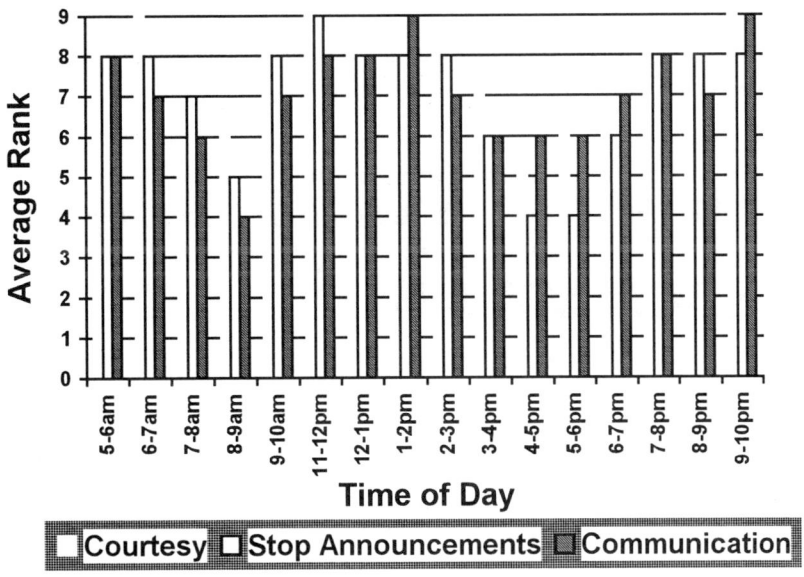

Figure 9-9. Driver Training Observations by Time of Day

CHAPTER 9 EVALUATING SUCCESS

Count passengers on the new routes and services.

Passenger Counts

Conduct counts of passengers on the new routes as well as on other routes that feed to the new ones or receive transfers from the new routes. The passenger counts may be of people with disabilities only, but it may be useful to count the overall number of passengers as well.

Count passengers at stops and on the specific routes that are implemented. Select sample times and compare the counts over time to determine if ridership increases. Conduct passenger counts when new routes are first implemented, then again after they have been in place for a time.

Survey riders on board the vehicles.

Rider Surveys

Take surveys of people with disabilities on board the vehicles. Include in the surveys, questions like the following:

- Did you ever ride [*name of fixed-route service*] before [*name of new service*] was implemented?
- How frequently did you ride [*name of fixed-route service*] before?
- Do you ride [*name of fixed-route service*] more frequently now that [*name of new service*] has started?
- Do you ride any other routes on [*name of fixed-route service*]? Which ones?
- Would you ride [*name of fixed-route service*] if [*name of new service*] was not available?
- How did you first learn about [*name of new service*]?

TRAINING DRIVERS

To measure the effects of driver training programs, conduct surveys and observe service.

Conduct Surveys

Survey all riders about driver performance.

Survey riders with disabilities as well as all other riders. The surveys can be conducted over the telephone or through mail-in surveys distributed at bus stops. Include questions on the

CHAPTER 9 EVALUATING SUCCESS

surveys which ask respondents how often they have seen drivers working with people with disabilities and what their opinions are of the service the riders received. Passengers with disabilities can also respond to questions about the service they have actually received.

Conduct surveys before a new driver training program is implemented and again after drivers are trained. Allow enough time after the training for the policies and practices of the training to become routine for the drivers. Compare the results before and after the training.

Analyze the survey results to determine if there is a pattern by time of the day, parts of the service area, or particular routes. Try to identify the cause of the variations and the solutions to identified problems. Solutions can include additional training, specific training, increased enforcement procedures, additional practice for drivers, or additional sensitivity training.

Compare the survey results on both accessible and non-accessible vehicles. Although vehicles may not have wheelchair lifts, people with disabilities may be riding. Ensure that drivers are well trained, even though they may transport relatively fewer people with disabilities than drivers on accessible vehicles.

Observe Service

Observe drivers in service.

Driver training is appropriately evaluated through observation of the service provided by drivers. Identify the objectives of the particular driver training program which is implemented. The objectives may include general sensitivity or specific skills for working with people with specific disabilities. The objectives may also include proficiency with securement systems, familiarity with mobility devices, and assisting riders to board and disembark. Analyze the training program to identify the most important objectives and include assessments of them in the service observation materials.

As for the surveys, analyze the service observation results to determine if there is a pattern of service variations and develop solutions to the problems.

CHAPTER 9 EVALUATING SUCCESS

PROGRAMMING ACCESSIBLE BUS STOP IMPROVEMENTS

To measure the success of a program to increase the accessibility of the fixed-route system, conduct passenger counts for people with disabilities and conduct surveys related to fixed-route use by people with disabilities.

Passenger Counts

Count passengers on newly accessible vehicles and at newly accessible stops.

Conduct counts of passengers with disabilities on vehicles and at stops on accessible routes. Conduct counts just after the implementation of accessible service, either by the deployment of accessible vehicles or the renovation or construction of accessible stops. Then, conduct the passenger counts 6 months to a year after the first implementation. Initially, people will not be aware of the new accessibility, but the success of the program can be measured through how many people have learned about the service and how many use it. Passenger counts can be simply the number of lift boardings or a more detailed procedure can be set up. Compare the same numbers over time to determine the success of the program.

Surveys

Conduct surveys at stops and on vehicles.

Survey riders with disabilities at the stops and on vehicles along the accessible routes. When asking riders about the service, ask questions about how often they use the service and how they feel about particular features of the service. Some potential questions are as follows:

- How often do you use [*name of fixed-route service*]?
- What routes do you ride?
- Do you only ride on accessible vehicles?
- Have you noticed [*name of a particular vehicle or stop feature*]?
- Does this feature help you to ride [*name of fixed-route service*]?
- Would you be able to ride [*name of fixed-route service*] without it?

CHAPTER 9 EVALUATING SUCCESS

TEACHING PASSENGERS TO USE THE SYSTEM

To evaluate the success of a program to teach passengers to use the system, survey people who have been taught and observe service for people with disabilities.

Surveys of Riders

Conduct follow-up surveys of riders who have been trained.

Follow up on travel training to determine if the people who participated are still using the service and how effective they feel the training was for them. Conduct training program evaluations immediately after any training takes place, either informally or formally, with those who participated. This helps in planning changes to a program and in identifying significant problems.

In addition, survey participants at regular intervals, perhaps every 6 months. Ask the participants how often they use fixed-route, whether they still use paratransit for some trips, and their opinion of the training they received. It is not necessary to survey all participants each time, but to select a sample at each interval. Some questions to include are as follows:

- How often do you ride [*name of fixed-route service*]?
- Please rate how valuable the travel training was for you.
- Would you have been able to use [*name of fixed-route service*] without the travel training?
- Is there something that you have learned since your travel training that should have been included in the training?

MARKETING THE FIXED-ROUTE SERVICES

Survey all riders about marketing effectiveness.

To evaluate the success of a marketing program, survey all riders about the effectiveness of the program. The surveys may take place on board vehicles, at stops, or over the telephone. Ask questions about the visibility of the program and whether or not the program encouraged the respondent to ride the service.

Figure 9-4 included questions for a survey to evaluate a marketing program. Include questions about particular aspects of the program, such as the features to which the most resources were devoted. Ask respondents about particular

CHAPTER 9 EVALUATING SUCCESS

aspects which may have been directed at people with disabilities.

CRITERIA FOR SUCCESS

There are two basic methods of determining the criteria for whether a program to attract people to fixed-route services has been a success. The first is to take measurements over time of the same standards and determine if there are changes showing that the program has had an impact. The second is to decide ahead of time what an appropriate level of a measure constitutes success. If the measure meets that level, then the program is a success. If it does not, then the program has not been a success.

Programs are affected by other programs and activities.

The difficulty with both types of criteria is that any program to attract people with disabilities to fixed-route service occurs in a variety of circumstances throughout the service area. It can be difficult to isolate the effects of the program and to measure them. For example, as part of a concerted effort to attract people from paratransit to fixed-route services, a transit system may implement a marketing campaign, an outreach or travel training program, and revisions to the eligibility determination procedures. The result may be an increase in the number of people with disabilities who use fixed-route, but the success may be attributable to the combination of efforts, rather than to one aspect.

Collect baseline measures before programs are implemented.

MEASUREMENTS OVER TIME

Measurements over time are best accomplished if the original, or baseline, measurement can occur before any programs have been implemented. Some of the baseline measures may be taken as part of the original market research, as described in Chapter 3 and the other chapters.

Take measurements consistently over time.

After the baseline measurements are taken, the same type of measures need to be consistently taken over time. For some programs, such as a driver training curriculum, annual surveys may be appropriate because it takes a certain amount of time to train all drivers and for them to learn to be comfortable and practiced with the training materials. Targeted measures, for example, surveys of residents in particular parts of the service area where additional accessible vehicles are being deployed,

CHAPTER 9 EVALUATING SUCCESS

can be made more frequently, to measure immediate and long-term impacts of the service changes.

However the measures are taken, it is important to be consistent. Passenger counts need to be taken in the exact same way each time. Surveys need to have identical questions. Service observations need to be conducted in a consistent manner. If the measures are not consistent, then variations may cause discrepancies in the results. The results would not accurately reflect the success of the program.

Changes over time reveal the success of programs.

As the measures are taken over time, they will reveal if additional people with disabilities have changed from paratransit to fixed-route services. The change may be attributable to a number of factors, but, if the measures are precise enough, then the contribution of specific programs can be determined. Over time, additional measures can be added to identify the effect of particular programs and of specific aspects of those programs. For example, if surveys are undertaken to measure people's perception of driver attitudes toward people with disabilities, then early surveys can ask general questions, and the later surveys can include more specific questions about some of the key training topics.

SETTING CRITERIA FOR SUCCESS

If the main purpose for a program is to attract people from paratransit services to fixed-route services, then the most objective measure is the one that would show that fewer people are using paratransit and more people with disabilities are using fixed-route services.

Decreases in paratransit ridership are not always realized.

There are two problems with achieving this measure. For most paratransit services, if some people stop riding for some or all of their trips, the capacity is easily filled with other people's rides. So, as some people take fewer rides, others take more rides, and decreases in paratransit ridership are not always realized.

Most paratransit service areas continue to experience unmet or latent demand. As paratransit space becomes available as people ride on the fixed-route, more of the latent demand can be met. While systems will not necessarily experience a decrease in paratransit ridership, they will have the opportunity to meet more demand without increasing paratransit capacity.

CHAPTER 9 EVALUATING SUCCESS

By attracting paratransit riders to fixed-route, transit systems can better satisfy the paratransit needs of riders who are unable to use the fixed-route at all. In this way, paratransit service will be more available and accessible to the people who need it, while other needs can be met on the fixed-route.

Not all new riders are from paratransit.

Second, although efforts to attract people with disabilities to fixed-route services may be directed toward paratransit riders, many of the new fixed-route riders may be people who never used paratransit.

Because funding is a major concern, the main question is whether the program has been successful in attracting paratransit riders from paratransit, which typically has a higher cost per trip, to fixed-route with a lower cost per trip. In addition, fixed-route services typically have a better farebox recovery ratio than paratransit. Figure 9-10 shows a method to calculate the net savings of increased boardings on fixed-route. From survey results, the number of trips that a person would have taken on paratransit instead of fixed-route can be calculated.

The calculations in Figure 9-10 are based on fictional estimates, but actual figures can be calculated from actual passenger counts and survey results. Be sure to include the appropriate questions in the surveys and service observation instruments. Other passengers than those who use wheelchairs also board the vehicles, so the number of boardings by people in wheelchairs, as used in Figure 9-10, is just one measure.

Calculation Step	Estimate	System Actual
1. Cost per paratransit trip	$15.00	
2. Paratransit fare	$2.00	
3. Net paratransit cost per trip	$13.00	
4. Last year fixed-route lift boardings	200	
5. This year fixed-route lift boardings	700	
6. Increase in fixed-route lift boardings	500	
7. Estimated number of fixed-route lift boardings by paratransit riders	300	
8. Cost per fixed-route trip	$7.00	
9. Fixed-route fare	$1.00	
10. Net fixed-route cost per trip	$6.00	
11. Net cost for 300 paratransit trips	$3900.00	
12. Net cost for 300 fixed-route trips	$1800.00	
13. Net savings for 300 trips on fixed-route instead of paratransit	$2100.00	

Figure 9-10. Calculating Savings of Increased Boardings on Fixed-Route

The question is then whether this amount constitutes success. A net cost savings is good, but it must be compared to the cost of the program itself. A marketing campaign or a travel training program has its own costs, calculated as described in the earlier chapters. However, it is important to remember that the cost savings may be realized year after year and may well increase over time as more people become aware of services and are comfortable using them. A one-time investment in accessible vehicles can yield cost savings over the life of the vehicle. Travel training and marketing costs may decrease over time yet still increase ridership by people with disabilities.

Many systems look beyond the actual cost savings and include in their evaluation the intangible benefits of the increased mobility of people with disabilities. The intangible benefits can yield goodwill from members of the community. This, in turn, can translate into support when financial and other difficulties arise. Those benefits cannot be easily calculated.

CONCLUSIONS

This chapter has presented methodologies for surveying riders and determining the level of success of efforts to attract paratransit riders to fixed-route service. Without a substantial effort, it may not be possible to demonstrate to decision makers and funders that efforts are worth the expenditure of resources. Ultimately, the evaluation program becomes the seminal source for future improvements. In this way, evaluation is not just a wise thing to do, but imperative to future activities.

APPENDIX A
SYSTEM DATA TABLES

APPENDIX A: SYSTEM DATA TABLES

Figure 1. System Data Tables for System 1: Data for East, High Density, Flat Topography, Hot Climate

Population, Trips, Productivity

NO.	STATE	97 ADA ELIGIBLE	SERV AREA POP	UZA POP	94 ADA PT TR/YR	97 ADA PT TR/YR	97 REV HRS	94 TOTAL PT TR/YR	97 TOTAL PT TR/YR	97 PRODUC-TIVITY
122	VA	6.50	500.00	1323.10	102	130	76	262	291	3.83
151	FL	22.98	1951.00	1914.66	1,357	1,936	890.4	1,357	1,936	2.17
152	FL	1.37	618.60	1708.71	35	147	49.12	35	147	2.99
153	FL	3.30	700.00	1238.13	50	175		572	697	
154	FL	13.70	800.00	887.13	78	257	496	574	826	1.67
155	FL	11.00	880.00	833.00	162	221	23.6	191	201	8.52
156	FL	31.10	536.40	794.85	390	430	1000	870	1,000	1.00
157	FL	5.60	65.00	738.41	101	247	312	101	247	0.79
159	FL	4.50	290.00	444.40	39	45	0	39	45	
160	FL	2.40	418.00	306.00	7	25	112	393	470	4.20
161	FL	1.05	200.00	253.56	21	27	3	27	43	14.33
163	FL	0.73	113.20	220.55	13	15	100.5	148	162	1.61
172	GA	1.60	161.00	198.63	42	62	28.3	42	62	2.19
192	NC	1.85	150.00	241.76	9	19	12.5	18	19	1.52
200	NC			101.36	8	13		8	13	

Vehicle Fleet

NO.	93 FR BUSES	97 FR BUSES	93 ACC FR BUSES	97 ACC FR BUSES	93 TOTAL FR BUS FLEET - % ACC	97 TOTAL FR BUS FLEET - % ACC	BOARD-INGS	93 ADA ACC FR BUSES	97 ADA ACC FR BUSES	93 TOTAL PT FLEET
122	151	151	81	127	54%	84%	0.325	81	127	60
151	618	616	181	389	29%	63%		88	296	88
152	177	186	98	186	55%	100%	3	0	136	59
153	189	195	149	195	79%	100%	8.77	40	110	4
154	139	281	30	228	22%	81%	0.3	12	210	162
155	145	173	63	151	43%	87%	0.7	41	151	119
156	74	145	74	145	100%	100%	3.34	18	145	194
157	172	172	43	90	25%	52%	0.808	23	70	160
159	34	41	18	40	53%	98%	1.124	18	40	28
160	29	35	29	33	100%	94%	1	0	8	32
161	30	30	13	21	43%	70%	0.25	12	20	41
163	36	37	3	37	8%	100%	0.01	3	37	70
172	57	61	11	28	19%	46%	0.29	11	28	12
192	18	20	6	20	33%	100%	0.7	0	8	5
200	NC									2

APPENDIX A: SYSTEM DATA TABLES

Figure 2. System Data Tables for System 2: Data for East, High Density, Flat Topography, Moderate Climate

Population, Trips, Productivity

NO.	STATE	97 ADA ELIGIBLE	SERV AREA POP	UZA POP	94 ADA PT TR/YR	97 ADA PT TR/YR	97 REV HRS	94 TOTAL PT TR/YR	97 TOTAL PT TR/YR	97 PRODUC-TIVITY
4	CT	0.90		413.86	16	24	12	34	39	3.21
5	CT	3.70	245.00	451.49	112	218	87	120	234	2.69
6	CT	2.45	265.00	187.00	38	77	36	39	79	2.19
15	MA	29.00	2308.00	2775.37	565	986	616	606	1,048	1.70
22	MA	4.50	305.85	139.08	83	111	20	83	111	5.45
39	NJ	6.74	5339.90		34	587	355	34	587	1.65
40	NJ	0.09	84.00	0.00	13	14	51	426	437	8.57
41	NJ	0.80	60.00	0.00						
42	NY	82.00	7321.07	16044.01	550	1,650	0	550	1,650	
43	NY	0.05	1068.00		0	2	1	0	2	2.00
45	NY	12.00	1150.00		38	123	96	38	123	1.29
46	NY	0.40	75.00		7	19	7	9	20	2.68
48	NY	7.60	1300.00		35	134	134	35	134	1.00
73	DC		1005.00	3363.03	0	449		0	449	
78	MD	0.25	64.00	78.59	2	2	0	16	22	
81	MD	0.15	99.50	0.00	2	5	16	33	36	2.25
85	PA	39.20	3200.00	4222.21	638	922	1176	1,601	2,298	1.95
94	PA	0.56	275.00	193.58	189	195	44	317	327	7.43
123	VA	4.22	421.00	589.98	216	370	75.2	216	370	4.92
124	VA	3.30	304.00	328.58	79	99	28	79	99	3.54
126	VA	0.75	43.00	103.53	11	11	3.7	11	13	3.38
130	VA	0.17	12.00	0.00	7	7	0	7	7	

APPENDIX A: SYSTEM DATA TABLES

Figure 2. System Data Tables for System 2: Data for East, High Density, Flat Topography, Moderate Climate (Continued)

Vehicle Fleet

NO.	93 FR BUSES	97 FR BUSES	93 ACC FR BUSES	97 ACC FR BUSES	93 TOTAL FR BUS FLEET - % ACC	97 TOTAL FR BUS FLEET - % ACC	BOARD-INGS	93 ADA ACC FR BUSES	97 ADA ACC FR BUSES	93 TOTAL PT FLEET
4	6	7	0	7	0%	100%	0	0	7	8
5	52	52	38	38	73%	73%	2.88	0	14	26
6	68	66	68	66	100%	100%	0.301	3	20	21
15	1,009	956	473	673	47%	70%	7.5	0	200	179
22	105	82	55	82	52%	100%	6	55	82	52
39	2,070	2,142	534	982	26%	46%	0	168	775	10
40	2	2	2	2	100%	100%	0.06	2	2	77
41	19	15	10	10	53%	67%	0.16	3	6	73
42										176
43	12	12	9	12	75%	100%	0	4	7	9
45	135	142	135	142	100%	100%	0	27	87	4
46	16	16	14	14	88%	88%	0.05	6	6	4
48	318	318	123	257	39%	81%	1.546	1	168	22
73	3	0	1	0	33%					0
78	14	14	0	8	0%	57%	0	0	8	4
81	7	10	5	10	71%	100%	0.2	3	10	9
85	1,441	1,441	688	988	48%	69%	4.1	240	746	355
94	41	45	3	28	7%	62%	0.45	3	28	31
123	191	191	129	190	68%	99%	3.053	0	80	29
124	110	129	39	82	35%	64%	2.17	39	82	28
126	12	12	12	12	100%	100%	0.006	12	12	3
130	6	6	1	6	17%	100%	0	4	6	4

APPENDIX A: SYSTEM DATA TABLES

Figure 3. System Data Tables for System 3: Data for East, High Density, Flat Topography, Cold Climate

Population, Trips, Productivity

NO.	STATE	97 ADA ELIGIBLE	SERV AREA POP	UZA POP	94 ADA PT TR/YR	97 ADA PT TR/YR	97 REV HRS	94 TOTAL PT TR/YR	97 TOTAL PT TR/YR	97 PRODUC-TIVITY
3	CT	10.00	702.00	546.20	73	115	58	73	115	1.98
16	MA	0.80	34.00		18	20	14	45	45	3.26
25	MA	0.01	104.00	68.00	0	1	74	191	221	2.99

Vehicle Fleet

NO.	93 FR BUSES	97 FR BUSES	93 ACC FR BUSES	97 ACC FR BUSES	93 TOTAL FR BUS FLEET - % ACC	97 TOTAL FR BUS FLEET - % ACC	BOARD INGS	93 ADA ACC FR BUSES	97 ADA ACC FR BUSES	93 TOTAL PT FLEET
3	114	114	88	114	77%	100%	1.805	0	26	0
16	10	10	2	10	20%	100%	0	0	10	20
25	7	7	5	7	71%	100%	0.75	0	7	43

APPENDIX A: SYSTEM DATA TABLES

Figure 4. System Data Tables for System 4: Data for East, High Density, Hilly Topography, Hot Climate

Population, Trips, Productivity

NO.	STATE	97 ADA ELIGIBLE	SERV AREA POP	UZA POP	94 ADA PT TR/YR	97 ADA PT TR/YR	97 REV HRS	94 TOTAL PT TR/YR	97 TOTAL PT TR/YR	97 PRODUCTIVITY
128	VA	0.14	53.00	54.32	8	9	0	8	9	
143	AL	3.10	426.00	622.07	82	77	25	82	77	3.06
168	GA	4.50	980.00	2157.81	268	901	355	268	901	2.54
169	GA	3.30	225.00		15	65	50	15	65	1.30
170	GA	0.76	120.00	286.54	12	15	10	12	15	1.50
171	GA	1.18	18.00	220.70	28	30	11	28	30	2.73
173	GA	0.43	119.00	129.50	3	5	4.6	3	5	1.00
175	GA	0.40	62.00	73.00	11	17	4.9	11	17	3.39
190	NC	6.90	428.00	455.60	102	370	100	105	381	3.81
191	NC	0.33	210.00	305.93	7	19	34	29	78	2.29
193	NC	1.80	140.00	205.36	53	84	32.3	54	84	2.60
194	NC	1.10	54.00		32	33	16	59	62	3.88
196	NC	0.19	148.00	185.18	11	15	26.5	170	191	7.20
197	NC	0.60	175.00	114.00	0	42	76	85	127	1.67
199	NC	1.60	62.50	108.69	35	39	18.35	44	48	2.62
213	SC	11.30	320.00	248.17	20	23	42.7	133	154	3.62
220	TN	4.75	702.00	825.19	126	138	40	126	138	3.44
223	TN	1.25	152.00	297.00	26	30	0.001	26	30	30000.00

APPENDIX A: SYSTEM DATA TABLES

Figure 4. System Data Tables for System 4: Data for East, High Density, Hilly Topography, Hot Climate (Continued)

Vehicle Fleet

NO.	93 FR BUSES	97 FR BUSES	93 ACC FR BUSES	97 ACC FR BUSES	93 TOTAL FR BUS FLEET - % ACC	97 TOTAL FR BUS FLEET - % ACC	BOARD-INGS	93 ADA ACC FR BUSES	97 ADA ACC FR BUSES	93 TOTAL PT FLEET
128	10	1	4	10%	40%	0.002	1	4	3	3
143	106	0	106	0%	100%	0	0	106	18	18
168	739	391	593	59%	80%	13	40	242	20	20
169	80	36	80	100%	100%	2.2	0	44	0	0
170	33	17	33	57%	100%	0.208	17	33	8	8
171	17	16	17	94%	100%	0.01	10	17	6	6
173	34	1	6	3%	18%	0.003	1	6	5	5
175	25	3	9	13%	36%	0.003	2	8	8	8
190	200	50	159	30%	80%	2.9	50	119	33	33
191									0	0
193	40	32	40	94%	100%	1	32	40	28	28
194	54	16	40	30%	74%	0.087	0	24	21	21
196	54	34	54	63%	100%	3.94	0	20	21	21
197	7	7	7	100%	100%	0.01	7	7	0	0
199	16	0	0	0%	0%	0	0	0	3	3
213	50	13	50	42%	100%	3.08	8	50	38	38
220	220	10	64	5%	29%	0	0	54	25	25
223	79	55	79	92%	100%	1	55	79	20	20

APPENDIX A: SYSTEM DATA TABLES

Figure 5. System Data Tables for System 5: Data for East, High Density, Hilly Topography, Moderate Climate

Population, Trips, Productivity

NO.	STATE	97 ADA ELIGIBLE	SERV AREA POP	UZA POP	94 ADA PT TR/YR	97 ADA PT TR/YR	97 REV HRS	94 TOTAL PT TR/YR	97 TOTAL PT TR/YR	97 PRODUCTIVITY
17	MA	3.20	551.50	533.00	54	74	125	265	286	2.28
75	MD	1.74	117.00		19	19	2.4	93	93	38.75
76	MD		78.00	1889.87	168	256	0	168	256	
88	PA		99.00	204.00	22	23	16	65	66	4.13
90	PA	5.50	538.00	410.44	159	190	1100	306	360	0.33
93	PA		391.00	292.90	7	7	3	7	7	2.33
104	PA	0.09	45.00		3	7	2	3	7	3.35
125	VA	0.85	100.00	178.28	17	23	14	17	23	1.61
127	VA	0.40	78.00	98.14	15	22	4.2	15	22	5.24
129	VA	3.00	68.00	0.00	65	73	0	65	73	
131	VA	0.06	22.00	0.00	4	4	3.2	4	4	1.34
134	VA		30.00	0.00	15	19	0	15	19	
177	KY	11.00	665.00	754.96	298	335	199	322	362	1.82
178	KY	4.50	225.00	220.70	99	102	35.3	35	35	1.00
195	NC	2.70	206.00	194.51	72	83	47	92	141	3.00
221	TN	8.00	510.00	573.30	124	164	67	134	174	2.60
222	TN	1.65	208.00	304.50	41	63	29.9	41	63	2.11
231	VA	0.03	18.40		25	40	80	25	40	0.50

APPENDIX A: SYSTEM DATA TABLES

Figure 5. System Data Tables for System 5: Data for East, High Density, Hilly Topography, Moderate Climate (Continued)

Vehicle Fleet

NO.	93 FR BUSES	97 FR BUSES	93 ACC FR BUSES	97 ACC FR BUSES	93 TOTAL FR BUS FLEET - % ACC	97 TOTAL FR BUS FLEET - % ACC	BOARD INGS	93 ADA ACC FR BUSES	97 ADA ACC FR BUSES	93 TOTAL PT FLEET
17	178	178	26	93	15%	52%	0.26	11	78	47
75	8	8	8	8	100%	100%	0.208	0	0	43
76	0	0	0	0						0
88	13	15	4	5	31%	33%	0.003	4	5	22
90	70	70	3	38	4%	54%	0.012	3	38	101
93	67	65	0	24	0%	37%	0	0	24	12
104	5	10	5	10	100%	100%	0.3	5	10	2
125	38	38	10	28	26%	74%	0.431	28	28	15
127	26	26	5	20	19%	77%	0.037	5	20	3
129	16	16	3	16	19%	100%	0.26	0	13	28
131	11	10	0	7	0%	70%	0	0	7	1
134	15	16	6	13	40%	81%	0	3	10	3
177	302	302	172	260	57%	86%	1.25	0	130	65
178	40	36	7	14	18%	39%	3.12	5	14	14
195	22	27	22	27	100%	100%	1.228	22	27	12
221	132	142	29	71	22%	50%	1	29	71	35
222	58	58	8	19	14%	33%	0	7	18	7
231	5	5	2	5	40%	100%	0	0	20	4

APPENDIX A: SYSTEM DATA TABLES

Figure 6. System Data Tables for System 6: Data for East, High Density, Hilly Topography, Cold Climate

Population, Trips, Productivity

NO.	STATE	97 ADA ELIGIBLE	SERV AREA POP	UZA POP	94 ADA PT TR/YR	97 ADA PT TR/YR	97 REV HRS	94 TOTAL PT TR/YR	97 TOTAL PT TR/YR	97 PRODUCTIVITY
1	CT	2.37	527.00		32	47	183	465	480	2.62
7	CT	2.75	197.00	175.07	37	50	24	37	50	2.08
9	CT	0.52	51.66	116.24	9	9	28	69	71	2.53
10	CT	2.20	170.31	92.42	0	44	0	0	44	
11	CT			88.00						
18	MA	3.10	282.70	315.67	33	75	103	300	300	2.91
19	MA	1.41	172.00	237.36	10	83	63	147	203	3.24
20	MA	0.09	194.70	181.65	2	4	34	88	95	2.81
21	MA	0.12	108.90	160.91	84	97	44	187	216	4.91
23	MA	0.71	99.40	82.25	24	27	118	607	683	5.81
24	MA	0.29	98.00	0.00	16	23	52	180	253	4.87
35	RI	12.00	846.00	846.00	69	279	140	69	279	1.99
44	NY	4.00	875.00		149	195	98	148	195	1.99
49	NY	2.00	1189.00	954.33	1	106	78	1	106	1.36
51	NY	2.60	431.00	509.11	87	118	72	89	120	1.66
52	NY	2.20	11.40	388.92	32	168	52	94	168	3.27
53	NY			264.00	0	0		0	0	
89	PA	12.00	1380.00	1678.75	480	538	913	2,206	2,299	2.52
91	PA	0.37	211.00	388.23	15	17	56	102	131	2.34

Figure 6. System Data Tables for System 6: Data for East, High Density, Hilly Topography, Cold Climate (Continued)

Vehicle Fleet

NO.	93 FR BUSES	97 FR BUSES	93 ACC FR BUSES	97 ACC FR BUSES	93 TOTAL FR BUS FLEET - % ACC	97 TOTAL FR BUS FLEET - % ACC	BOARD-NGS	93 ADA ACC FR BUSES	97 ADA ACC FR BUSES	93 TOTAL PT FLEET
1	236	236	161	236	68%	100%	6.1	161	236	133
7	34	34	2	34	6%	100%	0	2	34	8
9	20	20	10	20	50%	100%	0.03	0	10	31
10	20	20	10	20	50%	100%	0	0	12	41
11										0
18	65	65	19	57	29%	88%	1.431	0	38	94
19	45	45	41	45	91%	100%	0	0	19	121
20	35	35	22	35	63%	100%	0.375	22	35	31
21	52	52	35	52	67%	100%	1.985	29	46	92
23	25	25	5	10	20%	40%	0.336	5	10	103
24	20	20	14	20	70%	100%	0.056	0	14	36
35	234	234	234	234	100%	100%	21.6	73	73	0
44	330	347	8	113	2%	33%	0	0	113	41
49	354	354	344	354	97%	100%	4	97	256	0
51	227	228	30	167	13%	73%	2	2	139	23
52	18	28	8	25	44%	89%	0.789	8	25	15
53										0
89	895	853	278	773	31%	91%	3.2	278	773	498
91	37	36	0	4	0%	11%	0	0	4	19

APPENDIX A: SYSTEM DATA TABLES

Figure 7. System Data Tables for System 7: Data for East, Medium Density, Flat Topography, Hot Climate

Population, Trips, Productivity

NO.	STATE	97 ADA ELIGIBLE	SERV AREA POP	UZA POP	94 ADA PT TR/YR	97 ADA PT TR/YR	97 REV HRS	94 TOTAL PT TR/YR	97 TOTAL PT TR/YR	97 PRODUCTIVITY
144	AL			300.91	74	126	0	124	176	
158	FL	0.50	165.00	444.00	5	9	35.6	118	126	3.54
162	FL	0.49	204.00	221.34	37	50	16	37	50	3.14
164	FL	2.07	132.00	155.88	33	41	31.9	57	70	2.18
165	FL			147.63	42	49		70	82	
166	FL	2.00	184.00	126.00	42	43	23	111	112	4.87
174	GA	0.25	31.00	51.50	5	7	0	5	7	
176	GA	0.86	80.00	87.00	18	22	4.7	22	26	5.49
184	MS	0.45	85.00	179.64	3	4	26.8	143	147	5.49
202	NC	0.13	7.00	56.00	0	1	0.35	0	1	2.14
204	NC			51.00	0	5		0	5	
205	NC	0.20		0.00	2	13	0	2	13	
210	SC	3.30	250.00	393.96	30	37	35	30	37	1.06
216	SC	0.04	162.00	58.40	37	40	15	66	69	4.57

Vehicle Fleet

NO.	93 FR BUSES	97 FR BUSES	93 ACC FR BUSES	97 ACC FR BUSES	93 TOTAL FR BUS FLEET - % ACC	97 TOTAL FR BUS FLEET - % ACC	BOARDINGS	93 ADA ACC FR BUSES	97 ADA ACC FR BUSES	93 TOTAL PT FLEET
144	0	35	0	35		100%	0	14	35	10
158	14	14	14	14	100%	100%	1.8	6	14	23
162	37	45	18	26	49%	58%	1.269	0	13	7
164	54	68	20	68	37%	100%	2.6	15	68	15
165										0
166	43	42	7	38	16%	90%	0.015	0	31	14
174	35	28	0	5	0%	18%	0	0	5	2
176	11	11	5	10	45%	91%	0.384	0	5	21
184	22	26	13	17	59%	65%	0.1	8	13	20
202										1
204										0
205	7	6	5	5	71%	83%	0.03	5	5	0
210	53	53	10	44	19%	83%	2	10	44	12
216	22	38	3	25	14%	66%	0	3	25	14

APPENDIX A: SYSTEM DATA TABLES

Figure 8. System Data Tables for System 8: Data for East, Medium Density, Flat Topography, Moderate Climate

Population, Trips, Productivity

NO.	STATE	97 ADA ELIGIBLE	SERV AREA POP	UZA POP	94 ADA PT TR/YR	97 ADA PT TR/YR	97 REV HRS	94 TOTAL PT TR/YR	97 TOTAL PT TR/YR	97 PRODUCTIVITY
8	CT			156.00	79	79	0	79	79	
74	DE	1.23	460.50	24.00	137	151	87	233	277	3.18
84	MD	0.06	11.00	0.00	1	1	1.6	1	1	0.63

Vehicle Fleet

NO.	93 FR BUSES	97 FR BUSES	93 ACC FR BUSES	97 ACC FR BUSES	93 TOTAL FR BUS FLEET - % ACC	97 TOTAL FR BUS FLEET - % ACC	BOARDINGS	93 ADA ACC FR BUSES	97 ADA ACC FR BUSES	93 TOTAL PT FLEET
8										0
74	148	176	22	104	15%	59%	0	95	86	89
84	4	6	1	6	25%	100%	0	1	6	1

APPENDIX A: SYSTEM DATA TABLES

Figure 9. System Data Tables for System 9: Data for East, Medium Density, Flat Topography, Cold Climate

Population, Trips, Productivity

NO.	STATE	97 ADA ELIGIBLE	SERV AREA POP	UZA POP	94 ADA PT TR/YR	97 ADA PT TR/YR	97 REV HRS	94 TOTAL PT TR/YR	97 TOTAL PT TR/YR	97 PRODUC-TIVITY
28	MA	0.09	35.00	35.00	0	0	10	25	28	2.80
96	PA	1.10	188.00	177.67	10	42	40	22	42	1.05

Vehicle Fleet

NO.	93 FR BUSES	97 FR BUSES	93 ACC FR BUSES	97 ACC FR BUSES	93 TOTAL FR BUS FLEET - % ACC	97 TOTAL FR BUS FLEET - % ACC	BOARD INGS	93 ADA ACC FR BUSES	97 ADA ACC FR BUSES	93 TOTAL PT FLEET
28	5	18	1	14	20%	78%	0.003	0	13	7
96	62	62	24	42	39%	68%	0.882	16	34	32

APPENDIX A: SYSTEM DATA TABLES

Figure 10. System Data Tables for System 10: Data for East, Medium Density, Hilly Topography, Hot Climate

Population, Trips, Productivity

NO.	STATE	97 ADA ELIGIBLE	SERV AREA POP	UZA POP	94 ADA PT TR/YR	97 ADA PT TR/YR	97 REV HRS	94 TOTAL PT TR/YR	97 TOTAL PT TR/YR	97 PRODUCTIVITY
145	AL	3.30	142.00	210.01	11	94	33	12	94	2.85
146	AL	1.07	160.00	180.32	28	30	19	81	87	4.55
147	AL			106.43	0	0		0	0	
148	AL			71.00	0	0		0	0	
149	AL			56.50	0	0		0	0	
150	AL	0.19	30.00	68.00	3	3	3.66	3	3	0.93
183	MS	1.05	197.00	289.29	38	38	14	38	38	2.71
185	MS			60.00	0	0		0	0	
186	MS	0.07	41.00	0.00	6	6	2	6	6	3.10
201	NC	0.60	45.60	70.00	22	23	8.3	22	23	2.77
203	NC	0.50	28.50	29.00	10	21	11.5	10	21	1.78
211	SC	2.50	234.00	328.35	58	91	56.3	58	91	1.62
212	SC	0.11	68.00	286.54	3	3	0.76	3	3	3.82
214	SC		65.00	54.66	0	0	180	395	400	2.22
215	SC	0.27	65.00	104.80	7	14	4.2	7	14	3.33
217	SC	0.04	58.00	57.60	6	8	16	37	44	2.75
218	SC	0.25	50.00	59.00	2	3		2	3	
219	SC	0.30	58.00		3	3	0.9	1	1	1.00
225	TN	0.50	49.00	53.00	9	10	3.9	9	10	2.46
227	TN	0.50	85.00	97.58	13	15	7	14	15	2.14

APPENDIX A: SYSTEM DATA TABLES

Figure 10. System Data Tables for System 10: Data for East, Medium Density, Hilly Topography, Hot Climate (Continued)

Vehicle Fleet

NO.	93 FR BUSES	97 FR BUSES	93 ACC FR BUSES	97 ACC FR BUSES	93 TOTAL FR BUS FLEET - % ACC	97 TOTAL FR BUS FLEET - % ACC	BOARDINGS	93 ADA ACC FR BUSES	97 ADA ACC FR BUSES	93 TOTAL PT FLEET
145	40	40	6	17	15%	43%	0.15	6	17	9
146	4	9	4	9	100%	100%	0.01	0	5	8
147										0
148										0
149										0
150	5	11	3	9	60%	82%	0	3	9	4
183	42	39	15	39	36%	100%	0.01	0	39	10
185										0
186	8	8	3	5	38%	63%	0.024	1	5	16
201	5	5	0	0	0%	0%	0	0	0	4
203	6	8	0	4	0%	50%	0	0	4	6
211	50	50	14	34	28%	68%	0.015	14	34	13
212	3	3	3	3	100%	100%	0.001	3	3	5
214	6	6	2	2	33%	33%	1%	0	2	31
215	9	9	5	7	56%	78%	0	5	5	1
217	16	25	7	17	44%	68%	0	0	13	68
218										5
219	2	4	1	3	50%	75%	0	0	2	1
225	14	12	2	10	14%	83%	0	2	10	2
227	8	10	0	2	0%	20%	0	2	2	5

APPENDIX A: SYSTEM DATA TABLES

Figure 11. System Data Tables for System 11: Data for East, Medium Density, Hilly Topography, Moderate Climate

Population, Trips, Productivity

NO.	STATE	97 ADA ELIGIBLE	SERV AREA POP	UZA POP	94 ADA PT TR/YR	97 ADA PT TR/YR	97 REV HRS	94 TOTAL PT TR/YR	97 TOTAL PT TR/YR	97 PRODUCTIVITY
57	NY	7.00	259.00	148.53	3	28	39	84	112	2.87
58	NY	0.44	29.00		0	124	27	0	124	4.57
77	MD	0.25	41.00	114.00	2	15	0	18	27	
79	MD	0.60	121.00	70.21	4	23	0.3	14	35	116.67
80	MD	1.00	75.00	54.66	8	9	0	21	22	
86	PA	0.20	80.00	19.00	5	5	32	110	135	4.22
87	PA	0.50	289.00	392.00	3	5	3.7	3	5	1.38
95	PA	5.50	25.00	186.27	21	41	49	213	247	5.04
97	PA	0.05	173.00	142.68	2	3	3.85	6	7	1.82
98	PA	0.11	43.25	77.84	0	0	11.5	39	44	3.83
100	PA	0.49	65.00	65.07	0	1	1	0	1	1.30
105	PA	0.13	106.00	0.00	1	1	46.5	124	133	2.86
106	PA	0.10		0.00	0	0	13.8	57	59	4.24
107	PA	0.15	33.00	0.00	1	1		1	1	
108	PA	0.06	38.00	0.00	0	104	3.5	0	8	2.29
109	PA	0.02	11.00	0.00	0	0	18.5	59	61	3.30
113	PA	0.30		0.00	0	1	2	0	12	5.75
118	PA	0.05		0.00	0	1		0	53	
119	PA	0.04	89.00	0.00	0	1	10.5	36	42	4.00
121	PA	0.05		0.00	0	0	0.023	0	0	6.96
132	VA	0.16	35.00	0.00	9	10	2.4	9	10	4.08
135	WV		104.00	169.59	8	9	4	8	9	2.25
136	WV	2.00	183.00	164.42	28	30	20	563	495	24.75
137	WV	0.40	70.00	84.51	10	20	13	10	20	1.54
138	WV	1.00	45.00	58.68	17	20	5	18	20	4.00
139	WV		1.00	0.00	0	4		0	4	
140	WV		4.00	0.00	0	3		0	3	
141	WV	0.30	45.00	0.00	4	6	6	4	6	1.00
142	WV		4.00	0.00	0	3		0	12	
179	KY	0.06	25.85	170.00	8	8	1.8	8	8	4.44
180	KY	0.82	53.00	60.65	16	20	11	17	20	1.82
181	KY	0.03	24.00	0.00	7	8	2.76	7	8	2.75
182	KY	0.13	36.60	0.00	1	10	3.6	7	10	2.64
198	NC	1.16	66.00	110.43	23	30	9.8	23	30	3.10
206	NC	0.01	13.00	13.00	1	1	0.4	1	1	2.50
224	TN	0.12	10.90	87.40	1	1	0.85	1	1	1.65
226	TN	0.03	23.40	52.56	0	1	7.6	21	23	2.97
228	TN	0.73	45.40	82.38	17	22	8.3	18	23	2.80

APPENDIX A: SYSTEM DATA TABLES

Figure 11. System Data Tables for System 11: Data for East, Medium Density, Hilly Topography, Moderate Climate (Continued)

Vehicle Fleet

NO.	93 FR BUSES	97 FR BUSES	93 ACC FR BUSES	97 ACC FR BUSES	93 TOTAL FR BUS FLEET - % ACC	97 TOTAL FR BUS FLEET - % ACC	BOARD-INGS	93 ADA ACC FR BUSES	97 ADA ACC FR BUSES	93 TOTAL PT FLEET
57	15	15	0	15	0%	100%	0	0	15	24
58	8	8	8	8	100%	100%	0.208	2	7	0
77	5	9	5	9	100%	100%	1.2	0	9	4
79	14	14	9	14	64%	100%	0.5	0	14	4
80	12	12	7	12	58%	100%	0.012	0	6	9
86	11	11	1	3	9%	27%	0.005	1	3	6
87	22	22	18	18	82%	82%	0.1	2	10	10
95	56	56	35	44	63%	79%	0.65	35	44	35
97	22	22	19	22	86%	100%	4.69	1	15	6
98	34	34	31	34	91%	100%	5.178	4	20	8
100	14	21	10	21	71%	100%	0.137	10	21	0
105	12	13	7	13	58%	100%	1.4	5	6	42
106	0	0	0	0						19
107	3	3	3	3	100%	100%	0.09	3	3	6
108	12	12	0	12	0%	100%	0	2	12	13
109	5	5	4	4	80%	80%	0	4	4	19
113	4	8	0	4	0%	50%	0	0	4	0
118	0	0	0	0						0
119	9	10	9	10	100%	100%	3	3	5	11
121	2	4	2	4	100%	100%	0.036	2	4	1
132	28	30	3	16	11%	53%	0.008	3	16	4
135	29	32	0	30	0%	94%	0	0	30	5
136	58	55	8	35	14%	64%	3	8	35	9
137	20	20	14	14	70%	70%	0.08	2	6	5
138	15	14	5	5	33%	36%	0	4	4	2
139	0	0	0	0						0
140	0	0	0	0						0
141	7	7	0	0	0%	0%	0	0	0	2
142	0	0	0	0						0
179	6	6	3	6	50%	100%	0.072	3	6	1
180	8	8	8	8	100%	100%	0.1	0	2	4
181	5	5	5	5	100%	100%	0.3	0	0	1
182	8	8	3	5	38%	63%	0.025	0	4	2
198	25	20	0	16	0%	80%	0	0	16	17
206	12	12	1	12	8%	100%	0.003	1	12	3
224	2	5	1	4	50%	80%	0	0	3	3
226	4	4	4	4	100%	100%	0	4	4	3
228	10	10	2	2	20%	20%	0	2	2	4

APPENDIX A: SYSTEM DATA TABLES

Figure 12. System Data Tables for System 12: Data for East, Medium Density, Hilly Topography, Cold Climate

Population, Trips, Productivity

NO.	STATE	97 ADA ELIGIBLE	SERV AREA POP	UZA POP	94 ADA PT TR/YR	97 ADA PT TR/YR	97 REV HRS	94 TOTAL PT TR/YR	97 TOTAL PT TR/YR	97 PRODUCTIVITY
2	CT	1.20	71.00		42	49	30	62	71	2.37
12	CT	0.06	50.00	72.00	10	11	15	41	43	2.87
13	CT	0.04	29.77	20.00	1	2	8	30	30	3.59
14	CT	0.13	32.45	32.00	6	21	15	57	57	3.77
26	MA	0.12	90.40	55.05	3	5	18	78	84	4.69
27	MA	0.07	35.00	35.00	4	6	26	99	105	4.04
29	ME	0.60	104.00	120.22	4	8	4	48	54	13.50
30	ME	0.14	43.00	72.00	1	2	0	9	9	
31	ME	0.10	68.00	61.00	2	5	24	102	106	4.42
32	NH	0.95	63.00	114.96	1	13	0	1	13	
33	NH	0.35	101.00	114.92	25	25	1	50	50	41.67
34	NH	0.45	45.00	96.79	53	53	18	110	90	5.00
36	VT	0.63	82.00	87.09	7	10	8	7	10	1.25
47	NY	0.30	44.50		4	4	3	4	4	1.47
50	NY	3.10	577.00	619.65	200	212	55	200	212	3.85
54	NY	0.46	29.30		5	6	8	3	3	0.41
55	NY	0.59	115.00	158.55	23	24	16	23	24	1.52
56	NY	5.10	151.50	158.41	0	75	25	72	90	3.67
59	NY	0.59	95.00	66.61	86	94	16	86	94	5.88
61	NY	1.20	85.00	50.00	15	45	0	40	68	
62	NY			24.00	0	8		0	8	
63	NY	0.18	22.00	20.70	0	9	0	0	9	
64	NY	0.60	23.00	23.10	0	2	3	0	2	0.67
67	NY	1.00	31.40	16.70	27	28	0	27	28	
69	NY	2.10	86.00	2.00	0	2	1	0	2	2.10
71	NY	0.50	49.00	142.00	14	14	1	16	16	18.82
99	PA	0.55	70.00	76.55	10	9	2	10	9	4.50
101	PA	0.30	63.00	61.24	8	8	8	21	21	2.63
103	PA	0.15	38.50	52.82	1	2	0.9	1	2	2.22
111	PA	0.05	54.00	0.00	1	6	3.1	1	6	1.81
114	PA	0.20	60.00	0.00	3	3	0	6	8	

APPENDIX A: SYSTEM DATA TABLES

Figure 12. System Data Tables for System 12: Data for East, Medium Density, Hilly Topography, Cold Climate (Continued)

Vehicle Fleet

NO.	93 FR BUSES	97 FR BUSES	93 ACC FR BUSES	97 ACC FR BUSES	93 TOTAL FR BUS FLEET - % ACC	97 TOTAL FR BUS FLEET - % ACC	BOARD-INGS	93 ADA ACC FR BUSES	97 ADA ACC FR BUSES	93 TOTAL PT FLEET
2	9	9	9	9	100%	100%	0.036	9	9	25
12	2	2	0	0	0%	0%		0	0	10
13	6	6	5	6	83%	100%	0	5	6	11
14	5	5	2	5	40%	100%	0.8	1	5	15
26	22	22	22	22	100%	100%	0.855	13	13	16
27	23	23	12	22	52%	96%	0.05	0	20	35
29	28	28	28	28	100%	100%	0	0	0	16
30	10	13	10	13	100%	100%	0.01	0	8	26
31	11	14	11	14	100%	100%	1.6	11	14	38
32										0
33	21	21	5	11	24%	52%	0.349	1	7	4
34	7	7	0	0	0%	0%	0	0	0	12
36	29	29	29	29	100%	100%	2.5	14	29	18
47	9	10	5	6	56%	60%	0	5	6	2
50	215	215	75	187	35%	87%	3	39	151	21
54	8	9	3	9	38%	100%	0	1	9	3
55	38	38	9	35	24%	92%	1.228	0	26	13
56	40	40	0	23	0%	58%	0.002	0	23	13
59	27	27	19	24	70%	89%	24	9	14	8
61	49	61	15	44	31%	72%	1.14	15	44	24
62										0
63	4	5	1	5	25%	100%	0	1	5	1
64	4	5	4	5	100%	100%	0.001	3	5	3
67	5	6	1	6	20%	100%	0	0	0	0
69	9	9	2	7	22%	78%	0.002	0	5	0
71	6	6	1	3	17%	50%	0	1	3	1
99	31	31	11	15	35%	48%	0.02	11	15	42
101	44	40	0	40	0%	100%	0	0	40	3
103	4	4	4	4	100%	100%	0	4	4	20
111	10	10	2	10	20%	100%	0.05	0	8	0
114	10	10	5	10	50%	100%	0	0	10	0

APPENDIX A: SYSTEM DATA TABLES

Figure 13. System Data Tables for System 13: Data for East, Low Density, Flat Topography, Hot Climate

Population, Trips, Productivity

NO.	STATE	97 ADA ELIGIBLE	SERV AREA POP	UZA POP	94 ADA PT TR/YR	97 ADA PT TR/YR	97 REV HRS	94 TOTAL PT TR/YR	97 TOTAL PT TR/YR	97 PRODUC-TIVITY
167	FL	0.20	29.40	25.00	5	8	12.8	43	48	3.71
188	MS			0.00	9	9		9	9	
189	MS	0.07	65.50	0.00	1	1	30	28	48	1.60

Vehicle Fleet

NO.	93 FR BUSES	97 FR BUSES	93 ACC FR BUSES	97 ACC FR BUSES	93 TOTAL FR BUS FLEET - % ACC	97 TOTAL FR BUS FLEET - % ACC	BOARD-INGS	93 ADA ACC FR BUSES	97 ADA ACC FR BUSES	93 TOTAL PT FLEET
167	11	16	9	16	82%	100%	0.08	8	16	11
188	15	18	6	9	40%	50%	0.657	4	7	30
189	4	11	3	5	75%	45%	0.576	3	5	12

APPENDIX A: SYSTEM DATA TABLES

Figure 14. System Data Tables for System 14: Data for East, Low Density, Flat Topography, Moderate Climate

Population, Trips, Productivity

NO.	STATE	97 ADA ELIGIBLE	SERV AREA POP	UZA POP	94 ADA PT TR/YR	97 ADA PT TR/YR	97 REV HRS	94 TOTAL PT TR/YR	97 TOTAL PT TR/YR	97 PRODUCTIVITY
82	MD	0.06	5.20	0.00	2	2	2.9	3	2	0.79
83	MD	0.00	32.50	0.00	0	0	4.8	26	26	5.42

Vehicle Fleet

NO.	93 FR BUSES	97 FR BUSES	93 ACC FR BUSES	97 ACC FR BUSES	93 TOTAL FR BUS FLEET - % ACC	97 TOTAL FR BUS FLEET - % ACC	BOARDINGS	93 ADA ACC FR BUSES	97 ADA ACC FR BUSES	93 TOTAL PT FLEET
82	74	54	0	14	0%	26%	0	0	14	4
83	9	7	1	3	11%	43%	0	0	2	1

APPENDIX A: SYSTEM DATA TABLES

Figure 15. System Data Tables for System 15: Data for East, Low Density, Flat Topography, Cold Climate

Population, Trips, Productivity

No Systems Fit This Description

Vehicle Fleet

No Systems Fit This Description

APPENDIX A: SYSTEM DATA TABLES

Figure 16. System Data Tables for System 16: Data for East, Low Density, Hilly Topography, Hot Climate

Population, Trips, Productivity

NO.	STATE	97 ADA ELIGIBLE	SERV AREA POP	UZA POP	94 ADA PT TR/YR	97 ADA PT TR/YR	97 REV HRS	94 TOTAL PT TR/YR	97 TOTAL PT TR/YR	97 PRODUCTIVITY
187	MS	0.06	7.00	0.00	15	15	4.6	34	41	8.91

Vehicle Fleet

NO.	93 FR BUSES	97 FR BUSES	93 ACC FR BUSES	97 ACC FR BUSES	93 TOTAL FR BUS FLEET - % ACC	97 TOTAL FR BUS FLEET - % ACC	BOARDINGS	93 ADA ACC FR BUSES	97 ADA ACC FR BUSES	93 TOTAL PT FLEET
187	8	10	4	10	50%	100%	0.02	4	10	13

APPENDIX A: SYSTEM DATA TABLES

Figure 17. System Data Tables for System 17: Data for East, Low Density, Hilly Topography, Moderate Climate

Population, Trips, Productivity

NO.	STATE	97 ADA ELIGIBLE	SERV AREA POP	UZA POP	94 ADA PT TR/YR	97 ADA PT TR/YR	97 REV HRS	94 TOTAL PT TR/YR	97 TOTAL PT TR/YR	97 PRODUCTIVITY
102	PA	0.40	58.00	57.43	3	9	1	3	9	9.00
133	VA	0.08	7.00	0.00	0	1	4	0	1	0.25
229	TN		5.00	0.00	1	2		1	2	
230	TN		25.00	0.00	0	13	6.3	0	13	1.99

Vehicle Fleet

NO.	93 FR BUSES	97 FR BUSES	93 ACC FR BUSES	97 ACC FR BUSES	93 TOTAL FR BUS FLEET - % ACC	97 TOTAL FR BUS FLEET - % ACC	BOARDINGS	93 ADA ACC FR BUSES	97 ADA ACC FR BUSES	93 TOTAL PT FLEET
102	19	19	12	19	63%	100%	3	0	13	2
133	4	4	4	4	100%	100%	0.016	4	4	7
229	18	18	6	6	33%	33%	0	6	6	4
230	15	15	7	12	47%	80%	1	4	9	1

APPENDIX A: SYSTEM DATA TABLES

Figure 18. System Data Tables for System 18: Data for East, Low Density, Hilly Topography, Cold Climate

Population, Trips, Productivity

NO.	STATE	97 ADA ELIGIBLE	SERV AREA POP	UZA POP	94 ADA PT TR/YR	97 ADA PT TR/YR	97 REV HRS	94 TOTAL PT TR/YR	97 TOTAL PT TR/YR	97 PRODUCTIVITY
37	VT	0.03	25.80	18.00	0	0	14	59	65	4.57
38	VT	0.03	12.24	12.00	0	1	2	4	4	1.58
60	NY	0.25	56.00	56.48	3	3	2	3	3	1.68
65	NY	0.05	19.00	14.00	13	14	3	13	14	4.12
66	NY	0.12	8.00	8.00	0	1	1	0	2	2.40
68	NY	0.44	29.40	29.40	9	40	3	9	40	13.39
70	NY	0.05	16.00	12.00	0	0	1	0	1	0.71
92	PA	0.26	202.00	388.23	13	16	9	13	16	1.78
110	PA	0.05	37.00	0.00	0	1	2.5	0	1	0.20
112	PA	0.06	15.00	0.00	0	0	7.75	29	29	3.74
115	PA	0.05		0.00	1	3	24.4	84	86	3.50
116	PA	0.01	18.00	0.00	0	0	90.5	83	85	0.94
117	PA	0.02	25.00	0.00	0	0	7.9	58	62	7.85
120	PA	0.22		0.00	0	0	7.1	36	41	5.77

Vehicle Fleet

NO.	93 FR BUSES	97 FR BUSES	93 ACC FR BUSES	97 ACC FR BUSES	93 TOTAL FR BUS FLEET - % ACC	97 TOTAL FR BUS FLEET - % ACC	BOARDINGS	93 ADA ACC FR BUSES	97 ADA ACC FR BUSES	93 TOTAL PT FLEET
37	23	25	23	25	100%	100%	0.01	14	25	15
38	3	3	3	3	100%	100%	0	2	3	1
60	6	8	2	5	33%	63%	0.02	1	4	3
65										1
66	0	0	0	0			0	0	0	8
68	4	4	0	1	0%	25%	0	0	1	6
70	3	3	1	3	33%	100%	0.52	1	3	0
92	56	49	0	29	0%	59%	0	0	0	8
110	8	8	8	8	100%	100%	0.322	8	8	8
112	4	4	1	1	25%	25%	0	0	1	18
115	4	5	4	5	100%	100%	1.3	4	5	28
116	4	4	0	4	0%	100%	0	0	4	3
117	4	5	0	4	0%	80%	0.006	0	4	23
120	4	4	0	0	0%	0%	0.9	0	0	9

APPENDIX A: SYSTEM DATA TABLES

Figure 19. System Data Tables for System 19: Data for Central, High Density, Flat Topography, Hot Climate

Population, Trips, Productivity

NO.	STATE	97 ADA ELIGIBLE	SERV AREA POP	UZA POP	94 ADA PT TR/YR	97 ADA PT TR/YR	97 REV HRS	94 TOTAL PT TR/YR	97 TOTAL PT TR/YR	97 PRODUC-TIVITY
337	LA	7.50	601.00	1040.23	75	451	181.4	300	452	2.49
338	LA	3.30	397.00	365.94	52	104	25.9	54	109	4.21
340	LA	1.00	94.00	129.59	24	58	24.8	24	58	2.33
344	LA	5.50	386.00	0.00	72	78	43	72	78	1.81
349	OK	1.80	631.00	784.43	43	54	50.3	176	191	3.80
350	OK	5.00	362.00	474.67	185	214	0	185	214	
351	TX	6.50	483.00		251	379	112	251	379	3.38
352	TX	7.00		3198.26	846	1,007		936	1,097	
353	TX	6.00	1500.00	2901.85	706	775	531	867	1,061	2.00
354	TX	16.73	1045.00	1129.15	1,078	1,357	592	1,225	1,596	2.70
356	TX	7.60	551.00	562.01	410	540	255	473	623	2.44
371	TX	0.60	80.00	58.26	23	28	0	23	28	

Vehicle Fleet

NO.	93 FR BUSES	97 FR BUSES	93 ACC FR BUSES	97 ACC FR BUSES	93 TOTAL FR BUS FLEET - % ACC	97 TOTAL FR BUS FLEET - % ACC	BOARD-INGS	93 ADA ACC FR BUSES	97 ADA ACC FR BUSES	93 TOTAL PT FLEET
337	451	504	0	287	0%	57%	0	0	287	52
338	53	40	5	40	9%	100%	1.6	5	20	6
340	16	16	4	4	25%	25%	0.003	4	4	6
344	62	62	0	22	0%	35%	0	0	22	18
349	100	105	35	62	35%	59%	0.104	14	62	49
350										19
351	161	162	70	85	43%	52%	1.1	32	76	30
352										0
353	1,275	1,419	608	1,094	48%	77%	4.79	608	1094	131
354	529	668	30	312	6%	47%	1.03	0	282	157
356	367	367	367	367	100%	100%	44.4	30	142	45
371	14	14	14	14	100%	100%	2.61	14	14	3

APPENDIX A: SYSTEM DATA TABLES

Figure 20. System Data Tables for System 20: Data for Central, High Density, Flat Topography, Moderate Climate

Population, Trips, Productivity

NO.	STATE	97 ADA ELIGIBLE	SERV AREA POP	UZA POP	94 ADA PT TR/YR	97 ADA PT TR/YR	97 REV HRS	94 TOTAL PT TR/YR	97 TOTAL PT TR/YR	97 PRODUC- TIVITY
245	IN	0.50	116.60		11	36	5.75	11	36	6.26
246	IN	0.14	40.00		1	2	0.346	1	2	5.00
247	IN	4.80	786.00	914.76	91	162	202	91	162	0.80
250	IN	0.04	2.90	183.09	35	28	15	70	62	4.13
256	IN	0.27	89.00	0.00	3	4	0.69	3	4	5.22
290	OH	0.79	206.00		6	7	93	236	258	2.77
292	OH	8.70	868.00	1212.68	216	249	104	216	249	2.39
294	OH	16.00	883.00	945.24	88	176	101.5	97	176	1.73
295	OH	2.76	500.00	613.47	141	250	35	141	250	7.14
300	OH	0.78	226.00	224.00	9	20	26.5	41	101	3.81
301	OH	0.40	45.00	98.82	3	4	3.5	3	4	1.14
392	KS	2.40	308.00	338.79	100	75	20.2	100	75	3.71
394	MO	8.46	1390.00	1946.53	193	313	209	284	407	1.95
395	MO	4.17	600.90	1275.32	183	296	89	221	303	3.40

Vehicle Fleet

NO.	93 FR BUSES	97 FR BUSES	93 ACC FR BUSES	97 ACC FR BUSES	93 TOTAL FR BUS FLEET - % ACC	97 TOTAL FR BUS FLEET - % ACC	BOARD- INGS	93 ADA ACC FR BUSES	97 ADA ACC FR BUSES	93 TOTAL PT FLEET
245	37	37	22	37	59%	100%	0.5	13	37	6
246	5	5	0	2	0%	40%	0	0	2	2
247	157	157	0	69	0%	44%	0	0	69	24
250	26	26	0	26	0%	100%	0	0	26	11
256	11	11	11	11	100%	100%	0.003	11	11	2
290	10	24	8	24	80%	100%	0.3	4	24	52
292	379	415	20	210	5%	51%	2.227	20	210	34
294	342	310	108	243	32%	78%	9.685	108	243	22
295	249	246	249	246	100%	100%	23	249	246	19
300	8	8	8	8	100%	100%	0.038	2	8	9
301	6	6	6	6	100%	100%	1.44	6	6	0
392	53	53	16	30	30%	57%	1.02	16	30	26
394	644	644	475	604	74%	94%	17.669	187	412	59
395	254	254	165	228	65%	90%	7.9	32	95	35

APPENDIX A: SYSTEM DATA TABLES

Figure 21. System Data Tables for System 21: Data for Central, High Density, Flat Topography, Cold Climate

Population, Trips, Productivity

NO.	STATE	97 ADA ELIGIBLE	SERV AREA POP	UZA POP	94 ADA PT TR/YR	97 ADA PT TR/YR	97 REV HRS	94 TOTAL PT TR/YR	97 TOTAL PT TR/YR	97 PRODUC-TIVITY
232	IL	38.00	3318.00	6792.09	1,207	1,438	0	1,207	1,438	
233	IL	19.00	3271.00		282	897	444	1,553	2,168	4.88
236	IL	0.50	34.50		2	2	10	2	2	0.23
237	IL	1.87	173.30	207.83	34	30	12.9	34	30	2.33
248	IN	1.00	178.00	248.42	13	21	11	13	21	1.87
249	IN	1.80	178.00	237.93	28	40	11	28	40	3.64
268	MI		500.00		2	4	4	2	4	1.00
269	MI	17.00	2280.00		214	615	292	602	1,003	3.43
270	MI	5.60	1066.00	3697.53	207	441	135	207	441	3.27
271	MI	0.75	375.00	436.34	73	90	86	191	227	2.64
272	MI	1.20	227.00	326.02	76	97	131	272	309	2.36
273	MI	4.90	253.00	265.10	176	187	89	186	197	2.21
274	MI	2.90	200.00	222.06	169	210	156	272	321	2.06
275	MI	3.00	187.00	164.43	4	53	53	4	53	1.00
291	OH	5.89	1400.00	1677.49	0	288	138	400	288	2.09
296	OH	3.65	515.00	527.86	10	15	90	298	326	3.62
297	OH	3.30	418.00	489.16	44	54	28	44	54	1.93
299	OH	3.00	200.00	244.58	14	24	15	25	50	3.33
311	WI	0.50	209.00		6	7	2	22	26	12.85
312	WI	0.60	60.00		16	21	3.5	16	21	6.00
313	WI	21.00	965.00	1226.29	677	1,169	807	677	1,169	1.45
318	WI	1.20	132.00	121.79	17	17	34	31	31	0.91
319	WI	1.00	103.00	94.29	20	30	7	20	30	4.29
376	IA	1.10	269.00	293.67	11	34	47	252	316	6.72
400	NE	3.90	336.00	544.29	40	43	24	40	43	1.79

APPENDIX A: SYSTEM DATA TABLES

Figure 21. System Data Tables for System 21: Data for Central, High Density, Flat Topography, Cold Climate (Continued)

Vehicle Fleet

NO.	93 FR BUSES	97 FR BUSES	93 ACC FR BUSES	97 ACC FR BUSES	93 TOTAL FR BUS FLEET - % ACC	97 TOTAL FR BUS FLEET - % ACC	BOARD-INGS	93 ADA ACC FR BUSES	97 ADA ACC FR BUSES	93 TOTAL PT FLEET
232	2,101	2,101	946	1,741	45%	83%	0	470	1265	195
233	557	676	346	473	62%	70%	11	326	453	332
236	6	6	2	6	33%	100%	0.072	2	6	15
237	38	38	4	38	11%	100%	0.153	4	38	15
248	51	38	25	23	49%	61%	0.15	0	15	7
249	57	64	0	0	0%	0%	0	0	0	7
268	0	0	0	0			0	0	0	12
269	268	268	263	268	98%	100%	1.164	93	102	177
270	500	500	400	400	80%	80%	1.2	400	400	0
271	76	76	21	76	28%	100%	1	21	76	55
272	160	160	42	128	26%	80%	1	0	96	58
273	58	54	58	54	100%	100%	5.7	0	0	49
274	63	63	57	63	90%	100%	0.9	10	33	41
275	40	34	40	34	100%	100%	4.22	0	34	0
291	703	703	306	459	44%	65%	9.828	306	459	102
296	132	132	90	130	68%	98%	2.25	57	97	50
297	182	182	122	180	67%	99%	0	17	75	12
299	40	50	30	40	75%	80%	0.02	30	40	10
311	25	27	8	9	32%	33%	0	8	9	9
312	17	20	0	3	0%	15%	0	0	3	4
313	582	582	27	221	5%	38%	0.1	27	221	238
318	42	42	8	21	19%	50%	0.14	8	21	20
319	38	42	14	32	37%	76%	1.024	0	22	12
376	78	84	28	46	36%	55%	6.9	28	46	27
400	151	151	39	82	26%	54%	2.4	25	68	15

APPENDIX A: SYSTEM DATA TABLES

Figure 22. System Data Tables for System 22: Data for Central, High Density, Hilly Topography, Hot Climate

Population, Trips, Productivity

NO.	STATE	97 ADA ELIGIBLE	SERV AREA POP	UZA POP	94 ADA PT TR/YR	97 ADA PT TR/YR	97 REV HRS	94 TOTAL PT TR/YR	97 TOTAL PT TR/YR	97 PRODUC-TIVITY
332	AR	0.60	165.00	305.35	6	10	14	22	26	1.86
355	TX	7.50	540.00	571.02	250	936	314.6	250	936	2.98

Vehicle Fleet

NO.	93 FR BUSES	97 FR BUSES	93 ACC FR BUSES	97 ACC FR BUSES	93 TOTAL FR BUS FLEET - % ACC	97 TOTAL FR BUS FLEET - % ACC	BOARD-INGS	93 ADA ACC FR BUSES	97 ADA ACC FR BUSES	93 TOTAL PT FLEET
332	60	66	30	46	50%	70%	6	2	27	11
355	152	190	115	190	76%	100%	5.15	0	103	67

A-30

APPENDIX A: SYSTEM DATA TABLES

Figure 23. System Data Tables for System 23: Data for Central, High Density, Hilly Topography, Moderate Climate

Population, Trips, Productivity

NO.	STATE	97 ADA ELIGIBLE	SERV AREA POP	UZA POP	94 ADA PT TR/YR	97 ADA PT TR/YR	97 REV HRS	94 TOTAL PT TR/YR	97 TOTAL PT TR/YR	97 PRODUCTIVITY
266	KY	2.00	213.00	0.00	39	48	21	39	48	2.29
345	NM	5.00	385.00	497.12	179	239	64	180	239	3.73

Vehicle Fleet

NO.	93 FR BUSES	97 FR BUSES	93 ACC FR BUSES	97 ACC FR BUSES	93 TOTAL FR BUS FLEET - % ACC	97 TOTAL FR BUS FLEET - % ACC	BOARD-INGS	93 ADA ACC FR BUSES	97 ADA ACC FR BUSES	93 TOTAL PT FLEET
266	97	100	56	73	58%	73%	1.8	46	73	12
345	125	130	0	102	0%	78%	0	0	102	27

APPENDIX A: SYSTEM DATA TABLES

Figure 24. System Data Tables for System 24: Data for Central, High Density, Hilly Topography, Cold Climate

Population, Trips, Productivity

NO.	STATE	97 ADA ELIGIBLE	SERV AREA POP	UZA POP	94 ADA PT TR/YR	97 ADA PT TR/YR	97 REV HRS	94 TOTAL PT TR/YR	97 TOTAL PT TR/YR	97 PRODUC-TIVITY
285	MN	23.00	1506.00	2079.68	1,125	1,459	521	1,250	1,621	3.11
298	OH	2.50	300.00	361.63	34	40	0	38	44	

Vehicle Fleet

NO.	93 FR BUSES	97 FR BUSES	93 ACC FR BUSES	97 ACC FR BUSES	93 TOTAL FR BUS FLEET - % ACC	97 TOTAL FR BUS FLEET - % ACC	BOARD-INGS	93 ADA ACC FR BUSES	97 ADA ACC FR BUSES	93 TOTAL PT FLEET
285	982	1,045	187	615	19%	59%	0	165	593	444
298	0	0	0	0			0	0	0	5

APPENDIX A: SYSTEM DATA TABLES

Figure 25. System Data Tables for System 25: Data for Central, Medium Density, Flat Topography, Hot Climate

Population, Trips, Productivity

NO.	STATE	97 ADA ELIGIBLE	SERV AREA POP	UZA POP	94 ADA PT TR/YR	97 ADA PT TR/YR	97 REV HRS	94 TOTAL PT TR/YR	97 TOTAL PT TR/YR	97 PRODUC-TIVITY
341	LA	0.20	70.60	119.07	25	33	7.8	25	33	4.23
342	LA	0.75	55.00	110.74	3	9	0.5	3	9	18.00
357	TX	38.00	294.00	270.01	191	222	68	191	222	3.26
358	TX	0.68	661.00	263.19	3	3		3	3	
359	TX	0.88	183.00	187.91	43	50	21.9	45	51	2.33
360	TX	0.18	155.00	157.93	26	30	11.2	28	35	3.10
361	TX	0.35	103.60	144.37	21	29	19	21	29	1.53
363	TX	0.95	114.00	122.84	17	20	15.17	18	20	1.32
364	TX	0.50	117.00	117.68	31	35	16.35	31	35	2.14
365	TX	0.35	58.70	109.56	19	22	10	28	35	3.50
366	TX	0.73	106.70	107.84	26	31	13	26	31	2.38
367	TX	0.09	112.00	107.60	25	29	14.2	36	40	2.82
369	TX	0.50	75.00	79.70	24	25	7	24	25	3.57

Vehicle Fleet

NO.	93 FR BUSES	97 FR BUSES	93 ACC FR BUSES	97 ACC FR BUSES	93 TOTAL FR BUS FLEET - % ACC	97 TOTAL FR BUS FLEET - % ACC	BOARD-INGS	93 ADA ACC FR BUSES	97 ADA ACC FR BUSES	93 TOTAL PT FLEET
341	6	6	6	6	100%	100%	0.91	6	6	0
342	23	23	8	23	35%	100%	0.823	6	21	2
357	72	72	51	72	71%	100%	4.5	10	31	23
358	6	10			0%	0%				3
359	34	34	18	34	53%	100%	0.14	0	32	10
360	18	22	10	22	56%	100%	0.02	0	12	3
361	18	17	16	17	89%	100%	1.806	14	15	8
363	16	16	5	5	31%	31%	3	0	0	4
364										8
365	10	10	10	10	100%	100%	0.35	10	10	12
366	13	13	13	13	100%	100%	5.1	1	13	6
367	11	14	2	14	18%	100%	0	0	14	2
369	1	4	0	3	0%	75%	0	0	3	0

APPENDIX A: SYSTEM DATA TABLES

Figure 26. System Data Tables for System 26: Data for Central, Medium Density, Flat Topography, Moderate Climate

Population, Trips, Productivity

NO.	STATE	97 ADA ELIGIBLE	SERV AREA POP	UZA POP	94 ADA PT TR/YR	97 ADA PT TR/YR	97 REV HRS	94 TOTAL PT TR/YR	97 TOTAL PT TR/YR	97 PRODUCTIVITY
234	IL	0.50	32.00		0	26	9	0	26	2.93
235	IL	2.25	154.00	242.35	63	73	22	63	73	3.32
238	IL	1.10	127.00	124.52	52	64	44	52	64	1.45
239	IL	0.50	115.00	115.52	0	32	0	13	45	
240	IL	3.40	84.00	96.04	47	57	23	50	62	2.70
241	IL	0.40	98.50	94.19	27	27	6	28	28	4.67
251	IN	1.70	100.00	100.10	23	40	17.5	23	40	2.29
252	IN	1.00	71.00	88.07	36	38	21	49	52	2.48
253	IN			77.02	3	3	0	3	3	
254	IN			74.04	32	42	0	32	42	
255	IN	0.40	62.00	71.44	13	13	8	13	13	1.58
257	IN	0.05	20.00	0.00	0	0	0	0	0	
258	IN	0.07	41.00	0.00	10	10	?	27	26	
259	IN	0.10	35.00	0.00	6	6	4	9	10	2.50
260	IN	0.10	11.00	0.00	3	3	2	5	5	2.50
261	IN	1.00	36.00	0.00	4	5	5	4	5	1.00
263	IN	0.30	33.00	0.00	0	2	2	0	2	1.00
265	IN	0.20	129.00	0.00	2	6	3	49	50	16.67
293	OH	0.00		0.00	0	0	0.75	0	0	0.40
302	OH	0.65	70.50	88.70	8	11	8.7	8	11	1.26
303	OH	0.33	60.00	76.52	18	21	6.7	18	21	3.13
304	OH	0.19	26.00	69.12	2	7	647	2	7	0.01
305	OH	1.30	42.00	0.00	5	98	6.3	7	14	2.22
306	OH	0.50	30.00	26.70	12	13	5	12	13	2.60
307	OH	0.26	37.00	0.00	3	3	6	17	17	2.83
310	OH	0.40	22.00	0.00	8	9	5.8	16	17	3.00
377	IA	1.46	240.00	264.02	29	40	27.1	32	40	1.48
390	IL	4.00	240.00	0.00	70	70	48	85	89	1.85
391	IL	3.62			0	0		0		
393	KS	0.60	115.00	132.71	26	9	3.5	28	10	2.86
396	MO	0.50	140.00	159.09	17	17	11	18	17	1.57
397	MO	0.35	61.30	75.85	15	15	8.049	15	15	1.89
398	MO	0.75	71.80	75.40	14	14	4.4	14	14	3.18
399	MO	0.63	35.50	35.50	28	29	6.3	30	30	4.71
401	NE	2.30	197.00	192.56	75	78	17.5	95	101	5.77

APPENDIX A: SYSTEM DATA TABLES

Figure 26. System Data Tables for System 26: Data for Central, Medium Density, Flat Topography, Moderate Climate (Continued)

Vehicle Fleet

NO.	93 FR BUSES	97 FR BUSES	93 ACC FR BUSES	97 ACC FR BUSES	93 TOTAL FR BUS FLEET - % ACC	97 TOTAL FR BUS FLEET - % ACC	BOARD-INGS	93 ADA ACC FR BUSES	97 ADA ACC FR BUSES	93 TOTAL PT FLEET
234	5	6	5	6	100%	100%	0.156	5	6	0
235	49	49	20	49	41%	100%	0	0	29	14
238	46	46	24	46	52%	100%	6	1	23	10
239	75	80	65	80	87%	100%	12	15	40	0
240	24	28	0	26	0%	93%	0	0	26	4
241	25	25	25	25	100%	100%	1	25	25	5
251	49	48	6	12	12%	25%	0.463	6	12	5
252	27	24	27	24	100%	100%	9.88	1	13	11
253		10		10		100%		0	10	3
254	0	0	0	0			0	0	0	4
255	17	19	2	15	12%	79%	0.012	2	15	8
257	7	7	7	7	100%	100%	0.12	0	2	1
258	9	9	0	9	0%	100%	0	0	9	9
259	5	6	5	6	100%	100%	0.2	0	1	2
260	3	3	3	3	100%	100%	0	3	3	15
261	5	5	1	5	20%	100%	0.3	0	5	2
263	6	6	4	6	67%	100%	0.06	0	6	0
265	4	5	2	5	50%	100%	0	2	5	8
293	4	4	4	4	100%	100%	0.26	3	3	8
302	12	15	10	15	83%	100%	1.27	0	10	2
303	9	9	7	9	78%	100%	0.01	7	9	4
304	8	8	3	4	38%	50%	0.05	3	4	1
305	11	10	6	10	55%	100%	0	5	10	4
306	5	5	0	3	0%	60%	0	0	3	6
307	12	10	3	10	25%	100%	0	1	10	3
310	8	8	3	8	38%	100%	0	3	8	2
377	82	85	62	84	76%	99%	0.048	27	65	48
390	34	40	34	40	100%	100%	3.59	20	40	82
391										0
393	33	33	0	30	0%	91%	0	0	30	14
396	30	30	13	30	43%	100%	2.7	13	30	5
397	12	10	12	10	100%	100%	5.6	2	10	3
398	16	16	2	16	13%	100%	0	0	14	2
399	8	8	0	6	0%	75%	0	0	6	4
401	52	54	15	44	29%	81%	1.65	15	44	16

APPENDIX A: SYSTEM DATA TABLES

Figure 27. System Data Tables for System 27: Data for Central, Medium Density, Flat Topography, Cold Climate

Population, Trips, Productivity

NO.	STATE	97 ADA ELIGIBLE	SERV AREA POP	UZA POP	94 ADA PT TR/YR	97 ADA PT TR/YR	97 REV HRS	94 TOTAL PT TR/YR	97 TOTAL PT TR/YR	97 PRODUC-TIVITY
264	IN	0.20	20.00	0.00	10	11	4	39	43	10.75
276	MI	1.50	155.00	140.08	30	37	19	33	40	2.11
277	MI	0.04	71.00	106.25	3	4	5	10	11	2.20
278	MI		39.00	78.13	0	1	35	108	110	3.14
279	MI	0.06	70.00	77.92	13	29	13	36	39	3.00
280	MI	1.00	74.00	74.12	27	52	0	72	97	
281	MI	0.04	39.00	57.74	10	10	0	400	400	
282	MI	0.10	38.00	62.77	6	10	26	75	94	3.62
283	MI	0.10	29.00	0.00	5	9	28	119	124	4.43
308	OH	0.05	22.00	0.00	2	5	1.9	2	5	2.63
314	WI	4.00	200.00	244.34	224	256	87	232	267	3.07
315	WI	1.82	153.00	161.93	77	110	35	77	110	3.14
316	WI	2.20	177.00	160.92	53	81	51	131	161	3.16
322	WI	0.41	59.00	61.01	16	20	25	63	81	3.24
323	WI	2.90	60.00	58.94	19	24	104	66	76	0.73
325	WI	0.06	46.00	56.08	3	3	1	3	3	3.00
326	WI	0.08	54.00	53.00	3	3	1.3	3	3	2.31
329	WI	1.50	46.00	0.00	12	15	3.6	12	14.5	4.03
330	WI	0.68	43.50	0.00	17	19	7.4	18	20	2.66
378	IA	0.34	6.50	136.19	17	18	15.6	43	47	3.01
379	IA	1.02	108.00	108.26	45	48	24	69	72	3.00
380	IA	2.40	100.00	96.21	68	71	16.5	72	75	4.55
381	IA	3.20	71.70	71.37	73	78	31.5	73	78	2.46
382	IA	1.10	58.00	63.71	0	39	6.8	18	39	5.74
388	IA			47.00	11	11	0	12	12	

APPENDIX A: SYSTEM DATA TABLES

Figure 27. System Data Tables for System 27: Data for Central, Medium Density, Flat Topography, Cold Climate (Continued)

Vehicle Fleet

NO.	93 FR BUSES	97 FR BUSES	93 ACC FR BUSES	97 ACC FR BUSES	93 TOTAL FR BUS FLEET - % ACC	97 TOTAL FR BUS FLEET - % ACC	BOARD-INGS	93 ADA ACC FR BUSES	97 ADA ACC FR BUSES	93 TOTAL PT FLEET
264	4	4	2	4	50%	100%	0	2	4	10
276	44	44	44	44	100%	100%	0.02	44	44	7
277	20	20	20	20	100%	100%	4.35	2	4	4
278	37	42	37	42	100%	100%	3.744	7	35	23
279	19	20	12	17	63%	85%	0.05	0	4	9
280	15	15	13	13	87%	87%	0	0	0	5
281	2	2	2	2	100%	100%	0	0	0	12
282	9	9	9	9	100%	100%	0.02	4	9	10
283	10	10	10	10	100%	100%	0.1	0	10	15
308	6	6	0	1	0%	17%	0	0	1	0
314	166	184	22	109	13%	59%	6	22	109	118
315	34	40	0	38	0%	95%	0	0	38	15
316	40	40	10	20	25%	50%	0.72	10	20	37
322	33	34	0	11	0%	32%	0	0	11	11
323	19	19	19	19	100%	100%	3	11	11	8
325	13	13	3	13	23%	100%	0.02	3	13	3
326	24	24	14	19	58%	79%	0.654	0	3	4
329	9	9	9	9	100%	100%	0	7	7	23
330	8	8	6	8	75%	100%	0.153	6	8	4
378	38	38	1	32	3%	84%	1.02	0	32	24
379	22	17	4	17	18%	100%	4.7	4	17	15
380	25	26	3	16	12%	62%	0.01	2	16	0
381	47	47	2	41	4%	87%	0	2	41	4
382	26	18	4	9	15%	50%	0.05	4	9	27
388	15	25	0	12	0%	48%	0	0	12	0

APPENDIX A: SYSTEM DATA TABLES

Figure 28. System Data Tables for System 28: Data for Central, Medium Density, Hilly Topography, Hot Climate

Population, Trips, Productivity

NO.	STATE	97 ADA ELIGIBLE	SERV AREA POP	UZA POP	94 ADA PT TR/YR	97 ADA PT TR/YR	97 REV HRS	94 TOTAL PT TR/YR	97 TOTAL PT TR/YR	97 PRODUC-TIVITY
333	AR	0.07	29.50	74.88	10	11	5.9	10	11	1.86
335	AR	0.33	36.00	26.00	6	8	5.5	6	8	1.36
339	LA	1.10	251.00	256.49	34	68	48.3	34	68	1.41

Vehicle Fleet

NO.	93 FR BUSES	97 FR BUSES	93 ACC FR BUSES	97 ACC FR BUSES	93 TOTAL FR BUS FLEET - % ACC	97 TOTAL FR BUS FLEET - % ACC	BOARD-INGS	93 ADA ACC FR BUSES	97 ADA ACC FR BUSES	93 TOTAL PT FLEET
333	20	20	12	14	60%	70%	0.7	0	2	4
335	16	15	15	15	94%	100%	3%	2	5	2
339	45	45	13	28	29%	62%	0.025	8	23	11

APPENDIX A: SYSTEM DATA TABLES

Figure 29. System Data Tables for System 29: Data for Central, Medium Density, Hilly Topography, Moderate Climate

Population, Trips, Productivity

NO.	STATE	97 ADA ELIGIBLE	SERV AREA POP	UZA POP	94 ADA PT TR/YR	97 ADA PT TR/YR	97 REV HRS	94 TOTAL PT TR/YR	97 TOTAL PT TR/YR	97 PRODUC-TIVITY
267	KY				6	7	4.8	6	7	1.35
331	WV	0.02	24.00	24.00	0	0	0	0	0	

Vehicle Fleet

NO.	93 FR BUSES	97 FR BUSES	93 ACC FR BUSES	97 ACC FR BUSES	93 TOTAL FR BUS FLEET - % ACC	97 TOTAL FR BUS FLEET - % ACC	BOARD-INGS	93 ADA ACC FR BUSES	97 ADA ACC FR BUSES	93 TOTAL PT FLEET
267	6	6	3	5	50%	83%	1.3	0	2	2
331	3	0	2	0	67%		0	2	0	3

APPENDIX A: SYSTEM DATA TABLES

Figure 30. System Data Tables for System 30: Data for Central, Medium Density, Hilly Topography, Cold Climate

Population, Trips, Productivity

NO.	STATE	97 ADA ELIGIBLE	SERV AREA POP	UZA POP	94 ADA PT TR/YR	97 ADA PT TR/YR	97 REV HRS	94 TOTAL PT TR/YR	97 TOTAL PT TR/YR	97 PRODUC-TIVITY
288	MN	0.84	85.00	73.56	52	62	11.5	54	64	5.57
320	WI	1.00	63.00	80.29	40	40	11	40	40	3.64
321	WI	1.50	52.00	78.93	0	36	5.5	0	36	6.55

Vehicle Fleet

NO.	93 FR BUSES	97 FR BUSES	93 ACC FR BUSES	97 ACC FR BUSES	93 TOTAL FR BUS FLEET - % ACC	97 TOTAL FR BUS FLEET - % ACC	BOARD-INGS	93 ADA ACC FR BUSES	97 ADA ACC FR BUSES	93 TOTAL PT FLEET
288	24	32	10	20	42%	63%	0.193	5	15	9
320	16	16	0	8	0%	50%	0	0	8	6
321	22	20	16	20	73%	100%	3.068	12	18	0

APPENDIX A: SYSTEM DATA TABLES

Figure 31. System Data Tables for System 31: Data for Central, Low Density, Flat Topography, Hot Climate

Population, Trips, Productivity

NO.	STATE	97 ADA ELIGIBLE	SERV AREA POP	UZA POP	94 ADA PT TR/YR	97 ADA PT TR/YR	97 REV HRS	94 TOTAL PT TR/YR	97 TOTAL PT TR/YR	97 PRODUCTIVITY
334	AR	0.16	50.00	61.94	2	8	7.3	2	8	1.07
343	LA	0.15	93.00	86.00	9	11	6	9	11	1.91
362	TX	2.30	133.00	123.65	34	51	0	34	51	
368	TX	0.60	88.00	85.41	32	76	21	48	87	4.14
374	TX	0.13	30.00	30.00	1	1	3.7	3	4	1.08

Vehicle Fleet

NO.	93 FR BUSES	97 FR BUSES	93 ACC FR BUSES	97 ACC FR BUSES	93 TOTAL FR BUS FLEET - % ACC	97 TOTAL FR BUS FLEET - % ACC	BOARDINGS	93 ADA ACC FR BUSES	97 ADA ACC FR BUSES	93 TOTAL PT FLEET
334	10	10	10	10	100%	100%	0.16	0	4	0
343	19	22	1	4	5%	18%	0	0	3	2
362	18	19	6	19	33%	100%	0	13	13	7
368	7	8	4	8	57%	100%	0.05	4	8	7
374	4	5	0	5	0%	100%	0	0	5	4

APPENDIX A: SYSTEM DATA TABLES

Figure 32. System Data Tables for System 32: Data for Central, Low Density, Flat Topography, Moderate Climate

Population, Trips, Productivity

NO.	STATE	97 ADA ELIGIBLE	SERV AREA POP	UZA POP	94 ADA PT TR/YR	97 ADA PT TR/YR	97 REV HRS	94 TOTAL PT TR/YR	97 TOTAL PT TR/YR	97 PRODUC-TIVITY
242	IL	0.05	34.00	46.87	3	3	5.5	3	3	0.62
243	IL	2.40		33.50	11	12	4	11	12	3.00
244	IL	0.45	48.60	39.70	15	15	6.8	15	16	2.35
262	IN	0.08	11.00	0.00	2	2	2	2	2	1.00
309	OH	0.11	16.00	0.00	0	1	1.2	0	1	0.96
348	NM	0.28	44.60	44.60	6	7	2.4	6	7	2.71
386	IA	0.60	24.00	24.00	5	7	2.9	5	7	2.41

Vehicle Fleet

NO.	93 FR BUSES	97 FR BUSES	93 ACC FR BUSES	97 ACC FR BUSES	93 TOTAL FR BUS FLEET - % ACC	97 TOTAL FR BUS FLEET - % ACC	BOARD-INGS	93 ADA ACC FR BUSES	97 ADA ACC FR BUSES	93 TOTAL PT FLEET
242	8	8	8	8	100%	100%	0.103	7	7	4
243	4	4	0	0	0%	0%	0	0	0	3
244	11	11	9	11	82%	100%	0.025	0	6	4
262	2	2	2	2	100%	100%	0.01	0	2	1
309	3	3	1	3	33%	100%	0	1	3	2
348										10
386	7	9	7	9	100%	100%	8	0	9	2

APPENDIX A: SYSTEM DATA TABLES

Figure 33. System Data Tables for System 33: Data for Central, Low Density, Flat Topography, Cold Climate

Population, Trips, Productivity

NO.	STATE	97 ADA ELIGIBLE	SERV AREA POP	UZA POP	94 ADA PT TR/YR	97 ADA PT TR/YR	97 REV HRS	94 TOTAL PT TR/YR	97 TOTAL PT TR/YR	97 PRODUC-TIVITY
284	MI			22.00	28	31		48	51	
286	MN	2.11	86.00	122.97	27	32	13.5	30	35	2.59
287	MN	3.00	60.00	74.04	62	68	16	62	83	5.19
289	MN	0.25	48.50	31.50	10	11	5	10	11	2.20
317	WI	0.42	24.00		3	9	3.7	3	9	2.43
324	WI	0.82	40.00	57.35	14	26	8.5	14	26	3.06
327	WI	0.09	26.00	0.00	7	8	0	7	8	
328	WI		8.00	0.00	0	0	5	0	0	0.10
375	IA	0.33	55.00		11	8	5.6	11	8	1.50
383	IA	0.60	29.00	29.00	10	12	22	10	12	0.55
384	IA			25.00	9	9	0	9	9	
385	IA	0.70	26.00	26.00	5	6	3	5	6	2.00
387	IA	0.20	20.00	23.00	7	8	0	13	14	
389	IA	0.45	29.00	29.20	5	8	0	5	8	

Vehicle Fleet

NO.	93 FR BUSES	97 FR BUSES	93 ACC FR BUSES	97 ACC FR BUSES	93 TOTAL FR BUS FLEET - % ACC	97 TOTAL FR BUS FLEET - % ACC	BOARD-INGS	93 ADA ACC FR BUSES	97 ADA ACC FR BUSES	93 TOTAL PT FLEET
284										0
286	89	89	34	85	38%	96%	0.4	12	63	6
287	25	27	0	3	0%	11%	0	1	3	5
289	15	15	3	15	20%	100%	0	2	14	3
317	8	8	8	8	100%	100%	0.68	0	0	0
324	25	25	4	12	16%	48%	0.08	0	8	9
327	5	7	5	7	100%	100%	0.156	5	7	4
328	5	4	1	4	20%	100%	2	1	4	1
375	7	7	3	5	43%	71%	0.106	3	5	2
383	16	13	9	13	56%	100%	0.4	6	13	18
384										2
385	13	12	3	9	23%	75%	0.005	3	8	6
387	0	0	0	0			0	0	0	3
389										2

APPENDIX A: SYSTEM DATA TABLES

Figure 34. System Data Tables for System 34: Data for Central, Low Density, Hilly Topography, Hot Climate

Population, Trips, Productivity

NO.	STATE	97 ADA ELIGIBLE	SERV AREA POP	UZA POP	94 ADA PT TR/YR	97 ADA PT TR/YR	97 REV HRS	94 TOTAL PT TR/YR	97 TOTAL PT TR/YR	97 PRODUC-TIVITY
336	AR		2.00	2.00	1	1	1.9	1	1	0.63
346	NM	1.00	1300.00	81.47	15	15	3.3	15	15	4.67

Vehicle Fleet

NO.	93 FR BUSES	97 FR BUSES	93 ACC FR BUSES	97 ACC FR BUSES	93 TOTAL FR BUS FLEET - % ACC	97 TOTAL FR BUS FLEET - % ACC	BOARD-INGS	93 ADA ACC FR BUSES	97 ADA ACC FR BUSES	93 TOTAL PT FLEET
336	11	10	5	9	45%	90%	0.035	5	9	3
346	10	12	1	3	10%	25%	0.025	0	2	10

APPENDIX A: SYSTEM DATA TABLES

Figure 35. System Data Tables for System 35: Data for Central, Low Density, Hilly Topography, Moderate Climate

Population, Trips, Productivity

No Systems Fit This Description

Vehicle Fleet

No Systems Fit This Description

APPENDIX A: SYSTEM DATA TABLES

Figure 36. System Data Tables for System 36: Data for Central, Low Density, Hilly Topography, Cold Climate

Population, Trips, Productivity

NO.	STATE	97 ADA ELIGIBLE	SERV AREA POP	UZA POP	94 ADA PT TR/YR	97 ADA PT TR/YR	97 REV HRS	94 TOTAL PT TR/YR	97 TOTAL PT TR/YR	97 PRODUC- TIVITY
347	NM			63.06	0	41			41	

Vehicle Fleet

NO.	93 FR BUSES	97 FR BUSES	93 ACC FR BUSES	97 ACC FR BUSES	93 TOTAL FR BUS FLEET - % ACC	97 TOTAL FR BUS FLEET - % ACC	BOARD- INGS	93 ADA ACC FR BUSES	97 ADA ACC FR BUSES	93 TOTAL PT FLEET

A-46

APPENDIX A: SYSTEM DATA TABLES

Figure 37. System Data Tables for System 37: Data for West, High Density, Flat Topography, Hot Climate

Population, Trips, Productivity

NO.	STATE	97 ADA ELIGIBLE	SERV AREA POP	UZA POP	94 ADA PT TR/YR	97 ADA PT TR/YR	97 REV HRS	94 TOTAL PT TR/YR	97 TOTAL PT TR/YR	97 PRODUC- TIVITY
441	CA	2.34	563.50	2348.42	69	80	37.7	69	80	2.12
442	CA	11.30	1700.00		50	80	76	310	800	10.53
446	CA	7.00	931.00	1097.01	297	477	217	297	477	2.20

Vehicle Fleet

NO.	93 FR BUSES	97 FR BUSES	93 ACC FR BUSES	97 ACC FR BUSES	93 TOTAL FR BUS FLEET - % ACC	97 TOTAL FR BUS FLEET - % ACC	BOARD- INGS	93 ADA ACC FR BUSES	97 ADA ACC FR BUSES	93 TOTAL PT FLEET
441	149	149	149	149	100%	100%	10.1	29	66	20
442	555	619	441	619	79%	100%	49	0	239	28
446	200	200	147	200	74%	100%	55	70	123	136

APPENDIX A: SYSTEM DATA TABLES

Figure 38. System Data Tables for System 38: Data for West, High Density, Flat Topography, Moderate Climate

Population, Trips, Productivity

NO.	STATE	97 ADA ELIGIBLE	SERV AREA POP	UZA POP	94 ADA PT TR/YR	97 ADA PT TR/YR	97 REV HRS	94 TOTAL PT TR/YR	97 TOTAL PT TR/YR	97 PRODUC-TIVITY
405	CO	11.30	1800.00	1517.98	56	1,188	1024	56	1,188	1.16
438	CA	13.70	650.00		144	298	107	144	298	2.79
470	CA	0.00	44.00	44.00	0	0	4	7	9	2.25
507	OR	14.67	959.00	1172.16	479	580	375	719	952	2.54
518	WA	38.80	1564.50	1744.09	390	1,800	744	590	2,000	2.69
519	WA	2.00	170.00	0.00	90	120	43	90	120	2.79
523	WA	3.80	204.00	112.98	204	237	68	247	286	4.21

Vehicle Fleet

NO.	93 FR BUSES	97 FR BUSES	93 ACC FR BUSES	97 ACC FR BUSES	93 TOTAL FR BUS FLEET - % ACC	97 TOTAL FR BUS FLEET - % ACC	BOARD-INGS	93 ADA ACC FR BUSES	97 ADA ACC FR BUSES	93 TOTAL PT FLEET
405	626	585	569	573	91%	98%	69.35	180	303	21
438	304	317	217	317	71%	100%	550	0	209	66
470	7	11	6	10	86%	91%	0.008	4	8	3
507	580	614	484	614	83%	100%	85.7	163	293	152
518	1,164	1,145	986	1,145	85%	100%	220	0	565	170
519	81	99	17	60	21%	61%	4.6	17	60	13
523	51	66	28	66	55%	100%		10	66	30

APPENDIX A: SYSTEM DATA TABLES

Figure 39. System Data Tables for System 39: Data for West, High Density, Flat Topography, Cold Climate

Population, Trips, Productivity

No Systems Fit This Description

Vehicle Fleet

No Systems Fit This Description

APPENDIX A: SYSTEM DATA TABLES

Figure 40. System Data Tables for System 40: Data for West, High Density, Hilly Topography, Hot Climate

Population, Trips, Productivity

NO.	STATE	97 ADA ELIGIBLE	SERV AREA POP	UZA POP	94 ADA PT TR/YR	97 ADA PT TR/YR	97 REV HRS	94 TOTAL PT TR/YR	97 TOTAL PT TR/YR	97 PRODUC-TIVITY
433	CA	30.00	9800.00	11402.95	1,522	2,159	1796	3,826	4,490	2.50
434	CA	0.03	23.00		0	0	0.157	0	0	1.81
435	CA	9.00	2410.00		146	506	342	1,775	1,520	4.44
443	CA	9.00	1497.60	1435.02	358	890	0	358	890	
458	CA	2.40	132.60	132.60	29	29	26.6	80	80	3.00
497	HI	2.00	836.00	632.60	0	571	320	592	610	1.90

Vehicle Fleet

NO.	93 FR BUSES	97 FR BUSES	93 ACC FR BUSES	97 ACC FR BUSES	93 TOTAL FR BUS FLEET - % ACC	97 TOTAL FR BUS FLEET - % ACC	BOARD-INGS	93 ADA ACC FR BUSES	97 ADA ACC FR BUSES	93 TOTAL PT FLEET
433	3,634	4,096	3,594	4,096	99%	100%	0	533	995	1,698
434	11	11	8	11	73%	100%	0.002	2	9	0
435	441	497	441	497	100%	100%	80	10	230	464
443	464	456	464	456	100%	100%	74	91	234	20
458	15	22	15	22	100%	100%	2.4	2	16	16
497	475	550	0	332	0%	60%	9	0	332	87

APPENDIX A: SYSTEM DATA TABLES

Figure 41. System Data Tables for System 41: Data for West, High Density, Hilly Topography, Moderate Climate

Population, Trips, Productivity

NO.	STATE	97 ADA ELIGIBLE	SERV AREA POP	UZA POP	94 ADA PT TR/YR	97 ADA PT TR/YR	97 REV HRS	94 TOTAL PT TR/YR	97 TOTAL PT TR/YR	97 PRODUC-TIVITY
430	UT	2.64	1400.00	789.45	287	333	109.1	287	333	3.05
436	CA	24.00	1423.00	3629.52	338	969	577	523	1,153	2.00
437	CA	11.78	723.96		952	1,307	0	952	1,307	
439	CA	2.00	336.00		51	88	55.4	53	89	1.60
440	CA	5.90	418.00		49	134	53.6	98	134	2.50
457	CA	2.50	230.00	152.36	25	115	51.5	25	115	2.23
462	CA	5.30	317.20	99.96	87	131	69	211	259	3.75
467	CA	0.70	58.50	58.50	8	17	17	95	101	5.94

Vehicle Fleet

NO.	93 FR BUSES	97 FR BUSES	93 ACC FR BUSES	97 ACC FR BUSES	93 TOTAL FR BUS FLEET - % ACC	97 TOTAL FR BUS FLEET - % ACC	BOARD-INGS	93 ADA ACC FR BUSES	97 ADA ACC FR BUSES	93 TOTAL PT FLEET
430	459	508	251	482	55%	95%	11.4	124	355	138
436	797	809	797	809	100%	100%	29.6	560	764	29
437	474	455	455	455	96%	100%	42	455	455	107
439	277	274	256	274	92%	100%	4	0	88	15
440	112	128	112	128	100%	100%	0	0	90	24
457	79	79	79	79	100%	100%	6.4	4	58	22
462	78	95	63	95	81%	100%	12.8	30	73	25
467	14	14	14	14	100%	100%	0.1	2	2	10

APPENDIX A: SYSTEM DATA TABLES

Figure 42. System Data Tables for System 42: Data for West, High Density, Hilly Topography, Cold Climate

Population, Trips, Productivity

No Systems Fit This Description

Vehicle Fleet

No Systems Fit This Description

APPENDIX A: SYSTEM DATA TABLES

Figure 43. System Data Tables for System 43: Data for West, Medium Density, Flat Topography, Hot Climate

Population, Trips, Productivity

NO.	STATE	97 ADA ELIGIBLE	SERV AREA POP	UZA POP	94 ADA PT TR/YR	97 ADA PT TR/YR	97 REV HRS	94 TOTAL PT TR/YR	97 TOTAL PT TR/YR	97 PRODUC-TIVITY
402	AZ	15.80	1574.00	2006.24	208	651	278	790	1,018	3.66
426	NV	22.30	887.00	697.35	915	1,204	401	915	1,204	3.00
447	CA	1.50	124.40		33	35	12.7	40	42	3.27
449	CA	1.80	392.00	453.39	49	52	33.8	59	62	1.83
468	CA	0.70	57.90	57.90	19	22	11	24	28	2.55
484	CA	0.49	6.10	0.00	3	10	13.5	4	17	1.24

Vehicle Fleet

NO.	93 FR BUSES	97 FR BUSES	93 ACC FR BUSES	97 ACC FR BUSES	93 TOTAL FR BUS FLEET - % ACC	97 TOTAL FR BUS FLEET - % ACC	BOARDINGS	93 ADA ACC FR BUSES	97 ADA ACC FR BUSES	93 TOTAL PT FLEET
402	321	390	136	262	42%	67%	38.3	0	82	181
426	128	151	128	151	100%	100%	27	128	151	31
447	65	63	42	59	65%	94%	10.2	12	43	5
449	86	99	79	79	92%	80%	9.5	32	44	14
468	4	8	4	8	100%	100%	0.001	4	8	6
484	8	8	6	8	75%	100%	0.002	2	2	0

APPENDIX A: SYSTEM DATA TABLES

Figure 44. System Data Tables for System 44: Data for West, Medium Density, Flat Topography, Moderate Climate

Population, Trips, Productivity

NO.	STATE	97 ADA ELIGIBLE	SERV AREA POP	UZA POP	94 ADA PT TR/YR	97 ADA PT TR/YR	97 REV HRS	94 TOTAL PT TR/YR	97 TOTAL PT TR/YR	97 PRODUC- TIVITY
483	CA			7.00	0	0		0		
495	CA	1.30	55.00		29	37	17.65	74	74	4.19
516	WA	6.20	250.00		104	146	76	132	179	2.36
517	WA	1.60	85.00		31	35	17	42	47	2.76
520	WA	10.30	540.00	497.21	430	551	190	430	551	2.90
524	WA	2.00	160.00	95.47	71	106	60	120	131	2.18

Vehicle Fleet

NO.	93 FR BUSES	97 FR BUSES	93 ACC FR BUSES	97 ACC FR BUSES	93 TOTAL FR BUS FLEET - % ACC	97 TOTAL FR BUS FLEET % ACC	BOARDINGS	93 ADA ACC FR BUSES	97 ADA ACC FR BUSES	93 TOTAL PT FLEET
483										0
495	5	5	5	5	100%	100%	0	2	2	9
516	173	234	97	182	56%	78%	52	13	91	52
517	33	49	15	40	45%	82%	7.5	6	33	26
520	148	187	145	187	98%	100%	15	44	125	128
524	80	84	80	84	100%	100%	7.3	33	84	17

APPENDIX A: SYSTEM DATA TABLES

Figure 45. System Data Tables for System 45: Data for West, Medium Density, Flat Topography, Cold Climate

Population, Trips, Productivity

NO.	STATE	97 ADA ELIGIBLE	SERV AREA POP	UZA POP	94 ADA PT TR/YR	97 ADA PT TR/YR	97 REV HRS	94 TOTAL PT TR/YR	97 TOTAL PT TR/YR	97 PRODUC-TIVITY
428	SD	3.18	103.00	100.84	77	89	41	103	119	2.90
531	WA	4.00	58.00	0.00	20	21	0	20	21	

Vehicle Fleet

NO.	93 FR BUSES	97 FR BUSES	93 ACC FR BUSES	97 ACC FR BUSES	93 TOTAL FR BUS FLEET - % ACC	97 TOTAL FR BUS FLEET - % ACC	BOARD-INGS	93 ADA ACC FR BUSES	97 ADA ACC FR BUSES	93 TOTAL PT FLEET
428	27	17	0	17	0%	100%	0	0	17	17
531	9	10	9	10	100%	100%	0.8	9	10	7

APPENDIX A: SYSTEM DATA TABLES

Figure 46. System Data Tables for System 46: Data for West, Medium Density, Hilly Topography, Hot Climate

Population, Trips, Productivity

NO.	STATE	97 ADA ELIGIBLE	SERV AREA POP	UZA POP	94 ADA PT TR/YR	97 ADA PT TR/YR	97 REV HRS	94 TOTAL PT TR/YR	97 TOTAL PT TR/YR	97 PRODUC-TIVITY
445	CA	1.00	911.00		94	143	100.3	351	420	4.19
448	CA	3.30	305.70	480.48	42	45	18	42	45	2.50
451	CA	1.50	242.80	262.05	76	53	32.9	88	92	2.78
452	CA	4.17	191.00	230.61	50	53	5.3	115	115	21.70
455	CA	1.70	180.00	182.16	64	70	30	64	70	2.33
460	CA	0.60	238.00	129.03	41	59	21	68	65	3.10
461	CA	0.14	104.50	128.04	6	13	8.2	12	27	3.24
469	CA	0.16	50.00	50.00	20	22	8.84	20	22	2.49
471	CA	0.20	26.70	26.70	0	0	0.1	0	0	2.00
476	CA	0.03	7.60	8.00	3	3	6.65	23	25	3.80
488	CA	0.01	21.25	21.00	0	0	2.2	3.8	4	2.00

Vehicle Fleet

NO.	93 FR BUSES	97 FR BUSES	93 ACC FR BUSES	97 ACC FR BUSES	93 TOTAL FR BUS FLEET - % ACC	97 TOTAL FR BUS FLEET - % ACC	BOARD-INGS	93 ADA ACC FR BUSES	97 ADA ACC FR BUSES	93 TOTAL PT FLEET
445	63	88	63	88	100%	100%	14	15	61	43
448	37	37	31	37	84%	100%	6.15	31	37	0
451	66	87	47	87	71%	100%	0.8	47	87	17
452	34	38	14	29	41%	76%	1.4	0	15	24
455	72	74	72	74	100%	100%	5.5	72	74	36
460	47	40	27	40	57%	100%	5.1	0	40	21
461	9	9	9	9	100%	100%	0.25	0	0	13
469	3	3	3	3	100%	100%	0.2	3	3	0
471	1	1	1	1	100%	100%	0.01	1	1	2
476	1	2	1	2	100%	100%	0	0	2	10
488	3	4	3	4	100%	100%	0.2	0	2	2

APPENDIX A: SYSTEM DATA TABLES

Figure 47. System Data Tables for System 47: Data for West, Medium Density, Hilly Topography, Moderate Climate

Population, Trips, Productivity

NO.	STATE	97 ADA ELIGIBLE	SERV AREA POP	UZA POP	94 ADA PT TR/YR	97 ADA PT TR/YR	97 REV HRS	94 TOTAL PT TR/YR	97 TOTAL PT TR/YR	97 PRODUC-TIVITY
453	CA	1.60	120.00	194.56	25	30	21	25	30	1.43
454	CA	1.24	220.00		21	28	17.2	22	29	1.70
459	CA		270.00	122.00	56	73	27	56	73	2.70
463	CA	0.20	92.50	88.99	5	6	11	24	27	2.45
466	CA	3.20	147.00	71.80	80	85	61	184	195	3.20
473	CA	0.51	43.18	0.00	11	14	0	12	14	
490	CA	1.50	111.00	88.07	36	54	14	87	90	6.43
493	CA	0.40	64.00	77.17	4	14	13	65	65	5.00
504	ID	0.38	126.00	167.94	16	20	7.7	16	20	2.60
509	OR	3.00	168.00	157.08	0	120	48	0	121	2.52
512	OR	0.50	45.00	0.00	8	25	7.7	21	25	3.25
515	OR	0.30	16.00	0.00	1	1	2.1	3	3	1.43

Vehicle Fleet

NO.	93 FR BUSES	97 FR BUSES	93 ACC FR BUSES	97 ACC FR BUSES	93 TOTAL FR BUS FLEET - % ACC	97 TOTAL FR BUS FLEET - % ACC	BOARD-INGS	93 ADA ACC FR BUSES	97 ADA ACC FR BUSES	93 TOTAL PT FLEET
453	21	21	21	21	100%	100%	14.4	21	21	4
454	39	46	39	46	100%	100%	5.7	39	46	6
459	58	56	53	56	91%	100%	1.1	38	41	21
463	8	9	8	9	100%	100%	1.7	4	9	6
466	21	21	21	21	100%	100%	1%	16	21	29
473	7	7	7	7	100%	100%	1.85	7	7	7
490	18	23	18	23	100%	100%	3.342	0	13	13
493	6	9	6	9	100%	100%	1.032	0	9	9
504	26	30	2	30	8%	100%	5	2	30	8
509	50	59	37	59	74%	100%	7.7	4	35	0
512	5	7	5	7	100%	100%	2.5	2	7	12
515	2	2	2	2	100%	100%	0.016	1	2	1

APPENDIX A: SYSTEM DATA TABLES

Figure 48. System Data Tables for System 48: Data for West, Medium Density, Hilly Topography, Cold Climate

Population, Trips, Productivity

NO.	STATE	97 ADA ELIGIBLE	SERV AREA POP	UZA POP	94 ADA PT TR/YR	97 ADA PT TR/YR	97 REV HRS	94 TOTAL PT TR/YR	97 TOTAL PT TR/YR	97 PRODUC-TIVITY
406	CO	4.50	390.00	352.99	270	325	96	350	400	4.17
499	AK	1.30	241.00	221.88	69	94	36	69	94	2.61
521	WA		144.00	279.04	415	599	210	415	599	2.85

Vehicle Fleet

NO.	93 FR BUSES	97 FR BUSES	93 ACC FR BUSES	97 ACC FR BUSES	93 TOTAL FR BUS FLEET - % ACC	97 TOTAL FR BUS FLEET - % ACC	BOARD-INGS	93 ADA ACC FR BUSES	97 ADA ACC FR BUSES	93 TOTAL PT FLEET
406	45	45	31	45	69%	100%	4.7	0	29	88
499	52	62	0	42	0%	68%	0	0	42	10
521	144	136	53	107	37%	79%	7.5	0	54	71

APPENDIX A: SYSTEM DATA TABLES

Figure 49. System Data Tables for System 49: Data for West, Low Density, Flat Topography, Hot Climate

Population, Trips, Productivity

NO.	STATE	97 ADA ELIGIBLE	SERV AREA POP	UZA POP	94 ADA PT TR/YR	97 ADA PT TR/YR	97 REV HRS	94 TOTAL PT TR/YR	97 TOTAL PT TR/YR	97 PRODUC-TIVITY
403	AZ	7.00	506.00	579.24	0	589	278.35	310	589	2.12
456	CA	1.75	200.00	153.20	63	69	25.2	90	96	3.81
477	CA	0.25	26.00	21.00	6	15	7.5	28	38	5.07
480	CA	0.20	101.60	31.00	6	12	20	81	103	5.13
491	CA	0.08	10.00	0.00	0	2	1.8	11	13	7.00

Vehicle Fleet

NO.	93 FR BUSES	97 FR BUSES	93 ACC FR BUSES	97 ACC FR BUSES	93 TOTAL FR BUS FLEET - % ACC	97 TOTAL FR BUS FLEET - % ACC	BOARD-INGS	93 ADA ACC FR BUSES	97 ADA ACC FR BUSES	93 TOTAL PT FLEET
403	193	193	40	169	21%	88%	1.2	15	144	57
456	14	17	14	17	100%	100%	1.3	14	17	66
477	1	3	1	3	100%	100%	0.075	1	3	8
480	6	7	4	7	67%	100%	0.125	4	7	6
491	3	6	3	6	100%	100%	0.025	3	6	6

APPENDIX A: SYSTEM DATA TABLES

Figure 50. System Data Tables for System 50: Data for West, Low Density, Flat Topography, Moderate Climate

Population, Trips, Productivity

NO.	STATE	97 ADA ELIGIBLE	SERV AREA POP	UZA POP	94 ADA PT TR/YR	97 ADA PT TR/YR	97 REV HRS	94 TOTAL PT TR/YR	97 TOTAL PT TR/YR	97 PRODUC-TIVITY
407	CO	1.22	98.60	106.16	19	22	3.7	19	22	6.00
427	NV	3.20	79.00	213.75	163	188	79.4	191	209	2.63
514	OR	0.57	10.00	0.00	0	1	4	1	2	0.50
533	WA	1.00	18.00	0.00	14	20	9.7	15	22	2.27

Vehicle Fleet

NO.	93 FR BUSES	97 FR BUSES	93 ACC FR BUSES	97 ACC FR BUSES	93 TOTAL FR BUS FLEET - % ACC	97 TOTAL FR BUS FLEET - % ACC	BOARD-INGS	93 ADA ACC FR BUSES	97 ADA ACC FR BUSES	93 TOTAL PT FLEET
407	15	18	9	18	60%	100%	0.208	4	16	8
427	63	63	45	45	71%	71%	6.7	0	0	66
514	2	2	2	3	100%	150%	0.416	2	3	2
533	14	15	11	15	79%	100%	0.045	6	13	6

APPENDIX A: SYSTEM DATA TABLES

Figure 51. System Data Tables for System 51: Data for West, Low Density, Flat Topography, Cold Climate

Population, Trips, Productivity

NO.	STATE	97 ADA ELIGIBLE	SERV AREA POP	UZA POP	94 ADA PT TR/YR	97 ADA PT TR/YR	97 REV HRS	94 TOTAL PT TR/YR	97 TOTAL PT TR/YR	97 PRODUC-TIVITY
404	AZ	0.20	45.90	46.00	3	4	3.7	42	56	15.14
418	MN	0.30			6	7	5.5	11	12	2.22
423	ND	0.35	74.00	121.34	22	22	10.5	46	46	4.38
424	ND	1.50	59.00	58.10	49	54	10.5	49	54	5.14
425	ND	0.12	34.50	35.00	10	11	2	33	35	17.50
501	AK	0.03	3.50	0.00	2	2	7.2	15	18	2.43
502	AK	0.60	65.00	0.00	24	36	4.2	30	44	10.48
526	WA	3.00	59.00	59.32	93	97	39	109	114	2.92
532	WA	0.10	10.00	0.00	23	26	10	34	39	3.90
535	WA	0.60	63.00	0.00	72	79	25	145	158	6.32

Vehicle Fleet

NO.	93 FR BUSES	97 FR BUSES	93 ACC FR BUSES	97 ACC FR BUSES	93 TOTAL FR BUS FLEET - % ACC	97 TOTAL FR BUS FLEET - % ACC	BOARD-INGS	93 ADA ACC FR BUSES	97 ADA ACC FR BUSES	93 TOTAL PT FLEET
404	6	7	3	7	50%	100%	0.004	3	7	20
418	8	9	0	9	0%	100%	0	0	9	1
423	14	14	14	14	100%	100%	0.128	3	14	10
424	13	13	3	13	23%	100%	0	3	10	2
425	11	11	0	1	0%	9%	0	0	1	5
501	7	7	0	7	0%	100%	0	0	7	5
502	6	6	0	6	0%	100%	0	0	6	3
526	27	39	0	39	0%	100%	0	0	39	58
532	11	11	6	7	55%	64%	0.012	1	2	7
535	38	37	14	17	37%	46%	0.1	10	13	18

APPENDIX A: SYSTEM DATA TABLES

Figure 52. System Data Tables for System 52: Data for West, Low Density, Hilly Topography, Hot Climate

Population, Trips, Productivity

NO.	STATE	97 ADA ELIGIBLE	SERV AREA POP	UZA POP	94 ADA PT TR/YR	97 ADA PT TR/YR	97 REV HRS	94 TOTAL PT TR/YR	97 TOTAL PT TR/YR	97 PRODUC-TIVITY
444	CA	2.20	1140.00	1170.20	295	415	179	560	680	3.80
450	CA	1.20	303.00	302.61	44	50	18.2	44	50	2.73
464	CA	0.20	82.00	83.59	21	28	9.4	34	36	3.86
465	CA	1.80	93.00	78.36	42	80	40.5	42	80	1.98
474	CA	0.50	2.00	31.00	2	2	9	53	50	5.56
475	CA	1.10	48.60	33.00	10	11	0	62	68	
478	CA	0.10	129.00	0.00	3	4	11.25	41	45	4.00
479	CA			40.00	0	0		0	0	
482	CA	0.05	22.50	15.00	0	4	40	170	175	4.38
487	CA	0.05	16.50	16.50	2	2	3.5	48	64	18.29
489	CA	0.40	60.00	64.70	1	2	6.5	27	32	4.92
498	HI	0.30	51.20		3	3	17	26	32	1.88

Vehicle Fleet

NO.	93 FR BUSES	97 FR BUSES	93 ACC FR BUSES	97 ACC FR BUSES	93 TOTAL FR BUS FLEET - % ACC	97 TOTAL FR BUS FLEET - % ACC	BOARD-INGS	93 ADA ACC FR BUSES	97 ADA ACC FR BUSES	93 TOTAL PT FLEET
444	93	133	93	133	100%	100%	34.6	78	133	88
450	64	69	62	69	97%	100%	0	14	21	9
464	13	20	13	20	100%	100%	1	11	20	5
465	15	19	12	16	80%	84%	1.75	0	4	11
474	7	8	6	8	86%	100%	4.08	6	8	9
475	5	7	5	7	100%	100%		0	3	4
478	16	18	14	18	88%	100%	0.425	4	16	8
479										0
482	22	22	15	19	68%	86%	1.1	2	12	40
487	3	3	0	3	0%	100%	0.024	0	3	5
489	18	18	18	18	100%	100%	0.5	8	18	6
498	13	19	11	19	85%	100%	0.03	11	19	22

APPENDIX A: SYSTEM DATA TABLES

Figure 53. System Data Tables for System 53: Data for West, Low Density, Hilly Topography, Moderate Climate

Population, Trips, Productivity

NO.	STATE	97 ADA ELIGIBLE	SERV AREA POP	UZA POP	94 ADA PT TR/YR	97 ADA PT TR/YR	97 REV HRS	94 TOTAL PT TR/YR	97 TOTAL PT TR/YR	97 PRODUC- TIVITY
481	CA	5.50	193.00	44.00	64	78	23	64	78	3.39
486	CA	0.43	187.00	50.30	1	6	54.6	261	451	8.26
492	CA	0.41	43.75	20.00	46	58	21.4	51	64	3.00
494	CA	0.40	64.00		0	0	0	0	0	7.00
508	OR	3.70	234.00	189.19	51	68	30	77	92	3.07
510	OR	2.60	67.00	66.97	40	52	11	47	53	4.82
513	OR	0.20	32.00	0.00	12	16	2.75	12	16	5.82
522	WA	0.17	126.00	116.12	144	167	787	144	167	0.21
527	WA	0.75	44.00	57.12	23	30	14	23	30	2.14
529	WA	0.40	37.00	0.00	28	32	9	45	51	5.67
536	WA	1.00	19.00	0.00	3	4	2	5	6	3.00

Vehicle Fleet

NO.	93 FR BUSES	97 FR BUSES	93 ACC FR BUSES	97 ACC FR BUSES	93 TOTAL FR BUS FLEET - % ACC	97 TOTAL FR BUS FLEET - % ACC	BOARD- INGS	93 ADA ACC FR BUSES	97 ADA ACC FR BUSES	93 TOTAL PT FLEET
481	21	26	21	26	100%	100%	2.22	13	18	10
486	28	39	28	39	100%	100%	3.432	12	29	45
492	11	11	11	11	100%	100%	2.0951428	6	11	14
494	0	0	0	0			0	0	0	0
508	84	84	84	84	100%	100%	46	25	53	28
510	26	20	12	20	46%	100%	1.1	0	20	6
513	3	5	3	5	100%	100%	0.5	2	5	2
522	54	58	12	16	22%	28%	69	12	16	33
527	7	7	7	7	100%	100%	2	7	7	15
529	17	19	6	18	35%	95%	0.35	5	17	4
536	10	13	9	13	90%	100%	0.73	0	3	2

APPENDIX A: SYSTEM DATA TABLES

Figure 54. System Data Tables for System 54: Data for West, Low Density, Hilly Topography, Cold Climate

Population, Trips, Productivity

NO.	STATE	97 ADA ELIGIBLE	SERV AREA POP	UZA POP	94 ADA PT TR/YR	97 ADA PT TR/YR	97 REV HRS	94 TOTAL PT TR/YR	97 TOTAL PT TR/YR	97 PRODUCTIVITY
408	CO	0.61	106.00	105.81	23	25	39.1	32	35	0.90
409	CO	1.00	66.40	71.58	27	30	11	27	30	2.73
410	CO	0.61	21.00	7.00	0	0	0	0	0	
411	CO	0.20	5.10	5.00	0	0	1.5	4	4	2.73
412	CO	0.00	6.70	7.00	0	0	0	0	0	
413	CO	0.03		2.00	2	3	0	2	3	
414	CO	0.18	21.00	12.00	9	9	6	17	17	2.83
415	CO	0.03	30.00	30.00	0	0	0	0	0	
416	CO	0.04		4.00	0	0	0	0	0	
417	CO		1.31	1.00	0	0	0	0	0	
419	MT	0.50	81.00	88.18	57	59	19.4	80	82	4.23
420	MT	0.30	62.00	63.51	4	4	0	4	4	
421	MT	0.50	30.00	57.20	8	6	7.8	8	6	0.77
422	MT	0.23	33.50	49.00	4	8	3.1	4	8	2.48
429	SD	1.00	61.00	61.12	39	42	11.8	44	46	3.90
431	UT	0.36	50.00	50.40	6	7	4.5	6	7	1.56
432	UT	0.00	5.00	4.00	0	0	2	6	6	3.10
472	CA	0.05	11.75	11.75	5	5	2.85	6	7	2.35
485	CA		21.00	22.00	4	4	2.6	5	5	1.85
500	AK	0.14	29.40	0.00	14	16	13.5	26	28	2.07
503	AK	0.04	8.00	0.00	0	2		4	5	
505	ID	1.00	60.00	53.90	6	6	5.3	19	21	3.96
506	ID			0.00		0		0	0	
511	OR	0.44	42.80	0.00	9	13	9.4	26	33	3.51
525	WA	1.00	59.00	88.05	56	61	23	70	73	3.17
528	WA			0.00	86	104		92	112	
530	WA	1.00	23.00	0.00	3	3	4	10	10	2.50
534	WA	2.00	61.00	0.00	41	45	22	55	61	2.77

APPENDIX A: SYSTEM DATA TABLES

Figure 54. System Data Tables for System 54: Data for West, Low Density, Hilly Topography, Cold Climate (Continued)

Vehicle Fleet

NO.	93 FR BUSES	97 FR BUSES	93 ACC FR BUSES	97 ACC FR BUSES	93 TOTAL FR BUS FLEET - % ACC	97 TOTAL FR BUS FLEET - % ACC	BOARD-INGS	93 ADA ACC FR BUSES	97 ADA ACC FR BUSES	93 TOTAL PT FLEET
408	24	22	15	22	63%	100%	0	7	14	26
409	13	12	13	12	100%	100%	5.03	2	12	5
410	72	76	4	24	6%	32%	0.271	0	20	10
411	55	68	0	18	0%	26%	1	0	18	4
412	12	19	10	19	83%	100%	0	0	11	1
413	17	26	11	20	65%	77%	0.001	11	20	1
414	10	10	0	0	0%	0%	0	0	0	3
415	13	14	2	9	15%	64%	0.4	2	9	2
416	4	4	0	0	0%	0%	0	0	0	1
417	5	5	1	5	20%	100%	0	0	4	2
419	21	21	16	16	76%	76%	2.2	0	0	15
420	18	18	18	18	100%	100%	1.54	18	18	0
421	20	22	15	22	75%	100%	0.331	0	17	6
422	7	7	1	7	14%	100%	0.086	0	7	3
429	6	7	6	7	100%	100%	1.512	6	7	6
431	11	13	9	13	82%	100%	0.425	9	13	2
432	22	18	12	18	55%	100%	0.012	10	17	4
472	5	8	5	8	100%	100%	0.006	4	8	2
485	9	8	6	8	67%	100%	0.006	1	5	3
500	14	14	5	9	36%	64%	0	5	9	10
503										0
505	9	10	1	4	11%	40%	0	0	3	4
506										0
511	10	9	10	9	100%	100%	1.696	6	9	4
525	29	29	8	15	28%	52%	1	8	15	12
528										17
530	13	13	6	9	46%	69%	0.05	2	5	2
534	32	30	15	22	47%	73%		4	11	17

APPENDIX B

BIBLIOGRAPHY

APPENDIX B: BIBLIOGRAPHY

1. "Transportation for Individuals with Disabilities; Final Rule," 49 *Code of Federal Regulations (CFR)* Vol. 56, No. 173, Part 37, Subpart F, Subsection 37.123(e)(1-3), pg. 45634, September 6, 1991.

2. Atherton, T.J., Loudon, W.R., and Walb, C. A. *Transit Marketing: A Program of Research, Demonstration, and Communication,* Urban Mass Transportation Authority, Washington, DC 1985.

3. Ball, W. and Mierzejewski, E. A. *Transit Use Factors,* Center for Transportation Research, University of South Florida, Tampa, FL 1992.

4. Balog, J.N. "Emergency and Accident Procedures Training for: The Flxible Corporation Urban Transit Bus," "Emergency and Accident Procedures Training for: The Neoplan USA Corporation Urban Transit Bus," and "Emergency and Accident Procedures Training for: The General Motors Corporation RTS Urban Transit Bus," KETRON Division of The Bionetics Corporation, 1988.

5. Balog, J.N. *Conjoint Analysis of Paratransit System Features and Preferences for the Transportation Disabled Residents of New York City: Volume 3*, Office of Management & Budget, City of New York, KETRON, March 1987.

6. Balog, J.N. *Demand/Cost Model Technical Report and Programmers Manual - Planning, Development, and Implementation of a Paratransit Program for the Transportation Disabled Residents of New York City: Volume 5*, and *Demand/Cost Model Technical Report and Programmers Manual - Planning, Development, and Implementation of a Paratransit Program for the Transportation Disabled Residents of New York City: Volume 6*, Office of Management & Budget, City of New York, KETRON, February 1987.

7. Balog, J.N. *Final Report: Senior Citizen Free Transit Program Ridership Verification Study*, KETRON Division of The Bionetics Corporation, Pennsylvania Department of Transportation, Bureau of Public Transit & Goods Movement Systems, Harrisburg, PA September 1987.

8. Balog, J.N. *Market Survey - Planning, Development and Implementation of a Paratransit Program for the Transportation Disabled Residents of New York City: Volume 2,* and *Statistical Tabulations for the Market Survey - Planning Development, and Implementation of a Paratransit Program for the Transportation Disabled Residents of New York City: Volume 2*, Office of Management & Budget, City of New York, KETRON, February 1987.

APPENDIX B: BIBLIOGRAPHY

9. Balog, J.N. *Provider Survey - Planning, Development, and Implementation of a Paratransit Program for the Transportation Disabled Residents of New York City: Volume 4*, Office of Management & Budget, City of New York, KETRON, February 1987.

10. Balog, J.N. *Recommended Strategy for a Countywide Transportation System in Hudson County, New Jersey*, KETRON, February 15, 1985.

11. Balog, J.N. *Transportation Demand Estimates for the Elderly and Disabled Residents of Hudson County, New Jersey*, KETRON, February 4, 1985.

12. Balog, J.N. and Schwarz, A.N. *Shared-Ride of Philadelphia: Ridership Profile*, and Balog, J.N., *Philadelphia Shared-Ride Trip Distribution Analysis*, KETRON Division of The Bionetics Corporation, April 1990.

13. Balog, J.N., Schwarz, A.N., and Doyle, B.C. *Transit Security Procedures Guide*, KETRON Division of The Bionetics Corp., Volpe National Transportation Systems Center, 1994.

14. Balog, J.N., Schwarz, A.N., and Doyle, B.C. *Transit Security Program Planning Guide,* KETRON Division of The Bionetics Corp., Volpe National Transportation Systems Center, 1993.

15. Balog, J.N., Schwarz, A.N., Chia, D. and Gribbon, R.B. *Statewide Driver Training Program for Paratransit Rural/Small Urban and 16(b)2 Bus Operators: Passenger Sensitivity Instruction*, KETRON Division of the Bionetics Corporation, Malvern, PA January 1992.

16. Balog, J.N., Schwarz, A.N., Gribbon, R.B., and Chia, D. *Accessibility Handbook for Transit Facilities*, KETRON Division of The Bionetics Corp., Federal Transit Administration, July 1992.

17. Balog, J.N., Schwarz, A.N., Hood, M.M., and Rimmer, J.E., *ADA Public Participation Handbook*, KETRON Division of The Bionetics Corporation, Project ACTION, Washington, DC September 1993.

18. Bellucci, A. "Accessibility at a Price," *Mass Transit*, Vol. 17 No. 3, pg. 26, March 1990.

19. Benjamin, J. "A Least Absolute Deviations Critical Decision Path Analysis with Transport Applications," *Journal of Advanced Transportation,* 22:1, pp. 55-76, 1988.

20. Benjamin, J. "An Application of Multiple-Response Conjoint Measurement to Urban Regional Transportation," submitted to *Transportation Research*

APPENDIX B: BIBLIOGRAPHY

21. Benjamin, J. "An Introduction to Critical Decision Path Analysis with Consumer Marketing Applications," *Proceedings*, 25th Annual Meeting of S.E. TIMS, Myrtle Beach, SC October 1989.

22. Benjamin, J. "An Introduction to Critical Transportation Decision Path Analysis," *Preliminary Papers of the International Conference on Travel and Transportation*, Oxford, Eng. July 1988.

23. Benjamin, J. "How to Use a Consumer Information System to Improve Transit Performance," *Proceedings* of the ASCE Conference on Improving Urban Transportation Performance, pp. 103-118, July 1984.

24. Benjamin, J. "Structural Conjoint Measurement," *Proceedings*, the 5th International Conference on Travel Behavior Analysis, Aix-en-Provence, France October 1987.

25. Benjamin, J. "Utilization of Attitudinal Measurement Techniques to Analyze Demand for Transportation: Methods, Applications, and New Direction," *Proceedings* of the 4th International Conference on Consumer Behavior Analysis, Noordwijk, NE pp. 385-406, April 1985.

26. Benjamin, J. *A Consumer-Oriented Transit Information System,* UMTA/USDOT and NTIS, Washington, DC 1983.

27. Benjamin, J., "An Application of Multiple-Response Conjoint Measurement to Urban Regional Transportation: Some Preliminary Results," *Proceedings*, 6th International Conference on Travel Behavior Analysis, Quebec, Canada May 1991.

28. Benjamin, J. and Obeng, K. "An Analysis of the Effect of Policy and Background Variables on Total Factor Productivity for Public Transport," *Transportation Research*, B, 24B:1, pp. 1-14, 1990.

29. Benjamin, J.M. and Sen, L. *An Empirical Test of the Utility of Attitudinal Measures for Short-Term Public Transportation Planning*, US Department of Transportation, Research and Special Programs Administration, Washington, DC 1983.

30. Benjamin, J.M. and Sen, L. *Market Segmentation of the Transportation-Handicapped: An Assessment of Their Needs*, Urban Mass Transportation Authority, Washington, DC 1982.

31. Benjamin, J.M. and Sen, L. *A Manual of Procedures to Analyze Attitudes Toward Transportation,* United States Department of Transportation, Washington, DC 1982.

APPENDIX B: BIBLIOGRAPHY

32. Benjamin, J.M., Sen, L., Clark, J.E., Louviere, J.J., and Henshap, D.A. "Attitudes, Perceptions, and Constraints on Travel," *Transportation Research Record 890*, Transportation Research Board, National Research Council, Washington, DC 1982.

33. Black, W.R. *The Identification of Public Transit Needs in Indiana: Part 1 Urban Public Transit*, Indiana University Transportation Research Center, Bloomington, IN 1992.

34. Bogren, S. "ADA: The Real Story," *Community Transportation Report*, Vol. 10, No. 4, pg. 11, April 1992

35. Bower, M. "Factoring in Facilities," *Community Transportation Reporter*, Vol. 10, No.4, pg. 11, April 1992.

36. Chadda, H.S. and Noel, E.C. "Consolidating Elderly and Handicapped Transportation Services," *Transportation Quarterly,* Vol. 41, No. 2, pp. 229-245, April 1987.

37. Charles River Associates, Inc. *Characteristics of Urban Transportation Demand: An Update,* DOT-T-88-18, Urban Mass Transportation Administration, Washington, DC July 1988.

38. Coburn, N., Martin, C., Thompson, R., and Norstrom, D. *Guidelines for Improvements to Transit Accessibility for Persons with Disabilities*, Federal Transit Administration, pg. 28, September 1992.

39. Community Council Inc. *Community Council ON BOARD Project - Final Report,* Community Council Inc. for Project ACTION, Phoenix, AZ, pg. 6, March 1992.

40. Dabney, R.L., Henderson, W.H., and Thomas, D.D. *Passenger Assistance Techniques: A Manual for Vehicle Operators of Systems Transporting the Elderly and Handicapped*, Transportation Management Associates, Fort Worth, TX 1982.

41. Daucher, D.E. *Securement of Wheelchairs and Other Mobility Aids of Transit Vehicles*, Architectural and Transportation Barriers Compliance Board, Washington, DC September 1990.

42. Dornan, D.L., Middendorf, D.P., and Steinmann, R.P. *Cost-Effective Data Collection Process to Support Planning and Marketing of Transportation Services for Transportation-Handicapped People*, paper submitted to the Transportation Research Board, 1986.

APPENDIX B: BIBLIOGRAPHY

43. Edwards, A. *Handicapped Accessible Public Transportation: Mobility Device Lifts, Restraints, and Securement Devices,* Oregon State University, Department of Civil Engineering, Corvallis, OR 1991.

44. EG&G Dynatrend and Crain & Associates, *TCRP B-1: Transit Operations for Individuals With Disabilities, Phase I Report,* Transportation Research Board, National Research Council, Washington, DC December 1993.

45. Fricker, J.D. and Shanteau, R.M. "Improved Service Strategies for Small-City Transit," *Transportation Research Record 1051,* Transportation Research Board, National Research Council, Washington, DC 1986.

46. Frye, A. *Advantages and Disadvantages of Special Transport Services for the Handicapped. Comparisons with the Adaptation of Public Transport Vehicles. Viewpoint of Transport Policy,* Paper Presented at the ECMT Seminar, Berlin, Germany, May 3, 1987.

47. Grimes, G. *Michigan Small Transit System Management Handbook,* Michigan Department of Transportation, Lansing, MI, pg. 292, December 1985.

48. Hitlin, R.A., Spielberg, F., Barber, E., and Andrle, S.J. "A Comparison of Telephone and Door-to-Door Survey Results for Transit Market Research," *Transportation Research Record 1144,* Transportation Research Board, National Research Council, Washington, DC 1987.

49. Hunt, D.T., Still, S.E., Carroll, J.D., and Druse, A.O. "A Geodemographic Model for Bus Service Planning and Marketing," *Transportation Research Record N1051,* Transportation Research Board, National Research Council, Washington, DC pp. 1-12, 1986.

50. Hunter-Zaworski, K.M., Ullman, D.G., and Herling, D.E. *Application of the Quality Functional Deployment Method in Mobility Aid Securement System Design,* DOT-T-93-22, University Research and Training Program, Federal Transit Administration, Washington, DC December 1992.

51. Hunter-Zaworski, K.M., Zaworski, J.R., and Clarke, G. *The Development of an Independent Locking Securement System for Mobility Aids on Public Transportation Vehicles,* DOT-T-93-08, University Research and Training Program, Federal Transit Administration, Washington, DC December 1992.

52. Hunter-Zaworski, K.M. *Final Report and the Conference Summary Second Conference on Mobility Aids and Public Transportation, March 16-17, 1992, Portland, Oregon,* Transportation Northwest (TransNow), Seattle, WA October 1992.

APPENDIX B: BIBLIOGRAPHY

53. Jacobs, B.M. "Subway Security," *Mass Transit*, Vol. XIX, pg. 45, August 1992.

54. Katzman, R. A. "Transportation Policy," *Millbank Quarterly,* Vol. 3, No. 5, pp. 36-43, September 1980.

55. Kiersh, E. "Protecting the Commuter," *POLICE Magazine*, Vol.3, No. 5, pgs. 36-43, September 1980.

56. Kihl, M. "Marketing Rural Transit Among Senior Populations," *Transportation Research Record 1338*, Transportation Research Board, National Research Council, Washington DC, pg. 60, 1992.

57. Lave, R., Rose, K., and Sugrue, J. "Methodology for Conducting a Transportation Survey of Persons with Disabilities," *Transportation Research Record 1338,* Transportation Research Board, National Research Council, Washington, DC pp. 51-59, 1992.

58. Levine, N., and Wachs, M. *Factors Affecting the Incidence of Bus Crime in Los Angeles, Volume I: Final Report*, United Mass Transportation Administration, pg. ii, January 1985.

59. Maines, S. "The New Breed: Pierce Transit Provides Fully Accessible Service," *Community Transportation Reporter*, Vol. 9 No. 5, pg. 25, May/June 1991.

60. Market Strategies, Inc. *Transit Now: National Survey, June 1990,* American's Coalition for Transit Now, Washington, DC June 1990.

61. McGean, T.J. *Innovative Solutions for Disabled Transit Accessibility*, UMTA-OH-06-0056-91-8, Urban Mass Transportation Authority, pg. 10, October 1991.

62. O'Mahoney, T. "Keeping Watch Over Mass Transit," *Security Management*, Vol. 34 Co. 1. pgs. 50-55, January 1990.

63. Obeng, K., Assar, N., and Benjamin, J. "Total Factor Productivity in the United States Bus Transit Systems," *Transportation Research,* forthcoming

64. Office of Intermodal Programs. *Georgia State Management Plan and Administrative Guide for Rural and Small Urban Areas Section 18*, pg. 95, 1992.

65. Project ACTION, *Project ACTION - Local Demonstration Program - Phase I 1991-1992, Project Profiles*, Washington, DC 1992.

66. Raphael, D. "Minivans and Accessibility," *Community Transportation Reporter,* Vol. 10, No. 8, pp 14-15, March 1992.

APPENDIX B: BIBLIOGRAPHY

67. Retzlaff, J., Soucie, K., and Beimborn, E. *The Use of Market Research in Public Transit Final Report,* Urban Mass Transportation Administration, University Research and Training Program, Washington, DC 1985.

68. Rivas, E. "Elderly Transit and the ADA," *Community Transportation Reporter,* Vol. 10, No. 2, pg. 12, February 1992.

69. Rosenbloom, S. *Developing a Comprehensive Service Strategy to Meet a Range of Suburban Travel Needs,* DOT-T-91-06, Office of Technical Assistance and Safety, Urban Mass Transportation Authority, Washington, DC May 1990.

70. Rosenbloom, S. *Elderly and Handicapped Transit and Paratransit Services Across the United States: The Experience of Mid-Sized Cities,* Working Paper No. 022 in CRP Working Paper Series, University of Texas at Austin, 1990.

71. Russo, J.W. "Expanded Role of State Department of Transportation: New Jersey's Unique Joint Development Program," *Land Use and Transportation,* 1982.

72. Ryan, P.H. and Boyd, M.A. *Strategies for Implementing a Standee-on-Lift Program for Fixed-Route Bus Service,* Volpe National Transportation Systems Center, 1992.

73. Schauer, P. *Volunteers in Motion,* Brochure developed for Florida Transportation Disadvantaged Commission marketing program, 1991.

74. Schauer, P. *Mobility for Health,* Brochure developed for Florida Transportation Disadvantaged Commission marketing program, 1991.

75. Simon, R. *A Lift To Freedom: A Bus Everyone Can Ride, Final Report,* Mass Transit Administration (MTA) for Project ACTION, Baltimore, MD pg. 12, March 1992.

76. Simon, R. *Project ACTION: Annual Report 1992,* Project ACTION, Washington, DC 1992.

77. Simon, R. *Project ACTION: Local Demonstration Program - Phase 1 1991-1992, Project Profiles,* Project ACTION, Washington, DC 1992.

78. Smerk, G.M., Hendriksson, L., McDaniel, K., Perrault D., and Stark, S. *Mass Transit Management: A Handbook for Small Cities, Part 4: Marketing,* 3rd edition, USDOT-T-88-12, Urban Mass Transportation Authority, pg. 489, February 1988.

APPENDIX B: BIBLIOGRAPHY

79. Thatcher, R.H. and Gaffney, J.K. *ADA Paratransit Handbook: Implementing the Complementary Paratransit Service Requirements of the Americans with Disabilities Act of 1990,* UMTA-MA-06-0206-91-1, Urban Mass Transportation Administration, 1991.

80. Tischer, M.L. "Travel Analysis Methods for the 1980s. Workshop on Travel Behavior Characteristics and Analysis," *Transportation Research Board Special Report 201,* Transportation Research Board, National Research Council, Washington, DC 1983.

81. *Transportation Implications of the Americans with Disabilities Act: An Implementation Manual,* American Public Transit Association (APTA), Washington, DC 1992.

82. Vihmaa, J. *The Severely Visually Handicapped: Their Mobility and Willingness for Mobility Training,* Central Organization for Traffic Safety, Helsinki, Finland, 1987.

83. Walb, C.A. and Booth, R. "Transit Marketing: The State of the Art," *Transportation Research Record 1039,* Transportation Research Board, National Research Council, Washington, DC pp.9-16, 1985.

84. Walb, C.A. and Loudon, W.R. *Transit Marketing: A Review of the State-of-the-Art and a Handbook of Current Practice,* Urban Mass Transportation Administration, Washington, DC 1985.

85. Welch, W., Chisholm, R., Schumacher, D., and Mundle, S. "Methodology for Evaluating Out-of-Direction Bus Route Segments," *Transportation Research Record 1308,* Transportation Research Board, National Research Council, Washington, DC pp 43-50, 1991.

86. *West Virginia Transit Marketing Manual: "Get on the Bus and Ride,"* USDOT-I-85-23, United States Department of Transportation, Washington, DC May 1984.

87. *Wisconsin Transit System Marketing Manual,* USDOT-I-87-26, United States Department of Transportation, Washington, DC March 1987.

88. Worthington, H. "Low Cost Planning Techniques for Assessing Rural Transportation Needs," *Transportation Research Record 936*, Transportation Research Board, National Research Council, Washington, DC pp.55-60, 1983.